THE END OF FAMILY COURT

FAMILIES, LAW, AND SOCIETY SERIES

General Editor: Nancy E. Dowd

Justice for Kids: Keeping Kids Out of the Juvenile Justice System
Edited by Nancy E. Dowd

Masculinities and the Law: A Multidimensional Approach
Edited by Frank Rudy Cooper and Ann C. McGinley

The New Kinship: Constructing Donor-Conceived Families
Naomi Cahn

What Is Parenthood? Contemporary Debates about the Family
Edited by Linda C. McClain and Daniel Cere

In Our Hands: The Struggle for U.S. Child Care Policy
Elizabeth Palley and Corey S. Shdaimah

The Marriage Buyout: The Troubled Trajectory of U.S. Alimony Law
Cynthia Lee Starnes

Children, Sexuality, and the Law
Edited by Sacha Coupet and Ellen Marrus

A New Juvenile Justice System: Total Reform for a Broken System
Edited by Nancy E. Dowd

Divorced from Reality: Rethinking Family Dispute Resolution
Jane C. Murphy and Jana B. Singer

The Poverty Industry: The Exploitation of America's Most Vulnerable Citizens
Daniel L. Hatcher

Ending Zero Tolerance: The Crisis of Absolute School Discipline
Derek W. Black

Blaming Mothers: American Law and the Risks to Children's Health
Linda C. Fentiman

The Ecology of Childhood: How Our Changing World Threatens Children's Rights
Barbara Bennett Woodhouse

The Politicization of Safety: Critical Perspectives on Domestic Violence Responses
Edited by Jane K. Stoever

Living Apart Together: Legal Protections for a New Form of Family
Cynthia Grant Bowman

Social Parenthood in Comparative Perspective
Edited by Clare Huntington, Courtney G. Joslin, and Christiane von Bary

The End of Family Court: How Abolishing the Court Brings Justice to Children and Families
Jane M. Spinak

The End of Family Court

How Abolishing the Court Brings Justice
to Children and Families

Jane M. Spinak

NEW YORK UNIVERSITY PRESS

New York

NEW YORK UNIVERSITY PRESS
New York
www.nyupress.org

Some material in the book is adapted with permission from "When Did Lawyers for
Children Stop Reading Goldstein, Freud and Solnit? Lessons from the Twentieth Century
on Best Interests and the Role of the Child Advocate," 41 *Family Law Quarterly* 393 (2007),
Copyright 2007 American Bar Association and Jane Spinak; and "Family Court Reform:
Getting It Right between Rhetoric and Reality," 31 *Wash. U. J. L. & Pol'y* 11 (2009), Copyright
2009 Washington University Journal of Law and Policy.

Please contact the Library of Congress for Cataloging-in-Publication data.
ISBN: 9781479814084 (hardback)
ISBN: 9781479814107 (library ebook)
ISBN: 9781479814091 (consumer ebook)

This book is printed on acid-free paper, and its binding materials are chosen for strength
and durability. We strive to use environmentally responsible suppliers and materials to the
greatest extent possible in publishing our books.

Manufactured in the United States of America

10 9 8 7 6 5 4 3 2 1

Also available as an ebook.

For Warren and Briggin

and

In memory of Betty, Jay, and Michael

CONTENTS

Introduction   1

PART I: THE GREAT IDEA

1. The Great Idea of the Juvenile Court   17

2. The Great Idea and the Therapeutic Impulse   33

3. The Great Idea for Black Children   57

4. Rationalizing and Consolidating Court Power   80

5. The Great Idea Meets Due Process   100

PART II: THE FAMILY COURT RISES

6. Status Offenses and the Rise of the Family Court   127

7. Creating a Family Court Industry   163

8. The Federal Family Court   197

PART III: THE ROAD TO ABOLITION

9. The Failure of Reform   225

10. Abolition   255

Acknowledgments   295

Notes   299

Bibliography   325

Index   349

About the Author   369

Juvenile Court Committee

Chicago

INCORPORATED MARCH 26, 1904

MRS. JOSEPH T. BOWEN, President. 136 Astor Street.

Miss Julia C. Lathrop, Vice-President
Hull House, 335 South Halsted Street

Leroy D. Thomas, Vice President
204 Dearborn Street

Mrs. Charles Henrotin, Vice President
251 Goethe Street

Mrs. Frederick K. Tracy, Recording Secretary
545 Jackson Boulevard

Mr. James H. Eckels, Treasurer
President Commercial National Bank

Mrs. Theodore B. Wells, Assistant Treasurer
215 South Winchester Avenue

Mrs. George Bass, Chairman Court Committee
150 Lincoln Park Boulevard

Miss Julia C. Lathrop, Chairman Conference Committee
Hull House, 335 South Halsted Street

Mrs. Sadie T. Wald, Chairman Detention Home Committee
3958 Michigan Avenue.

In order to continue the work of the Juvenile Court in a satisfactory manner, it is necessary to raise the sum of $15,000 annually.

The Committee in charge of this work is incorporated. We employ fifteen probation officers, without whose services the Juvenile Court would be useless.

We have assumed the management and certain expenses of the Detention Home, 625 West Adams Street.

We are asking every church in Chicago to give us $10 per annum, and it is earnestly requested that every pastor will put this matter before his congregation and urge upon them the necessity of supporting this most important institution. There is no better mission work than this saving of children; it is keeping them from becoming criminals; it is making them honest citizens. We look to you to do your share in guiding the children of this city towards clean and and reputable lives. If you are able, support a probation officer at $720 a year. If you are unable to do this, give us something—at least $10.

Make cheques payable to James H. Eckels, Treasurer, and send to Mrs. F. K. Tracy, Secretary, 545 Jackson Boulevard.

LOUISE DE KOVEN BOWEN,
President Juvenile Court Committee.

Figure I.1. Juvenile Court Committee Flyer. Courtesy of Chicago History Museum.

Introduction

Juvenile court, the predecessor of family court, was one of the grand public institutions established by American social reformers around the turn of the twentieth century to address massive changes in urban life. Families affected by problems of poverty, crime, immigration and migration, sweatshop labor, and scarce access to education and health care began to experience these newly created public institutions, which included public schools, hospitals, mental institutions, reformatories, settlement houses, playgrounds, libraries, and specialized courts. They were designed not only to provide needed assistance but also, more notably, to assimilate these families into the prevailing culture and, at times, to alter their perceived harmful or disruptive conduct.

Juvenile court—still known variously as "family," "dependency," "domestic relations," or "children's" court—began as a benevolent alternative to adult criminal court for children in trouble with the law. Over a century later, they have expanded to include multiple areas of jurisdiction regarding family life including child protection, child support and paternity, status and family violence offenses, divorce, custody and visitation, and guardianship and adoption. The creators of the juvenile court had imagined a court where informality, specially trained public servants such as probation officers and social workers, and a kindly, all-knowing judge would wisely assist children and families. The harshness and formality of the adult criminal court would be replaced by a court system capable of responding to the immediacy and intimacy of family life by identifying its problems and providing services to solve them. The judge would serve as the benevolent leader of the court.

The Great Idea of the juvenile court was conceived in cities to protect children. Cities were teeming with immigrants whose children worked in factories, lived in crowded and unsanitary tenements, and suffered from diseases that swept through neighborhoods. Miriam Van Waters, an early juvenile justice theorist and prison reformer, captured the progressive sentiment that was championed largely by white female reformers, or *child-savers*: "Children should deal with the elemental things of the world—earth, stones, trees, animals, running water, fire, open spaces—instead of pavements, signboards, subdivided lots, apartment houses, and electric percolators."[1] A key purpose of the court was to make the lives of immigrant children better by transforming them into *real* Americans. An equally essential purpose was to protect young women flooding in from the countryside from the temptations of city life.[2] This jurisprudence intended to do good by saving these children, even if that meant saving them from their families and communities.

In investigating the roots of the current courts that evolved over time from the original juvenile court—and will be referred to most often in this book as *family court*—I examine the court's role as a central actor in the history of state intervention in family life. When the court began, the reasons that children found themselves before a judge were not divided into jurisdictional categories. The court did not differentiate between children getting into trouble and parents failing in some way to prevent that trouble. Children could be brought to the court if they committed a crime, what we now label "juvenile delinquency"; if they disobeyed parents and teachers by engaging in behavior that was not criminal but was prohibited only because of their age—like having sex or drinking alcohol—what we now call "status offenses"; or if their parents couldn't control them, failed or were unable to provide for them, or actually hurt them, what we now call "child protection" or "child welfare." These three categories of *family regulation* were not formally differentiated because the role of the court was to help the child so that she would desist from troublesome behavior and her parent would provide proper care. If trouble continued, the state would take over the parental role. As Justice Frederick Cabot of the Boston juvenile court wrote of the early court in 1925:

> The State first exercises its power as a super-parent when the parent or guardian fails in duty in aiding the child, in fulfilling its responsibility of services to the community, or when, disputing such natural, proper aid from its natural parents, the child fails in those duties. The court is empowered and has the duty to act as a parent should for the welfare of the child, and the court must exercise these powers through intimate talks with the child and by acting directly upon the child.[3]

Legal designations of the reasons why children were brought to court were unnecessary because the court's purpose was considered preventive or rehabilitative in order to achieve what came to be called *personalized justice* for the child.[4] This was the Great Idea. By talking with the child "and by acting directly upon the child," the court would find a solution; the court would solve the problem.

Progressive activists at the turn of the twentieth century proposed their ideas at a previous high point of income inequality in the United States. This was a moment when immigration sustained the industries producing Gilded Age wealth yet frightened the descendants of earlier immigrants who had created a more homogeneous sense of community in and around the great cities of the North and Midwest.[5] The differences newer white immigrants presented in language, dress, food, custom, and skin and hair tone—and compounded with their pervasive poverty—spurred progressive reformers to create institutions to help these new-comers and guide them out of their precarious lives into middle-class morality and stability. They were driven by what political scientist Andrew Polsky identified as a *therapeutic impulse*—an impulse to do good by fixing children and families—exemplified in the new juvenile court.[6] Instead of formal judicial proceedings, harsh punishment, and incarceration, judges would guide children to become law-abiding and productive by using benevolent methods of instruction, surveillance, and detention. Judges would solve the problems that brought these children and their families to the court. Judges would lead.

That this foundational impulse—this *mandate*—to do good was never accomplished, not then and not now, is the reason for this book. One hundred and twenty years later, we are still sending children and families into a court that thinks it is doing good and the consequence is that, by trying to do good, it fails to do justice and often does great harm.

This is a serious claim to make at a time of many serious claims about intrusive and destructive state action. The grassroots advocacy that produced Black Lives Matter, Occupy Wall Street, and #MeToo has been studied and embraced by academics and theorists who are increasingly allied with and contributing to movement actions. On the streets, in classrooms, and increasingly in state and local legislatures, the consequences of a massive carceral system that leads directly from slavery through Jim Crow to the present phenomenon of militarized police and mass incarceration are no longer being ignored or denied. Reparations, defunding the police, and prison abolition have entered mainstream conversations. The ideas of closing jails like Rikers Island in New York, eliminating cash bail, and decriminalizing low-level nuisance behavior have found root not only in major cities but also in small towns and county seats. And state intervention in family life through child protection systems—what is now increasingly labeled "family regulation" or "family policing"—has also begun to be challenged more forcefully for its systemic and persistent attacks on families experiencing the greatest precarity in our society: low-income, marginalized, and disproportionately Black and Native American families. These movements are growing despite a persistent, xenophobic populism that has unearthed an ugly racism too hastily considered dead and buried and a sexism that is recriminalizing women's reproductive health.

Family court has yet to feel the depth of scrutiny generated around these many sites of social and institutional injustice. Most people have no idea what happens in family court today and know even less about its historical role in developing and sustaining a system of official and often destructive intervention in family life. The procedures and policies of modern family court reflect some of this country's worst afflictions—not only racism and a deep mistrust and disdain for lives lived in poverty but also a perverted approach toward equality and well-being that holds individuals rather than our neoliberal state responsible for why some children and their families fail to flourish. These children and families find themselves in family court.

When I began writing this book, I had no intention of calling for the abolition of family court. I believed that, if the court would safeguard constitutional constraints on state intervention into families' lives and champion due process protections in its proceedings, then the court could fulfill a modern-day obligation to provide children and families with a fair judicial process when state intervention in family life becomes necessary. Over the forty years that I have been practicing in and teaching about family court, I have met hundreds of dedicated people who work in the court, in the systems around the court, and in systems trying to fix the court. This book is not a condemnation of their work or dedication. It is, instead, a way to reimagine the history of family court and to confront its future. I no longer believe a court originally created to save children from their own families and communities can shed its historical mandate. At multiple points during the last century, neither efforts to limit the court's discretionary reach nor attempts to overlay the court's purported therapeutic, problem-solving character with due process protections have succeeded in constraining the court's fundamental belief in its power to do good whether by therapeutic or, if necessary, punitive means.

Do these failures lead inevitably to *abolishing* the court? My answer is "yes." Contemporary investigations into the country's continuing struggles with racism, poverty, inequality, and the separation of children from their families and communities have solidified my belief that family court cannot simply be remade into a better version of itself. Its heritage is too entwined with our history of slavery, mass displacement of indigent populations, discrimination, and inequality; its purpose is too tethered to assimilationist norms intent on fixing children and families who are different; and its practices are consistently punitive when those children and families fail to be fixed. This book concentrates on children and families most likely to be in family court because the state has determined to intervene in their lives, as opposed to when the court is called upon in paternity, custody, and support proceedings to rearrange families' lives and assets. While cases of state intervention most clearly reveal the reasons to abolish the court, Jane Murphy and Jana Singer's examination of family dispute resolution reinforces how family court has also largely failed to effectively resolve private family disputes through either formal or informal means.[7]

Prison abolitionists distinguish an abolitionary agenda from simply tearing down prison walls. The former provides a mindset for how we think and act to eliminate the carceral state that is our current approach to safety and security; the latter is a logical consequence of that mindset.[8] Abolishing family court embraces a parallel theory and approach by rejecting the interventionist tenets upon which it was built and has been maintained. The abolitionist mindset requires us, as a start, to drastically reduce the court's jurisdiction by narrowing the types and scope of the cases it has authority to adjudicate—to embrace what in 1973 the sociologist Edwin Schur labeled "radical non-intervention."[9] This means letting go of—leaving alone—those family problems that rarely if ever need court intervention to solve. Radical nonintervention embraces developing systems of support and problem-solving in neighborhoods and communities instead of in court. As I will trace in this book, soon after the court's founding, reformers like the sociologist Thomas D. Eliot were already recommending that most of what families need should be developed and provided outside the court, in the neighborhoods and communities where families feel supported and understood,[10] places where the threat of punitive sanctions and the fear of family destruction are removed.

Abolition also means shifting resources away from a largely ineffective and bloated court-based approach to family need or dysfunction. The result of this reduced scope of jurisdiction would be a smaller court-related bureaucracy, a smaller number of professions that operate predominantly in a court-based setting, and an increased awareness of and respect for the abilities of communities—if given the chance and resources—to create solutions. Ultimately there is no need for a court attempting to do good by fixing families.

Framing Tenacity: The Invention and Reinvention of Family Court

There are many stories to tell about the family court and many ways to tell them. As the sociologist and historian Charles Tilly observed, we choose to tell a story in order to make sense of the world.[11] There is the straight *chronological* approach marching through time; a more *sociological* approach looking at individual families or groups; a *biographical* approach highlighting court leaders over the decades; and a *jurisprudential* approach analyzing the meaning and impact of law on families. While I draw from each of these, I have chosen to frame this story around *the tenacity of the idea of a court invented to do good by intervening in family life*, despite its ongoing inability to accomplish its interventionist goals.

One reason family court remains so entrenched as a legal institution—despite its failures—is that it seems like such a good idea, even a great idea. A great idea can become a powerful story that is hard to abandon; we hold onto ideas that feel right, even in the face of contrary evidence. A court that cares—a court that eschews adversarial methods, embraces therapeutic paradigms, and champions judicial beneficence—is a powerful story that resonates emotionally and prevents us from seeing the harm that it may be causing. We may be unable to reject a discredited idea because of our pride or our public commitment to it. Our collective conservatism also keeps us tethered to established arrangements even when those arrangements are now doubted or new needs have been identified.[12]

And there is the sheer difficulty of radical change in a complex bureaucratic system, particularly a court system with so many intersecting yet independent parts: multiple government agencies with their own professional rules and norms, court administration structures, publicly funded and private law firms, powerful unions, and legions of local, state, and national organizations involved in maintaining or reforming these systems.[13] As one commentator expressed at the court's fiftieth year in 1949: "The foolishness of abandoning midstream a reasonably good ship is not hard to discern. This is so, even if it seems at the moment not to be moving ahead altogether satisfactorily."[14] We're still sailing that ship seventy years later, and it is still not moving ahead "altogether satisfactorily."

Moreover, court observers and scholars have noted how effective family court has been in reinventing itself to remain indispensable. Unlike the playwright Lillian Hellman's famous remark that she "cannot and will not cut my conscience to fit this year's fashions," the family court has been remarkably adept at reconfiguration. The court has routinely adopted and then abandoned fundamental missions when they proved problematic to the court's continued existence. One of the key justifications for the court in its early decades was that it would significantly reduce delinquency recidivism.[15] When that claim was soundly disproven, court supporters in the 1930s either declared that the court had never proffered that justification or that, if it had, it really didn't matter because the court was successfully accomplishing other important missions, such as diagnosing the reasons for delinquent behavior and providing specialized supervision and treatment.[16] One set of observers at the centennial commemoration in 1999 marveled at the juvenile court's ability to use its broad discretionary authority to retool its work to fit the latest theory of intervention or to serve a revolving cast of clientele. Possessing "almost complete control over its own survival," the court changes "the playing field whenever the footing becomes precarious."

These observers concluded that the court, depending on whether society is clamoring to protect children or shrieking to control them, is an "institutional chameleon" able "to intone, without blanching, whatever bromide suits the moment."[17]

The time has come to challenge the Great Idea of the family court, to reject its foundational premise that it can do good, and to stop its endless reinvention to survive. Instead, an abolitionist agenda demands meaningful, community-developed and -based resources, shifting most family assistance out of the court's sphere, shrinking the types of matters that need court intervention, and ensuring that any family-related case that requires legal adjudication safeguards all necessary due process protections in a court of law. By doing so it helps set in motion a commitment to a political and economic democracy that cares about all families.

Part I: The Great Idea

Chapter 1, "The Great Idea of the Juvenile Court," introduces the founding period of the juvenile court and the key concepts that undergirded the court's formation and remain animate in the court's current work. The court's founders believed that children could be saved from wretchedness, crime, and poverty by being brought to a new *socialized court* where the judge would employ informal processes to focus on what the child needed rather than the legal question of what the child had done. Volunteers were instrumental in creating the court and in administering the court's services. Once the court survived initial challenges to its constitutionality as a *social* court, it worked to solidify its place within a more unified court system.

Chapter 2, "The Great Idea and the Therapeutic Impulse," explores how the original juvenile court's mandate to save children is rooted in the broader therapeutic, but also xenophobic and classist, impulse of the late nineteenth century to fix families who were different. This impulse was directed at immigrant families especially but also the urban poor more broadly, seeking to assimilate them into middle-class respectability, reduce their "disruptive behavior," and maintain public order. The judicial team of judge and probation officer was tasked with figuring out what was ailing the child—and, soon after, the family—and respond with appropriate treatment or, when treatment did not work, with punishment. Coercion was always part of the court's remedial instruments even if many of the court's founders despaired the use of punishment. By the court's twenty-fifth anniversary, the disparity between the court's aspirations and its reality led some of its supporters to wonder whether a preventive approach outside court—as well as more limited interventions once the child was in court—was a better philosophy.

Chapter 3, "The Great Idea for Black Children," retraces the juvenile court's trajectory through the first half of the twentieth century to explore how Black children were either ignored by the court or treated far more harshly once they came under court authority. The chapter also explores the role of the Black community historically in supporting and protecting Black children as they began to come under the court's jurisdiction. Professionals and community volunteers were intimately involved in the efforts to provide a place for Black children in the family court while simultaneously challenging its discriminatory and punitive practices. As the court expanded to supervise the whole family—especially in child welfare cases—these families were disproportionately brought into the court and their children were removed. Finally, this chapter provides background for better understanding the choices the United States Supreme Court made when it began requiring due process in juvenile court, which is the subject of chapter 5. While the Supreme Court had the opportunity to consider the role of racial injustice in determining what due process protections should be given to children in juvenile court—especially the right to a jury trial—the Court failed to do so. As a result, the role of the juvenile court in oppressing Black children was largely ignored.

Chapter 4, "Rationalizing and Consolidating Court Power," traces the many ways the court revised its goals and tools during its second quarter-century to pledge allegiance to the Great Idea in words if not in actions. In the 1930s, judges began an organized, systematic campaign to justify and maintain the court's helping role in the face of substantial evidence that the court was not achieving its therapeutic mission. Ultimately, after the court's fiftieth anniversary celebrations were over, the juvenile court began in earnest to reinvent itself more fully by evolving into a family court with even greater jurisdictional authority over children and families. Any check on that authority would not be a serious threat to the court's existence until the late 1960s.

Chapter 5, "The Great Idea Meets Due Process," examines the Supreme Court's so-called due process revolution as it determined which procedural protections would apply to children as well as adults. During the 1960s, there was serious concern that the juvenile court was not living up to its ideals and that more regularized procedures would complement the court's treatment goals. The Supreme Court concluded that some procedural rights were necessary to ensure that juveniles received "fundamental fairness" in delinquency proceedings. These due process decisions made many juvenile court judges nervous about the future of the court. They feared that overlaying the court with procedural regularity, especially requiring jury trials, would destroy its ability to function as a therapeutic court. In 1971 in *McKeiver v. Pennsylvania* and its companion cases, the Court decided that jury trials were not mandated. Because the Court focused on what happened to Joseph McKeiver after he was arrested for stealing a quarter rather than on Barbara Burrus and her fellow young civil rights activists in *McKeiver*'s companion case, *In re Burrus*, these cases became a rumination on the ideal of the juvenile court—even with its flaws and punitive outcomes—without seriously addressing the juvenile court's long history of deeply discriminatory and punitive practices against Black children. If the Court had done so, the juvenile court might not have survived and continued its transformation into a family court encompassing even greater jurisdictional authority over families.

Part II: The Family Court Rises

Chapter 6, "Status Offenses and the Rise of the Family Court," begins with one more foray into the juvenile court's founding history to understand the court's power over children who get in trouble but don't break the law. These young people came under the court's authority in delinquency proceedings for much of the century until they began to be defined as "status offenders" instead. Important national commissions and projects deliberated whether the court should continue to have any authority over misbehaving youth who were not lawbreakers, proposing instead that children and families would be better off with voluntary, community-based assistance. Judges were horrified with what they considered a radical and dangerous idea of removing these youth from court jurisdiction entirely. They had already lost a major battle with the imposition of due process requirements in delinquency proceedings. They fought back and won. In the ensuing years, however, the court's role over status offenses has continued to be central in the battle over the appropriate boundaries of justifiable state intervention in family life.

Chapter 7, "Creating a Family Court Industry," introduces changes initiated in child welfare practices in the 1950s and 1960s that were aligning with new federal child protection mandates in the 1970s to transfigure the court into a machine processing hundreds of thousands of cases each year. The traditional process of a judge determining whether delinquent, destitute, or dependent children should be declared "wards of the court" and given services or sent away from home was reconstituted into a complex family regulation system. Federal and state child protection initiatives increasingly shifted decision-making to the family court in larger and larger numbers of cases, spurring both intended and unintended consequences for families, government agencies, and the court itself. Just as the children in the early juvenile court came from the most marginalized families, the family court's child welfare jurisdiction manages predominantly poor families and disproportionately poor families of color. States developed vast child protection systems during the 1980s and 1990s, and courts became flooded with cases that propelled litigants, caseworkers, attorneys, treatment-providers, and volunteers into court for ever more complicated and prolonged proceedings. The number of judges expanded along with the apparatus of increasingly adversarial hearings, creating an immense court industry.

Chapter 8, "The Federal Family Court," identifies how the federal government in the 1990s and early 2000s transformed family court into a full partner with state child protection systems in monitoring families. Federal funding mandates that had shaped state child welfare and foster care systems since the early 1970s began to be applied more purposefully to address the role of family court in supervising those systems. In 1990, the U.S. Advisory Board on Child Abuse and Neglect declared that "child abuse and neglect now represents a national emergency" and that the approach by federal and state governments needed to be radically changed away from punitive investigations and surveillance to community-based help and support. Its recommendations were ignored by both the George H. W. Bush and Bill Clinton administrations. The

Clinton administration instead developed and implemented the Adoption and Safe Families Act of 1996 (ASFA) as a mechanism to harness the runaway size of the nationalized child protection system. ASFA was a time-limiting remedy to accelerate decision-making by child protection authorities and family court judges, focused especially on achieving adoptions. Preventive efforts to keep families safely together or to reunite them were abandoned. Instead, vast numbers of families were torn apart permanently through termination of parental rights and many of those anticipated adoptions never happened, leaving thousands of children ageing out of foster care without a legal family. The community-based, intensive services approach the advisory board had recommended was ignored. And the family court largely abandoned its independent decision-making authority under this new collaborative and monitoring regime.

Part III: The Road to Abolition

Chapter 9, "The Failure of Reform," considers how the key elements of the original juvenile court have remained animate despite layering on greater formality and adversarialism in an ever-expanding family court. Preferences endure for informality, judges with broad authority to fix families, therapeutic solutions (which often turn punitive), and a reaffirmation of the court as being the place to solve family problems. Whatever reform does occur is framed around responding to back-end crises with calls for more resources (especially more judges) and more efficiency. Model courts (and best practices) are heralded as the way to improve family court and the systems that feed into it. But these administrative adjustments have not succeeded as planned and sometimes have made it worse, expanding the court's authority and enabling judges to employ significant discretion, even beyond lawful boundaries. In delinquency, status offense, and child welfare cases, judges remain rooted in their belief that they know best—that they can do good—and thereby thwart alternative approaches to reform—especially outside the court's realm—and obstruct fundamental change.

Chapter 10, "Abolition," provides a road map to the demise of the family court through a mindset of abolition. That mindset adopts the proposition that a court is not the place to solve family problems but instead is the place to adjudicate those cases that can be resolved only through a judicial solution. This in turn requires a reassessment of what types of cases belong in a court at all: what have we labeled a "legal controversy" that requires adjudication and what have we labeled a "legal controversy" that is really something else? For too long the idea of a therapeutic court has blurred this distinction, structuring responses to marginalized families around court processes that focus on intervention and otherwise ignoring the grossest inequalities that propel those families into court. This mission to do good has drained resources out of communities and into the court or the government agencies that report to the court, undermining the ability of communities to create solutions. The goal of abolishing the family court must be consonant with the experiences and agendas of the children, families, and communities most deeply affected by court intervention, and the solutions proposed for shrinking and then abolishing the court likewise contain lessons from community advocacy and activism. Finally, the mindset of abolition requires a radical reimagination that embraces and supports all families in a fair and equal economic and political democracy.

I

The Great Idea

Figure 1.1 Ben Lindsey, Denver's first juvenile court judge.
Courtesy of Library of Congress.

1

The Great Idea of the Juvenile Court

The original juvenile court had few of the trappings and practices of late nineteenth-century criminal courts. There was a judge but rarely lawyers. Probation officers decided whether to bring a youthful troublemaker before the judge. The child and probation officer might stand in front of the judge seated on the bench, or all parties might sit at a table to encourage the child to talk. Some early courtrooms resembled crowded dining rooms overflowing with families and hangers-on. Even rudimentary notions of due process for criminal proceedings were anathema to the purpose of the juvenile court to solve the problems that led children into trouble or caused them harm. The bargain made between a youth, her parent, and the state permitted a judge to substitute his judgment for the parents' judgment in exchange for not treating the youth as an ordinary criminal.[1] Instead, the judge would shoulder parental responsibilities fully, acting "as the wise parent or the natural parent . . . to undertake successfully to guide the child along the right way."[2]

This was the core of the Great Idea of the juvenile court: some social problems—especially those that occurred in and around families—did not belong in an adversarial setting that could identify but not resolve the problem. Instead, the state (in the guise of the kindly and committed judge and a trusty helper, the probation officer) would intervene compassionately and knowledgeably to leave the child—and even the family—better off.

Writing in 1925 about the creation of the juvenile court, Judge Charles Hoffman of Cincinnati, Ohio, declared that the court would "mark the inauguration of a new social order founded on the principles of humanity and love rather than that of retribution and hate." He lauded the pioneers who, barely twenty-five years earlier, "devised the best plan for the conservation of human life and happiness ever conceived by civilized man."[3] Judge Hoffman's remarkable description was predicated on investigations that "have brought to light a body of scientific knowledge and information which, if applied, will relieve mankind of much of its wretchedness and misery." He reflected the optimistic attachment to new behavioral sciences at the time and the ability of judges to apply them, declaring that "children by the cold processes of science can be saved from pauperism and crime and the fate of a wretched existence prevented."[4] This therapeutic impulse will be explored in depth in chapter 2. First, I provide a short introduction to the other key elements of the juvenile court that remain animate today.

The Juvenile Court as a Socialized Court

The juvenile court was novel not in its concern about children but rather in its formation to situate government-funded and -regulated assistance under court authority. Such assistance included probation services to guide children and their parents; detention facilities if the child failed to be guided; and the meager financial assistance disbursed to impoverished families, or "mothers' aid."[5] While there were private charitable agencies providing limited financial or casework assistance at the end of the nineteenth century, the juvenile court was created specifically as the site of government-supported assistance for these children. At the time there were no state child protective services, no state or federally funded foster care, no state-run institutional care facilities except the adult jails and prisons or the detested houses of refuge in which delinquent children were then committed. Orphanages run by charities were little better.

Some private charitable organizations and societies like the Society for the Prevention of Cruelty to Children would become affiliated with the court to enhance their authority to work with the families now coming under the court's jurisdiction. Many of them would later be considered part of the court's services or be available only through court authority. This affiliation established an early and persistent pattern of drawing resources that might have otherwise reduced court involvement or surveillance out of the community and into the court's purview.[6]

Children were sent to juvenile court because they were considered at risk for three categories of adversity:

(1) dependent or neglected children, that is, children who are destitute or homeless;

(2) truant children, children who have not attended school as the compulsory education law requires; and

(3) delinquent children, children "who violate any law, who are incorrigible, who knowingly associate with vicious persons, who are growing up in idleness and crime, who knowingly frequent a disorderly gaming house."[7]

Whether the child was categorized delinquent, dependent, destitute, or abandoned, the judge's solution emerged out of a resolution to fix whatever was the matter.[8] Formal rules and processes would stymie the judge's ability to determine what the child—and later the rest of the family—needed. In 1910, Judge Harvey Baker of Boston captured the judge's duty:

> The court does not confine its attention to just the particular offense which brought the child to its notice. For example, a boy who comes to court for some such trifle as failing to wear his badge when selling papers may be held on probation for months because of difficulties at school; and a boy who comes in for playing ball on the street may . . . be committed to a reform school because he is found to have habits of loafing, stealing or gambling which can not be corrected outside.[9]

This broad mandate to fix the child situated the solution process firmly in the court. Julia Lathrop, the first director of the United States Children's Bureau and the first woman to head *any* federal agency, acknowledged the novelty of a court offering a child "the best chance of wholesome life without regard to previous offense" in the introduction to a series of papers titled *The Delinquent Child and the Home*. The authors of that volume, Sophonisba Breckinridge and Edith Abbott, conceded that the lack of clear categories for intervention might be confusing but that its purpose was "[to] treat children according to their needs, unhampered by any arbitrary system of definition or classification."[10] As such, the juvenile court became the first dedicated problem-solving court.

The creation of a specialized court for children was part of a larger institutional reform movement of so-called *socialized* courts. Begun at the

end of the nineteenth century, these newfangled courts substituted informal dispute resolution processes for adversarial hearings in order to
resolve the issues of ordinary people without the costs and requirements
of traditional court formalities. The most vocal proponent of socialized
courts of this sort, the Harvard professor Roscoe Pound, envisioned in
the juvenile court a benevolent judge shaping an outcome of personalized justice for the child. Pound traced parallels between his quest to
move minor business disputes out of the courts and into arbitration
or other informal dispute resolution mechanisms and the impetus to
have judges use their discretion to determine what was best for children
and families. The goal was to make informal processes a key element of
shouldering the difficult task of administering order and control among
the urban poor.[11]

To accomplish this orderly administration, a judge, a probation officer, and perhaps a social worker would question a child, her parent, the
local cop on the beat, or the schoolmistress to ascertain what had really
brought the child before the court. Juvenile courts were encouraged not
to look like courts but rather "just a room with a table and two chairs,
where the judge and the child, the probation officer and the parents,
as occasion arises, come into close contract, and where in a more or
less formal way the whole story may be talked over."[12] Even today when
more formal courtrooms are constructed for family courts, roots of the
informal court's physical configuration remain. In the New York County
Family Court, for example, courtrooms are designed in a circle around
the central (though higher) seat of the judge, emphasizing the conversa-
tional objective of the proceedings.

This well-meaning movement to *delegalize* certain issues glorified informality as nonadversarial, preventive, and rehabilitative. Even so, the
early juvenile court faced skeptics who questioned the constitutionality
of a tribunal bereft of procedural formalities and the protections of lawyers and juries against the tyranny of judges. Their concerns, however,
were fairly rapidly dismissed as irrelevant to the purpose of the court: to
save children from criminal misbehavior and misery rather than prosecute them for their actions. "[The] common law court is not equipped
nor is it competent to deal with problems of this nature . . . [because] it
is neither a social nor a scientific institution. It is a legal institution, with

the legal mind in the saddle."[13] Neither legality nor due process was the point of the juvenile court.

The 1905 appellate decisions in *Commonwealth v. Fisher* are representative of the sleight-of-hand approach to considering the constitutionality of juvenile court. Fourteen-year-old Frank Fisher was indicted on three counts of larceny and pleaded not guilty. After the indictment, the district attorney indicated that he would not prosecute the case, thereby avoiding the possibility of criminal condemnation and prison for Frank, and instead turned over the case to the juvenile court for resolution. No testimony appeared to be taken, nor did Frank ask for a jury trial. There was nothing in the record before the appellate courts to indicate that Frank consented to his case being sent to juvenile court or to a "deal" being made with the district attorney. Frank was committed to the house of refuge instead of prison and the indictments were dismissed. The intermediate appellate court determined that Frank could have asked for a jury trial, but not having done that he could not later argue that this made the subsequent juvenile court process unconstitutional. The criminal and juvenile proceedings had two different purposes. A criminal trial established innocence or guilt. As for the juvenile process:

> It is to save, not to punish; it is to rescue, not to imprison; it is to subject to wise care, treatment and control rather than to incarcerate in penitentiaries and jails; it is to strengthen the better instincts and to check the tendencies which are evil; it aims, in the absence of proper parental care, or guardianship, to throw around a child, just starting in an evil course, the strong arm of the parent patriae.[14]

In its subsequent affirmance, the Pennsylvania Supreme Court concluded that, since all children under sixteen are entitled to this beneficence and children can and are treated differently than adults, such distinctions present no constitutional challenges. Nor did Frank lack due process because there was *no* process due to be had. Frank could be brought "into one of the courts of the state without any process at all, for the purpose of subjecting [him] to the state's guardianship and protection. . . . [When] the child gets there, and the court, with the power to save it, determines on its salvation, and not its punishment, it is immaterial how it got there." The court further explained that Frank would have had a right to a jury trial if this had been a criminal case. Since there was no crime taken to trial, there was no need for a jury: "Whether the child deserves to be saved by the state is no more a question for a jury than whether the father, if able to save it, ought to save it."[15] This question of jury trials in juvenile court would arise out of Pennsylvania again—in *McKeiver v. Pennsylvania*—and reach the U.S. Supreme Court sixty years later. There the same question of whether a child was being punished or saved in juvenile court would be determined in language infused with less religious fervor but similar meaning. In the meantime, constitutional challenges to the very existence of the juvenile court were repeatedly rebuffed; the court would not be significantly challenged again until the 1960s, during the due process revolution of the Supreme Court under Chief Justice Earl Warren.

The Structure of the Early Juvenile Court and Its Lasting Influence

The early juvenile court was constructed around three interwoven concepts. The first was giving the court jurisdiction over a specialized set of issues related to the family: determining whether a child was a delinquent, truant, destitute, or dependent child. The second was saving that child through the informal processes of a socialized court. The third situated this informal, specialized, child-saving court within an efficient and well-managed unified court system. As constitutional challenges receded as an impediment to the juvenile court's development, supporters and detractors argued instead about these three concepts. They deliberated the correct boundaries of the court's authority, the best methods to assert that authority, and the potential limits of the court to resolve family issues and save children.

The juvenile court's jurisdiction over family matters evolved and expanded during the twentieth century. Specialized court names—the most common being juvenile court, children's court, dependency court, orphans' court, domestic relations court, and family court—are still used across the country today to signify that the court is addressing only family-related issues. Such a contemporary court may adjudicate one or more and sometimes all of the issues that bring family members to court: divorce, custody, support, delinquency, status offenses, domestic violence, child protection, and foster care and adoption. States continue to vary tremendously on which types of family matters are adjudicated in one or more specialized courts, but all states have carved out some family-related matters to be heard in a specialized court apart from other civil or criminal matters.

These specialized family courts continued to use informal processes of questioning, cajoling, and sometimes threatening a child or parent in order to determine how to save the child (and, later on, the entire family). The court's investigative methods were intended to substitute for formal adversarial and litigious practices. These informal practices also became increasingly cloistered over the court's first quarter-century, diminishing the ability of the public and the press to monitor the court and leading later court reformers to assume that juvenile court proceedings had always been out of the public eye.[16]

The third concept of situating the juvenile court within a unified court system has two meanings for this specialized court. As a general goal, "court unification" means rationalizing how an entire court system fits together to run more efficiently and fairly. Unification may lead to resources being apportioned more equitably among the myriad types of cases being heard within a court system. Applied specifically to courts addressing family issues, unification has also meant gathering all of the issues that might bring members of a family into court and assigning them to a single judge. This broad authority permits the judge to, for example, adjudicate a child delinquent, determine whether that child's parent is also neglectful, issue a financial support order for the parent no longer living in the home, and enter an order of protection against a violent grandparent.

Not surprisingly, specialization and unification have often been in tension, balancing the desire for a more efficient system for the court to assist a family while being skeptical about too much power in the hands of a single judge. Reform efforts have also vacillated between informality and formality within these varied unified court processes. Even after specialized courts were required to adopt greater formality to comply with procedural due process mandates in the 1960s and 1970s—the right to counsel for juveniles in delinquency proceedings being the most prominent—they have retained a preference for sidestepping formal and generally more adversarial proceedings. This preference to minimize formality requirements was reinforced by Supreme Court decisions that specifically carve out when due process protections are unnecessary in family court—especially the assignment of counsel for adults in civil matters—in what the Supreme Court has characterized as "routine" cases. Yet the cases that the Court has identified as so routine that counsel is not obligatory are not routine at all, applying to determinations as consequential as the termination of parental rights and imprisonment for nonpayment of support.[17] As a result of defining family-related cases as less worthy of heightened due process requirements and more suited for informal procedures overall, the concept of informal personalized justice with significant judicial discretion in a specialized forum has remained remarkably intact in family court for over a hundred years.

Court Jurisdiction and Authority over the Family

In 1914, the sociologist and court observer Thomas D. Eliot of Oregon noted with concern the range of responsibilities juvenile courts around the country were shouldering, some purposefully trying to be "all things to all men" instead of determining whether assistance to the family would be better found in a school, a hospital, a charity, or a church.[18] That same year, writing of his experience as a lawyer in Pennsylvania, Edward Lindsey cautioned about the "arbitrary powers of the court" over the status of children and rejected the idea that the juvenile court judge's actions on behalf of the state were consistent with earlier equity powers in courts of chancery. Rather, the power of the juvenile court judge was far greater, for such a judge could interfere with a child's liberty without trial and without requiring parental consent.[19]

Judges of the first courts responded to these warnings by justifying their role to "adjust the relationships in family life." The first job of the juvenile court was to determine through scientific inquiry "what judgment of the court would best serve the interest of the individual child."[20] This naturally and necessarily led to shifting assistance from the child to her lawful guardian and to recognizing that the family is the basic unit of society in need of the court's intervention. Writing in 1928, Judge L. B. Day of the domestic relations and juvenile delinquency court in Omaha, Nebraska, noted the intersecting impact of desertion, divorce, custody, and support with dependency, delinquency, and adoption. These matters required the intervention of the court to protect the child and to ensure not only that the state's legal obligations to children were met but also that the state was not too greatly burdened financially by family disruption or dissolution. Judge Day believed the ideal family court would have broad jurisdiction to include all those categories and more: domestic violence, unwed mothers, mothers' pensions, and guardianship. Working with the expertise of probation officers, physicians, psychiatrists, and charitable social welfare institutions, Judge Day trusted that the court would approach "the adjustment of family disorganization in a friendly, sympathetic and intelligent manner," diminishing if not eliminating the family's disruption.[21]

Several years earlier, in 1923, Judge Edward Waite of Minneapolis responded to an attack on the early court by surveying the literature about the court during its first two decades. While the court was in many ways still in its infancy and those writing about the court were few, Judge Waite asked that it be "judged at the highest point of its present normal development" before outlining the justifications for the court—justifications that read remarkably like those asserted across the country today.[22] Judge Waite began with acknowledging that the court is neither a complete success nor a complete failure. Rather, where it is not a success, it can be fixed rather than abandoned. Many urban courts are more successful, he noted, because they have more resources. As they continue to improve, urban courts will serve as a model for rural areas still developing. Better judges can be identified, replacing judges unwilling to embrace the mission of a socialized court that intervenes to solve a family's problems.

Judge Waite championed expanded jurisdiction over the family to draw better judges into the court who would be challenged by greater complexity. He also emphasized that the court must retain the ultimate authority to identify and supervise the agencies providing assistance to the families. Judge Waite believed giving such authority to these agencies without judicial supervision would be unwise, because if they fail to engage the family there would be no way to coerce success. Schools or other agencies may serve preventive functions, but only a judge can order the supervision or institutionalization identified for the child's or the family's good. Only a judge has the power to order the child into school, into detention, or into reform school. And the child's own good is the only purpose of the judge's order. When a judge of the juvenile court punishes a child for misbehaving, the punishment must "be administered in the true parental spirit, as an obligation due to the child, not as a penalty exacted from him."[23]

The ultimate solution for a successful court governing the family is to expand, not contract, court jurisdiction, even if some of the boundaries of authority are questionable or controversial. Judge Waite acknowledged that bringing families into the court under dependency grounds—essentially because the family is poor—is not ideal yet was justified "for the purpose of making sure that no destitute and unprotected child shall fail to find custody and support." He then posed the rhetorical question that judges are still asking and generally answering affirmatively today: "Is not this the safer policy?"[24]

Poor Mothers, Their Children, and the Juvenile Court

The scope of the court's jurisdiction—over whom the court has authority—cannot be isolated from how and when the court chooses to assert that authority. When the Pennsylvania attorney Edward Lindsey was despairing over the legality of the juvenile court in 1914, he quoted disdainfully from a 1905 Illinois Supreme Court decision upholding its juvenile court and delinquency statute, noting that the Illinois court asserted: "This law applies, with equal force, to the son of the pauper and the millionaire, to the minister's son (who is sometimes the wolf among the flock), as well as to the son of the convict and the criminal." In response, Lindsay protested: "As a matter of fact, however, it is not applied to the dominant social class and if ever it is so applied it will undoubtedly be largely modified."[25] Monrad Paulson drew the same conclusion when he surveyed the court over fifty years later, noting "[the] upper and middle classes show surprising agility in keeping their delinquent children out of the court."[26] Paulson had recently come across a confidential study of the court that cautioned against using the same kind of intervention against wealthy families for maltreating their children. The study noted: "According to statistics, many child abuse cases come from within families well-placed financially and of repute. In considering help to such families, reporting to the police[] and taking court actions right away may not be appropriate."[27]

The jurisdiction of the original juvenile court over families not "well-placed financially and of repute," especially the immigrant and migrant families of the industrial centers, reflected the strong belief that the children of these families needed court intervention not only to be saved from destitution but also to be made into the progressive reformers' understanding of Americans—that is to say, white Americans. As Katherine Bullard has persuasively asserted, the progressives' work helped to define "the racialized child citizen" who was white, even when their intent was to protect all children.[28] Most children of color at the time— African American, Native American, Mexican American, and Asian American—were not considered worthy of this citizenship project even if they found themselves in the early court.[29] When the juvenile court seriously turned its attention to children of color, citizenship assimilation was not among its goals.[30]

The poor children and children of color who find themselves in the family court today have something in common with the white immigrant children of the 1900s: they bring with them significant and even intractable problems that cannot be solved in the cases of child protection or truancy or support that currently trigger court jurisdiction. Those problems of poverty, racism, sexism, and a slew of inequalities in housing, employment, education, child care, nutrition, health, and mental health have always been beyond the authority and capacity of any court to resolve. Our national aversion to identifying positive rights within the Constitution that ensure basic shelter, nutrition, health, and education is an aversion that has been rightly called the "deconstitutionalization of poverty," which leaves family courts ordering ineffective or irrelevant assistance as if they that assistance could substitute for a what a child or family truly needs.[31] The personalized justice that the court's founders envisioned has never been able to grapple with these structural and systemic barriers, not only limiting the solutions a judge can provide but also leaving the court perpetually in a bind. As the New York judge Justine Wise Polier wrote in 1941:

Children's Courts cannot supply adequate parents, minimum economic security, good schooling, proper medical care, sanitary housing conditions, or any other basic needs for wholesome family life. They can seek to discover what has brought each child to Court, and enlist appropriate community facilities to grapple with causative factors or ameliorate their effects. This is their strength and their weakness. The high purpose of the founders of these Courts can be realized only as the community assumes greater responsibility for every one of its children.[32]

During its earliest years, the juvenile court administered mothers' aid, a practice that early court observers found unwise, cautioning against bringing children under court jurisdiction who were dependent or destitute but not maltreated. Writing a decade earlier than Judge Waite, the prominent civil rights lawyers Bernard Flexner and Roger Baldwin advised in 1914 against drawing children and families into the court for reasons of poverty alone and identified the harm of separating children from their families because they were poor.[33] This was consistent with the position taken at the 1909 White House Conference on the Care of Dependent Children, convened by President Theodore Roosevelt. Attendees strongly favored keeping children at home with subsidies rather than removing them from their parents. Widowed, divorced, or abandoned white and European immigrant mothers were to be supported in raising their children as long as they were considered worthy of their motherhood. Many mothers were not—especially in the South and Southwest—where the neediest mothers were Black and Mexican. For poor mothers who led lives that were considered "unsuitable" or "immoral," their children were far more likely to find themselves in juvenile court and taken away "for urgent and compelling reasons."[34] Despite the general agreement that poverty alone did not indicate unfitness, children continued to be removed from their families for poverty alone throughout the century. In 1962, Margaret Keeney Rosenheim, the great chronicler of the juvenile court, commented on Flexner and Baldwin's concerns about this practice fifty years earlier, noting that this remained a perennial issue for the court.[35] For the creators of juvenile court, the issue of poverty could not be separated from its role in fomenting delinquency. The broad definitions assigned to the terms "delinquency" and "dependency" purposefully allowed for poor children to be brought to court as a preventive measure. There the socialized court would save the child through personalized justice administered by a caring and wise judge with the aid of willing helpers.

The Role of Volunteers in Creating and Sustaining the Juvenile Court

Volunteers were central to creating and sustaining the original juvenile court and retain a critical role today. This is in contrast to a general aversion to the public knowing too much about what goes on in courts addressing family matters. The extent to which juvenile court proceedings have been open to public and media scrutiny has varied over the decades. Even today, states and localities follow a variety of rules for allowing the public and the media to observe and report on court proceedings. Some courts are presumptively open, with procedures in place to request closures; others are presumptive closed, with ways to ask the judge to open the courtroom. Public-minded volunteers, by contrast, have always been welcomed into the court.

The first juvenile court in Chicago—and the other early courts that soon followed—was founded in large part through the efforts of public-minded women who championed a separate court and probation service for children, and they labored tirelessly for many years to secure its creation. The Chicago philanthropist Lucy Flowers, for example, has been called "the mother of the juvenile court" for ensuring its creation.[36] Julia Lathrop, the first director of the Children's Bureau, recounted that, to protect delinquent children, there "came a body of women, many of unusual cultivation and public spirit, who had given earnest study and hard personal work to the social and civil problems of their city" and were intent on creating a children's court with a children's judge.[37] These same volunteers worked cooperatively first to secure legislation to create the court, and then, in concert with court officers, "worked and sacrificed" to ensure the court's survival.[38] The Chicago Juvenile Court Committee—in large part comprised of delegates of various white women's clubs—also established the "Detention Home" to house and care for children involved in court. Unable to get funding from the city to transport the children, the committee bought "its own omnibus, its own horses, renting its own stable and furnishing its own horse-feed."[39] Fur-

Figure 1.2. Julia Lathrop, first director of the federal Children's Bureau. Courtesy of Library of Congress.

thermore, the members of the committee vetted prospective judges and even "sat beside the judge to advise or assist in anyway possible."[40] Looking back at that work twenty-five years later, Louise de Koven Bowen, a former president of the Juvenile Court Committee, lamented that, when the committee eventually stepped back from day-to-day involvement, the Detention Home became nothing better than a jail staffed by political appointees with little care or experience dealing with children.[41] Even with such setbacks, the involvement of volunteers in juvenile court became an accepted and promoted practice.

At times, volunteers were the only source of potential personnel.[42] Until the robust advancement of social work as a profession and probation services as sufficiently paid employment, the "friendly visitor" could be almost any reputable person. In Cincinnati, "[the] Rotary and other civic and luncheon clubs assist[ed] in caring for particular groups of both delinquents and dependents."[43] If free labor were not enough of an incentive for the court system, supporters of volunteers also lauded the spontaneity and worldly experience of amateurs: "[T]he person who made a success in life would make the greatest success in probation work."[44] Volunteer advocates in family courts today are similarly acknowledged for their life experiences.[45] Those early volunteers—and many volunteers today—came to the work to save children. In the early days they applied Christian beliefs to redeem depraved families: "The visitor saw in her client less an equal or potential equal than an object of charitable reform whose unfortunate and lowly condition resulted from ignorance or deviations from middle-class values and pattern of life organization."[46] That volunteers (as well professionals) want to save children from their families and communities still animates significant work in and around the court.

Yet as early as 1910, court observers warned against overreliance on volunteers. Bernard Flexner of Kentucky believed that the juvenile court's success depended on a well-funded and -staffed probation department. He noted with concern the number of courts continuing to rely on private donations to fund paid probation officers, as well as the number of courts relying in whole or in part on volunteers. Flexner identified multiple problems for volunteer offices: the difficulty in identifying volunteers with the right attributes; the ability to supervise them sufficiently; the extremely limited number of children a volunteer should oversee; and the challenge of standardizing volunteer work. All these factors counseled against "indiscriminate use of volunteers."[47] As time passed, concerns about the motives of volunteers became even more blunt. In his chronicle of the early Chicago court, the historian David Tanenhaus noted that, by the 1920s, volunteers were often "unwelcome outsiders in the neighborhoods that they investigated, surveyed and policed."[48] He quoted from a contemporary report about many volunteers in the Juvenile Protection Association: "[T]he appeal which it uses to get its funds . . . applies the mores of a small New England community to a great cosmopolitan city."[49]

While the juvenile court came to rely increasingly on professional staff, the role of the volunteer remained an acceptable substitute when public coffers were closed to further funding. Looking at juvenile probation in New York City in the early 1950s, for example, the social work professor Alfred Kahn warned that, while "unskilled assistance of enthusiastic volunteers" may have a role, "treatment responsibility" should be administered by "personnel who have been suitably prepared" and "have the ability to develop, understand and control personal relationships with the children they are trying to help."[50] While greater professionalization and formality infused the family court in the 1960s and 1970s, as the court became overwhelmed with cases in the 1980s the role of the volunteer reemerged forcefully through the court's engagement of *guardian ad litem* (*GAL*) and court-appointed special advocates (CASAs), two types of volunteers looking out for a child's "best interests" in dependency and/or maltreatment proceedings. As the national CASA organization proudly notes on its website: "These children, who had experienced abuse or neglect, needed trained volunteers speaking up in the courtroom for their best interests."[51] Volunteerism historically was about saving children. Today volunteers are supposed to protect the best interests of children. In both instances, their families are seen as unable to care for them. From the earliest days of the court, poverty, disfavored behavior, ethnicity, and eventually race indicated who would find themselves in proceedings that interrogated their lives and justified strangers—judges and volunteers alike—controlling their lives.

The basic concepts that animated the original juvenile court remain embedded in the family court more than a century later. The court is still a socialized court, routinely employing informality in its proceedings. The judge continues to have broad discretion over many aspects of the court's processes and in the dispositions that are meted out to both children and parents. Court reform efforts continue to try to consolidate all family issues before a single judge. And the families who find themselves in the court today are still overwhelmingly impoverished and marginalized and now disproportionately Black, Brown, and Native American. Chapter 2 explores the nature of the court's therapeutic impulse—its alleged ability to do good—and considers how that impulse has helped maintain the court's mandate to problem-solve even as more coercive and punitive dispositions came to dominate its work.

2

The Great Idea and the Therapeutic Impulse

In 2004, Judge Leonard Edwards received the William H. Rehnquist Award for Judicial Excellence. The prize is bestowed each year by the National Center for State Courts to a state court judge who "exemplifies the highest level of judicial excellence, integrity, fairness, and professional ethics."[1] Judge Edwards, a distinguished and dedicated California jurist, was the first juvenile or family court judge to receive the award, a testament to his national leadership on behalf of these courts. On receiving the award in the Great Hall of the United States Supreme Court, Judge Edwards took the opportunity to remind his august audience of the critical work done by his colleagues throughout the country while also lamenting how infrequently the Supreme Court has acknowledged that work. Judge Edwards captured these judges' distinctive role:

> Judges in the juvenile court are charged with keeping children safe; restoring families; finding permanency for children; and holding youth, families, and service providers accountable. . . . We have to convene child- and family-serving agencies, schools, and the community around the problems facing our most vulnerable and troubled children. . . . The role of the juvenile court judge is unlike any other. In the traditional judicial role, deciding a legal issue may complete the judge's task; however, in deciding the future of a child or family member, the juvenile court judge must, in addition to making a legal decision, be prepared to take on the role of an administrator, a collaborator, a convener, and an advocate.[2]

Judge Edwards is proud of these multiple roles with broad responsibility for children and families, a significant departure from the impartial, restrained, and objective judge in the common law tradition. As the ultimate authority in the courtroom, judges in all trial courts today assume a leadership role to make sure cases move along expeditiously, that due process protections are upheld, and that everyone in the courtroom is working. Professor Judith Resnik calls this modern decision maker the "managerial judge."[3] The family court judge is given a different, more comprehensive managerial role. Under New York law, for example, the family court judge has "a wide range of powers for dealing with the complexities of family life so that its action may fit the particular needs of those before it."[4] Judge Edwards described that power as "the legal equivalent of an emergency room in the medical profession. We intervene in crises and figure out the best response on a case-by-case, individualized basis."[5]

When the juvenile court was created at the beginning of the twentieth century, juvenile court judges were similarly described as "doctor-counselors" or "judicial therapists" who are "specialists in the art of human relations."[6] The judge's task was to "get the whole truth about a child" just as "a physician searches for every detail that bears on the condition of a patient."[7] The medical metaphor stands in stark contrast to a judge who is asked to determine whether a child committed a crime or whether a parent is neglectful. Those determinations rely on evidence of acts and intent rather than what the best response to those acts might be. Judge Harvey Humphrey Baker, the first judge of the Boston Juvenile Court, used medical metaphors to explain why the juvenile court doesn't "confine its attention to just the particular offense which brought the child to its notice."[8] Judge Baker believed "it is helpful to think of [court officials] as physicians in a dispensary,"[9] referring to both the physical arrangement in a juvenile court but also to the way in which the court conducts its business:

> In determining the disposition to be made of the case the procedure of the physician is very closely followed. . . . The judge and probation officer consider together, like a physician and his junior, whether the outbreak which resulted in the arrest of the child was largely accidental, or whether it is habitual or likely to be so; whether it is due chiefly to some inherent physical or moral defect of the child, or whether some feature of his environment is an important factor; and then they address themselves to the question of how permanently to prevent the recurrence.[10]

And whereas a doctor may have a duty to minimize pain, the judge and probation officer "from time to time deliberately cause the child discomfort, because the discomfort of punishment affords in some cases an indispensable stimulus or moral tonic which cannot be supplied in any other way."[11]

Judge Baker was providing the prescription for the therapeutic impulse that continues to govern the family court today. The Great Idea of the juvenile court was not only to treat children differently than adults when they misbehave or are dependent but also to intervene in the child's life in a way that would eliminate or at least diminish the underlying causes of the misbehavior or dependency. Judge Baker's description of the judge and the probation officer examining the cause of the "outbreak" and then finding an individualized remedy, even one that might hurt, became the basic formula for treating the problem child or family. That framework remains today.

The Therapeutic Moment

The original juvenile court was born at a therapeutic moment, when there was a strong belief that wedding treatment for social ills to public authority could normalize children and families who occupied the edges of society. The political scientist Andrew Polsky called this the "therapeutic impulse."[12] Using "scientifically" endorsed casework techniques in conjunction with judicial oversight, the probation officer (and, later, the psychiatrist and social worker) would uncover the underlying causes of a child's misbehavior and, in conjunction with the judge, create an individualized treatment plan. Children and their parents would be expected to embrace the judge's determination and abide by his directives. Ideally, the initial efforts would be the least intrusive or restrictive. Children and parents would meet with probation officers; children would attend school; and parents would be expected to share their concerns freely with the clinic treatment staff. Resistance to these more "benign" interventions could lead to increasingly coercive and punitive sanctions, including removing children from their homes, sending them to special schools, or confining them in institutions.[13] Only a year into its work, the Chicago juvenile court was negotiating with the United States Navy to send older boys to training ships to "greatly lengthen the period for discipline and increase the chances of thoroughly reforming wayward youths"[14] Some of the pioneering child-savers emphasized removing children from "undesirable surroundings" rather than strengthening families.[15] Even the most punitive steps, like institutionalization, were considered part of treatment or, as Judge Baker described, "an indispensable stimulus or moral tonic which cannot be supplied in any other way."[16] Moreover, this tonic was ever-flowing: the child and family would remain under surveillance and supervision until the judge was satisfied that the patient was cured.

The court's therapeutic mantle was a disguise—not just of punishment but also of the state's failure to address the inequities suffered by most of the families finding themselves at the courtroom door. To be sure, progressive reformers identified the concrete dangers of an increasingly urbanized life and sought to address them by eliminating child labor, championing public schools, and tearing down slums. Yet their central purpose was to uplift the family morally despite the social ills and economic hardships they faced.[17] The therapeutic impulse of the day did not include wealth redistribution. The meager mothers' aid distributed by the juvenile court to the deserving few at the beginning of the twentieth century came with an expectation that such financial aid would normalize the family and create the proper environment for children.[18] Mothers were expected to comply with their caseworkers' requirements for how to run their households and raise their children in exchange for inadequate but desperately needed sums that could be snatched away at any time. The coercion inherent in this method was central to the court's treatment approach. Very few of the reformers at the time understood how coercion would compromise the therapeutic relationship being developed between the child and the probation officer or the judge. Coercion remained a central feature in a "continuum of remedial instruments" readily at hand.[19]

The therapeutic mantle was also intended to substitute for the routine legal processes of other courts. In addition to jettisoning the blame and retribution of criminal proceedings, the juvenile court permitted the state to intervene in family life with little more than good intentions. Referring to the 1899 statute that created the juvenile court in Chicago, the first assistant State's Attorney for Cook County, Albert Barnes, explained the impetus for preventive action in deterring the child from a life of crime or destitution:

[The] State must step in and exercise guardianship over a child found under such adverse social or individual conditions as develop crime. To that end it must not wait as now to deal with him in jails, bridewells and reformatories after he has become criminal in habits and tastes, but must seize upon the first indications of the propensity as they may be evinced in his conditions of neglect or delinquency.[20]

Seizing upon the first indications of misbehavior or maltreatment meant that "any reputable person" could initiate cases by filing a petition alleging that the child needed court supervision.[21] The child did not have to commit an offense, and her parent did not need to maltreat her, for the court to intervene if there was a problem at school or rumor of an immoral environment at home.[22] Instead of collecting evidence of an offense before a court hearing, the probation officer would investigate the child's condition and the family's social circumstances in order to recommend the desired outcome to the judge. Even prior to a court order, the probation officer might supervise a child, even removing her from the home, in order to start her on the right path.[23] In 1910, Grace Abbott, the second director of the federal Children's Bureau, wrote that the desired language of juvenile delinquency statutes "make the definition much more inclusive so that the court will not be unable, because of any technical lack of jurisdiction, to place a child under the care of the court."[24] Many of the early child-savers were equally concerned that the state might miss an opportunity to set the misbehaving youngster on the right path as they were that the child would be punished as an adult.[25]

A New Kind of Judge: General Supervisor and Mentor of the Home

The expansive authority of the court to supervise a child was in stark contrast to the common law tradition in which the judge's "sole duty is to determine under the law and the facts the questions presented."[26] Most publications examining the early court reassured readers that the *parens patriae* power vested in the judge drew on powerful precedents in the chancery courts of England, which emphasized equity outcomes and could be distinguished from criminal court—a "complicated legal machine"—that emphasized punitive results.[27] They lauded the potential of joining legal apparatus with scientific findings to justify the court's therapeutic role. As introduced in chapter 1, the juvenile court was an early attempt to embody the legal scholar Roscoe Pound's "sociological jurisprudence" model of dispute resolution that favored informality and discretion in judicial decision-making. Consistent with other progressive ideals of the time, Pound proposed diminishing contentious court procedures to serve individual and societal interests simultaneously. Pound's call for greater government intervention to protect workers and public safety extended "to administer justice in relations of family life, where conditions of crowded urban life and economic pressure threaten the security of the social institutions of marriage and the family."[28] "Personalized justice" administered on behalf of children required scientific expertise that included understanding the factors that had led a youth to misbehave. The judge, the probation officer, and, within a few short years, the psychiatrist, psychologist, and social worker engaged in a process to investigate and respond to the underlying causes of the child's misbehavior. This occurred on both the individual and systemic levels.

Dr. William Healy, the first director of the Juvenile Psychopathic Center of the Chicago Juvenile Court, developed a system of examining and recording information about children in court to provide the judge with constructive recommendations for the particular child as well as to test the delinquency theories then in vogue, including genetic ones (something that he later regretted).[29] By the time he delivered his findings to the Children's Bureau in a 1922 report titled *The Practical Value of Scientific Study of Juvenile Delinquents*, he had studied children in Chicago and Boston courts and had concluded that if the treatment is to effect a cure—the cessation of delinquency or dependency—then the intervention "must balance carefully what is causative and alterable in the environment and what is not, and what is causative and possible to influence in the inner mental life and what is not."[30] Healy recognized how exceptional a judge would have to be to craft such an intervention, concluding that "[it requires] of the judge more thoughtfulness, a wider education in the human sciences, more shrewd discernment, more close reasoning on the relation of theory, fact, and proposed treatment to outcomes than is demanded in any other court."[31] Healy's archetype juvenile court judge would also have to be given far more power than the typical common law judge.

Judge Willis B. Perkins, a prosecutor and later a Michigan circuit court judge early in the twentieth Century, proposed adopting the inquisitorial tradition of the civil law courts of continental Europe to justify the judge's scrutiny deep into a family's life:[32]

> The judge of a family court must have larger powers than [a judge of a common law court]. He must be at liberty to investigate or cause to be investigated every anti-social or abnormal act growing out of family disturbances. His duties must necessarily be inquisitorial rather than accusatory. . . . To empower a judge to act on his own initiative immediately and without pleadings; to authorize him to become the general supervisor and mentor of the home and its several occupants, will be a new thing in our jurisprudence.[33]

Judge Perkins was concerned that society would not tolerate these "tyrannical methods unless they are fruitful of good results," so he set the standard for this new kind of judicial officer very high:

> It is apparent, therefore, that a judge who is given these extraordinary powers must be a man well versed in the law, of large experience, unswerving firmness, broad sympathies, and clear, quick and accurate judgments. Wanting in any of these elements, his work must fail.[34]

Judge Perkins was right to be concerned about the methods and character of the judge. From the beginning of the juvenile court movement, there had been resistance to eliminating the formalities of courts to permit unfettered intervention in family life through chancery-type procedures.[35] Nevertheless, the justification of a court process in which the child is not *tried* by the judge but is *saved* by him prevailed. As Ben Lindsey, Denver's first juvenile court judge, explained, "more is accomplished through love than by any other method."[36] Any other method included the rule of law.

Probation: The Physician's Junior

The judge utilizing the extraordinary powers that Judge Perkins identified required more than character, learning, and understanding. He also needed help. Judge Perkins understood that "adequate probation departments, departments for investigation, medical and other treatment, and the carrying on of such scientific and other investigations as are essential to get at the root of the disturbances."[37] "[Like] a physician and his junior," the judge employed a probation officer to complement his work. As the eyes and ears of the judge, the probation officer considered complaints from schools, police officers, and parents; decided whether to send the complainants away with words of advice or referrals for assistance; and conducted initial investigations to determine whether to bring the child before the judge and, pending that appearance, whether to keep the child in detention to observe his behavior. In this way the probation officer was characterized as a "social physician."[38] And if court intervention was needed, the probation officer presented the case to the judge, and they would determine together the "personalized justice" needed to straighten the child's path.[39]

The probation officer's work was to be based on the newest scientific knowledge and administered in a therapeutic casework model. Mary Richmond, an early theorist of social work as a profession and the greatest progenitor of the casework model, "emphasized systematic, efficient, and accurate record keeping along with an attitude of scientific investigation and understanding of the client's problems."[40] But probation was a particular kind of casework. After a lifetime of studying the juvenile court, Professor Thomas D. Eliot noted in 1937 that probation was "a new type of case work: namely, probation not merely as legal status, but as a social process and as a special educational treatment."[41] This social process was a "system of reporting and of home visits; their purpose was not only supervision to keep the child from doing wrong, but constructive effort to enrich his interests, implant right ideals and encourage the formation of sound habits."[42] This model remains extant today.

Probation was an integral part of the Great Idea. The statute establishing the first juvenile court, in Chicago, included a provision for the court to appoint "one or more discreet persons of good character" to serve as probation officers.[43] Initially these probation officers were funded through private donations, but as the need for a larger professionalized staff grew, public funding was authorized with a requirement that probation officers be administered civil service examinations. Yet despite an overall commitment to the role of probation in facilitating individualized responses to children's needs, there were concerns about just how much power probation officers should have to investigate families' lives, how effective community supervision was, and when it was appropriate to institutionalize children who did not respond to a probation plan.[44]

There was also disagreement about where probation departments should be situated. Today probation departments are part of the executive branch in almost every state. However, when the U.S. Department of Justice investigated the St. Louis County Family Court in 2012, it found that probation officers were court employees, raising serious questions about the separation of executive and judicial powers.[45] Such concerns would have puzzled early court supporters because a majority of probation officers were appointed by the judge and served at his pleasure.[46] The symbiotic relationship between the judge and the probation officer was key to effecting real change in the child and to protecting the probation department from political patronage.[47] Having a probation service was considered one of the hallmarks of a true juvenile court—"an essential feature of adequate juvenile court organization."[48]

Yet not every jurisdiction followed this model. In 1920, the Children's Bureau published the first national survey of juvenile courts. To the dismay of the researchers, although every state but Wyoming had legislated juvenile probation, only 45 percent of the responding courts had a probation service, and fewer than half of these had full-time officers on the payroll.[49] In response, a national campaign was launched to spur the development of probation services as a profession. The professionalization of probation was intended to improve the quality of the officers so that children would not just be sent back into their communities to cause more trouble. The probation officer was intended to become more than "a jack-of-all-trades or first-aid man," because his role was not simply to secure "for the child shoes, job, club, book, medicine, as the case demanded" but to dig beyond the immediate needs of the child into his deeper soul.[50]

The National Probation Association (NPA) was founded in 1907 to develop national standards for intervention, especially for young people

Figure 2.1. Children's Court. Courtesy of Library of Congress.

in juvenile court.[51] Over the next two decades the NPA, in concert with the Children's Bureau, rallied to transform probation from a volunteer, privately funded, haphazardly utilized program into a standardized, professional, and integral part of the juvenile court system.[52] These changes were considered essential for the survival of the court at a time when its founders still retained optimism for its ultimate success. As Evelina Belden, the chief researcher for the Children's Bureau's 1920 survey of the courts, emphasized: "Without definite provision for the investigation and supervision of children's cases [by probation] an attempt to socialize the treatment of children who reach the courts would be fruitless."[53] By 1923, the NPA and the Children's Bureau had jointly published a formal set of standards for the juvenile court and distributed them across the country, reiterating the centrality of the probation officer to a court focused on a child's social condition and needs.[54]

The Child, the Clinic, and the Court

Professionalizing probation services was only one of the efforts aimed at maintaining the court's therapeutic purpose. By the second decade of the twentieth century, concerns about the court's effectiveness in deterring delinquency and normalizing youth behavior had already surfaced.

Response to these concerns can be sorted roughly into three overlapping categories. The first was ensuring a therapeutic approach rather than a punitive one. The strongest supporters of the court wanted to improve its ability to intervene effectively using the most up-to-date theories of behavioral practice. These supporters were dismayed at the failure of courts to embrace what Judge Edward F. Waite of Minnesota identified as "doing something for a child because of what he *is* and *needs*" rather than "doing something *to* a child because of what he *has done*."[55] They wanted a recommitment to the therapeutic model and a rejection of the punitive tendencies of judges they were observing across the country. The 1923 proposed Standard Juvenile Court Act, which provided a basic model of what a proper juvenile court required, strongly backed the therapeutic ideal. The act recommended broad jurisdiction over all children under eighteen; a specially trained judge familiar with the behavioral sciences and the social problems of the day; continued use of informal procedures; diminished use of punitive rather than preventive institutions; and finally, increased resources for this complex system of treatment and care.[56]

Securing resources was the second category of concern. Court supporters understood well that resources were limited, but the model could not succeed without both government and philanthropic resources. Judges, probation officers, and psychiatric staff overwhelmed by cases were unable to offer individualized treatment based on careful diagnoses and investigations. Without sufficient staff, supervision of the home became perfunctory; the likelihood of steering a child away from delinquency was diminished; and as the child got into more trouble, he would more likely find himself punished rather than treated.[57]

The last category of concern was jurisdictional and administrative. Studies of the early court led some researchers to question the expansive nature of the court's jurisdiction and wonder whether much of the work the court shouldered—like dealing with youth getting in trouble but not breaking the law—would be better situated in community agencies like public schools or settlement houses. A corollary concern was whether the court should be administering services at all. Perhaps probation, the psychiatric clinic, and court-based material aid would be administered better by independent agencies. This was not a rejection of the therapeutic impulse per se but a dawning recognition of the limited role the court should or could play in effectuating it. Each of these categories—holding onto the therapeutic purpose of the court, securing sufficient resources for the court's work, and defining the jurisdictional and administrative limits of the court—has remained part of every reform effort since the court began, including today.

The founders of the court were most worried about holding on to the original therapeutic purpose of saving children. They had begun to despair that the curative ideal they had championed was not coming to fruition and questioned whether it was not time to redouble their efforts "to awaken fresh interest in a nation-wide realization of its ideal of justice."[58] Their anguish permeated a series of papers presented at the joint commemoration of the juvenile court's twenty-fifth anniversary and the fifteenth anniversary of the first juvenile psychopathic institute, both founded in Chicago.[59] Titled *The Child, the Clinic, and the Court: A Group of Papers*, the contributions reviewed contemporary knowledge of child behavior and the ways to approach that behavior through psychopathic and judicial interventions. Many of the authors had been deeply involved in the creation of both the clinic and the court (in Chicago or elsewhere) and had written widely about their beliefs in the therapeutic role of judges trained as "specialists in the art of human relations."[60] As explained in some of these papers, trying "to reach into the soul-life of the child" through court machinery was proving harder to accomplish than first envisioned.[61]

Grace Abbott, the second director of the federal Children's Bureau, noted the gap between the explosion of the juvenile court in all but two states in the United States and on every continent and the failure of those states and nations to live up to the principle of therapeutic intervention.[62] Abbott expressed deep concern about the disparity between the courts created in U.S. cities—especially those that included probation departments and applied social and behavioral knowledge—and the almost nonexistence of these specialized courts in rural areas, where 50 percent of the population then lived. She lamented the inadequacies of much of the legislation establishing separate juvenile court systems around the country and the world and the "widespread failure to live up to the principle of scientific care and treatment which is embodied in the excellent laws that have been passed."[63] Nevertheless, she remained hopeful that, in the following ten years, states and counties

Figure 2.2. Grace Abbott, second director of the federal Children's Bureau. Courtesy of Library of Congress.

would expand and improve their work in a greater number of rural areas while applying therapeutic principles more fully in the courts already established.[64]

In his contribution to the paper series, the sociologist Thomas D. Eliot felt compelled to reassure his fellow participants that he was not calling for the destruction of the juvenile court but was instead proposing a "new life for the principles and spirit" that had animated the court in its first generation.[65] As early as 1914, Eliot had begun analyzing how juvenile courts across the country understood their mission and organized their work. In multiple publications he outlined an alternative way of understanding the juvenile court. While he supported the fundamental principles of therapeutic casework, he rejected the court as the best place to exercise those principles.[66] He saw juvenile court as a necessary response to a criminal justice system in which children were being tried and punished as adults instead of being treated as children. This response was in large part necessary because the services that should have "kept the child normal" in the community were lacking. Instead, the court was providing material assistance as well as shouldering medical, mental health, and even educational responsibilities through its clinics, probation officers, and close relationships with charitable organizations.[67] Eliot found the court ill-suited to accomplish those laudable goals. A court "represents society's powers of adjudication and compulsion" but not the power to administer "the machinery of treatment" itself.[68] Situating services within the court might have been expedient when the courts were first established, but, given their educational and curative nature, that historical accident should not govern the courts going forward. Eliot argued that probationary and psychiatric adjustments were better suited in community agencies—even when the court compelled participation—rather than the court apparatus.[69]

Community-based treatment would achieve another of Eliot's goals: reducing the court's jurisdictional reach. Eliot believed, contrary to the decisions that had upheld the juvenile court's power to intervene to save the incorrigible or misbehaving child, that troublesome behavior did not belong within a court's jurisdiction. There was no need to brand a child a delinquent unless he had clearly broken the criminal law; only then "should it be necessary to bring a child's case to court in order to get the treatment needed to keep it normal."[70] Eliot first wanted the intervention to be conducted through educational methods. The "pupil-patient delinquent" had to be given the opportunity to change his habits, character, and attitude through interaction with the "adjustment" officer in educational or welfare settings. If the officer or child or parent could not be reconciled to the treatment methods, whether the case had begun in the community or in the court, they could then appeal to the court for resolution. In this way, "the basis of social control [would be] shifted from compulsion and punishment to treatment and adjustment."[71]

That shift from punishment to treatment and adjustment through court intervention had not occurred in the way the founders had hoped. As one pioneering judge of the juvenile court, Julian Mack, had warned: "We think that because this fine conception of dealing with the little human beings has come into the law that everything connected with it must in practice be equally fine." But he was unsure if "we have just cause for a spirit of pride or whether we should not be extremely humble, recognizing how far, far from complete have been our endeavors; valuable as has been the work, how much remains undone."[72] While Judge Mack didn't outline the specific failures seen during the first twenty-five years of the Chicago court he helped to build, he alluded to what Professor Anthony Platt would describe in his landmark study of that court a half-century later. In *The Child Savers*, Platt depicted children subject to severe punishment, institutionalization, and imprisonment with adults even as efforts were being made by well-meaning citizens to improve institutions like probation services and juvenile homes.[73] He found that little to no distinction had been made between children misbehaving, children without adequate parental supervision, and children breaking the law. Platt established that the court's therapeutic mandate to save children enhanced the state's ability to reach delinquent and dependent children more easily through the juvenile court. The consequence: many more children became subject to state intervention in the very harsh forms of punishment that the child-savers themselves abhorred.[74]

Why was punishment rather than treatment so persistent? One reason was that the treatment ideal needed greater resources. The historians Platt and, more recently, David Tanenhaus described the struggles of the founders of the Chicago Juvenile Court to secure funding and support not only for the court itself but also for its various services like probation, detention, transportation, and reform schools. County boards and state legislatures reluctantly provided partial funding, but the founders continued to plead for funding from private philanthropies to supplement meager public dollars.[75] This pattern was repeated throughout the country. In her 1920 countrywide study of the juvenile courts for the Children's Bureau, Evelina Belden had found an amalgam of private and public resources available for the court and its services. The report described most court systems as cobbling together a combination of volunteers and part-time employees—including judges—without sufficient resources to maintain the court.[76] A more in-depth study of ten juvenile courts a few years later also found this pattern of part-time employment in the court, reliance on public and private coffers, and underpaid court personnel.[77]

But having insufficient treatment resources was not the only reason that punishment prevailed. Even when treatment was available, if it failed or if the child was not "cured," then the judge could still compel the child to comply. Compulsion now had different names: jail was the "detention home"; prison was the "reform school" or later the "vocational" or "industrial training" school.[78] And some children were simply being jailed and imprisoned with adults. This punitive justice was costly for young lives. George Kirchwey, a prominent criminologist at the time, despaired of the number of children being institutionalized. His studies of imprisoned adults found that most of them had been in juvenile homes, reform schools, and institutions and there, under brutal conditions, had learned the criminal trade. He warned judges that there is no ideal institution to send children to and that, even if there were, it "would still be a rotten place to send a growing child to."[79] But that is where children went. Belden's 1920 study found children housed in jails, often with adults, instead of in separate facilities throughout the country.[80]

Of the 175,000 cases of children being brought to court in 1918, over 50,000 were in courts not adapted to deal with children.[81] In the early part of the twentieth century, most African American children lived in rural jurisdictions where fewer than half had created juvenile courts and children continued to be treated as adults—with adult punishments. Even in jurisdictions with juvenile courts and attendant services, with rare exceptions, African American children were denied access to the burgeoning juvenile court system, experiencing even harsher treatment and punishment than their white inner-city and immigrant counterparts.[82] The plight of Black children in the early juvenile court will be examined in chapter 3.

How had the reality already strayed so far from the ideal? Judge Mack holds the judge ultimately responsible:

> I know—and the other judges have told me the same thing—that the good people of the community think that every judge of the juvenile court must necessarily be a fine fellow, filled with the wisdom of the ages, capable of dealing with all the children that come before him. That sort of a genius does not exist. He may in the course of time, through unusual experience and opportunity, gain considerable wisdom. . . . But few judges are really temperamentally fitted, and few are so eminently endowed as to be able to do the juvenile work and the probation work and all the other work that must be done if the court is to be really successful.[83]

The extraordinary judge not only had to be endowed with those characteristics; he also had to be willing to embrace the philosophy of the court and reject harsh punishment. Belden's study found that judges frequently declined to differentiate between adults and children, failing "to recognize the cardinal principle of juvenile courts—that the purpose is not punishment but education and discipline suited to the needs of the child."[84] Instead they punished, administering whippings and sending children to jails and prisons, work farms, reformatories, and chain gangs.[85]

The contributors to *The Child, the Clinic, and the Court* remained committed to achieving the Great Idea even as they described its failures. They recognized that future efforts would have to include more prevention, more resources, and a reconfigured administration of services. The court was still young and the proposals for improvement hardly begun; many jurisdictions had no probation or clinical services. Specialized detention and correction facilities developed just for children were mostly in the future. Judges were still transitioning from conducting trials and meting out punishment to determining children's needs and providing treatment. There was much work to be done to complete the project.

The Future of the Juvenile Court as a Casework Agency

Barely a decade had passed before this optimism soured. At the end of her long career at the Children's Bureau, Grace Abbott proposed a diminished role for the juvenile court. She was discouraged that the court had been unable to prevent delinquency after thirty years.[86] The Children's Bureau's reports during the 1930s advocated "something of the newer philosophy in regard to the whole problem of delinquency," shifting treatment and supervision of children away from the court and into community-based and publicly funded social welfare departments being developed around the country.[87] This shift would maintain the court's role "to understand why the particular child is delinquent, and, on the basis of this understanding, to attempt intelligent treatment for proper adjustment toward responsible future living," but only after family and community efforts had failed.[88] When a child must be legally separated from her parents or when disputes concerning the child cannot be resolved except through a court process, then the court is necessary to further ensure the child's treatment and cure.[89] Abbott was keenly aware that the most recent studies showed that judges were unqualified, in both training and experience, to identify and order what the child needed. Most of the supervision the child received was structured more like punishment. And parents and teachers waited too long before turning to the court, so the assistance the child required often came too late.[90] The Children's Bureau began pursuing more robust prevention alternatives than the court, building on Professor Eliot's earlier recommendations that as much treatment as possible be conducted outside the court.

The court instead should become part of a treatment social service system, but not the center of one. In a 1939 article titled *The Future of Juvenile Court as a Case Work Agency*, Alice Scott Nutt of the Children's Bureau showed how this could be achieved. She maintained that casework responsibility of any sort should be removed from court administration. The court had shouldered treatment and administrative responsibilities by historical default. When the court was created, there were often no other public authorities available to administer mothers' aid, investigate family life, or provide foster homes. The court had become a social agency rather than a "socialized court."[91]

During the ensuing years, public and private agencies had developed casework expertise that would allow them to provide preventive services "pre-delinquency" in community settings. These preventive programs could be accessed voluntarily without the stigma of being hauled into court. Nutt was concerned that children are "suspicious and resistant to treatment" administered by the court. Children are unlikely to distinguish treatment from punishment, and they know that the court is likely to threaten some form of punitive placement for failure to improve.[92] Nutt's solution was to remove the court from being "the central agency around which is built the whole child welfare program," instead becoming the venue "for determining issues, for settling controversies, for deciding need for treatment and the agencies best able to meet that need."[93]

Relegating the court to its more clearly judicial functions reflected the broader changes occurring in public welfare practice at the time. Abbott and her successor at the Children's Bureau, Katherine Lenroot, had participated in drafting the New Deal's Social Security Act, which included

Figure 2.3. Katherine Lenroot, third director of the federal Children's Bureau. Courtesy of Library of Congress.

several provisions that purposely shifted responsibility for delinquency and dependency casework out of the court's sphere and into the new public welfare systems that were being created throughout the country. The goal was to provide community-based prevention so that fewer cases would reach the court, where punitive rather than therapeutic sanctions were more likely to be handed out. Proponents like Abbott and Lenroot were disappointed and frustrated with the court's inability to be the benevolent leader of an effective treatment system and saw the new public welfare agencies as a mechanism more likely to employ the best social work practices to create effective solutions for children and families.[94]

Judges Fight Back

Nutt's proposals to shift the court away from being a social agency had been prepared as remarks for the National Probation Association's national conference in 1939. Two judges in attendance—George W. Smyth and Alton Westwick—responded to Nutt's remarks. Their responses captured the early optimism of judges like Mack, Perkins, and Baker, but they did more: they staked out a claim for the judge's role going forward. They argued that the court must remain a key—if not the central—therapeutic intervention for children and families, because only a judge has the power to coerce. Judge Smyth, a children's court judge and vice president of the NPA, insisted that judges wanted prevention as much as the Children's Bureau and the social workers at the public welfare agencies. But "no judge can sit complacently on the bench" and see the results of inadequate public services and not do "his level best to remedy the omission."[95] Judges had learned enough about social work practice, which, combined with their legal training, prepared them to receive advice from the clinic and other agencies to craft and enforce productive outcomes. Even if they left the supervision of most cases to probation or child welfare agencies, judges must be ready to supervise and consult on the most difficult cases. Judge Smyth insisted that, compared to other agencies involved in antisocial conduct of children or parents, the juvenile courts, despite all their faults, "are doing a far better job than any other agency that I know could do in the treatment of these cases." He contended that progressive courts were doing the work that the Children's Bureau wanted but "so quietly their achievements are not more widely understood."[96]

Nutt's findings that too many juvenile court judges were punishing rather than treating children belied Judge Smyth's remarks, but his fellow responder had the answer. Judge Westwick, a California juvenile court judge, was a fierce opponent of punishment. He believed that only juvenile court judges who remained true to their mission would be able to hold back the tide of "far too many judges, legislators, teachers and even probation officers" who insisted on punishing young offenders.[97] Even if current judges were failing in their therapeutic mission, they remained the best possible solution for too much punishment. Judge Westwick argued that the juvenile court is the first tribunal "where law and science would or *could work* side by side and hand in hand . . . to make decent, humane and sensible human adjustments."[98] That the studies up to that time revealed that the court had not prevented delinquency was a disappointment but did not mean the court's role should be curtailed. Instead, by expanding jurisdiction to all the issues the family suffered, the court could achieve its objective "to protect, to remedy and to save."[99]

Judges Smyth and Westwick were staking out ways for the court to justify its continued relevance as the nation prepared for war. The quiet achievements that Judge Smyth alluded to were not readily apparent to a dissatisfied public. Many court supporters became increasingly worried about being able to justify the court if it was unable to prevent delinquency. The juvenile court became part of debates during World War II about the best way to balance individual rights and social control. Roscoe Pound, now dean emeritus of Harvard and vice president of the NPA, had often mined the juvenile court for answers to getting these balances right. Now the absolutism that had infested the world in the previous decade affected Pound's thinking. His address, titled "The Juvenile Court and the Law," at the NPA's thirty-eighth annual conference, held in Cleveland in May 1944, exhorted the need to continue to find the right balance between individual rights and a socialized approach to families. But he was less enamored with broad court discretion and informal procedures than he had been at the beginning of the century. He now saw greater purpose in a juvenile court that favored procedural regularity, organizational reliability, and consolidated jurisdictional authority over the family within a unified court system.[100] A court that acted like a court—even a court solving family problems—was more likely to strike the right balance among important but competing societal values when compared to the informal administrative approach that favored greater discretion. Pound now came down on the side of law and regularity in protecting children and fortifying community security, including procedural measures like more specificity for bringing children to court and the right to appeal. While he continued to acknowledge the social work component of a socialized court to achieve individualized justice for the child, he was impatient with a solution to delinquency that required more long-term preventive measures to improve the social and economic life of families—the measures the new social welfare authorities back in Washington were championing. Like Judge Smyth, Pound no longer was prepared to await the results of social work programs while the public clamored for court action to protect society from danger.[101]

Many juvenile court judges who listened to Pound's remarks at the NPA meeting had remained in Cleveland after attending the annual meeting of the recently created National Council of Juvenile Court Judges (NCJCJ).[102] The relationship between the NPA and the NCJCJ was complicated and, in many ways, reflected the divide between Nutt's proposal to diminish the primary preventive role of the court and the judges' cry to maintain the court as the central therapeutic authority. Pound's remarks would have reassured the judges of their primary role and perhaps reassured them of the NPA's continued support at a time when the missions of the two organizations were diverging

Some of the tension was apparent almost from the beginning. While juvenile court judges had been actively involved in the creation of the NPA in 1907 and had served as officers and committee members over several decades, the NPA's central concerns had shifted away from the court as probation had developed into a social work profession. Probation officers were anxious to focus on the institutions and methodologies of their new trade. The NPA had been the only national organization with which juvenile court judges had been affiliated, and by the 1930s this affiliation was insufficient to fight the battles on behalf of their courts.[103] What was called a "minor crisis" became a serious rift between the NPA and juvenile court judges, spurring the judges to create their own national organization, the NCJCJ.

In 1934, Drs. Eleanor and Sheldon Glueck published their book *One Thousand Juvenile Delinquents*, which studied boys in the Boston juvenile court and its affiliated Judge Baker Foundation Clinic. The Gluecks would continue to follow those boys for the next twenty-five years. Remarkably, their studies continue to provide insight into effective interventions with young people in trouble to this day.[104] A colleague of the Gluecks at Harvard, Dr. Richard C. Cabot, reviewed their original study and concluded that they had proven that the juvenile court had entirely failed to prevent delinquency. Cabot's article was widely circulated and quoted (and misquoted) throughout the country, frustrating juvenile court champions and challenging juvenile courts to justify their existence more publicly. Court defenders were unhappy that Sheldon Glueck agreed to address the NPA's 1934 annual meeting, spurring Judge Harry L. Eastman of Cleveland to propose that he defend the court in response. Glueck insisted in his remarks that they had not been on a headhunting expedition against the juvenile court. Instead, they were gravely concerned that, if a court and clinic with the reputation of Boston's Judge Frederick Cabot and Drs. William Healy and Augusta Bronner were unsuccessful in curtailing delinquency, then the burden was on juvenile courts throughout the rest of the country to prove their own effectiveness.[105]

Judge Eastman's response indicated how desperate judges were to reposition and defend their work. Eastman directly attacked the reputation of the Boston court and challenged Glueck's assertion that other juvenile courts should be measured by what the Boston court had failed to achieve: "That they have made a partial survey of one of the nation's inferior juvenile courts and found it inadequate to meet the needs of its community. That this situation was the result of a lack of community interest and support, and the failure of a judge to adapt his office to the needs of the community."[106] After that blow directed at prominent colleagues, he then boldly contended—contrary to the founding mission of the court—that the "juvenile court was never designed to prevent delinquency" and that its mission had always been "diagnostic and not prophylactic."[107] He asserted that Cabot's review of the Glueck study had been "used by unscrupulous persons and organizations as propaganda for their own purposes and to the detriment of the progressive juvenile courts of the country."[108] Eastman argued that this propaganda included that the role of the court was to treat children and insisted that blame for the lack of treatment belonged to community agencies and not the court. Instead of acknowledging that these expectations *were* part of the court's original work and that practices had begun to shift over time to reflect more proscribed jurisdiction and a more rational distribution of responsibilities between social work agencies and courts, Eastman instead declared that the original purposes had never existed, asserting that if researchers had just studied the right courts and the right types of outcomes—even failures—he was sure the results would be different.[109]

Eastman was proclaimed a hero for his defense of the juvenile court, and in the wake of his remarks several judges drafted a resolution deploring the misunderstanding for the NPA to adopt. The NPA refused to pass the resolution, sorely disappointing the judges and leading directly to Eastman's subsequent efforts to create a national organization to represent judges' interests. Judges realized that neither the NPA nor the Children's Bureau could be counted on any longer to support their court.[110] Juvenile court and its judges now had their own national defender organization as the court entered another phase of its existence.

To understand further the evolution of the court midcentury, another story first has to be told. Black children had a very different experience in the court, one that illuminates the racism deeply embedded in the court from its beginnings and that remains today. This is the story presented in chapter 3.

3

The Great Idea for Black Children

From her position as director of the federal Children's Bureau in 1925, Grace Abbott had observed that juvenile courts were urban inventions at a time when half the nation's population lived in rural areas.[1] Cities were absorbing new immigrants and rural white Americans drawn to industrial employment, while Progressive Era reformers were creating institutions to assist this new population in adopting the values and mores that had characterized American middle-class life in the latter part of the less industrialized nineteenth century. This backward-looking practice was fed by many impulses. For some, it was a wish to hold on to rural, white Protestant, middle-class traditions in the face of the urban chaos exemplified by the jumble of immigrants crowding city neighborhoods. Other reformers embraced the professionalism of a new middle class in which rational and scientific thought, combined with administrative expertise, would address escalating social problems. The white child-savers who were part of this movement used their growing understanding of child development to champion protective labor laws, compulsory school attendance, early childhood programs, and the rehabilitative ideal of the juvenile court.[2]

Whatever the impetus for this movement, Black children did not fit into the picture at all. In his pivotal work to uncover the place of race in the early history of juvenile justice and to connect that place to what has happened since, Professor Geoff Ward has insisted that all students of today's juvenile legal system reckon with the exclusion of Black children from the citizen-building impulses of most of the white child-savers, specifically the rehabilitative ideal of the juvenile court. Ward's reexamination of the early juvenile court also revealed the role of Black child-savers, those community leaders, especially Black women, whose goal for Black children was no less than first-class citizenship in a racially and ethnically diverse democracy. The Black child-savers identified the "refusal to extend the rehabilitative ideas and resources [of the juvenile court] as a denial of equal protection and a form of structural violence" that maintained the second-class status of Black children. They reimagined institutional and community resources not as a source of state control but as an essential step toward securing racial equality.[3] This was not only a tall order but one largely unseen by white child-savers.

An Ugly Reality from the Start

Black children emancipated from slavery remained subject to brutal forms of punishment when convicted of crimes. They suffered severe corporal punishment, imprisonment that led to convict leasing—an especially inhumane punishment that often resulted in death—and lynchings.[4] They were excluded from houses of refuge for most of the nineteenth century, and when they were admitted it was only grudgingly and with far fewer resources and spaces than those provided for white children.[5] These so-called colored units were justified by decision makers to avoid white children being tainted by contact with Black children, who were also excluded from the same rehabilitative educational services as white children in the same institutions. Black boys were relegated to learning manual labor skills, and Black girls were trained to be maids, cooks, laundresses, and seamstresses.[6] In communities with no separate facilities for children, Black children were simply sent to jail or prison, just like most white children had been before the new juvenile court system was created.[7]

When the juvenile court was first being established, most Black children still lived in the South, where the violent racial backlash against Reconstruction had destroyed nascent Black rights and most Black children remained untouched by the court's rehabilitative prospects. Juvenile courts in the South were slow to be created for *any* children, and even where such courts existed, Black children either remained outside their purview or were subject to far more severe judicial sanctions—whippings, imprisonment, convict labor—than white juveniles. The juvenile court's disregard for the welfare of Black children was reflective of the national approach to child protection at the beginning of the twentieth century. In 1909, President Theodore Roosevelt convened the White House Conference on the Care of Dependent Children. Of the hundreds of attendees, only two Black men were invited to attend: Dr. Booker T. Washington and Richard Carroll, both of whom were accepting of the segregationist policies practiced nationwide and did not advocate for white child welfare institutions to be responsible for Black children.[8] Other than their two contributions, little attention was paid to the needs of Black, Mexican, and Native American children.[9]

Black Communities and a Different Meaning of the Great Idea

From the founding of the juvenile court, Black community leaders conceded the realities of the Great Idea for Black children. The juvenile court either excluded Black children or failed to provide the individualized rehabilitative services that justified the court's purpose. As Ward has chronicled so thoroughly, early individual and collective action by the Black community on behalf of Black children was intended to save them from the horrors of the worst punishments imposed on them and to provide them with segregated institutions. This would offer them rehabilitation built on Dr. Booker T. Washington's theory of racial uplift through industrial education.[10] The predominantly female Black activists negotiated through lethal territory on behalf of the children, where Jim Crow reigned and any improvements provided to the Black community were considered suspect. While these reformers were remarkable as individuals and organizations—especially the local, state, and national Black women's clubs that powered the greatest progress—they were armed with few political and economic resources and remained dependent on convincing hostile white authorities to sustain their efforts. They opened their own homes to children who would otherwise have been imprisoned, started small and poorly financed houses of refuge, and worked tirelessly to establish public rehabilitative institutions that would accept Black children.[11]

Examples of early efforts occurred in Memphis. The Negro Reform Association of Memphis was created in 1908 to raise money and press for facilities for Black children. After raising sufficient funds from Black citizens for a home for delinquent Black children, Julia Hooks, a prominent Black reformer, became its matron and chief probation officer. More years of activism resulted in the county creating a "Negro department" within the industrial school for white delinquents, but even here

Figure 3.1. Julia Britton Hooks. Courtesy of Memphis
Public Library.

the Black boys were routinely sent to do agricultural labor while the
white boys received industrial training. Charges of peonage brought
by numerous grand juries did not stop the juvenile court from sending
boys, especially Black boys, to the state industrial school to work on
farms in abject slavery until the school was finally closed in the 1930s.[12]

The Black child-savers' initiatives "focused on securing equal protection, opportunity, and influence within the arms of the parental state."[13]
And despite the knowledge that their communities "lacked equal social,
economic and political opportunities, and rigid barriers denied their
black humanity and democratic standing," these "early Black child-
savers toiled on at the speed of molasses, lifting as they climbed."[14] Nevertheless, before 1920 most Black children in the North and the South
would be untouched by these efforts to hold juvenile courts accountable to them. As the century progressed, Southern juvenile court judges
continued to authorize whippings for Black children. Tragically, the

percentage of Black youth executed in the South increased well after juvenile courts were established, 70 percent of them occurring between 1931 and 1959.[15]

Ugly Realities in the North

Punishment of Black children in the North was less horribly violent but hardly represented the ideals of the Great Idea in its first decades. As Blacks migrated northward to fill inner cities and eventually replace white immigrant populations, the juvenile courts routinely discriminated against Black youth in ways still resonant today. Philadelphia, the City of Brotherly Love, established a juvenile court in 1903. By 1920, when Black youth represented 3 percent of the state's males ages fifteen to nineteen, they represented 30 percent of the midteens sent to prison.[16] Early studies of the juvenile court in Chicago and the children's court in New York exposed unequal patterns of treatment between white and Black youth at every step of the juvenile court process. This disparate treatment was built on popular eugenic theories that Black children were inherently degenerate, more prone to immorality and delinquency, and thus less likely to benefit from rehabilitative rather than punitive interventions.[17]

Even the hallowed juvenile court in Chicago brought Black children disproportionately under its control. Following the 1919 race riots in Chicago, the Chicago Race Commission Report—*The Negro in Chicago: A Study of Race Relations and a Race Riot*—applied the following finding to juvenile courts as well as adult criminal courts: "[Negroes] are more commonly arrested, subjected to police identification, and convicted than white offenders; that on similar evidence they are generally held and convicted on more serious charges, and that they are given longer sentences. This bias, when reflected in the figures, serves to bolster by false figures the already existing belief that Negroes are more likely to be criminal than other racial groups."[18] The superintendent of the Chicago and Cook County School for Boys, O. J. Milliken, testified about the disparate treatment of Black and white children: "You don't find any of the $900,000 school buildings in the colored population district." He went on to lament that the police know the boys who end up in court and that, especially for the Black boys, he had to issue letters for them to carry to prove they are allowed to go to work. Referring to "one of the finest lads we have had," he noted "I think probably within the last three months I have had to get him out of the hands of the police by calling up the police department twenty times, to get him to work."[19]

Louise de Koven Bowen, a white philanthropist associated with Jane Addams's and Julia Lathrop's Hull House in Chicago who served for many years as president of the Juvenile Protective Association (JPA), produced numerous investigations into the status of children and families in Chicago in the early twentieth century, often highlighting the discriminatory treatment suffered by Black families. In *The Colored People in Chicago*, Bowen makes palpable the discouragement that infiltrates every condition of Chicago's Black population—from inadequate and demeaning educational and work opportunities to housing segregation and disproportionate policing—and its impact on the large number of Black children finding themselves in juvenile court on charges of prostitution, theft, school truancy, and vagrancy. She writes how the JPA was "much startled by the disproportionate number of colored boys and young men [in the county jail]; for although the colored people of Chicago approximate 1/40 of the entire population, 1/8 of the boys and young men and nearly 1/3 of the girls and young women who had been confined in the jail during the year were negroes."[20] Bowen did not ignore the role of the juvenile court in perpetuating discrimination; she found that the court acquiesced to protestations by administrators of reformatories that "we have no room" for Black children.[21] While her reports provide multiple concrete solutions like day nurseries for the overwhelming number of Black mothers who worked, and equal access to public beaches and parks for Black children, she saw the real solution to Black delinquency as far more monumental: "In suggesting remedies for this state of affairs [the JPA] finds itself confronted with the situation [that] the life of the colored boy and girl is so circumscribed on every hand by race limitations that they can be helped only insofar as the entire colored reputation in Chicago is understood and fairly treated."[22]

New York City suffered from the same faults as Chicago. Black children were not receiving their fair share of education and training and were barred from many children's institutions. The children's court, which had been created first as a separate section of the criminal court and eventually became an independent court, was unable "to deal constructively with colored children under sixteen years of age," according to the presiding justice of the court, Franklin Chase Hoyt.[23] In response to Justice Hoyt's concerns, two civic organizations in New York City, one Black and one white, prepared the "Joint Study on the Negro Child in New York," which thoroughly examined the racial practices of the children's court in the mid-1920s. The 1920 federal census showed that, at a time when only 152,467 Black people out of 5,620,048 lived in New York City, 4.2 percent of the cases in children's court involved Black children. By 1925 that percentage had more than doubled.[24] Not only the percentage of children but also the sources of court jurisdiction differed by race. While white boys found themselves in court predominantly for *actual* crimes—especially stealing and burglary—African American boys were more often running away from home or charged with disorderly conduct. African American girls were "ungovernable and wayward" or brought in as runaways.[25] The distinction in charges reminds us that the court had broad jurisdiction over youthful misbehavior (some of which was criminal and some not), and a finding of delinquency could stem from normal adolescent behavior, like arguing with parents or staying out past curfew. While there was adequate provision of services for white children experiencing what the joint study called "mild delinquency," the Black children who were far more likely to find themselves in this category had little access to such services. Like their peers in Chicago, for Black children the key causes of delinquency included few recreational opportunities, truancy, lack of home supervision (because their mothers were working), and overall neighborhood conditions. They were not in court due to "dangerously anti-social behavior."[26] Even though Black children were, for the most part, engaging in less serious misconduct, they were more likely to be brought to the court by police. The joint study expressed concern that "the disproportion in offences of Negro children which may be classed as serious[] suggests that these children get into the courts more readily."[27] And the study understood the real problem:

> To an extent evidenced probably by no other racial group in the city, the Negro finds himself with inadequate facilities in the recreation field and in the field of care of dependent and delinquent children. Unlike certain other racial groups the Negro has not accumulated sufficient wealth as yet to make it possible for him to do much toward meeting the problems of his own People.[28]

Today, parents with few other resources still turn to the family court to help them control their children. They file "status offense" petitions, hoping the court can talk sense into their misbehaving child or just find somewhere for her to stay until she stops being angry. Black parents in New York City who did that in 1925—who relied on the court as a resource to treat or discipline children—ended up instead losing control or even custody over them. Institutions that could assist children prior to court involvement were entirely inadequate.[29] The recommendations presented in the joint study noted the "special problems Negros have to face," including the facts that "certain agencies and institutions make no provision for them" and that society generally created for white children "an environment in which [they] had a fairer chance."[30] Without programs to engage and treat Black children, as a group they were far more likely simply to be punished.

Then and now, New York has relied on religious-affiliated agencies to provide placements for children subject to court jurisdiction. However, not only were these agencies free to reject children of a different religion; the law favored placing children in homes and institutions of the same religion, practices that continued for decades until a federal lawsuit challenged them in the 1970s.[31] The largest and best-funded agencies were Catholic and Jewish, religions that serviced few Black children due to religious matching. Moreover, not all the Protestant agencies accepted Black children; neither did some nonsectarian agencies, and in the publicly run training schools few spaces were allotted for Black children.[32] In 1924, the Children's Village, a nonsectarian agency founded in 1851 that is still in existence today, reversed its policies and began taking only white children.[33] The court often placed Black children charged with delinquency with neglected or dependent children in the Colored Orphan Asylum because there was no other place to put them. Just as frequently, Black children lingered in temporary shelters run by the Society for the Prevention of Cruelty to Children for weeks or even months only because no suitable place could be found for them. Or they were just sent to the House of Refuge.[34]

The 1925 joint study urged New York to recommit its efforts to develop community-based services for children and families in the areas that Black families lived. These were to include boys and girls clubs, recreational activities under local leadership, and after-school programs and summer camps to supervise children whose parents worked. The report also urged social work assistance for the entire family in addition to centers created for young people. These preventive services would serve to divert many children out of the court entirely, but if court jurisdiction was necessary, Black children also needed foster care, institutional placements, probation services, and access to mentoring through organizations like Big Brothers and Big Sisters—all services and assistance far more readily available for white children.[35] The available evidence about the disparate treatment of white and Black delinquent children across the country during the 1920s indicated that Black children consistently received fewer alternative services to reduce the likelihood of their being placed in institutions for children. Yet crucially, the "greatest discrimination" was that Black children were sent to prison with adults 50 percent of the time, while white children were incarcerated with adults 20 percent of the time.[36]

Race and the Lack of Progress

Henry W. Thurston had a long and storied career in social welfare, including as the chief probation officer of the Chicago juvenile court. Writing in 1930 in his best-known publication, *The Dependent Child*, Thurston posited that the short distance between the end of slavery and the present day explained the lack of progress for delinquent and dependent Black children. The lack of progress was certainly apparent at the 1930 White House Conference on Children; Thurston attended that conference and served on several committees on dependent children.[37] The direct relationship between discrimination against Black families and outcomes for Black children, along with concerns about other children of color, began to receive attention. This was in marked contrast to Theodore Roosevelt's 1909 White House conference on dependent children, which had essentially ignored children of color. A special subcommittee of the conference addressed "Child Dependency as Affected by Race, Nationality or Mass Migration," highlighting how "Negro, Mexican, Porto Rican and Indian dependent children present special problems of great importance."[38] The final report of this subcommittee included a section titled "The Negro in the United States" written by Dr. Ira De Augustine Reid, a key representative of Black children at the conference.

Dr. Reid addressed four areas of discrimination against Black parents that had the greatest impact on the Black family overall: income maintenance, medical care, services to unwed mothers, and day-care services. Like advocates before and long after him, Dr. Reid emphasized that the lack of these services for all children was harmful but was particularly harmful for Black children. He noted that the disregard for Black children "has resulted in an aggravated condition of dependency which has not received it fullest attention in the first instance, and which has been handled unwisely and unscientifically in many other instances." At the same time, he lauded the readiness of Black "kin to stick together" and the solidarity of Black families in caring for each other's children.[39]

Mothers' aid was still the only governmental income assistance program at the time, but the states with the largest Black populations either failed to enact enabling laws to provide the aid or denied benefits to Black families outright. Public services to assist unwed Black mothers were virtually nonexistent. Black infant mortality far exceeded the overall rates for whites, as did the death rates for Black people in general, because of the lack of medical and health facilities. Finally, discrimination in the workplace against Black men meant that Black mothers desperately needed child care so they could work. The paucity of nurseries and day-care facilities available for Black children intensified the problem; at the time only forty day-nurseries existed in the entire country for Black children.[40]

What is most chilling reading Dr. Reid's 1933 report and the recommendations of the conference overall is how the language so closely mirrors findings and concerns being made today. These same conditions continue to send more Black children and families into court with the same underlying "cause and effect":

> The presence of these conditions find both their cause and effect in the existing racial attitudes of the nation. While these attitudes themselves involve the problem, the amelioration of the social ills aids in their reformulation. Thus, a group facing the social handicaps described here presents a more greatly complicated situation than that presented by any other racial stock forming the total population. The social antecedents of the Negro's dependency problems are common to all racial stocks, but when they are complicated by the manifestation of psychological pro-

cesses whereby the Negro is classed as inferior they become most singular. The Negro 's presence here resulted from his having been brought into the lowest possible social class—that of the slave. The attitudes and habits which were generated during the two centuries of slavery have formed a culture complex in both races for which color has become an inescapable sign. This leering gargoyle of race and its potential combination with social handicaps then becomes the heritage of the Negro child. For it the child is not responsible; because of it the child suffers.[41]

The 1930 White House conference may have clearly highlighted what needed to be done, but the Depression decade that led toward World War II held little promise for Black children or their families. Throughout the country, what progress was being made for Black children relied on segregated systems and the gradual provision of Black probation officers and social workers in segregated facilities. Northern juvenile court judges had acquiesced to or actively supported this segregation, even reassuring protesting white parents that they would not send their children to integrated facilities.[42] Despite the recommendations of the New York joint study in 1925 to improve the provision of services to Black children, less than a decade later advocates were again challenging segregation and disparities in services in New York facilities, where Black girls in "juvenile court communities suffered fewer educational opportunities, inferior vocational training, far more crowded conditions[, and] frequent corporal punishment."[43] Twice as many Black children were arraigned as delinquent as white children in 1930. That disparity continued through the decade.[44]

The "So-called Negro Problem"

A 1934 study commissioned by the presiding justice of the New York City domestic relations court, Edward Boyle, highlighted the rapidly increasing numbers of Black children and families flooding the court while noting that the city was failing to address the disproportionate impact of the Great Depression on the already suffering Black community. The report was written by a former probation officer, Katherine Hildreth, and was titled *The Negro Problem as Reflected in the Functioning of the Domestic Relations Court of the City of New York*.

It emphasized: "Negro cases in the Children's Court in this city have increased out of proportion to the increase in negro population."[45] This disproportionality was the "so-called negro problem" that Justice Boyle argued had to be addressed and, as he noted, had already been studied for over a decade. Boyle reminded Mayor Fiorello La Guardia when he sent him the Hildreth report: "There are more negro children in New York City than in any other city in the world." Justice Boyle's concerns were blunt and emphatic, highlighting the significant disproportionate numbers of Black children brought to court and their unequal treatment in subsequent placement outcomes. The percentage of Black children in children's court in Manhattan was two times the percentage of the Black population in the borough, in Brooklyn three times, and in the Bronx and Queens four times. Boyle emphasized the need for preventive resources for Black families to reduce the need for court corrective intervention at all and concluded: "Failure of the community to meet [the report's] reasonable demands would be indefensible; unthinkable."[46]

Boyle was equally concerned about the state of institutional placements, warning that the new Warwick State Training School would soon become "an institution for negro boys and the harder cases of white children" if greater attention were not paid to securing less restrictive foster homes.[47] As in the 1920s, a significant percentage of the "crimes" being committed by Black boys and girls were not crimes at all but misbehavior characterized as delinquency: disorderly conduct, deserting home, and being ungovernable. One of the recommendations in Hildreth's report was to send younger Black delinquent boys to the "parental" boarding school in Queens to address truancy before the boys committed more serious offenses.[48] That turned out to be a problematic solution. Only three months after Hildreth's report was sent to the mayor, a Queens County grand jury "caustically denounced the conduct and management" of the parental school, where "children are improperly fed, poorly treated, beaten without cause, and given inadequate formal and vocational education."[49]

Hildreth's report also noted an alarming pattern of treatment at the Hudson Training School for Girls. The New York state attorney general had already ordered the training school to stop "classifying" girls by race. In defiance, the school instituted a system that paroled Black girls in order to take new ones, keeping the number of Black girls who allegedly needed such a placement disproportionately low.[50] Given the punitive nature of such training schools, Black girls were probably much better off not finding themselves there or leaving sooner.

Some of Boyle's and Hildreth's recommendations were based on a 1932 report, titled *The Negro Children of New York*, by the Children's Aid Society; it repeated many of the findings of the 1930 White House conference. The Children's Aid Society report does not shy away from identifying that "a certain bias is not infrequently detected which if absent might cut down" the disproportionality. Even "throughout the North," noted the study, "courts are less patient with the colored or foreign offender than with one of their own race or color." It was common knowledge that "a larger percentage of Negro than white delinquents" were sent to jails, workhouses, and reformatories, either because they don't have the ability to pay fines or because agencies won't cooperate to find and develop suitable alternatives for Black children. To counter the persistent idea that "the Negro is just naturally bad," the report traces the horrors of the slave trade, the Middle Passage, bondage, and sudden emancipation as if it had happened to Europeans instead of Africans and positing that the conclusion would be that "Nordics are bad." Surveying the mass of available evidence, the report blames environmental conditions for delinquency occurring within Black families: segregated and crowded housing, lack of employment opportunities, marginalized and criminalized communities, nonexistent or insufficient services and care, and lack of recreational spaces.[51] The same evidence, the same conclusions, and no change.

Harsh treatment of Black youth and families and the paucity of services available to them were replicated in juvenile courts from the Eastern Seaboard through the Midwest to the Pacific Coast. A late 1930s national survey of fifty-three juvenile courts found Black children to be involved in 22 percent of the delinquency cases even though they constituted only 7 percent of the youth population under twenty-one. The survey found that Black children were brought to court at an earlier age and that Black boys were more likely to be detained and institutionalized after a delinquency finding and less likely to have their cases dismissed.[52] The survey's author, Mary Huff Diggs, sees real children behind the numbers and describes them affectionately as children and not delinquents:

Take, for instance, three Negro boy [referred for larceny]. We shall refer to them as Frank, Ted, and Luther. . . . Frank's stealing was his response to his deep feeling of need for recognition . . . he was, an undersized, little person, placed in a position in which his group of playmates demanded of him a demonstration or proof of the fact that he was a "regular feller." [Ted] stole to punish his parents-to wreak vengeance so to speak. But Luther's stealing was entirely different. His was of a compulsive nature, the delinquency itself being rather obviously a neurotic symptom, which in a measure solved his unconscious conflict for him. Thus, these three boys had practically nothing in common except their racial identity, and identical reasons for reference to court.[53]

Diggs sees three boys in need of assistance but little need for court intervention. In a pattern established by reformers before her, she urged greater attention to preventively addressing the social, economic, and community conditions that triggered delinquent behavior so that children could remain in their homes and neighborhoods. She pressed for the disparities between the services and assistance afforded Black and white children to be eliminated and that the juvenile court improve and professionalize its staff. She was especially concerned that Black caseworkers or probation officers be employed to link with Black families. In the end, she despaired: "Added to this is the fact that the juvenile court itself, as it exists today in most communities, has never been, and is not now an agency equipped to render specialized service to children who come in contact with it."[54]

Our Delinquent Children

Like earlier generations of Black child-savers, African American advocates in the mid-twentieth century transcended class and economic barriers that separated them from many of the children they were assisting. Their own experiences with racial discrimination in its myriad forms fueled not only a greater understanding of the barriers Black families faced but also a belief that the Black community itself was a central resource to assist families and children through a preventive and rehabilitative process.[55] The Black women's clubs worked to counter stereotypes about Black boys and girls as well as Black women. The women club members had moral and self-interested reasons for stand-ing with the "most illiterate and vicious representatives" of their race and sex because they knew they would be judged not by their own status and achievements but by their less fortunate sisters.[56] They understood that the racial, economic, political, and structural conditions of Black families were used to justify treating Black children as delinquent. As Professor Cheryl Butler posits: "[T]he society from which the juvenile court emerged had already equated [Black] neighborhoods, culture, customs, and families as synonymous with delinquency itself."[57] Black activists well into the twentieth century found themselves with two con-tradictory goals: to improve the way in which the juvenile court treated Black children, and to protect Black children from that same court.[58]

Elaine Ellis, a frequent contributor to the official NAACP publication, *The Crisis*, published "Our Delinquent Children" in 1937. The title re-flected the Black community's sense of responsibility for the Black chil-dren in the juvenile court. Ellis knew that white prejudice blamed Black children for their delinquency (i.e., "the Negro is a born criminal"). She chronicled the legacy of slavery and Jim Crow justice on every aspect of the vast majority of Black families' lives in the 1930s, leaving most of them in "miserable subjugation."[59] The multiple causes of delinquency cannot be effectively distinguished for any particular child, but the de-grading impacts of racism and poverty are especially relevant to delin-quency and dependency within the Black community. The ability of families with means, especially white families, to avoid court remained a crucial distinction as well. Ellis quoted from a contemporaneous Chil-dren's Bureau report: "It is doubtless true that many children of the well-to-do are saved from coming before the courts because their families have greater resources and are often able to obtain special care for their children whereas the children of the poor are more likely to be referred to courts or committed to institutions when they develop serious behav-ior problems."[60]

This distinction, however, doesn't justify the court's role once the child was brought to court. After giving a nod toward those few courts "doing commendable work," Ellis then chronicles again the barbaric treatment of Black children by the courts and the institutions to which judges sent Black children. Citing a study in North Carolina, Ellis noted that, for the same offenses, twice as many Black as white children were in the state's prisons. From 1919 until 1929, corporal punishment was permitted for white children in seven counties but for Black children in twenty-two. A North Carolina judge ordered three Black boys publicly whipped for breaking into a house in 1932. Over five times as many Black boys as white boys were whipped, what one attorney general in the state called "the grossest kind of racial discrimination."[61] In Alabama, in the infamous Scottsboro case, the youngest boy, Roy Wilkins, was only thirteen and two others, Olen Montgomery and Willie Roberson, were fifteen and seventeen. As Ellis recounts: "For six years, these three children, who should have been in school and living the happy lives to which all children are entitled, were subjected to the brutality of the prison system before they were released." Everywhere in the South, Black children were lynched. Ernest Collins and Benny Mitchell, fifteen and sixteen, were lynched because they were picking pecans near where a dead white girl had been found. Picking pecans while Black was their crime.[62]

World War II Fails to Change America

The period spanning World War II and its aftermath intensified the Black community's concern for their children as rural Black families crowded into the Northern industrial centers. Racial unrest in major cities reflected the anger and despair at the continuing segregation and inequities, conditions that Black communities had anticipated would have diminished following Black participation in the war effort. The Double V campaign—"victory over our enemies at home and abroad"— begun under the auspices of the largest Black newspaper in the country, the *Pittsburgh Courier*, challenged the nation's leaders to see the parallels between the Nazis' treatment of the Jews and the continuing segregation of and discrimination against Black people.[63] Youth were frustrated with persistent discrimination and its impact on their schooling, jobs, and basic needs. The continued migration of Black people into cities with segregated and restricted housing opportunities forced greater numbers of them into limited neighborhoods where dance halls, bars, clubs, and brothels were permitted to flourish for customers both criminal and not. Police presence then grew in these communities, creating an upward spiral of surveillance and arrests.[64]

Figure 3.2. Judge Jane Bolin. Courtesy of Library of Congress.

Black activists continued to challenge the disparate treatment of Black children. Black reformers who secured positions of power, like the New York City family court judge Jane Bolin—the first African American female judge to sit on any American court—used their positions to keep pressure on the juvenile court system to follow the law. Judge Bolin "wanted to bring Harlem and the concerns of its black youth within the purview of city responsibility."[65] From the time of her appointment in 1939 by Mayor La Guardia, she worked tirelessly against the persistent discrimination in the court, including advocating against public funds being used to sustain court-related institutions and agencies that discriminated on the basis of race or that maintained segregated facilities. In fighting for all facilities to be desegregated, Judge Bolin realized this meant dismantling some of the few facilities providing services and placements for Black children. This, she believed, was the price of integration.[66]

Judge Bolin—who retired from the bench in 1978, the year before I began to practice in her former court—boldly confronted the inequities she found from the very beginning of her tenure. She challenged the routine assignment of probation officers only to children who shared the same race, threatening to sue the court system if it continued the practice. She advocated for an amendment to the city charter that would prohibit discrimination by race in private child care agencies receiving public funds, and years later, when she discovered that white children were continuing to receive preferential placements, she successfully confronted the child welfare commissioner to end the practice. In the early 1960s, Judge Bolin discovered that the probation department identified children by race, making it easier for placement agencies to accept or reject children without appearing to discriminate. Once again, she succeeded in stopping the practice.[67]

Judge Bolin's concern for the welfare of all children in the city who appeared before her was exemplified in her objection to New York's sharp punitive turn the year she retired from the bench. A new juvenile offender law would treat younger and younger children as adult offenders with far more serious punishments. Judge Bolin called instead for "a many-faceted, highly financed attack on the social, economic, and family problems . . . to rehabilitate and reclaim our children," echoing similar calls throughout the century.[68] Despite some of Bolin's achievements in reducing the discriminatory practices of the court, the decades leading up to the juvenile offender law in 1978 were already increasingly dangerous and punitive for New York's Black children.

The end of World War II and the years immediately following it saw an uptick of criminal activity in large cities across the country. Attention to crime in New York was driven by print media sensationalism heralding a crime wave that would inspire a warlike response among public officials. Billboards scattered around the city in the 1950s screamed "Crime Is Juvenile Delinquency Grown Up" and "Juvenile Delinquency Is the Hard Way to Get Nowhere!"[69] Across the country headlines barked "Why the Young Kill: Prowling the Juvenile Jungles of the Big Cities" and "Arsenal of Delinquency."[70] Newspapers were quick to emphasize crimes committed by Blacks or in Black neighborhoods like Harlem. Roy Wilkins, then the executive secretary of the NAACP, chastised newspaper editors for blaming children of color for delinquency. In a speech that "electrified the annual meeting of the New York State Welfare Conference," Wilkins declared: "If one were to believe much of today's literary output on delinquency, one would conclude (a) that it is a development peculiar to our times, and (b) that Negroes and Puerto Ricans are responsible for its appearance in our midst."[71]

It is worth pausing for a moment to consider the stereotypes of Black youth, especially Black boys, that animated Wilkins's charge and that we know from recent research informs stereotyping and cognitive bias today. The history of Black youth characterized as "violent, immoral and degenerate" has been sanitized by less provocative language, but the racialized perception of them remains deeply rooted.[72] Black boys are seen as less innocent than white boys, and they are seen and treated as older and more dangerous than they really are. In school, they are considered less competent; suspended and expelled more frequently at younger ages for minor infractions; and suffer from mental health challenges linked to the trauma and stress of racism. They are diagnosed with conduct disorders that mask their true mental health issues and that steer them into the juvenile legal system.[73] When I represented youth charged with delinquency, I do not remember a single Black male client who wasn't diagnosed as "undersocialized/aggressive" no matter what the charge. This narrative of Black youth had always instilled fear in the public, but at the time Wilkins was speaking the press was transforming general crime into "Black crime" and juvenile crime into "Black youth crime."[74]

In his recent account of delinquency in New York in the late 1940s and early 1950s, the historian Carl Suddler illuminates how Black youth were transformed into "hoodlums" and fueled a panic of Black youth lawlessness that created predictable patterns of response. Calls for prevention efforts and services essentially triggered the belief that a crime wave was occurring. Rather than responding to the complex needs of the community and the youth themselves, these calls generated greater police presence that resulted in sending increasing numbers of Black youth into juvenile court in two ways. The first was that the police simply arrested more Black youth because those were the neighborhoods where they were policing. The second was that juvenile prevention programs affiliated with the police, such as the Juvenile Aid Bureau and the Police Athletic League, widened the net of police surveillance and increased the likelihood that neighborhood youth who participated in the programs could be identified as potentially delinquent.[75] Given the extremely broad legal definition of delinquency at the time—including everything from serious felonies to incorrigibility, habitual disobedience, habitual truancy, running away from home, working illegally, associating with immoral or vicious persons, begging, using profanities, and/or endangering the morals of others—merely being observed as an adolescent became perilous.[76] The white immigrant children who had previously been scrutinized were scattering to the more secluded suburbs, leaving in their place Black children whose opportunities to join them in leafier confines continued to shrink.[77]

The 1957 *Fact Book on Children in New York City* confirmed this demographic shift. Between 1920 and 1950, the number of children in the city increased by 3.8 percent. The number of white children *decreased* by 6 percent, and the number of nonwhite children *increased* by 500 percent.[78] Even so, the proportion of Black children charged with delinquency and the proportion of Black children in foster care by the mid-1950s were far greater than their proportion in the population generally. A third of the children in children's court on delinquency charges were Black, as were 29 percent of the children in foster care. The 1957 *Fact Book* noted that the economic deprivation of these families, the strain of moving into an urban environment, and "that they are still, even in New York City, subject to discriminating pressures" all contributed to the disproportionality.[79] This discrimination spilled over into the services these children needed. While securing services and assistance to prevent placements or institutionalization would have been most beneficial for all families, foster care remained the available option. Yet foster care placements were inaccessible for Black (and Puerto Rican) children, who represented 70 percent of the children awaiting placements, many of them very young. Adoption options remained woefully inadequate for Black children, leaving most of them in foster care for years.[80] This discrimination was inextricably tied to the religious matching policies that had long governed volunteer foster care agencies and excluded Black children despite efforts of judges like Jane Bolin, Justine Wise Polier, and Hubert Delaney to change these practices from the 1940s onward.[81]

Grappling with the "Negro Is a Born Criminal" Stereotype

The Supreme Court, in *Brown v. Board of Education*, relied on Dr. Kenneth Clark's doll studies to show the pernicious impact of segregation on Black schoolchildren. Five years later, Dr. Clark contributed to a 1959 symposium issue on juvenile delinquency in the *Journal of Negro Education*. Clark's goal was to firmly situate the relationship between minority status, economic deprivation, and delinquency in social science research going forward. He noted that social scientists increasingly rejected the interpretation that the disproportionate numbers of crimes committed by Black people result from their being—as Elaine Ellis had despaired— "born a criminal." Instead, investigators like Clark looked to the complex environmental and individual reasons in their lives to explain behavior. By the time Clark was writing, he could conclude uncontrovertibly that, while social scientists may emphasize one factor more than others, there was a lengthy list of factors at play: community disorganization, economic disadvantages, poor housing and generally depressed living conditions, the cultural shifts from rural to urban living, the less inhibited lifestyles of the lower classes, and, increasingly, "social psychological interpretations which stress the inevitability of aggressive and antisocial reactions to the racial frustrations, deprivations, discrimination, and segregation of the Negro."[82]

Relying on two studies of delinquency, Clark posited that, if the studies' findings were consistent around the country, Black children would be committing three times as many crimes as white children and brought to court two and a half times more often. Rather, the significant amount of delinquency—in both the white and Black communities— came from the children with the lowest socioeconomic status; in the case of Black children, this meant 85 percent of them. For Clark, the disproportionality made perfect sense. Deprived Black children in poor urban neighborhoods were shaped by their reaction to the discrimination, segregation, and economic barriers that molded their feelings of self-worth. They were burdened by feelings of inferiority and the denial of dignity in the broader society. Antisocial behavior was triggered not only as a response to the society that rejected them and prevented them from accruing social and economic benefits but also as a way to have status within their own peer communities. This led to a vicious cycle in which the larger white society saw this behavior as justification for labeling these youth as delinquent rather than taking responsibility for the deep and pernicious structural barriers that these youth were flailing against.[83]

Clark's insights into middle- and upper-class Blacks and privileged whites provide a deeper understanding of who didn't find themselves in court. Clark believed that Black families who acquired middle-class values taught their children not to act like their lower-class brethren. These children instead internalized their ambivalence about self-worth, which deeply harmed them but was less likely to lead them to delinquent behavior and court. His most profound insight, however, is about privileged *white* children. Here his self-admitted hypothesis (since these children weren't studied in the same way) goes beyond the usual observation that their families had resources and stature to keep them out of court. Clark said instead that much of their bad behavior—what he labels "privileged delinquency"—was not treated by society as delinquency at all. Their patterns of social cruelty with a subculture of cliques were as vicious as any gang's. "If delinquency is to be defined in terms of its essentials of lack of social sensitivity, lack of empathy, a callous disregard for the humanity and dignity of others, a punitive and seductive approach to others who are considered weak and defenseless," then these children would certainly find themselves counted in the court statistics, diminishing disproportionality in a novel way.[84] Whatever Dr. Clark's insights on the true nature of delinquent behavior, poor and marginalized Black children would remain disproportionately the objects of the juvenile court's work. Clark concluded, with a clear touch of irony: "When the privileged delinquent exercises his power in the middle-class society to deny others this right to full social participation on arbitrary grounds of color, class, or caste, he contributes directly to the increasing rate of delinquency among the underprivileged and he makes it impossible for the problem of juvenile delinquency to be effectively controlled."[85]

The juvenile court had a deplorable history with Black children. For much of the twentieth century, Black children were either ignored—leaving them to the sanctions of adult courts and punishments—or disproportionately accounted for in delinquency proceedings and treated far more punitively. At the same time, study after study and report after report identified how Black children were captured within a structural racism that denied them access to the opportunities, assistance, and support that would diminish the likelihood that they would be considered "born a criminal" and be thrust into the juvenile court system.

The prospects for Black children in the juvenile court would not improve as the century progressed and the court expanded its jurisdictional authority and became a family court in many jurisdictions, the focus of chapter 4. Neither would the Supreme Court's due process mandates rendered in the 1960s and 1970s protect them sufficiently from punitive outcomes, as chapter 5 highlights. Yet these children were not abandoned by their communities. Instead, against tremendous barriers, Black communities continued to advocate for "our delinquent children," holding on to the goals of racial and economic justice.

4

Rationalizing and Consolidating Court Power

Great ideas continue not only because of their emotional power and our collective conservatism but also because of an optimistic belief that errors can be corrected over time to create a better system. The sociologist and historian Charles Tilly posited that we reform only at the edges of what we know. We frame our efforts in ways that fit into our conventional idea of things, rarely breaking entirely with the ways in which we have ordered our structures. We hang on not only because the idea is powerful but also because we see our options for reform mostly in relation to that powerful idea.[1] Katherine Lenroot, the third administrator of the federal Children's Bureau, reflecting on the juvenile court in 1922, captured Tilly's proposition perfectly:

> The juvenile court is a living and growing institution, that has experienced both failure and success during its comparatively short history. Whatever form its future development may take, if it advances steadfastly in the scientific, yet sympathetic and understanding, study of the children with whom it deals, and in the perfecting of the remedies it offers, it cannot fail to contribute to individual happiness and social welfare.[2]

The fiftieth anniversary of the court in 1949 was an obvious occasion to reflect on whether the court was contributing to individual happiness and social welfare. During and after World War II, juvenile delinquency had become an issue that received renewed attention as the types of crimes and their frequency raised concerns about public safety.[3] Some of the court's early supporters and advocates remained engaged in the court's work. Katherine Lenroot was in her last years at the Children's Bureau; Charles Chute was finishing his long tenure at the National Probation Association; and Dr. Thomas Healy, though retired from directing court psychopathic clinics, was still advocating systemic studies of treatment methods and outcomes. Colleagues who had come to their work more recently, especially judges, were anxious to enhance the court's role within a more uniform court system without diminishing its ability to provide personalized justice. The rhetorical flourishes about the court as one of the great achievements of mankind were gone. Nevertheless, there remained an adherence to the court's therapeutic potential—symbolically and in practice—at the fiftieth anniversary commemorations.

The symbolic role for the court was its enduring commitment to the ideal of therapeutic intervention. As the pretext that the court could prevent delinquency was abandoned, supporters like Lenroot sought to imbue the court with figurative importance. "The great primary service of the court is that it lifts up the truth and compels us to see the wastage of human life whose sign is the child in court."[4] A child in court now meant society's failure to prevent court intervention, not the expansive opportunity for the court to prevent such damage. The underlying philosophy of the court's therapeutic intervention was credited for influencing states to create other treatment institutions, like youth correction authorities, and for transforming the idea of adult probation from a roll-call tool to an investigative sentencing mechanism.[5]

Imbuing the court with wide-ranging symbolic importance as a treatment ideal helped to ensure its continuance. "The Juvenile Court is here to stay," reaffirmed Dr. Healy, as it had "hardly begun to embrace its opportunities."[6] He urged a healthy exchange of ideas to reconstruct the court's underlying purpose, abiding by the American propensity of "building up rather than tearing down."[7] Nevertheless, there were warnings about arrogance. As one commentator noted: "[T]he pace of progress during the last half-century gives us no cause for smug satisfaction."[8] The metaphor advanced by Professor Harrison Dobbs in his defense of the court as a "reasonably good ship" finding itself in still waters seemed to be enough justification for the court to exist.[9] No one was prepared to abandon ship. Instead, as Tilly posited, they began reforming at the edges of what they knew to sail the ship forward.

The NPA's Charles Chute recommended what had become a predictable set of measures: First, shift preventive efforts back into the community with enhanced funding and trained social service providers in order to limit the need for court intervention; second, provide more resources for the court to do its job; and third, reassess what kinds of children still belonged in court. He joined these recommendations with the proposed conversion from a juvenile to a broader family court to enhance the court's ability to correct the underlying family problems. This reconstructed court "is to deal with cases needing authoritative treatment and the enforcement of the state's parental powers."[10] Community prevention efforts would keep all but "the most aggressive youth" out of court, whose job now "as an authoritarian agency" included protecting society.[11] If families were unwilling or incapable of correcting their children, the new family court would step in to do the job.[12] The war years had seen a spike in youth crime, which, despite dropping after the war, had taken its toll.[13] The "safety, protection[,] and welfare of the community" was no longer to be subordinated to the welfare of the individual child. As Pound had advised in 1944, the court's obligation now ran equally to the best interests of the child and the community.[14]

Toward a Family Court (with More Criminal Roots)

The call for a juvenile court more like other courts within a unified court system resonated with reformers who were anxious to expand the jurisdiction of the juvenile court to include many, if not all, of the issues that brought children and families to court. Many jurisdictions in the first three decades of the century had created multiple specialized courts modeled on the juvenile court—domestic relations courts, women's and girl's courts, conciliation courts, children's courts, home courts, truancy courts—to tackle broader family problems in an effort to address the myriad issues of marriage and divorce, support and custody, abandonment of wives and children, dependency, guardianship and adoption, and even probate. Like the original juvenile court, these courts emphasized the social rather than the legal character of the issues, drawing on social science expertise to resolve conflict through informal procedures and by eschewing adversarial processes. They were seen as shouldering the job that used to be done more privately within families and communities and now had become a public responsibility.[15] Given the similarities in purpose and approach among these socialized courts, consolidating their work was a predictable solution.

Yet consolidation also brought criminal court elements more straightforwardly into the courts being unified. Scholars examining these parallel and sometimes overlapping socialized courts have emphasized the centrality of their criminal roots. Professor Elizabeth Katz, for example, described how criminal nonsupport laws morphed into civil processes heard in family courts beginning in the 1930s while still retaining their "criminal bite." In New York, for instance, judges had the authority to transform civil support proceedings into criminal ones, and a judge could use either civil contempt procedures or a criminal conviction of nonsupport to exact payment—and in both cases could impose jail terms of up to a year for noncompliance.[16] Similarly, Professor Mae Quinn has upended the presumed novelty of current criminal problem-solving courts in her study of the first criminal domestic violence court created within New York City's magistrate court system in 1946. This court was one of several therapeutic projects within the magistrate system that had been created by Judge Anna Moscowitz Kross. Judge Kross had experimented ten years earlier with combining social services as a first alternative to criminal sanctions in her Wayward Minors Court for Girls. Young women would be given the opportunity to change their ways as "sex delinquents," but if they did not comply with treatment and had "no prospect of an adjustment pursuant to the plans suggested," then they would be tried and sentenced.[17] Judge Kross went on to create the Home Term Part of the magistrate court to address domestic violence first as a social problem with conciliating solutions before using criminal sanctions. Like juvenile court, the Home Term courtroom was a table and chairs, but it also had a waiting room with homey furnishings. This therapeutic approach to criminal court matters was controversial for some of the same reasons juvenile court had been: the lack of formality and due process, the limitless discretion of the judge and probation officers in attempting to use treatment in a court setting, and the potential that defendants were innocent but nevertheless were labeled in need of treatment and required to comply with curative solutions or face criminal sanctions.[18] While Kross's approach can be considered holistic in its openness to solutions that strengthened the family, being situated within the court system rather than the community meant that the "stick" of prosecution and sentencing remained always available.

When a unified family court was eventually created in New York, the Home Term Part was incorporated and morphed into "family offense" civil proceedings with fewer curative aspects. The support proceedings

JUDGE PAUL W. ALEXANDER
of the Family Court Center

Figure 4.1. Judge Paul W. Alexander. Courtesy of Library of Congress.

described by Katz also became part of the family court. Both types of cases brought their criminal court roots with them, and contempt sanctions were available that could lead to fines and also jail.[19] These examples show how the therapeutic processes of socialized courts could so easily devolve into highly discretionary, invasive, and punitive interventions, especially in "poor people's" courts. As with the juvenile court, a punitive result was always animate in the developing family courts.

Dean Pound's original objective of using socialized courts to control the urban poor was enhanced because these courts increasingly handled overlapping problems like custody, support, and abandonment. As dockets swelled, informality was justified not only to use social workers and probation officers to investigate family issues but also to simplify processes and minimize the need for lawyers and formal adjudications.[20] As Professor Elizabeth MacDowell has argued, despite the justifications offered by court reformers that these socialized processes offered greater access to justice, what they actually did was intensify the state's intervention in the lives of poor, urban immigrant and Black families. Like the founders of the juvenile court, judges, social workers, and probation officers continued to employ white middle-class values in their discretionary determinations of family matters regarding marital and parental fitness. In Cincinnati, for example the information in divorce cases included, "in addition to the facts of the dispute, a complete personal history, including such matters as church membership, moral character, temperance, mentality, occupation, a statement as to the character of the home, its sanitation, cleanliness, and order."[21] Creating family courts to consolidate the issues that drove poor and marginalized families into courts intensified the scrutiny of these families and facilitated greater interference into how they chose to live their lives. Many of them were left with punitive consequences rather than the therapeutic outcomes promised.

Family Court Judges: The "Keystone of the Arch"

Calls for a court with broad and exclusive jurisdiction over family matters had first been made early in the century, most prominently by Judge Willis Perkins of Michigan, who identified the family rather than the individual as the basic unit of society and emphasized how "these matters can be traced to some defect in the administration of the family."[22] Judge Perkins had written that unified family courts would provide judges with extraordinary inquisitorial and supervisory powers, and therefore they must be "well versed in the law, of large experience, unswerving firmness, broad sympathies, and clear, quick and accurate judgments," or their work would fail.[23] When states and localities finally began in earnest to consider consolidation, the role of the judge in wielding such tremendous authority in forums that were defined by informality, social solutions, and continuous monitoring became a central issue.

Judge Paul Alexander exhorted creating family courts with powerful judges. Judge Alexander spoke at the same NPA conference that Dean Pound had addressed in 1944. He called on juvenile court judges to resist political control and improve themselves through learning to fulfill their jobs of redirecting lives, reforming attitudes, alleviating distress and emotional misery, and protecting society against incipient crime.[24] He believed so strongly in the therapeutic power of the judge that he

Figure 4.2. Family Court of Lucas County, Toledo, Ohio. Courtesy of Library of Congress.

would later propose a therapeutic divorce system that would allow the judge to deny a divorce if he believed the marriage could be saved. The judge would rely on scientific knowledge and expertise to heal the marriage instead. Judge Alexander employed a long-used medical metaphor to emphasize this point: "[T]hough pain drives [the patient] to demand amputation of his shattered leg, the surgeon won't amputate if the leg can be repaired."[25] Judge Alexander's therapeutic divorce movement was short-lived, but his other passion—the creation of family courts—proved more durable. Judge Alexander led the movement for family courts from the 1940s until the 1960s, using the model of his own court in Toledo, Ohio, through his leadership of multiple national organizations including the NCJCJ and the NPA and by speaking and writing widely about the benefits of a consolidated family court.[26]

Consolidating disparate proceedings concerning the same family under one roof was the most widely expressed purpose of creating a family court. Overlapping or conflicting jurisdiction too often resulted in contradictory decisions and orders, confusing and frustrating the family and challenging the effective provision of services. Multiple proceedings were a waste of time and resources for the families and the court. Organizing connected cases in one court would improve interagency cooperation, ensure complete and consistent records, and diminish mistakes. Specialized judges focusing on the family would maintain the therapeutic philosophy of the juvenile court and its informal approach to adjudication and resolution.[27] And they would have far greater authority over the entire family.

The juvenile court founders had purposefully left vague the reasons why a child could be brought to the court. "Delinquency" and "dependency" were imprecise terms that included almost any wayward action by a child or parent that might implicate the child's care and protection. Now, the time had passed when "any reputable person" could initiate a case alleging that the child needed court supervision.[28] Even so, "thousands of juvenile are being processed by the courts as 'unofficial cases' without benefit of the due process of law . . . [and] judges apparently often take account of rumor, gossip, opinion, and others forms of hearsay in regular court hearings."[29] The Model Standards Acts written in the late 1950s for both the juvenile court and the family court struggled with language that would establish more concrete bases for state intervention and give clearer notice to families. Jurisdiction over dependent children would now require a finding of neglect or abuse by a parent. Delinquency would require an actual violation of the law. Only youth sixteen or older who committed a felony could be transferred to adult court after a determination that it was in the youth's or the public's best interest to transfer.[30]

Yet even here, the Model Standards' drafters could not agree on how to classify children being brought into court because they were truant or not following their parents' rules. Leaving those children out of the court's reach was inconsistent with the mandate to expand and consolidate the court's jurisdiction to "best serve the legal-social problems of children and families."[31] Most juvenile court judges at the time supported broad jurisdiction over "pre-delinquent" youth in an apparent design "to inhibit the exuberance of the slum-dwelling child."[32] As the sociologist Paul W. Tappan wrote in 1962:

A child may be a candidate for redemption if he associates with neighbors or schoolmates who are "vicious" or "immoral" persons . . . [or absents] himself from his home or school. He would do well not to express an unfavorable estimate of his parents or oppose their "reasonable and lawful commands," but he should not permit them to neglect him. He must not idle or loiter when he should be at work, or work at unapproved occupations when he should, presumably, be idle. He must shun gaming places, policy shops, dram shops, railroad yards and tracks, streets at night, public pool rooms or bucket shops . . . [he] should also avoid "indecency," "disorderliness," sex, cigarettes, liquor and obstinacy in general. . . . The zealous court can in fact intervene in any case in which the condition of the child, his parents, or his neighborhood attracts the solicitude of its personnel.[33]

In effect, despite some clearer definitions of what constituted behavior justifying the court's intervention, the new family court would continue to reach deeper, more efficiently, and with greater authority to reshape lives.

Judge Alexander believed fully in the power of scientific casework to join with the compassion of a knowledgeable judge to correct the mistakes afflicting families. He believed that all judges would come to the same conclusion if they would follow his example and become "the keystone of the arch [because] no court can be expected to rise above its judge."[34] He recounted that he had convinced lawyers appearing before him that "the philosophy of the family court actually is preventive and not punitive" and that the complete social history of the family "will never be used against the client but always in the best interests of the entire family."[35] Handling all family cases together in one court would in time lead lawyers to be able to counsel their clients to trust the court. Judge Alexander provided an example of this trust, saying that a lawyer would be able to urge a client, for example: "Don't worry, Mrs. Jones. The court won't send your boy away unless it's absolutely necessary for his own good. You just go over there and tell them the whole story. You needn't cover up anything."[36] Like many of his juvenile court predecessors, Judge Alexander minimized the coerciveness of a court to reshape people's lives. He is not concerned that, when Mrs. Jones tells him the whole story, he will have the exclusive power to decide what's "absolutely necessary" to be done because he knows best.

Judge Alexander acknowledged the barriers to creating the type of family court he envisioned and spoke widely and forcefully to advocate for more resources, better status for family judges, and the appointment of judges willing and able to shoulder the burden of human welfare. He readily believed that these obstacles could be overcome, just as he had overcome them. Like many of his colleagues anxious to imbue the juvenile and family courts with success, he encouraged studying the courts and insisted that they had been successful even if he couldn't prove it.[37] Stories from Judge Alexander and his colleagues extolling the court further embedded the Great Idea into the public realm and were rarely challenged. One exception was a scathing law review article in 1955 by the sociologist William M. Kephart denouncing the extravagant claims, including Alexander's, of the effectiveness of family courts. Kephart put it bluntly:

> In the absence of statistical and research information which might substantiate some of the otherwise extravagant claims made by proponents of the family court, there has arisen a fairly extensive body of verbally eloquent, albeit non-documented, literature. Extolling the alleged virtues of the family court, this material abounds in legal journals and is usually, though not always, written by members of the judiciary or legal personnel connected with such a court, or by social workers directly or potentially involved in family court procedures. There is nothing wrong with salesmanship of this kind; in fact, the pleading of one's case in the absence of supportable facts is an old human custom and privilege.[38]

Kephart lamented the use of "case histories," wherein reliance on storytelling without statistical support "continues to be the stock-in-trade of marriage counselors, psychiatrists, social workers, and others engaged in remedial family-problem work." He encouraged them instead to build a body of knowledge to solve the problems they routinely faced. Kephart was sympathetic to the hard work done on behalf of children and families but, like the Gluecks before him, believed that the proponents of these courts had the burden of proving their success. He urged bar associations to study contemporary juvenile and family courts to determine whether demonstrated results justified their existence.[39]

The New York Model of a Family Court

The Association of the Bar of the City of New York (now the New York City Bar Association) was following Kephart's recommendation to study the various courts dealing with family issues. The organization engaged Professor Walter Gellhorn of Columbia Law School to conduct a study "to inquire into the manner in which each court has discharged its duty to the family and to society at large [as] a step toward considering whether improvements in law administration are possible."[40] When Gellhorn conducted his study in the early 1950s, his conclusion that the disjointed ways in which child and family problems were parsed out to at least six different courts and several divisions of those courts led easily to the determination that this was not a productive way to get the work done. For Gellhorn, who is credited as one of the creators of modern administrative law, a unified family court was necessary to do the job. Yet efficiency turned out to be a byproduct of his conclusions because "[t]here is more to this suggestion than a mere aesthetic impulse to create an orderly pattern. It rests on the solid proposition that familial controversy can best be handled by judges who specialize in the family."[41]

Like other court reformers in the 1950s, Gellhorn remained committed to the therapeutic ideal within a more rationalized and regularized court process. A comprehensive family court would allow the judge to provide an opportunity for the family to address their problems in a constructive rather than punitive way while using "skills drawn from the social and biological sciences."[42] Staff would be trained in these scientific skills, and judges would have to be willing to adopt this approach. Gellhorn believed that judges should not be assigned to the court unless they are "particularly understanding of the methods it must employ," and if assignments to the court were to be rotated among judges, then they needed enough stability to learn this methodology and to develop relationships with the other staff.[43]

Gellhorn's central point was that the many courts that addressed family issues were not set up for success to do this job well. He also realized that many judges in the courts he reviewed were not suited for the unified family court he was proposing. He offered a stark assessment about judges presiding in the children's court—which was then adjudicating delinquency in New York City with few attorneys present, infrequent appeals taken, and the public barred from entrance: "Each of these men and women is the monarch of the court while sitting on its bench." Some of them "are humble enough to recognize their limitations, supple enough to absorb learning from fields other than the law, and warm enough to know that they are dealing always with human beings and not with 'cases.'" However, other judges "are confident in their righteousness, suspicious or at least skeptical about disciplines other than their own, and insensitive to the feelings of those who come before the court." He pointed to one judge consigning a delinquent boy to two different institutions without ever reading the psychiatric reports that had been prepared, another judge arbitrarily fluctuating between benignity and punitive orders, and a third never listening to his probation officer's recommendations.[44]

Nevertheless, Gellhorn was circumspect about the quality of the judges he was observing in his report. His goal was to change the structure of the system and, by doing so, change the quality of the judiciary. Gellhorn did not doubt that suitable judges could be found and trained to do the work. In fact, he had found them in the separate School Part of the children's court that dealt with truancy. Gellhorn was impressed with the expertise of the four judges in that part and with the fact that children did not seem to feel stigmatized by attending it. He feared that the helping functions that seemed so successful in the specialized School Part were not sufficiently understood or implemented by the bench in the rest of the children's court. Gellhorn concluded that the School Part should remain a separate entity until the community supported—and the bench fully embraced—the treatment function of the new family court exemplified by the judges in that section. Even here, the quality of the judge trumped the consolidation of the court.

Gellhorn drew significantly for his report on a study just completed by Dr. Alfred Kahn, his Columbia colleague in the School of Social Work. Kahn's study of the children's court had been labeled "controversial and provocative" because Kahn "[gave] us facts which are not sugarcoated and which are not pleasant to take."[45] Dr. Kahn, the social scientist, was less convinced that structural change was the main impediment to an effective family court judge. He agreed with Gellhorn that judges with specialized knowledge in a better-structured and -resourced court would do a better job, but he was also alarmed at the judge-as-monarch who, "in too many instances[] consciously or by implication [see] themselves as *the Court*."[46] The litigants also experienced the judges in this way: "For the majority of parents and children, the significance of the entire court is largely decided on the bench."[47]

Kahn wanted to hold on to the Great Idea of the juvenile court—but on different terms. Fifteen years before the Supreme Court would grapple with the meaning of due process for children in court, Kahn asserted that a judge lacks the legitimacy to enter into the dispositional phase of a proceeding unless the adjudicative phase is conducted with the basic due process protections of a common law court. Informality had a place in making children and families more comfortable in court and in integrating the opinions of the social service or mental health experts, yet to Kahn informality was not a substitute for fairness at either the adjudicative or dispositional phases of hearings. Neither was the judge's innate sense of what to do. Kahn put it bluntly: "Judges are prone to a major occupational hazard—the feeling that they can readily appraise a situation and regularly make wise decisions not subject to question."[48] Like Gellhorn, Kahn believed that a court with few lawyers, no oversight by the public and the press, or regular appellate review "lends itself particularly to such hazards."[49]

Kahn found these hazards throughout his study. Some judges failed to inform litigants of their limited due process rights. Parents often found that their child was adjudicated delinquent without the opportunity for an adjournment to seek witnesses or evidence. Judges routinely asked frightened children what they had done without any warning of the consequences. One judge, with no knowledge of the family, lectured a boy on how good his mother was to him. Another judge did the same— until it turned out that the woman accompanying the boy was the foster mother he had met recently. Kahn recounted stories of judges chiding children for bad spelling or for not going to church. Judges often ordered children they had just met to promise good behavior. One judge told a boy that he couldn't know the difference between right and wrong without knowing the Ten Commandments and repeated that admonition to his mother, who began to cry in court. Parents were chastised for their clothes or demeanor. A father was accused of being a gambler by the judge because he had no visible means of support. One judge even called a young boy into the courtroom to introduce him for the first time to his putative father and then sent the boy home to live with him![50] Judges also regularly meted out punishments for their young charges, who were often detained or placed in crowded facilities unsuitable for their needs. One judge compared the State Training School with "a good private boarding school [which] will be good for him to go somewhere where he can't have his way and will be made to learn what was wrong with what he did."[51] To be fair, other judges tried but failed to provide the type of disposition best suited for the child because of the limitation of services or facilities.[52]

Recognizing the occupational hazard of judges' thinking that they were wise and would always make the right decisions, Kahn urged restraint on the use of the court's power:

> It is clear that, even within a juvenile court concerned with arranging treatment, the process which considers intervention (judicial steps) must be carefully separated procedurally from treatment planning (disposition) since the court properly should assert jurisdiction only in clearly defined situations and not simply because a judge considers a particular child to need treatment.[53]

Kahn believed that this constraint on court intervention would more likely lead to "a refined instrument of social control and treatment, used only when appropriate and then with adequate legal safeguards."[54] The judge who is given the power to exercise such instrumental authority must understand the grave implications of that power in order to make wise findings and proper dispositional orders. Kahn wanted the judge to be the leader of a court team, but most of the judges he observed didn't define their roles in ways "consistent with the intent of the law" or "fail[ed] to implement [the law] successfully."[55] Kahn understood that resources both in and out of court were essential to assist families with complex issues and that those resources had never been sufficient. He reluctantly concluded that "[many] children and parents known to the Court require a complex range of services and facilities, but only a minority are well served. Hence from the perspective of the aspirations of the juvenile court movement and the expressed goals of court leadership, the accomplishments are outweighed by the inadequacies."[56] Perhaps with greater legal safeguards, improved resources, and consolidation of family issues, the court could fulfill "a dream still unrealized," which was the title of one of the last chapters in Kahn's report.[57]

Within ten years of Kahn's and Gellhorn's reports, the New York State Family Court had been created. Gellhorn's recommendations for a unified court helped create a path to the passage of the 1962 New York Family Court Act, which combined most, but not all, family proceedings in a single, unified family court.[58] The proceedings would now look far more like Kahn recommended, with less informality and an adjudicative process that incorporated more procedural regularity. Treatment would also play a far greater role after the court made a determination of responsibility on the part of a child or parent. Judges, however, once jurisdiction was established, were given "a wide range of powers for dealing with the complexities of family life so that its action may fit the particular needs of those before it."[59] The new act also addressed Gellhorn's proposals that "legal training and experience should be required before any person may assume the office of family court judge" and that judges of the family court "should also be familiar with areas of learning and practice that often are not supplied by the practice of law."[60]

Three lessons can be drawn from New York's new family court system, which was being replicated in reforms in several states at the time. First was a recommitment to the court's continuing power to shape the type of services and assistance children and families would receive once the purpose for intervention was established. The therapeutic impulse of the juvenile court requiring personalized justice remained intact. Second, while the court would have broader jurisdiction over the entire family through a more integrated court, the proceedings themselves would be less informal than previously, incorporating at least some of the formal aspects of trial courts as the cases became more complex. And third, the judge remained the "keystone of the arch" in a more effective, if less freewheeling, therapeutic court.

Serious Rumblings of Concern about the Great Idea

While Judge Alexander and the National Council of Juvenile Court Judges worked to solidify the centrality of judge-led therapeutic family courts midcentury, many court observers and participants began to question the very basis of the juvenile court concept. The bargain made between a youth, her parent, and the state, which permitted the judge to substitute his or her judgment for a parent's in exchange for not treating the youth as an ordinary criminal, had not been kept.[61] Could an expanded family court with even greater jurisdictional authority over the family be built atop this failing idea? Good intentions were insufficient justifications for court intervention if, after six decades of adjudicating youth matters, most courts were "not equipped to diagnose their problems, prescribe remedies suited to the individual needs, or provide the treatment necessary to help them."[62] Young people were being treated as junior criminals by law enforcement and corrections agencies; court proceedings were not only informal but also chaotic; and children were being institutionalized in appalling detention centers or adult jails before any adjudication and were similarly incarcerated in horrific institutions if found delinquent. Children removed from their homes rarely improved.[63]

Centering the court as the hub of a system to address children in trouble and their parents was becoming unrealistic. The judge was less directly involved with the mechanism of treatment, as it was state child welfare agencies that increasingly distributed public assistance and shouldered many of the services previously situated in the court.[64] That being said, the court was not seen as obsolete. An expanded and unified family court was considered the best solution for consolidating jurisdiction that may affect a child and her family, especially if detailed laws established clearer classifications for the reasons families were in court. There was greater recognition that delinquency was not the same as dependency or neglect or abandonment. The time had passed when judges were supposed to decide only what the child needed.

In 1961, California established different dispositional rules for neglected, misbehaving, and delinquent children, rules that were designed to limit placing neglected children alongside children in trouble or who were breaking the law—especially commitment to a youth correctional facility.[65] At the same time, judges still retained tremendous power over children and families. Writing in the early 1960s, Professor Monrad Paulson used several examples of judges abusing their discretion to deliver unwarranted severe punishments "as a reminder of the human limitations of judges and social workers."[66] Such cases had convinced Paulson to change his mind about relying solely on judicial discretion for dispositional orders, fearful of the inclination of many judges to "get tough" and aware of how few courts provided any due process protections to children or parents. In a West Virginia case Paulson cites, a fourteen-year-old boy made a crank call on a dare saying a bomb was placed in a school (at a time when school safety did not have a legacy of school shootings). He was sent to the state reform school until he was twenty-one; if he had been an adult, he would have received a fine or thirty days in jail.[67] This case is remarkably similar to *In re Gault*, where the Supreme Court would hold in 1967 that youth at risk of losing their liberty were entitled to a lawyer. Gerard Gault was also found to have made a crank call—this time a lewd one—and was sentenced to six years in the Arizona Industrial School; had he been an adult he would have paid a fine or spent a short time in jail.[68] Concerns like Paulson's would be reflected in the Court's opinion in *Gault* and several other cases in the 1960s that began to layer due process protections onto juvenile court proceedings; these will be discussed in chapter 5.

Paulson and other prominent commentators also worried about judicial discretion in proceedings where specific definitions of neglect and abuse were replacing dependency. Despite those clearer classifications, children were still being taken from their families because of poverty, the inability to access services, and the belief that it was in their "best interests" because of a parent's lifestyle.[69] For many parents, even when their children weren't removed, the court was "taking my child away from me" by reducing their ultimate parental authority. Elliot Studt, who worked directly with children and parents, noted "the child's perception of his parent's worth may be seriously damaged by court action unless steps are taken to recognize and support the parent's continuing function."[70] In looking at the future of what the court might accomplish, Studt was remarkably progressive in his call to seek answers from the people who appeared there—"to take these crucial participants into consideration" by asking them, "How do they see this organization under whose guidance they are expected to solve problems? What structural arrangements invite regression, diminish self-respect, or encourage vindictiveness within families? What arrangements, on the other hand, support the fullest acceptance of responsibility of which the clients are capable? Where is clarification needed? And how can pathways for improved communication be devised?"[71] Despite Studt's recognition of the formative role parents and children could play in changing the court, their opinions about solutions would not be solicited for another half-century.

The Great Idea Persists

The Great Idea of the juvenile court had withstood sixty years of investigations, critiques, denunciations, despair, and reformulations. Every state had adopted some form of juvenile or family court; many would consolidate additional family proceedings later in the century. The growing and living institution that Katherine Lenroot had described in 1949 had incorporated some but not all of the lessons of its history, continuing to reform around the edges. Kahn's formulation of the court as "a refined instrument of social control and treatment, used only when appropriate and then with adequate legal safeguards," left many questions for the court's future unresolved.[72]

The court remained tethered to the belief that, with sufficient scientific knowledge applied by a capable and caring judge, the right intervention was possible. Nevertheless, the bargain made originally to reduce formality and punishment for personalized justice was being challenged on many fronts. The court was now explicitly responsible for community safety, having to balance the child's or family's interest with the community's concerns. This led to calls for less informality and more procedural regularity in the court's proceedings. There was also more explicit acknowledgement that the court was an instrument of coercion that often was unable to achieve its therapeutic goals without sufficient resources within the court or in the community. Too frequently this resulted in relying on punitive rather than therapeutic outcomes. The court had become less central to delivering the treatment children and families needed and more likely to be monitoring the results of its orders. The rise of public welfare agencies had accelerated the transfer of most services and assistance from the court itself into those agencies and their community partners. The extraordinary judge nevertheless remained the keystone of the court. And yet most judges had not been a Judge Mack or a Judge Edwards or the four judges sitting in New York's special School Part; most judges had failed to accomplish the court's therapeutic goals. As William Kephart had observed, the wonderful case stories did not suffice to justify courts that had never been proven to accomplish their own missions. Their continuation needed to be justified by greater proof.

When Professor Francis Allen considered the juvenile court as part of a series of extraordinary essays on criminal justice in 1964, he cautioned that "in reacting against old errors we are constantly in danger of being enslaved by our emancipation."[73] He warned that holding on to the original idea of the juvenile court could obstruct needed reforms. By the early 1960s many reformers, like Allen, were reevaluating the Great Idea with increased awareness of what terrible outcomes had befallen so many children when the idea had not been implemented in the ways it had been conceived. To accomplish the goals of a juvenile or family court more tempered by law and regularity, these reformers were scrutinizing the extent to which the due process rights of adults should be introduced to the juvenile court. This would not only protect individual rights; it would satisfy the public that the court could keep the community safe while implementing therapeutic goals. Allen, like many observant commentators before him, admonished the court and its supporters to recognize the complexity of the reasons children and families found themselves in this court. Fundamental solutions were not to be found in the court but rather "in the direction of integrating our alienated populations into full participation in the social, economic, political and cultural life of our communities [even though] such measures run afoul of the interests, attitudes and prejudices of the dominant segments of our population." The court's defenders had "to distinguish between wish and reality and to determine with reasonable accuracy the limits of our powers and capabilities."[74]

At the same time, judges deeply committed to the therapeutic ideal, like Judge Alexander, were expressing outrage that the introduction of procedural due process rights would deny "the juvenile court a fair trial [which is] to deny the child himself a fair trial." To "deprive the court of its rightful status" would "impair its intended effectiveness" and "deprive the child not merely of constitutional rights but of many invaluable rights regarded as the birthrights of every American child." Invoking the medical metaphor once more, he declared: "It is like denying a sick child the right to a good hospital." Judge Alexander believed that four institutions protected the child: home, church, school, and the juvenile court.[75] He foresaw only injustice for children in transforming the juvenile court into a court of law. He could not see the injustice that had already been done to children in the juvenile court that he loved.

5

The Great Idea Meets Due Process

The last great public pronouncement about the role of the juvenile court took place in 1971 when a boy from Philadelphia named Joseph McKeiver asked to be tried by a jury after being charged with robbery, larceny, and receiving stolen goods for stealing twenty-five cents. Joseph was fifteen years old in 1968 when he was arrested for participating in a robbery against three other teenagers. The teens were playing in a park when a large group of youth pursued them on foot and by bicycle and managed to steal a quarter from one of the victims. Soon after the incident, the victims were driven around the neighborhood in a police patrol car and identified Joseph as their mugger. Joseph had never been arrested before and already had a good employment history. Five months later, Joseph's case was heard in Philadelphia's juvenile court before Judge Theodore S. Gutowicz.[1] He met his lawyer on the day of trial and spoke to him for five minutes before the court insisted on proceeding. Two of the victims testified, giving a jumbled account of how many teens were involved, whether they were on foot or bikes, and what actually happened to them. On only one point they were clear: the mugger did not wear glasses. Joseph, it turns out, had worn glasses since he was a small boy. At the end of the testimony, Joseph's lawyer argued that the case should be dismissed. The eyewitness account was incredible and unreliable and certainly did not establish Joseph's guilt beyond a reasonable doubt. Judge Gutowicz disagreed, found Joseph to be a "delinquent child," and placed him on probation.[2]

Joseph's case would have been long forgotten, along with thousands of similar cases across the country, but his lawyer decided to appeal a motion he had made before the hearing began: that Joseph be given a jury trial. Judge Gutowicz had denied the motion and, when the lawyer renewed the request at the end of the short hearing, denied it again. The denial was upheld on appeal to the superior court and to the Pennsylvania Supreme Court before reaching the United States Supreme Court in December 1970.[3]

Several cases considering the due process rights of children had been heard by the Supreme Court during the 1960s. The call for more regularity in juvenile and family court proceedings that had infused reform efforts in the 1950s intensified during the following decade under the Warren Court's "due process revolution." Not only in criminal trials but also in other state actions—like securing public benefits or facing involuntary commitment—the Court was requiring public officials to have processes that gave an opportunity for the people affected to participate and be heard. This had a profound impact on the goals and meaning of the juvenile court. As Professor Barry Feld has chronicled so thoroughly, the therapeutic justification for the juvenile court lost most of its luster during the tumultuous 1960s. Progressives' justification for *parens patriae* intervention and benevolent coercion was being challenged by critiques of the progressives' assimilationist ambitions for families and the state's failed rehabilitative practices for children. The rise of pluralism and diversity rather than assimilation into white middle-class norms diminished the acceptance of therapeutic professionals fitting a misbehaving youth into an assigned way of being cured. The civil rights movement had resurfaced the deep racial injustices that permeated the country's policies and practices, including within its criminal and juvenile legal systems. As Feld noted, the Court chose to use procedural safeguards in both the adult and juvenile systems "to limit the state, to constrain discretion, and to protect people's freedom and liberties."[4] That this did not happen in quite the same way for adults and children can be attributed in large part to the unwillingness of the Supreme Court to abandon totally the ideal of the juvenile court.

The Constitutional Domestication of the Juvenile Court

By the time Joseph's lawyer requested a jury trial, the Supreme Court had taken a hard look at juvenile court procedures. In the first case, *Kent v. United States* (1966), Justice Abe Fortas, writing for the majority, was stymied from conducting a full review of juvenile court procedures and practices by the limited nature of the issue before him.[5] Morris Kent had originally been charged in juvenile court (because he was sixteen years old) with robbery and rape. Without holding a hearing or conducting any sort of investigation, the judge waived jurisdiction of the juvenile court and sent Kent directly to adult criminal court. Juvenile court judges had transferred some youth into adult court throughout its history, often in response to public concerns about safety and the fear of mounting youth crime, but also as a way to protect the court's central mission to protect those children most likely to be amenable to help. Judges considered transfer powers to be part of their exclusive control over what factors to consider in determining whether a youth would continue to be treated as a child—with the full panoply of rehabilitative opportunities—or was no longer suited for this specialized assistance.[6] Even if juvenile court judges retained exclusive statutory power to make that determination, the Supreme Court held that they could not do so without some regularized procedure that included a hearing with the opportunity to present and examine evidence that would form a sufficient basis for the juvenile court's determination and be reduced to a written statement. This was because the decision to deny a young person the right to the special protections of juvenile court jurisdiction was a critical one that required more than the judge's personal opinion.[7]

While the Court ruled on the narrow question of what process was due before a youth could be waived to adult court for criminal prosecution, Justice Fortas used the opportunity to express his concerns about the juvenile court more generally, including his most perceptive observation: "There is evidence, in fact, that there may be grounds for concern that the child receives the worst of both worlds: that he gets neither the protections accorded to adults nor the solicitous care and regenerative treatment postulated for children."[8] He would write about the evidence for those grounds the following year when the Court squarely faced what due process was necessary in the juvenile delinquency hearing of Gerald Gault.

In re Gault (1967) reached the Supreme Court in a time of turbulence but also optimism. Justice Fortas recounted what had happened to Gerald and how Gerald's story fit into the larger context of how juvenile courts operated. His harsh opinion of the juvenile court nevertheless contained a hopefulness that the imposition of due process procedures would protect a boy like Gerald while also allowing the juvenile court to reinvent itself. At age fifteen, Gerald had been charged with making a lewd phone call. He was picked up at home with no notice to his parents; no formal petition was filed against him; the complainant didn't appear at either of the two short proceedings; no record of the proceedings was kept; and no lawyer appeared for Gerald. At the end of the second proceeding, Gerald was found delinquent and committed to the Arizona State Industrial School for his minority—the next six years—unless the authorities discharged him earlier. If Gerald had been an adult, he would have been subject to either a small fine or up to two months in the county jail.[9] Instead Gerald was sent to spend the rest of his childhood in state custody. Eventually, with the assistance of an experienced attorney associated with the American Civil Liberties Union, Amelia Lewis, a habeas corpus petition was filed seeking Gerald's release. When that and subsequent appeals failed, Lewis and the ACLU shepherded the case to the Supreme Court.[10]

Justice Fortas again wrote the majority opinion. This is not surprising, as he has been considered in the Court's history to be the justice who was most focused on children's rights.[11] The juvenile court was the subject of Justice Fortas's opinion, if not its holding. The original purpose of the juvenile court, he wrote, was driven by "the highest motives and most enlightened impulses" that led to creating a specialized court "unknown to our law in any comparable context" for its focus on individualized treatment. Not only was this kind of court unknown; Justice Fortas also noted that "[t]he constitutional and theoretical basis for this peculiar system is—to say the least—debatable."[12] Moreover, he observed how the history of juvenile court showed repeatedly that "unbridled discretion, however benevolently motivated, is frequently a poor substitute for principle and procedure."[13] Nevertheless, Fortas was very aware that every state had created a juvenile court and that the constitutionality of the juvenile court had been repeatedly upheld.[14] He purposefully narrowed the Court's investigation to examining the extent to which due process protections apply to an adjudicative hearing that determines whether a child is delinquent and subject to consequences that could include commitment. While he filled his text and footnotes with the most recent reports of how poorly the juvenile court was achieving its therapeutic goals, how unfit most judges sitting in the court were for their positions, and how euphemisms like "training schools" did not hide the fact that children were being confined with harsh treatment, he was not prepared to limit the discretion of the "kindly judge" once a more constrained adjudicative process was completed. The disposition remained fully within the discretion of the judge: "[T]he features of the juvenile system which its proponents have asserted are of unique benefits will not be impaired by constitutional domestication."[15] Many juvenile court judges disagreed. Writing only two years later in the *Juvenile Court Journal*, a well-respected California family court judge, William E. MacFaden, described *Kent* and *Gault* as nuclear explosions dropped on the juvenile court.[16]

What was actually dropped on the court was the incorporation of regularity that had been gaining ground for over a decade. To be fair to Judge MacFaden, what Fortas required was, if not a nuclear explosion, certainly a repudiation of the omniscience of therapeutic intervention. Fortas insisted that children charged with delinquency needed to know specifically why they were there, not vague allegations that they were in need of the court's intervention. They were in court for what they had alleged done, not for who they were. Once the child was there, the probation officer was no longer responsible for protecting the child's interests; children needed a lawyer to protect their rights first and, if they were indigent as many were, a lawyer appointed by the state to represent them. Fortas cited the most recent edition of the Children's Bureau's Model Juvenile and Family Court Standards as well as the recently enacted New York Family Court Act—both of which had endorsed legal counsel for children—as authority for his decision. The best he could get from the National Council of Juvenile Court Judges was a tepid statement that, at the NCJCJ's 1965 national convention, the judges "found no fault" with the Model Standards' recommendations on providing counsel.[17] That was because, as Judge MacFaden would later write, *Kent* and *Gault* were about to be a nuclear disaster for juvenile court judges who wanted to retain their full powers.

Justice Fortas drew on the Model Standards as well to require sworn testimony and competent evidence in a juvenile court hearing. His conclusion that children were also protected from self-incrimination drew on the Court's recent adult cases, like *Miranda v. Arizona*, and he concluded that there was no basis for carving out an exception to the protections against self-incrimination under the Fifth Amendment for children. Fortas rejected family court judge Paul Alexander's recent plea—"To help the child change his attitude, a confession is a primary prerequisite"[18]—relying instead on recent studies indicating that confessions weren't aiding in individualized treatment.[19] *Gault* did not, however, incorporate all of the due process protections in the Bill of Rights that had been found applicable to adults in criminal proceedings. Instead, Justice Fortas created a specific approach to juvenile delinquency proceedings to protect youth from too much arbitrariness and discretion. With the addition of specific due process rights—notice of the charges, counsel, confrontation and examination of witnesses, and privilege against self-incrimination—the Court afforded what it considered "fundamental fairness" in a juvenile proceeding. The due process protections and fair treatment of the Fourteenth Amendment were sufficient for Justice Fortas to ensure that "the condition of being a boy does not justify a kangaroo court."[20] Justice Hugo Black, in his concurrence and dissent, pointed out that the holding "strikes a well-nigh fatal blow to much that is unique about the juvenile courts in the Nation." He, like Justice Potter Stewart, would have preferred to wait to pass on all of these issues, but if the Court chose to strike that blow, Justice Black would have preferred a knockout: he believed juveniles deserved all the protections of the Bill of Rights, not just a limited version of adult protections.[21] Justice Stewart, however, rejected the Fortas analysis entirely. Juvenile courts may need some due process constraints, but they remained an agency "of correction of a condition" and not a criminal process, despite "the reality has sometimes not even approached the ideal."[22]

Between the time that *Gault* was decided in 1967 and Joseph McKeiver's request for a jury trial reached the Supreme Court in 1970, the Court had also determined that the adjudicative phase of a juvenile court proceeding required a standard of proof beyond a reasonable doubt.[23] In Justice John Harlan's concurrence *In re Winship* (1970), he sought to reassure juvenile court judges that,"[t]oday's decision simply requires a juvenile court judge to be more confident in his belief that the youth did the act with which he has been charged."[24] In his dissent, the new Chief Justice, Warren Berger, disagreed. Weighed under by "an avalanche of cases" and inadequate staff and facilities, the juvenile court instead needed "breathing room and flexibility in order to survive, if it can survive repeated assaults from this Court."[25] Contrary to historical fact, Chief Justice Berger insisted that juvenile courts had been able to work effectively without the need to address constitutional issues before they were faced with their current problems.[26] *Winship* did not change Justice Fortas's approach to incorporating only "the essentials of due process and fair treatment" into the adjudicative phase of a delinquency proceeding. Requiring a higher standard of proof for a finding of delinquency could be absorbed into established routines. Holding jury trials was another matter.

The Paradox of *Gault*

Judge Gutowicz's decision to deny Joseph McKeiver a jury trial was upheld by an intermediate appellate court and then by the Pennsylvania Supreme Court, in an opinion by Justice Samuel J. Roberts on two consolidated cases (Joseph's and *Edward Terry's*). Prior to sitting on the state supreme court, Justice Roberts had served as president judge of the Orphan's Court of Erie County, a specialized court whose responsibilities included looking out for the best interests of minors in termination-of-parental-rights and adoption proceedings. *Gault* frustrated Roberts, who labeled the case a paradox for trying to hold on to the original purpose of the juvenile court while recognizing that young people still needed due process protections. If the *Gault* opinion had required that adults and juveniles charged with crimes receive the same due process protections, Roberts would have had little difficulty determining that Joseph should have received a jury trial. Instead, he found himself stuck in the same paradox for which he would fault the Supreme Court: making sweeping statements about the purpose and practice of juvenile court before deciding whether fundamental fairness included a jury trial. And while Roberts was in fact quite disturbed by the way in which Joseph's hearing was conducted—including no time for Joseph to consult with his lawyer and very weak evidence—that wasn't the issue before him.[27]

The balance Roberts sought reflected the *Gault* mandate to provide sufficient procedural protections to ensure that the juvenile court "will operate in an atmosphere which is orderly enough to impress the juvenile with the gravity of the situation and the impartiality of the tribunal and at the same time informal enough to permit the benefits of the juvenile system to operate."[28] Roberts didn't want to give up on his colleagues in the juvenile court even as he acknowledged that "the quality of the juvenile bench is not an entirely satisfactory substitute for due process,"[29] He lamented the lack of resources for the juvenile court, which limited its effectiveness, while acknowledging that it had never really accomplished its central goals of treatment and rehabilitation. Those goals, more than any other, "constitute the single best reason for preserving the juvenile system. Properly operated, the juvenile system is capable of giving understanding and sympathetic treatment for each juvenile by providing the correctional, rehabilitative and instructional attention appropriate to each case."[30] Roberts nevertheless cited sources that challenged the hallmarks of the juvenile court system—a combination of "kindness, expertise, and discretion"—in an increasingly diverse and divided urban landscape in which those qualities were not likely to engender a child's trust in the juvenile court judge.[31] On the one hand, he fretted that a jury trial, more than any other due process right, would turn the juvenile court judge into a technician and potentially destroy "the traditional character of juvenile proceedings."[32] On the other hand, Roberts wasn't sanguine about how this tradition had worked so far following a determination of delinquency. He lamented that the post-adjudication process "has fallen far short of its goals, and its reality is far harsher than its theory."[33]

The failures of the original juvenile court that the historian Anthony Platt would recount a year after Roberts's decision—harsh and lengthy incarceration, severe punishment, inadequate or nonexistent education or training, forced labor—had also been revealed in subsequent investigations into the juvenile justice system throughout the century.[34] During the period Roberts struggled with his decision he had been well aware of the recent and dismal findings about the juvenile court system included in *The President's Commission on Law Enforcement and Administration of Justice* (Johnson Commission) and its accompanying *Task Force Report: Juvenile Delinquency and Youth Crime* (Task Force), both cited heavily by Justice Fortas in *Gault*. Despite the bleak descriptions in these two reports of the ways in which the juvenile court had failed to serve children, and Roberts's own dissatisfaction with *Gault's* fundamental fairness construction, in the end the Great Idea won. Jury trials would destroy the juvenile court. Roberts concluded: "[We] are not yet convinced that the current practices do not contain the seeds from which a truly appropriate system can be brought forth."[35]

The lone dissenter was Justice Herbert Cohen, a former Pennsylvania attorney general. Justice Cohen was not persuaded that jury trials were the Armageddon of juvenile court. In Cohen's view, while "due process and parens patriae have come into direct conflict," they don't have to. The beneficial aspects of the juvenile system—informality and flexibility—could be maintained in the pre- or post-adjudicatory stages, where, "hopefully, some rehabilitation can be accomplished." He firmly rejected the idea that informality and flexibility at the adjudicatory stage "can have much effect on molding the juvenile's outlook so that his conduct will be in conformity with the rules society has established." Cohen saw the trend in Supreme Court decisions toward greater due process protections in the adjudicative part of delinquency proceedings and saw no basis for distinguishing jury trials from this trend.[36] Cohen also urged restraint. The Supreme Court had recently accepted a case from North Carolina, *In re Burrus*, on the issue of juvenile jury trials, and Cohen wanted to wait until hearing from the Supreme Court. *Burrus* instead would become one of the companion cases to *McKeiver* and provide an opportunity for the Supreme Court to consider the impact of juvenile court in perhaps an even more profound way than it ever had before by reckoning with the court's racist history. The Court failed to grasp that opportunity and instead chose Joseph's story to end this chapter in the procedural due process saga of the juvenile court.

The Supreme Court Wills the Patient to Live: The Great Idea Holds On

Joseph McKeiver's lawyers saw their opportunity. Just the year before, the Supreme Court had dismissed a challenge on procedural grounds to Nebraska's failure to provide jury trials to youth charged with delinquency. In dissent, Justices Hugo Black and William O. Douglas would have ruled in favor of trial by jury.[37] In granting certiorari in *Burrus*, the Court was clearly ready to address the question of whether its understanding of fundamental fairness in juvenile proceedings included the right to a jury trial. Joseph's case and two companion cases, *In re Burrus* and *In re Terry*, were argued in early December 1970.

Justice Fortas was gone. Caught up in a failed nomination to be named Chief Justice amid political and ethical scandals, Fortas resigned and was replaced by President Nixon's appointee, Justice Harry Blackmun. Justice Blackmun took his place next to Justice Roberts at the bedside of the juvenile court to determine whether the patient would survive. Despite attempts by both the concurring and dissenting opinions to make trial by jury the central question of these cases, Blackmun was more concerned with the impact on juvenile proceedings. After reviewing the facts and procedural history of the three consolidated cases,[38] Blackmun began his analysis by repeating the substance of Roberts's opinion with its on one hand/on the other description of juvenile court, including Roberts's confident conclusion "that a properly structured and fairly administered juvenile court system can serve our present societal needs without infringing on individual freedoms."[39] It can do so, Blackmun insisted, by not trying to fit the court into a civil or criminal box but by following *Gault*'s precept to determine whether a particular due process right is necessary to preserve fundamental fairness in the court proceeding. In short order he concluded that our system of justice permitted judges as well as juries to be the triers of fact, so having a jury isn't a necessary component of fundamental fairness for juvenile court trials.[40] After quickly dispatching with the due process issue, Justice Blackman turned sadly toward the lingering patient:

> We must recognize, as the Court has recognized before, that the fond and idealistic hopes of the juvenile court proponents and early reformers of three generations ago have not been realized. . . . Too often the juvenile court judge falls far short of that stalwart, protective, and communicating figure the system envisaged. The community's unwillingness to provide people and facilities and to be concerned, the insufficiency of time devoted, the scarcity of professional help, the inadequacy of dispositional alternatives, and our general lack of knowledge all contribute to dissatisfaction with the experiment. To say that juvenile courts have failed to achieve their goals is to say no more than what is true of criminal courts in the United States. But failure is most striking when hopes are highest.[41]

Blackmun then warned that, if trial by jury were found to be constitutionally required, the patient would surely die. Relying on the Johnson Commission report that Justice Fortas had previously cited, Justice Blackmun concluded: "Had the Commission deemed this vital to the integrity of the juvenile process, or to the handling of juveniles, surely a recommendation or suggestion to this effect would have appeared. The intimations, instead, are quite the other way."[42] He was correct in the specifics: the Johnson Commission did not recommend trial by jury as a necessary component to fundamental fairness in a juvenile proceeding. The recommendations were written before *Gault* had been decided, and whether applying *Gault*'s concept of fundamental fairness would have made a difference in their recommendations is speculation. At the same time, the Johnson Commission had rejected Blackmun's belief that making the adjudicative phase of the proceedings a fully adversarial proceeding would destroy the purpose of the court. Neither did it equate improved due process as the equivalent of returning juveniles to criminal court, as Blackmun suggested.[43] The intimations, in fact, were not the other way.

The Johnson Commission was clear that children should not be tried as adults in an adult court but in a court for children that provided extensive due process protections. This was to shield them from the adult system and, as Justice Cohen had suggested in his dissent below, to use the preventive and rehabilitative potential of the court prior to or after adjudication. But the Johnson Commission went further, warning that unfettered discretion by the court that had so far resulted in little rehabilitation and significant punishments for young people needed to be curtailed significantly if the juvenile court were to remain viable. In its struggle to balance the preventive and rehabilitative purposes of the juvenile court with the need for fair processes, the Johnson Commission's strongest recommendation was to narrow the court's jurisdiction significantly to minimize the number of children who would face adjudication. This was applicable especially to children brought to the court not because they had broken the law but because they had misbehaved in ways that worried parents, teachers, and police officers.[44] The Johnson Commission recommended rigorous attention to community-based assistance and diverting children away from the court. The court would then adjudicate only those few youth who had "already proved resistant to helping services or whose conduct was so repetitive or so clearly dangerous to the community that no other alternative seemed feasible."[45] And while the Johnson Commission was not specific in how this particular (and much smaller) group of youth would be tried, it concluded: "For this group, as to whom the condemnatory, deterrent, and incapacitative functions of judicial dispositions would appear to predominate, the use of more structured adjudicatory procedures destined to insure fairness and reliability of determinations is singularly appropriate."[46]

Nevertheless, since Justice Blackmun equated the imposition of jury trials on states with the eventual demise of the court, he urged the states to continue to experiment with new, better, and more medicines: "So much depends on the availability of resources, on the interest and commitment of the public, on willingness to learn, and on understanding as to cause and effect and cure."[47] Unlike Cohen and the Johnson Commission, Blackmun did not distinguish the adjudicative from the treatment and rehabilitative functions of the court: "If the formalities of the criminal adjudicative process are to be superimposed upon the juvenile court system, there is little need for its separate existence."[48] Blackmun, like Roberts before him, willed the patient to live on. The time may come, he wrote at the end of his opinion, when the difference between adult and juvenile tribunals becomes so scant that the entire endeavor might end. For Justice Blackmun, trial by jury appeared to be the process that maintained the distinction. He ended with a sigh: "Perhaps that ultimate disillusionment will come one day, but for the moment we are disinclined to give impetus to it."[49]

When Professor Allen cautioned that "in reacting against old errors we are constantly in danger of being enslaved by our emancipation," he warned that holding on to the original idea of the juvenile court could obstruct needed reforms half a century after its founding.[50] Holding on certainly underlay much of Justice Roberts's and then Justice Blackmun's opinions. They believed that, at some point, the right balance would be found between procedural protections and benevolent supervision, and between adversarial formality and therapeutic informality, to accomplish at least some of the original purposes of the juvenile court. As Professor Feld later noted, the *McKeiver* decision "uncritically accepted the assertion that juvenile courts rehabilitate rather than punish delinquents, failed to inquire about a need for procedural protections against 'benevolent' coercion, and ignored the role of constitutional procedures to prevent governmental oppression."[51]

The facts in Joseph McKeiver's case could explain—though not justify—Robert's opinion. A boy is charged with stealing a quarter and

Figure 5.1. Hyde County Peace March. Courtesy of State Archives of North Carolina.

is put on probation after a hurried hearing. Even the Pennsylvania companion case to *McKeiver*, *In re Terry*, which resulted in a harsher punishment, involved a street fight that got out of control. Both could be seen as characteristic juvenile court cases that would have resulted in fairer determinations without the need for a jury trial if some of the other due process protections recently required by the Supreme Court in *Gault* had been more firmly in place. Perhaps this is why Justice Blackmun failed to see the coercion and oppression that Feld asserts was so clearly before him.

Fundamental Fairness and Race: Considering *In re Burrus*

As it turned out, Justice Blackmun was presented with a far more complicated scenario in which Allen's warning of the juvenile court becoming an obstacle to reform was prescient and Feld's conclusions about government coercion and oppression were clear. *In re Burrus*, the third companion case, originating in North Carolina, was not a typical juvenile court case. Most of the young people in *Burrus*, more than forty of them, were charged with willfully impeding traffic during what the Court described as "a series of demonstrations . . . by black adults and children protesting school assignments and a school consolidation plan."[52] The children marched almost daily for two months. Highway patrolmen testified that "on various occasions the juveniles and adults were observed walking along Highway 64 singing, shouting, clapping, and playing basketball."[53] The marchers would be asked to leave the road and either did so and returned or just continued to march. The state district judge, Hallett S. Ward, sitting as a juvenile court judge, found that all the youth had committed acts "for which an adult may be punished by law," declared them juvenile delinquents "in need of more suitable guardianship," and put them on probation after suspending an order to commit them to a state institution.[54] One of the conditions of probation for every child was to "attend some school, public or private, or some institution, offering training approved by the Hyde County Director of Public Welfare."[55] In other words, they were being ordered back into schools they believed violated their civil rights. All the children, who ranged in age from eleven to fifteen, were represented by a prominent civil rights lawyer, James E. Ferguson II, who requested a jury trial and objected to the exclusion of the general public in each case.[56] The intermediate appellate court characterized the actions of the youth as "as a concerted demonstration by Negroes of Hyde County to assert their defiance of law and order and to disrupt the normal economic and social life of Hyde County by a willful, intentional and flagrant disregard and violation of laws duly enacted by the governing bodies of the State for the public welfare and orderly conduct of human affairs for all citizens of the State."[57] In fact, the children were protesting that the county had created an unlawful and failed desegregation plan.[58] Their request for the public to be permitted into their hearings or to be afforded a jury trial, as Justice William Brennan would later write in his concurrence and dissent, would protect "the petitioners against misuse of judicial process."[59] The North Carolina appellate court saw the request quite differently: "In the instant case, it is true that such a provision [of an open court] thwarted the hopes and desires of those instigating and promoting these unfortunate children in their public demonstrations. The deprivation of a public forum to further their misguided and antisocial conduct does not make it wrong or illegal in a constitutional sense."[60]

The North Carolina Supreme Court also ignored the civil rights context of the children's cases. Justice J. Frank Huskins, who wrote the opinion, was not a fan of the Warren Court's expansion of due process rights in criminal cases. He once gave a speech to the North Carolina Bar Association admonishing activist judges who got lost in the technicalities of trials rather than simply determining guilt or innocence.[61] He dismissed the requests for a jury trial or an open court with the same alacrity as the court below. Two justices dissented without writing opinions, including Susie Sharp, the first woman to serve on the North Carolina Supreme Court and its first female chief justice.[62] If they had been provided as written dissents, these opinions may have been able to form the basis for a stronger appeal and even provided the Supreme Court with an alternative perspective on the issues being considered. (However, this is just speculation, as there is no mention of the case in Sharp's papers or biography.) In addition, Justice Sharp had a racist history, including describing the *Brown v. Board of Education* decision "the greatest calamity to befall the South since reconstruction," so her reasons for dissenting were unlikely to be based on understanding the political nature of the children's protests.[63]

As Professor Robin Walker Sterling has pointed out in her analysis of the *Gault* and *McKeiver* cases, the Supreme Court's criminal due process revolution was closely tied to racial injustice and states' institutional failures.[64] Here could have been another opportunity to present the Court with that connection. But surprisingly, the NAACP Legal Defense Fund lawyers who appealed the *Burrus* case to the Supreme Court—some of the most important civil rights attorneys of the time including Julius Chambers and Jack Greenberg—crafted a brief that did not dwell long on the civil rights context of the youths' hearings and the fact that these were Black children being adjudicated in the Jim Crow South. With the exception of noting several studies of police and judicial discretion that had resulted in disproportionately arresting, charging, and adjudicating Black youth, the brief did not overly emphasize the racial component of juvenile court actions or discuss findings from an earlier report of the United States Commission on Civil Rights on the juvenile court's treatment of Black youth asserting their constitutional rights to peacefully protest.[65] This was especially surprising given that Justice Fortas had cited that report in his *Gault* opinion. The brief did raise the concerns that the considerable discretion of the juvenile court judge had been "employed to the detriment of racially and economically disadvantaged groups" and that a jury trial including representatives of the community was as important for Black youth as for Black adults.[66] Only in their reply brief were they more explicit about the sharp discrepancies between how the court treated white and Black children, asserting that rehabilitation for Black children was more likely to mean incarceration.[67] Overall, the arguments were far more focused on the ways that jury trials would not sound the death knell of the juvenile court (in much the same way Joseph McKeiver's lawyers had argued). They thereby forfeited the opportunity to expose the deeply discriminatory nature of juvenile courts both at the time they were writing and earlier in the court's history—a different kind of leverage for arguing the need for jury trials in juvenile proceedings.

In re Burrus in Context: The Juvenile Court and Black Children Again

Contemporary scholars have been investigating the place of Black children in the early juvenile court, revisiting and unearthing both the appalling way that Black children were treated (or ignored) by the early juvenile court as well as the role of the Black community, especially Black women's clubs, in creating an alternative version of "child-saving."[68] One reason for this reexamination is to link the treatment of Black children and families from the founding of the court to the present day as proof of a deep and continuing discrimination inherent within the legal system against the Black community. A second is to highlight what needs to be done to eliminate the disparate treatment suffered by children and families of color—especially Black Americans—in every step along the way to and through this system. And a third is to celebrate the efforts of the Black community to provide for its children when most of the white "child-savers" historically and today have failed them. Professor Walker Sterling, for example, uses the specific context of the Supreme Court's constitutional domestication of the juvenile court as a moment when the Court could have linked the civil rights of Black children to their miserable treatment in the juvenile court in much the same way that the Court had linked racial injustice to its criminal due process decisions for adults.[69]

Certainly Burrus, more than any of the other juvenile court due process cases, put race squarely before the Court. These Black children were protesting discrimination in their education, and yet the juvenile court not only found them in violation of the law but also that they were "in need of the care, protection and discipline of the State, and [were] in need of more suitable guardianship and [were] delinquent"[70] before placing them on probation (with a suspended commitment order) under the supervision of public welfare authorities. Judge Ward could have found them in violation of the traffic law and yet not found them in need of any type of care, protection, or discipline by the state. They were not maltreated by their parents, they had not committed the type of crime that could justify supervision or punishment, and they were not the "wayward" youth that the juvenile court had traditionally tried to protect from themselves. These were young civil rights activists at the height of the civil rights movement being declared delinquent. This lens offered an opportunity for the Supreme Court to revisit its recent decisions parsing out what due process rights are necessary for youth charged with delinquency and subject to their liberty being curtailed. The justices could have asked themselves what they really meant when Justice Fortas had written in the *Kent* case that children seem to receive the worst of the juvenile and adult court systems.[71]

In a charitable moment in his decades-long study of the juvenile court, Feld suggested that we know more today about how little difference there is between treatment and punishment in the juvenile court and how the *McKeiver* justices may not have had as much empirical or practical information about the daily workings of the juvenile court system to enable them to reject outright the high-flying rhetoric of the *parens patriae* ideal.[72] Certainly, in retrospect, the lawyers for the children in *Burrus* presented less of that information than seemed wise, even if they admonished the Court at one point in their reply brief not to "simply ignore the grim reality of 'rehabilitation': that the poor and the black are those usually incarcerated; that they are treated as if they have broken society's rules; and held for long periods of time-to emerge older, but basically unchanged, for the experience."[73] More recent scholarship offers a less charitable explanation for the Court's decision, one more consistent with Feld's overall assessment of Supreme Court jurisprudence on the juvenile court: the justices were ignoring the deeply punitive nature of the juvenile court, permitting the rhetoric and high hopes of the Great Idea to mask how profoundly coercive and retributive the court was in 1970 and had been since the court's creation.[74] The critical point in reassessing *McKeiver* is how the juvenile court had always disproportionately penalized Black children.

Burrus and the Opportunity to Challenge the Great Idea

Following the Supreme Court's monumental decision in *Brown v. Board of Education*, sustained state and federal litigation challenged the failure of so many states to integrate their juvenile justice institutions.[75] This raised the contemporary profile of racial discrimination in the juvenile legal system, even though the long history of the juvenile court's discriminatory policies and practices were less widely known. In 1965, the United States Commission on Civil Rights issued a scathing report, titled *Law Enforcement: A Report on Equal Protection in the South*, which painstakingly confirmed the discriminatory and illegal actions to prevent and punish civil rights activists for exercising their constitutional right to peacefully demonstrate. The report included a special section titled "Juvenile Proceedings" that described the actions of juvenile court judges to strip children of their rights and to impose harsh punishments. The greatest irony was that juvenile court judges used the absence of constitutional safeguards in juvenile proceedings (this being pre-*Gault*) to exert their discretionary power to impose excessively harsh treatment on Black juveniles.[76] The report noted: "In Jackson, Americus, and St. Augustine, juveniles who had been arrested in demonstrations were threatened with imprisonment and, as a condition of exoneration or release, were forced to promise that they would not participate in future civil rights activities."[77] Some of the children were put on probation on the condition that they would not associate with known civil rights leaders; if they violated this probation mandate, they would be sent to the state detention home. Juvenile court judges would hold children without bail or hearings for long periods of time. One fourteen-year-old Black girl was arrested and then stated that she was seventeen so that she wouldn't have to appear in front of the juvenile court judge who had ordered her not to participate in any other demonstrations. When her age was eventually revealed, she was sent back to that juvenile court judge, who kept her in jail for eighty-seven days without a hearing. Youth who would not agree to conditions that they not be involved in civil rights activities were sent to adult jails and segregated juvenile facilities (in one case for nearly six months).[78] In Florida, 234 children were arrested; when they were eventually released per federal court order, the federal judge observed:

> The customary procedure with respect to juveniles in Florida charged with misdemeanors is to release them to parents' custody to await trial. . . . Their detention without bond or release was an arbitrary and capricious act of harassment and cruel and unusual punishment on the part of [the juvenile court judge] Mathis.[79]

The Supreme Court knew about these findings when deciding *McKeiver*. Justice Fortas had cited them in *Gault*; he had also cited Professor Monrad Paulson's 1966 law review article, which cautioned that the vague phrases defining "delinquency"—such as "engaging in conduct harmful to himself or others," "incorrigible," or "a child who is beyond the control of his parents or other custodian"—have "formed the basis for adjudications of delinquency in the case of Negro children engaged in civil rights demonstrations."[80]

The children in the *Burrus* case faced similar treatment three years after the Commission on Civil Rights report was issued and five years before the case reached the Supreme Court—sufficient time for the Court to absorb and consider the role the juvenile court played in denying these youth their constitutional rights to free expression through arbitrary and capricious actions. This legacy should have helped the Court shift the focus away from the narrower question of jury trials destroying the Great Idea to the broader issue of whether the juvenile court should be mandated to provide the full panoply of due process rights that adults then received because children were being routinely punished (and in the case of Black children, in particularly harsh and disturbing ways). This was the opportunity to rethink what "fundamental fairness" meant in the larger context of how these youth—protesting illegal and discriminatory school placements—were being treated as criminals. The Court couldn't eliminate juvenile courts in their ruling, but in finding that a jury trial was a necessary component of fundamental fairness, the Court could have signaled that the juvenile court system had failed to accomplish its goals and had to be reconsidered in fundamental ways in light of the "devastating commentary upon the system's failure as a whole," which the Court acknowledged, and the deeply discriminatory practices that *Burrus* had helped to reveal. Instead of lamenting what had not yet been attained, the Court could have signaled that the pretense of hope should be abandoned for a more realistic assessment of what juvenile court can and should be. The justices needed to grapple with the way juvenile court handled itself beyond the adjudicative process. There was punishment when there was supposed to be treatment; there was prison or its juvenile equivalent when there was supposed to be rehabilitative placements; there were indeterminate and disparate dispositions when there was supposed to be individualized—but fair—proportionate and compassionate justice. The Court did not contend with these realities.

The Legacy of *McKeiver*

In the decades following *McKeiver*, the juvenile court's jurisdiction over delinquent behavior changed in striking ways. From the late 1970s until the late 1990s, states revised their juvenile justice schemes to respond to what they saw as the rise of more violent and sustained criminal activity by young people. This happened in several ways. Youth involved in the most serious crimes, like Morris Kent, were likely to be transferred to adult criminal court either automatically or through discretionary waiver systems. More vigorous transfer schemes began to be adopted by state legislatures in the late 1970s and fully flourished in the 1990s; these have been described as symbolizing a fundamental change from rehabilitation to retribution, shifting "individualized justice to just deserts, from offender to offense, from amenability to treatment to public safety, and from immature delinquent to responsible criminal."[81] Some transfer legislation is categorical, requiring youth of a certain age or who have committed particular crimes or who have committed multiple crimes (or a combination of these factors) to be automatically charged as an adult in criminal court. Other states permit prosecutors to determine whether to file charges in juvenile or adult court, shifting considerable power away from juvenile court judges. While judicial waiver remains available in forty-six states, categorical and prosecutorial exclusions likely affect far more young people.[82] In the get-tough era of the 1990s, legislatures added more crimes to the list of excludable offenses—including nonviolent property and drug offenses—and continued to lower the minimum age of transfer to adult court for certain crimes.[83]

Transfer policies that were predominantly under the control of prosecutors built upon an unintended result of *Gault*'s promise of "fundamental fairness." If lawyers were necessary to protect child defendants, then prosecutors were necessary to represent the state. Their presence in juvenile courts increased dramatically at the expense of the traditional power of juvenile probation to determine whether to divert a youth out of court or send him before the judge, as well as the traditional power of the judge herself, who now awaited the prosecutor's decision. Even the judge's role in crafting dispositional outcomes was supplanted in many states by statutes permitting or requiring her to combine juvenile and adult punishment in so-called blended sentences.[84] Blended sentences could impose either a juvenile or an adult sentence; impose both, with the possibility of suspending the adult sentence; or impose a juvenile sentence beyond the limit of juvenile court jurisdiction.[85] The stated mission of the court had shifted. While this transformation has been characterized as a cultural shift in how we construct our understanding of youth and the court's response to that understanding, that is only part of what happened. Equally important is the shift of power within the juvenile court from probation and the judge to the prosecutor.[86]

Many states also revised their juvenile court "purposes" clauses to include community safety as a central tenet and explicitly acknowledging that youth could be punished as well as treated by the juvenile court. Since 1997, seventeen states have incorporated their concerns about public safety, punishment, and accountability into their purpose clauses. States also began to incorporate victim rights guarantees into juvenile statutes, often tracking language contained in the criminal codes, thereby diminishing the traditional confidentiality rules of the juvenile court and welcoming victims into the various stages of juvenile proceedings.[87] These changes also reflect the tenets of the restorative justice movement, which advocates for a balanced approach among individual accountability to the victim and the community, public safety, and the opportunity for the individual to be restored to law-abiding and productive lives.[88] While many states' purposes provisions maintain a commitment to the original ideal of the juvenile court as a place to protect and improve children, the laws on the books—from transfer provisions to blended sentences to revised purposes clauses—increasingly challenged the continuation of the system itself—or perhaps protected it.

The centennial mark of the juvenile court at the end of the twentieth century provided another convenient opportunity to reevaluate its purpose and meaning. While a small number of scholars presented justifications for abolishing the court—justifications that we'll seriously reconsider in chapter 10 ("Abolition")—others acknowledged that the flexibility of the court ensured its durability. Transfer statutes, for example, satisfied the public's concern that the most heinous crimes would be dealt with in an adult court. Blended sentences acknowledged the ability of the juvenile court judge not only to get tough but also to exercise discretion. State legislators, rather than abolishing the court and sending all youth to adult court, instead changed purposes clauses to reinforce the community's desire for punishment in addition to rehabilitation. At the same time, there was no viable movement to lower the age of responsibility overall, thereby reinforcing the acceptance of the continuing role for the juvenile court for most youth until majority.[89] Recommendations for court reform during the 1990s acknowledged these safety-valve features as a necessary component of an evolving court while continuing to emphasize that judicial leadership and discretionary decision-making from the bench were at the core of protecting and rehabilitating children.[90]

Reforms to ensure the continuity of the court were not only related to shifting the most serious crimes or habitual delinquents to adult court. At the other end of the spectrum, many reformers lamented courts punishing children for noncriminal misbehavior like truancy, drug use, and sexual activity. The court had addressed these behaviors as delinquency for most of its history, as chapter 6 will trace. By the early 1980s, such behaviors had been reconceived as status offenses instead—actions that could still be addressed by the court because of the youth's minority but not as criminal offenses. This led to various ways of treating young people in what were considered more enlightened ways—from diversion from the court entirely to preventing status offenders from being institutionalized with delinquent youth. Status offenses preserved the court's protective and guiding roles, which had been diminished in many delinquency matters. The sharp rise in child protection cases in the 1980s, which mirrored public concern about the rise in crime and the deterioration of communities, also reinforced the perceived need for the court's intervention, as chapter 7 will address.

The most critical observers of the juvenile court, however, lamented the court's ability to reinvent itself as a survival measure. Taking advantage of "the ambiguity and diversity of [its] mission, the broad range of behavior over which it has jurisdiction, the limitless number of young people who exhibit [bad] behavior, the powerlessness of its clientele, and societal disinterest and inattention to its mission and mandate all operate[d] to entrench the juvenile court."[91] These critics saw the American disinclination for radical change being reinforced by the idea of the court as a power to do good; equally responsible is the court's ability to respond to society's wants of the moment, whether for control or punishment, and to shift its emphasis within the complex system of public and private institutions over which it presides.[92] As Professor Allen warned several decades earlier, our "tendency to attribute capabilities to the court that it does not possess" can stand in the way of more painful but essential reform.[93]

Calls for abolishing the court receded as the twenty-first century began, but not the conditions that had led to the *McKeiver* case. The "fundamental fairness" due process protections demanded by *Gault*— notice of charges, a fair hearing, assistance of counsel, opportunity to confront and cross-examine witnesses, and privilege against self-incrimination—remained elusive across the country, in large part because of the lack of assistance of counsel. Studies during the 1970s and 1980s found that throughout the country youth lacked counsel, often because juvenile court judges ignored the right or allowed waiver of counsel in their courtrooms without first explaining what the youth was giving up.[94] Those judges who did explain applied the adult standard for waiver—"knowing, intelligent, and voluntary under the totality of the circumstances"—without considering how children are different than adults.[95] States also established barriers to indigent youth being assigned counsel, including high fees to prove indigency.[96] In 1988, Feld compared appointment of counsel in six states, finding highly variable appointment rates from a low of 38 percent in North Dakota to a high of 96 percent in New York. The federal General Accounting Office reconfirmed Feld's results in 1995, finding that rates of representation varied widely among and within states and that juvenile courts tried and sentenced many unrepresented youth.[97] In the same year, a comprehensive study found widespread examples of youth throughout the country waiving their right to counsel.[98] In the early 2000s, similar studies continued to find as many as 80–90 percent of juveniles in some states appeared without counsel.[99] Attorneys who did represent youth were severely burdened with high caseloads, limiting their ability to take the necessary steps to effectively represent their clients.[100]

Judges were routinely not protecting juveniles' basic due process rights. There were several possible explanations: inadequate or nonexistent public defender services; judges easing the administrative burden of the court, including by implying that counsel was not needed; judges who wanted to retain their full discretionary authority; or judges who didn't see the need for counsel if they weren't intending to impose a custodial sentence.[101] Whatever the reason, this failure to protect constitutional rights meant that judges were continuing to use their power as they saw fit, harkening back to the type of court that *Gault* was supposed to tame and *McKeiver* determined should remain a viable mechanism for treatment.

Whether youth were subject to transfer laws, blended sentences, or the amplified punitiveness of the juvenile court, they found themselves increasingly at risk of incarceration. The last census in the twentieth century counted 134,000 juveniles in residential placement facilities in October 1999.[102] Sixty-two percent of these youth—six out of ten—were youth of color, and nearly four in ten were African American. Throughout the country, youth of color were placed at twice the proportion of their population, with Black youth in some states eight times more likely to be placed than white youth.[103] These were not bucolic boarding schools. Seven out of ten youth were in some form of locked facility, with 75 percent of Black and Hispanic youth behind locked doors.[104] Moreover, almost eight thousand youth treated as adults were detained in jails during the first months of the twenty-first century while over five thousand youth were in adult prisons in 1999 in the thirty-seven states reporting youth imprisonment.[105] Between 1985 and 2000, there was a 70 percent overall increase of youth in prison. As prison admissions increased until 1995, they did so disproportionately for Black males; as they began to decrease after 1995, the declines were greater for white males than for Black males.[106] While imprisonment for young adults in adult court doubled from 1971 until 1991 and imprisonment for adolescents remained flat during this same period—giving credence to the protective role of the juvenile court during a particularly harsh period—this does not diminish the overall punitive reaction to juveniles during this period, particularly regarding the treatment of children of color.[107]

The first part of this book has recounted the historical examples of the juvenile court's failure to provide individualized prevention and rehabilitation, to treat Black children (and later other children of color) equally, or to provide due process. This leads to asking whether the time for Justice Blackmun's "ultimate disillusionment" has come. That question cannot be answered without first examining the court's historical and current role in addressing misbehaving youth considered "status offenders" and, second, the court's rapid growth in the last quarter of the twentieth century as it tackled child protection. These two phenomena are also instrumental in the transformation of the juvenile court into a broader family court that maintains the therapeutic impulse, the initial hallmark of the juvenile court when it was created.

11

The Family Court Rises

Figure 6.1. "Incorrigibles." Courtesy of Alison Cornyn.

6

Status Offenses and the Rise of the Family Court

Nowhere has the Great Idea been more tenacious than in the context of *status offense jurisdiction*. The very purpose of the court is deeply intertwined with its ability to control disruptive children and assist desperate families. As the juvenile court lost some of its therapeutic rationale in delinquency cases, it doubled down on its authority over misbehaving children. The statutory classifications of status offenses have defined the role of the court in addressing such youthful behavior, essentially determining how much state power can be brought against a child (and sometimes against her parent) for behavior that does not break the law. Similarly, status offense jurisdiction provides insight into the authority that the family court would more fully develop in child protection proceedings in the last three decades of the twentieth century and discussed in chapters 7 and 8.

Bringing children into court for misbehavior is a political decision. The first choice is to permit parents (and their surrogates, like schools) to appeal to the court to control youth behavior. The second choice is to provide the court with broad discretion to respond to those appeals. In both instances, society has decided that judicial intervention is more helpful than not and that bringing the power of the state to bear on these youth through the court is warranted for their own good. Status offense jurisdiction is also the clearest example of the tenacity of family court to sustain its discretionary authority to fix children and mend families even in the face of overwhelming evidence that the court's prescriptions have failed.

Helen Geddes

Helen Geddes was a bit tipsy as she and her sister headed toward Washington, D.C.'s Chinatown, where they were meeting two boys they knew. Helen was fifteen at the time, her sister a little older. After her mother died, Helen had begun drinking and hanging out with friends, getting into deeper trouble with her father. When Officer Davis noticed that the sisters seemed to be intoxicated as they walked down the street, he stopped to talk to them. They told him where they were going, and he encouraged them to go home instead. They initially protested but eventually agreed to let him walk them home. Their father was outside the house when they arrived, and he thanked the officer for bringing them home. Mr. Geddes was worried about them, especially Helen, who had stopped going to school and helping around the house; she wasn't violent, but he knew she was drinking and no longer listening to him. He decided that the only solution was to send her to a place where she would be closely supervised and (hopefully) get the help she needed to straighten out. And although he acknowledged that some of her problems were his fault—he hadn't really been there for her since her mother had died, and some of his own friends weren't the most well behaved—he saw no alternative. Even one of his friends, a knowledgeable reporter for the *Baltimore Sun*, agreed he had no other option. Soon, he sent Helen away.[1]

This is a familiar story of adolescent misbehavior and parental response. Parents with sufficient resources will send their child to therapy or substance abuse treatment, try a new school or activities, and, if necessary, send the child away from home to a boot camp or a boarding school. Charles Geddes didn't have the resources to try these options—in fact in 1901 most of these options didn't exist—so he sent Helen to the Reform School for Girls for the District of Columbia. He didn't ask Helen if she wanted to go, and it wouldn't have mattered. One of the provisions establishing the reform school permitted the superintendent to accept any girl under seventeen at the request of a parent or guardian if the girl was "incorrigible or habitually disregards the commands of her father and mother or guardian, who leads a vagrant life, or resorts to immoral places or practices, or neglects or refuses to perform labor suitable to her years and condition or to attend school." Unlike girls placed in the school who had been found by a court to have committed a crime, a girl like Helen could be taken into the school solely on her father's written request and the superintendent's agreement.[2] The idea was that the state would help a parent keep a young person on the straight and narrow before she could get into real criminal trouble. Such "wayward youth" laws had deep historical roots in legal practices to control children and families, especially poor and "different" children and families, for their own good and for the good of the state.[3] They also provided further justification for the juvenile courts that were just starting to be created in Helen's time and were considered revolutionary because of their broad powers over youthful misbehavior in a court setting.[4]

In today's parlance, Helen would be a "status offender," a young person in need of supervision, treatment, and/or placement. Being incorrigible, a truant, drinking, drugging, and committing "immoral acts" is still sufficient for parents, schools, and police to instigate proceedings against a minor in family court. The laws are called "status offenses" rather than "crimes" because the "status" is being a minor; an adult could not be taken in for the same behavior unless it was also defined as a crime. Today's version of the statute that governed Helen requires a juvenile court to determine when a child is "habitually disobedient of the reasonable and lawful commands of his parent, guardian, or other custodian and is ungovernable."[5] The statute clearly expresses the concern that "[j]uveniles who are not under proper supervision or control . . . are likely to endanger their own health, morals and welfare and the health, morals, and welfare of others."[6]

Like Helen, a youth today remains subject to the concept of *parens patriae*, that is, when the state steps in to assist or replace parental decision-making. In Helen's case, the state first assisted and then replaced Mr. Geddes. His original request was granted and Helen was sent to the reform school, thereby providing her father with the assistance he said he needed. Two years later, Mr. Geddes changed his mind and decided that Helen should leave the school and live with her sister and brother-in-law. The school superintendent disagreed, believing that Helen was better off remaining at the school, in essence substituting a state agent's judgment for her father's. Helen's brother-in-law filed a writ of habeas corpus on Helen's behalf, demanding her release and alleging that she was being unlawfully held without due process of law. But the power of *parens patriae* to substitute the state's power for that of an ineffective parent was firmly established, thwarting the writ.[7]

Early in the nineteenth century, a Pennsylvania court rejected a similar writ by a father attempting to have his daughter released from a house of refuge after her mother had brought a claim of "incorrigibility" and the girl had been committed. In extolling the state's responsibility to ensure the moral well-being of young people as well as their ability to earn a living, the court posed in conclusion: "[M]ay not the natural parents, when unequal to the task of education, or unworthy of it, be superseded by the *parens patriae*, or common guardian of the community?"[8] Wanting the state's help while losing decision-making control over one's child remains a core tension of status offense jurisdiction today, especially for parents with no other means to get the assistance they believe their child needs. With no appropriate or readily available community-based services, failing schools, and slashed budgets for therapy and treatment, even parents fearful of the court substituting its decision-making for their own may see no other option. They lose control of the process and of the ultimate decision—whether or not they agree with it.

Helen, of course, never wanted to go to the school. But she had no say over the matter; no one asked her opinion. When her family decided to retrieve her and the school refused, the appeals court that ultimately determined Helen's fate declared that Helen had no right to a hearing because her placement was not a punishment following adjudication. She lost her writ and was ordered to remain at the school until she was at least eighteen and maybe until she was twenty-one.[9] There was no juvenile court in Washington, D.C., at the time, but a youth found guilty of committing a crime in adult court and punished by incarceration would have been placed, like Helen, in the reform school. Ironically, if Helen had been placed after being found guilty of a criminal offense, she would have received her hearing. But she wasn't charged criminally; in fact, she wasn't charged at all. Her father had sworn that he needed the state to help him take care of his wayward child, and as the court denying her release declared:

> Unable to assert his own legal power of restraint, and apprehensive of the ruin to which his child seemed drifting, he appealed to the State to assume the functions of guardianship and take her into its protection during her years of nonage. . . . The child herself, having no right to control her own action or to select her own course of life, had no legal right to be heard in these proceedings. Hence, the law which does not require her to be brought in person before the committing officer or extend her the privilege of a hearing on her own behalf cannot be said to deprive her of the benefit of due process of law.[10]

In essence, Helen didn't need due process to protect her because the state wasn't punishing Helen but placing her in reform school for her own good.[11]

That justification would have likely surprised Helen, since she was living with girls who had been found to have broken the law and been punished by being sent to the institution. Her life in the school was no different than theirs. To the girls, what the place was called couldn't have mattered very much; they were being held against their will, and none were free to leave. Today, the dispositional alternatives in status offense cases are still not called "punishments," though many youth subject to these dispositional orders, like Helen, feel punished. The language of therapy or treatment—in Helen's day, of "refuge" or "reform"—doesn't diminish the punitive nature of the institutions.

Camille Sippy

The reform school admission process that Helen experienced remained in place until 1953, when the Municipal Court of Appeals for the District of Columbia proclaimed that the intervening Juvenile Court Act precluded such placements in a case remarkably similar to Helen's.[12] Camille Sippy was a couple years older than Helen, almost eighteen, when her mother applied to have Camille committed to Washington, D.C.'s Board of Public Welfare for placement in a psychiatric school in Philadelphia. Camille protested. The appellate court declared that Helen's case, *Rule v. Geddes*, was no longer good law. By this time Washington, D.C., like many jurisdictions around the country, had codified a limited version of due process for youth that included, in Camille's case, a right to appeal the decision placing her with the Board of Public Welfare. Camille did appeal; unlike Helen's request, hers was granted.

Camille's successful appeal provides some insight into the evolution of status offense jurisdiction in the middle of the twentieth century. The absolute power of Helen's father to place her in reform school had diminished by 1953. The creation of the juvenile court in D.C. provided Camille with some means to contest her placement. The Juvenile Court Act didn't distinguish between delinquency and status offenses; as in most other states at the time, both criminal and noncriminal misbehavior by youth were still defined as "delinquency."[13] Camille had a lawyer she seems to have secured on her own, fourteen years before the Supreme Court would mandate lawyers for children in most delinquency matters. Her lawyer objected to hearsay evidence offered to establish her need for placement and objected to her doctor breaching confidentiality by providing testamentary evidence that had not been subject to cross-examination. The court agreed and even went further, declaring that the adversarial nature of the proceeding, which pitted mother against daughter, precluded Mrs. Sippy from asserting her traditional legal right to waive her minor daughter's privileged communications with her doctor. These procedural rulings protected Camille, preventing her placement against her wishes.

The vehemence of the court's determination is still surprising for the time. The juvenile court provided only limited due process protections for youth like Camille; informality and broad court discretion were still the norm in juvenile courts throughout the country.[14] Perhaps because Camille was just days from turning eighteen, the court rejected a pure *parens patriae* approach to Mrs. Sippy's request. Yet the court never intimated that Mrs. Sippy didn't have the authority to bring her daughter to court for being habitually out of control; the court just determined that Mrs. Sippy hadn't *proven* that Camille was beyond her control. The nature of a parent's control over a child was less unconditional in the early 1950s than in 1901. The trend was toward providing greater procedural protections for youth brought to juvenile court for reasons like being out of control.[15] Mrs. Sippy was the petitioner/mother; Camille was the respondent/daughter. They were now formally fighting in court over what was best for Camille. While Mrs. Sippy was trying to establish that Camille was out of control, Camille defended herself by alleging that "'both she and her mother had strong tempers and wills and that both had difficulty in avoiding clashes.'" The trial court judge noted "'that the situation probably was not respondent's fault alone, indicating that some responsibility was with the petitioner [mother].'" The appeals court further mentioned that a psychiatrist was also treating Mrs. Sippy. Mrs. Sippy was being judged along with her daughter.[16] When parents today bring their problems to court voluntarily, they still face the possibility that they, and not their child, will be held responsible. For example, a status offense case in some states can be converted into a neglect proceeding against a parent.[17] The court's ability to change the nature of the proceeding while arbitrating a family dispute reinforces the extensive discretionary power of the court over the families appearing before them.

In the decades since Camille successfully challenged her placement, most noncriminal misbehavior is no longer categorized as "delinquency." Every state has created some variation of status offense jurisdiction focusing on the misbehavior of youth: not listening to their parents, truancy, use of forbidden alcohol and drugs, sexual activity, and running away.[18] Even with today's expanded diversion programs for status offenders, states have not yet eliminated the ultimate availability of the court to hear the complaints of parents, schools, and law enforcement officers when they believe there is no other effective alternative.[19] Once court jurisdiction is triggered, not only the youth but also whoever brought the case—parents, school, police—is subject to the judge's decision of what is best, including a decision with which the petitioner disagrees. After a hearing or settlement, the court then has broad discretion to decide the appropriate disposition. And while the court's power to lock up a youth in a status offense case has been curtailed, it remains available in many states among the dispositions at the court's disposal, which also include probation, treatment, rules of behavior, and placement outside the home.[20] These dispositions frequently are punishments by other names.

Presidential Commissions Weigh in on Wayward Youth

The first serious proposal to eliminate status offense jurisdiction was introduced by Lyndon Johnson's 1967 Presidential Commission on Law Enforcement and Administration of Justice.[21] The Johnson Commission's report, *The Challenge of Crime in a Free Society*, dedicated a chapter to "Juvenile Delinquency and Youth Crime," a far-ranging riff on mid-1960s youth culture and the disintegration of traditional controls over adolescent behavior. Crime-ridden, inner-city "slums" were of special concern. Parents, teachers, and police had been losing control and now were in free fall. Yet once the inflammatory rhetoric describing these horrors subsided, the chapter offered a clear-eyed blueprint for seeking solutions to youth crime and misbehavior rather than merely assigning blame. It was almost as if the commission used a narrative that would resonate with the public—a story of scary youth culture—before relaying a more nuanced and fact-based story that outlined key components of youth behavior. The commission recognized first that almost any adolescent misbehavior could be the basis for arrest and thus most adolescents could be arrested; second, that the youth most likely to be arrested for misbehavior lived in communities where poverty and the failure to maintain basic services like decent housing and education were widespread; third, that the traditional migration out of "slum life" for generations of immigrants was different for African Americans, whose paths were blocked by explicit racism and structural segregation; and fourth, that the juvenile justice system—and the court in particular—had failed in its promise to help children and families. These findings resonate today because they represent one of the most comprehensive governmental efforts ever undertaken to analyze the juvenile court system. The commission not only used the best research available at the time; it spurred further research and analysis that resulted in the call for eliminating all noncriminal misbehavior from the court's jurisdiction. Their underlying rationale remains as cogent today as it was half a century ago.

Of course, if the chapter on juvenile delinquency and youth crime had been written today, the commission would have used the behavioral and psychological language of adolescent development and the newest brain research to talk about how adolescence is different than adulthood.[22] But even without that scientific knowledge and language, the report recognized that adolescence is a time of experimentation and growth, testing independence and identity, making mistakes and learning from them. By definition, every adolescent will be incorrigible, fail to listen to a parent or teacher, and consider running away (or do so). Most will try drinking or drugs, have sexual intimacy of some kind, skip school or work, or otherwise test the limits of parental and societal authority. As the commission concluded, by making normal adolescent behavior the basis for state control and punishment, "[s]tatutes often define juvenile delinquency so broadly as to make virtually all youngsters delinquent."[23]

The commission also determined that these statutes were not applied equally. Today we use the language of disproportionate minority representation to describe the disparate impact of coercive state intervention on children and families of color (particularly poor ones). And we can identify the structural racism that has shaped and maintained this deep inequality. At the time, the commission simply stated that "slum offenders are more likely than suburban offenders to be arrested and referred to juvenile court."[24] They were right.

The Johnson Commission's recommendations took the juvenile court head-on. The reasons for the court's failures are again told in two stories. The first—and the most popular and persistent to this day—is that the court, with enough resources, enough good judges, and enough dispositional alternatives, could fulfill the hopes and dreams of its founders. But the commission realized the limitations of that story. Court reformers had been asking for those resources from the day the first court was founded in Chicago, and those pleas remain largely unheeded today. There isn't a family court reform report that I know of—including one I've written—that doesn't pin many of its hopes on more resources and more and better judges.[25] Perhaps because of the depth of its research, the commission didn't stop with that unproductive suggestion but took on the harder, more fundamental questions of the court's job. Members of the commission or its staff clearly had read, and indeed cited, Professor Francis Allen's formidable essay on the juvenile court in which he extols reformers to be willing to "subject cherished presuppositions to the hazards of inquiry and analysis" to determine the purpose of the court.[26] And even if the commission couldn't quite bring itself to abandon the court in its entirety—not unlike Justice Blackmun's decision to hold on to the juvenile court in the *McKeiver* case discussed in chapter 5—it bravely asked whether the court was doing more harm than good. And if it was doing harm, what steps needed to be taken to reconsider the court's jurisdiction and authority so that it could do good instead?

The analysis that the Johnson Commission used and the answers that it reached were, in part, a product of its time when scholars like Allen were disputing the fairness and effectiveness of the rehabilitative ideal. In one essay, Allen raised several broad concerns that directly applied to jurisdiction over status offenders. The rehabilitative ideal was based on human behavior having antecedent causes that may be subject to scientific control, most commonly some form of treatment or therapy. This is an attempt to cure someone or force an adjustment to societal norms— what Professor Andrew Polsky termed the "therapeutic impulse"—and remains a key element of state intervention to control youth. But which

youth qualify for the cure? Those whose behavior is defined as "delinquent" or later as a "status offense"? As Allen pointed out, "[the] juvenile
court is authorized to intervene punitively in many situations in which
the conduct, were it committed by an adult, would be wholly ignored
by the law or would subject the adult to the mildest of sanctions."[27] As
long as statutes define youth as needing control, they can be candidates
for a cure.

And what happens if the cure doesn't work and the youth doesn't
conform to the required norm? One result is that the cure can go on
indefinitely, resulting in longer or more severe intervention or—setting
aside the therapeutic language that masks reality—harsher punishment.
Helen Geddes was held against her will (and then her father's) because
the reform school superintendent thought she needed more supervision
and help. She hadn't yet been cured (however that may be defined or justified). As Allen noted: "Experience has demonstrated that, in practice,
there is a strong tendency for the rehabilitative ideal to serve purposes
that are essentially incapacitative rather than therapeutic in character."[28]
Judges had little scientific basis for deciding who was cured, subjecting
many young people to indeterminate control. Allen cogently summa-
rizes the core of this dangerous policy:

> Measures which subject individuals to the substantial and involuntary
> deprivation of their liberty contain an inescapable punitive element, and
> this reality is not altered by the facts that the motivations that prompt in-
> carceration are to provide therapy or otherwise contribute to the person's
> well-being or reform. As such, these measures must be closely scrutinized
> to insure that power is being applied consistently with those values of the
> community that justify interference with liberty for only the most clear
> and compelling reasons.[29]

The Johnson Commission's recommendations were deeply affected
by this critique of the rehabilitative ideal, especially around youthful
misbehavior that could not be defined as criminal for an adult. The
commission urged juvenile and family courts to recognize that the rehabilitative ideal of the courts' founders had collapsed into a system of
punishment that was neither rehabilitative nor fair. For the vast number
of youth—and the fact that almost any young person *could* be arrested

under this system for bad behavior—the court system was the wrong place to address this conduct. The court's business should be only to deal with charges against youth that would be crimes regardless of the age of the offender. Young people who broke the law should have available to them effective court diversion services, due process trial protections, rehabilitative efforts, and, if necessary, clear punishment. These were required elements of a juvenile system that recognized that young serious offenders could change but also acknowledged society's concerns for safety and, when necessary, incapacitation. For all those other youth who found themselves in court because of their age and not for criminal actions, the commission recommended a significant contraction of the court's jurisdiction and urged serious consideration of eliminating all jurisdiction over noncriminal misbehavior.[30]

The importance of the Johnson Commission's recommendations to spurring serious reconsideration of juvenile court cannot be understated. The commissioners, who included Republicans like the future Supreme Court justice Lewis Powell and future secretary of state William Rogers, were not a bunch of radicals. The commission and its staff were predominantly lawyers, yet the analysis of the juvenile court went far beyond children possessing procedural due process rights.[31] The Supreme Court had already issued its first juvenile due process decision in *Kent v. United States*, requiring a formal hearing with counsel before a child could be transferred to adult court. Justice Fortas famously wrote of the juvenile court in *Kent*:

> There is evidence, in fact, that there may be grounds for concern that the child receives the worst of both worlds: That he gets neither the protections accorded to adults nor the solicitous care and regenerative treatment postulated for children.[32]

The commission recommended several other due process rights for children, including the right to counsel, which the Supreme Court subsequently ordered in *In re Gault*.[33] Yet these procedural protections were not the central focus of the commission's attention. These protections were imperative for fundamental fairness, but the commission was far more concerned with the many children who did not belong in court in the first place.

The commission's single-most serious problem with court juris-diction was that it accepted far too many youth into the system and encompassed forms of control that relied predominantly on institu-tionalization. The commission worried that this process may "actually help to fix and perpetuate delinquency in the child through a process in which the individual begins to think of himself as delinquent and orga-nizes his behavior accordingly."[34] Being defined as "delinquent" allowed the child's family, school, and community to perpetuate this label and to reinforce expectations of this behavior. One of the unintended con-sequences of the court system is that "[the] most informed and benign official treatment of the child therefore contains within it the seeds of its own frustration and itself may often feed the very disorder it is designed to cure."[35] Since at the time most states still defined status offenses as delinquency, the self-fulfilling "delinquent" label would be stuck on the vast majority of youth moving through the court system. This was ex-actly what the sociologists who had developed "labeling theory" feared: being called a delinquent made you a delinquent.[36]

To minimize such destructive labeling, the commission recom-mended restricting official contact with the court by eliminating almost all noncriminal misbehavior from the court's jurisdiction and creating more effective forms of diversion for those youth whose criminal be-havior did not justify immediate court intervention. It urged the cre-ation of voluntarily accessed, community-based services and assistance for noncriminal youth as an alternative to the failed service attempts accessed through the court system. While acknowledging the potential for discretionary abuse in creating service systems beyond the direct control of the court or even state agencies, the commission nevertheless believed that these services had far greater potential for success than the failed attempts of the juvenile court. Even after listing all the fears associated with a voluntary, discretionary system (including insufficient guidelines and supervision, discretion with too little accountability, and the potential for illegal or discriminatory results "by the ill-intentioned, the prejudiced, [and] the overzealous "), the commission nevertheless pinned more hopes on "informal pre-judicial handling . . . [to] formal treatment in many cases . . . [because the] possibilities for rehabilita-tion appear to be optimal where community-based resources are used on a basis as nearly consensual as possible. The challenge is to obtain the benefits of informal pre-judicial handling with a minimum of its attendant evils."[37] At each step of the process from police contact, to determining whether formal hearings were necessary, and finally to disposition, utilizing the community to engage youth was the central goal. The commission sought to circumscribe the hazards of discretion at every point by developing guidelines and standards for each decision maker.[38]

What the commission was trying to accomplish with its recommendations has been interpreted several ways.[39] Its focus on the social causes of delinquency—like poverty, racism, and failed public systems—fell squarely into a liberal reform agenda that believed "that the most significant action that can be taken against crime is action designed to eliminate slums and ghettos, to improve education, to provide jobs, to make sure that every American is given the opportunities and the freedoms that will enable him to assume his responsibilities."[40] But at the same time, until this "war on poverty" agenda could be accomplished, the juvenile legal system that neither rehabilitated, nor stemmed "the tide of delinquency," nor brought "justice and compassion to the child offender" had to be fixed because it was still better than sending youth to adult court.

The Johnson Commission must also be credited with spurring serious consideration of "radical nonintervention" in children's and families' lives by proposing that most social services and treatment programs be voluntarily accessed and that noncriminal juvenile misbehavior be removed from the court's purview to minimize the harm done through any formal processing. These ideas would, quite remarkably, be adopted by yet another crime commission, the 1973 National Advisory Commission on Criminal Justice Standards and Goals, established by a very different kind of president, Richard Nixon. A quarter of the members of the Nixon Commission were politicians at a time when fear of youth crime was a political hot potato. Unlike the Johnson Commission, its work was not original but cumulatively built on what had come before; its objective was to establish specific standards and goals for reducing crime over ten years.[41] As Michael Tonry points out in his review of three presidential crime commissions between 1931 and 1976, the Nixon Commission nevertheless took an even more sweeping transformational view of adolescent behavior than the Johnson Commission when it acknowledged:

There are a number of studies which suggest that many children mature out of delinquent behavior. If this is true, the question is whether it is better to leave these persons alone or put them into the formal juvenile justice system. Because there are no satisfactory measures of the effectiveness of the juvenile justice system, there is a substantial body of opinion which favors "leaving alone" all except those who have had three or four contacts with the police.[42]

Some aspects of "leaving alone" that the Nixon Commission endorsed, like diversion and the voluntary use of community-based youth bureaus, reinforced the earlier findings of the Johnson Commission that the juvenile court and its attendant systems had failed in reducing delinquency and in "providing . . . special treatment in an adequate, fair, and equitable manner."[43]

Still, the Nixon Commission wasn't quite sure what to do with misbehaving youth beyond not treating them as delinquents. Despite its embrace of the earlier findings of the Johnson Commission, the Nixon Commission sidestepped the most fundamental conflict it faced about youth behavior: who should be subject to court jurisdiction. A recommendation to remove noncriminal misbehavior from juvenile court jurisdiction would have gone a long way toward changing the juvenile court from an interventionist court to a criminal court with special protections for children. Instead, the Nixon Commission proposed to reassign at least some of that behavior to a new entity: the family court. And that reassignment helped to create and solidify the interventionist family court we have today:

> The Commission recommends that jurisdiction over juveniles be placed in a family court which should be a division of a trial court of general jurisdiction. The family court should have jurisdiction over all legal matters related to family life, including delinquency, neglect, support, adoption, custody, paternity actions, divorce, annulments and assaults involving family members. Dependent children—those needing help through no fault of their parents—should be handled outside the court system.[44]

In proposing a family court, the Nixon Commission noted favorably the few family courts already created, including New York's ten-year-old unified family court, which had already separated delinquency and status offenses into two categories of court jurisdiction. Status offenders in New York are called "persons in need of supervision" (PINS), but the Nixon Commission declined to take a position on whether to extend jurisdiction of its proposed new family court to include what it generically labeled "the PINS category."[45] Instead, over the next decade, that battle would be fought over the development of a comprehensive set of standards about how the law should treat children (and their parents) who find themselves in court. The winner of the battle, and ultimately of the war, was a family court with enhanced jurisdiction over myriad aspects of family life, including the "dependent children—those needing help through no fault of their parents." The loser was radical nonintervention in the lives of noncriminal youth and their families.

Radical Nonintervention and the Juvenile Justice Standards Project: Eliminating Status Offense Jurisdiction

"Radical nonintervention," as the sociologist Edwin Schur christened it in 1973, starts with the premise that our values, attitudes, and approaches to youthful behavior define what we mean by "delinquency."[46] Defining youth behavior remains a political choice with political solutions. In his book *The Child Savers: The Invention of Delinquency*, Anthony Platt posited that the founders who created the juvenile court were also inventing the very concept of delinquency.[47] Helen Geddes, Camille Sippy, and millions of other youth would not have traveled through the juvenile legal system at all if the purpose of the juvenile court had been solely to divert youth who committed crimes from the adult criminal justice system. The decision to intervene in the lives of some youth who were misbehaving in ways that all youth misbehave gave them an identity and a way of interacting with the rest of society that Schur argued was far beyond the needs of a smooth-running society.[48]

And it had failed miserably. What society needed was to change its approach radically: *to leave kids alone whenever possible*. "Leaving alone" didn't mean "abandonment" but rather smarter, narrower approaches to youth behavior that recognized the danger of messing with people's lives. The first step was to take misbehavior out of the definition of delinquency entirely. Schur rejected simply recategorizing misbehavior from delinquency to status offenses and sending those status offenders through a different door in the courthouse. The second step was to take young people more seriously by strengthening their bonds to society in two ways: first by engaging them in creating a more just society, and second by creating a court system worth respecting for those who belonged there. That court system would have explicit rules and punishments. These would not be "get tough" rules but "deal evenly" rules that diverted or included youth based on their illegal actions and not on what was good for them. The third step was to accept that no single solution, or even an identifiable combination of solutions, would quickly or effectively reduce delinquency. Instead, approaches that maximize community-based, voluntary, noninstitutional programs were more likely to engage youth over traditional, court-based processing and services for all but the most serious offenders.[49] This is "leaving alone" with benefits.

Radical nonintervention was seriously considered during the most sustained fight over whether to retain status offense jurisdiction in the 1970s. About twenty years after Camille Sippy won her case, the way our juvenile and family courts—and their attendant systems—intervened in the lives of children and families was thoroughly examined. It was a "perfect storm" moment when in 1971 the Institute of Judicial Administration (IJA) at New York University School of Law decided to expand its work on adult criminal justice standards to create a Juvenile Justice Standards Project (JJ Standards Project). Two years later the American Bar Association (ABA) became a cosponsor of the JJ Standards Project, with a combined governing board of illustrious experts in law and the disciplines most relevant to families, such as psychology and sociology. For over a decade the standards created by the JJ Standards Project would be drafted, edited, presented for comment, revised, re-presented, and ultimately put before the ABA House of Delegates for approval. The Juvenile Justice Standards (JJ Standards) considered virtually every issue related to youth at risk—coinciding with the Supreme Court's decisions in the late 1960s and early 1970s that established what constituted procedural "fundamental fairness" for youth charged with crimes. Ultimately, twenty of the twenty-three published volumes of the JJ Standards would be approved by the ABA and distributed around the country "for consideration and implementation by the components of the juvenile justice system in the various states and localities."[50]

One volume, *Schools and Education*, was withdrawn from consideration for being too specialized. A second volume, *Abuse and Neglect*, was not completed in time for the ABA House of Delegates to approve.[51] The fight over that volume and the meaning of "child protection" will be discussed in chapter 7. One—and only one—volume was "tabled" by the ABA delegates for being too controversial. That volume was *Noncriminal Misbehavior*, which called for the elimination of status offense jurisdiction.[52] Most states at the time still defined criminal and noncriminal misbehavior of juveniles as "delinquency." The recommendation was to eliminate behavior from the court's delinquency jurisdiction that did not constitute a crime. No longer would youth like Helen Geddes and Camille Sippy be taken to court for being incorrigible, for being truant, running away, having sex, drinking, or drugging. No longer would age alone, rather than criminal action, be the sole basis for state intervention and control.

How had the JJ Standards drafters revived this unconventional and radical conclusion? The JJ Standards are, in many ways, a triumph of what the Nobel Prize winner Daniel Kahneman has labeled "System 2 thinking" in his book *Thinking Fast and Slow*. System 2 thinking is the "thinking slow" of the title, a way of approaching problems and their solutions that challenges our implicit and explicit assumptions about what we are addressing. System 2 thinking recognizes the limitations of expertise in order to reconsider all we know (or think we know) in light of our conscious and unconscious biases; that is to say, using the best available knowledge to make decisions.[53] Here, from the 1982 edition of the "Summary and Analysis" of the JJ Standards, is an explanation of this often-painful process of thinking slow:

> Contrary to the usual experience of projects of this sort, many participants found their views changed as they reconsidered the validity of their assumptions. They found some of their most cherished ideas challenged and ultimately vanquished by exposure to unexpected formulations and findings concerning the performance and goals of the juvenile justice system. Agreement on principles was the primary concern, although once basic positions were adopted, the Commission was exhaustively conscientious in hammering out the precise language to be adopted in the individual standards.[54]

This extraordinary process of reconsidering the basic principles and goals of a powerful system created over seventy years earlier resulted in recommendations that one of the directors of the JJ Standards Project, Barbara Flicker, called "revolutionary."[55]

Whether any reform—including the creation of the juvenile court—is truly revolutionary is an open question.[56] The sociologist and historian Charles Tilly contended that we reform only around the edges of customary patterns.[57] The historic roots of controlling misbehaving children stretch back several centuries before the juvenile court was created. As Professor Allen noted: "No institution as complex as the juvenile court emerges suddenly and fully formed," listing several nineteenth century innovations leading to the juvenile court, including separating juveniles from adults in correctional institutions and developing probation services.[58] Nevertheless, I think Flicker was right to label nonintervention as revolutionary. A proposal that the state *not* intervene when children misbehave challenges the basic premise of *parens patriae* intervention as an overall good. That a nonintervention proposal ultimately failed may be proof of its revolutionary power.

Another Misbehaving Girl: Cindy Snyder and the Juvenile Justice Standards

By the time the *Noncriminal Misbehavior* volume of standards was being drafted in the early 1970s, an estimated one-third to as many as one-half of the juvenile court docket in the United States included cases involving youth like Helen and Camille—girls who had committed no crimes but whose incorrigibility invoked state action.[59] Cindy Snyder of North Seattle, Washington, was one of them.[60] Cindy's parents were strict: no smoking, no dating, and severe limits on friendships and extracurricular activities. Cindy remained a good high-school student, but these limitations were unbearable for her. Hostilities grew so much that Cindy and her parents stopped communicating; in desperation Mr. Snyder delivered Cindy to the Youth Service Center. Cindy was placed in a temporary home; not wanting to return to her family, she filed a petition in the juvenile court asking that she be declared a dependent child, what today would be categorized under "neglect." Several months later the court determined that Cindy didn't meet the statutory requirements of dependency because her parents were not unfit and sent her home. That lasted barely a month before Cindy fled back to the Youth Service Center. The director of the center's intake office filed another dependency petition, this time alleging that Cindy was incorrigible by being beyond control of her parents. Cindy agreed; her parents did not. They challenged the court's finding once they realized that the court intended to keep Cindy in foster care instead of sending her home.

As Helen Geddes's father had discovered seventy years earlier, invoking the state's coercive help can backfire. Mr. Snyder thought the court would help him control his daughter, not take her away. Having a full evidentiary hearing made no difference. When Helen Geddes's brother-in-law filed a writ of habeas corpus to get her released from reform school in 1903, the court held that she had no right to a hearing. In 1973, the Snyders had a right to hearing, with lawyers and sworn witness testimony. One witness, the psychiatrist hired by the Snyders, testified that Cindy shouldn't go home until everyone in the family could back away from their rigid positions. And Cindy, now represented by counsel, testified that she refused to return home. When her parents' lawyer objected that Cindy's opinion about returning home was irrelevant, he was overruled. The case made its way to the Washington Supreme Court. That court noted:

> It is implicit in the record that the petitioner parents believe the juvenile court has given sympathy and support to Cynthia's problems in disregard of their rights as parents, and that the juvenile court has failed to assume its responsibility to assist in the resolution of the parents' problems with their minor child. We find this presumption of the petitioners to be unsupported by the evidence.

The supreme court then described the efforts made by the juvenile court judge to facilitate reconciliation, including sending Cindy home and urging counseling for the family. But the high court also noted that some of these efforts were interrupted by the Snyders' decision to use the adversarial process to appeal the juvenile court's decision. Asserting their parental rights was used against them.

The JJ Standards Project's drafters knew about the Snyder case and believed that Cindy's situation would have been very different if she and her parents had not had access to the court. Reviewing the Snyder case soon after it was published, they wrote:

> Had resort to the court not been possible and had there been available the sorts of crisis intervention services and voluntary alternative residential placements or mechanisms for emancipation of older youth, the minor, her family, and the community in which they lived would have been spared the invidious spectacle which the record presents. It is perfectly true that "hard cases make bad law." *In respect of status offense cases, it is not beyond the mark to conclude that they are all hard.*[61]

In proposing an alternative to court intervention for noncriminal misbehavior, the JJ Standards Project provided substantial justification for why these cases are so hard, building on the findings of the commissions under Johnson and Nixon but going beyond them to challenge the very purpose of the juvenile court:

> These standards take the position that the present jurisdiction of the juvenile court over noncriminal misbehavior—the status offense jurisdiction—should be cut short and a system of voluntary referral to services provided outside the juvenile justice system adopted in its stead. *As a general principle, the standards seek to eliminate coercive official intervention in unruly child cases.*[62]

The twenty volumes of JJ Standards that were eventually approved by the ABA outlined a carefully constructed, re-envisioned juvenile legal system. But when Barbara Flicker published the second edition of the summary of the JJ Standards in 1982, she acknowledged that all that work would have little meaning without addressing "the most sensitive task: to define the boundaries of justifiable state intervention in the lives of families and children. That task was fundamental to the project; in a sense, everything else was mere detail."[63]

The boundaries the JJ Standards recommended were considerably narrower, and the most significant boundary kept youth who hadn't committed any crime out of court. The message could not have been clearer:

[Allowing] formalized coercive intervention . . . in unruly child cases undermines family autonomy, isolates the child, polarizes parents and children, encourages parents to abdicate their functions and roles to the court, may blunt the effectiveness of any ameliorative services that are provided, and cuts against the development of controls and means within the family for the resolution of conflicts.[64]

Permitting intervention when children hadn't broken the law was bad for children and bad for their families. The JJ Standards compared legal compulsion to restore parent–child understanding to "surgery with a spade."[65] They rejected the assumption that court intervention in these cases would do more good than harm. Citing a contemporary California legislative report, they noted: "[Not] a single shred of evidence exists to indicate that any significant number of [beyond control children] have benefited [by juvenile court intervention]. In fact, what evidence does exist points to the contrary."[66]

If that evidence of harm weren't sufficient justification for eliminating misbehavior jurisdiction, the JJ Standards reiterated the concern expressed by both presidential crime commissions: youth exhibiting noncriminal misbehavior are treated differently depending on their race, economic standing, family composition, and community.[67] As Professor Allen had earlier recognized, "[these] are children alienated from the legitimate institutions of society, lacking in opportunities for employment and goal satisfactions, victims of discrimination and cultural deprivation. The behavior of such children, even that which contributes most to community concern and insecurity, may often reflect normal adaptation to the conditions of life to which they are subjected."[68]

This inequality is intolerable when every youth is known to misbehave in ways that could, but doesn't, result in intervention. The outcomes for those youth who were drawn into the system at the time the JJ Standards were being crafted were staggering: "[In] the great majority of American jurisdictions, status offenders are subject to exactly the same dispositions as minors who commit crimes, including commitment to state training schools."[69] Or to put it more bluntly: a youth could receive the same punishment for parental defiance or burglary or armed robbery. Helen Geddes's 1901 institutionalization with girls who had committed serious crimes was still occurring routinely in the early 1970s.

Trying Radical Nonintervention

What would have happened to Cindy Snyder if her father could not have turned to the court for help in 1973 and if, instead, Washington State had adopted the proposed standards for noncriminal misbehavior? Cindy was living at home and attending school even though hostility was high and all communication seemed to have deteriorated between her and her parents. Cindy and her parents (alone or together) would have had a range of options under the standards' proposals. They could start with a call to a well-publicized twenty-four-hour hotline or a crisis walk-in center. If Cindy's parents contacted the police or her school for information about what they could do, they would be referred to the crisis walk-in centers for first-line assistance. The school or the police could have taken no coercive action themselves, and they would have urged the Snyders to seek appropriate voluntary help rather than court assistance. All efforts would have been made to connect them quickly with centers that could either offer short-term assistance or make referrals to more specialized support for the family, including relief the family might identify themselves, like their own religious assembly or another community-based group. Available services could be short-term crisis intervention, including voluntary residential care in the home of a relative or friend or in a family or group home setting. But equally important would be connecting the family quickly with skilled professionals or trained volunteers to help them communicate so that any out-of-home option would be considered only as a respite. Crisis intervention or long-term assistance could include medical, educational, social welfare, or legal services to assist the family. Services would have to be funded sufficiently to be able to respond expeditiously. Without sufficient funding and marketing for community services, families would be reluctant to abandon a court-based approach. In Cindy Snyder's case, there was no evidence that voluntary efforts were tried before the family turned to the court. And the court process itself had hardened everyone's position to the point where even the examining psychiatrist said no progress could be made until everyone backed off.

Cindy wasn't a runaway or a danger to herself or others. If she had been, the proposed JJ Standards recognized that, if voluntary efforts failed, the safety of the young person would present a significant challenge if there were no alternative placements. Even here, though, the standards focused on a family-based solution with short-term custody or placement only after every effort was made to reconcile the family or the court determined that the parents were actually unfit.[70] The standards framed the solution as being voluntary, family-centered, supported by adequate services, and conciliatory—not coercive, punitive, or court-based. When children are really in danger by being with their families, they must be swiftly protected, but the worst-case scenario is not allowed to define the solution for the overwhelming number of families who, with some meaningful expeditious help, would resolve their own problems. Court intervention was recognized as the last, most detrimental solution.

This approach is what the juvenile justice scholar Margaret K. Rosenheim would have called "normalizing" rather than "problematizing" most of the issues that families face at some point during a child's adolescence. Rosenheim coined the phrase "juvenile nuisances" to describe much of the youthful misbehavior that she believed was inappropriately deemed "delinquent" and that led not only to court intervention but also to creating a professional, specialization-driven social service system to "solve" the problems of delinquency. Instead, by recognizing how normal these issues are for families and providing them with readily available, proximate, and simple responses first, she believed that most families would resolve their issues; those with more serious needs could be provided with more targeted, long-term, and specialized professional assistance.[71] In the normalized juvenile nuisance world, Cindy Snyder would not be defined as a dependent or incorrigible child, and her parents would not be at risk of losing their child because they didn't have access to help that was immediate, noncoercive, and respectful.

While the *Noncriminal Misbehavior* standards were never formally approved by the ABA, they remained in the public imagination; several states, including Washington, used them as the basis for revamping their delinquency systems. Soon after the Snyders' experience, Washington virtually eliminated status offense jurisdiction as part of a broad reconstruction of the state's juvenile legal system. Prior to the law's enactment, a study of Washington's training schools found that on average "incorrigibles" stayed inside the institutions for fifteen months, whereas "the armed robbers and the murderers" averaged only seven and a half months—a clear example of the rehabilitative ideal run amuck.[72] The initial legislation tracked the language of the *Noncriminal Misbehavior* standards verbatim—which still permitted very limited commitments to protect a youth in serious danger—but in the following legislative session even these interventions were "quietly and without discussion" repealed. The goal was to move the juvenile court from its *parens patriae* origins of "benevolent coercion" to being a court of law.[73] Children who were incorrigible, ungovernable, or fighting with their parents could no longer be brought to court for misbehaving. The legislation nevertheless allowed law enforcement to take youth into temporary custody if they were in serious danger, had run away, or were truant and the officer could not resolve the conflict after making "all reasonable efforts."[74]

The new system anticipated a set of crisis intervention services and refuges in the community for these youth, but in the initial years many youth were either left to their own devices or placed in foster care.[75] Concerned that law enforcement was getting it wrong at both ends of the intervention spectrum—doing too little or too much—the statutes were rewritten to require officers to take all youth in serious danger into custody but to turn them over to crisis intervention quickly. Truancy was eliminated as a ground for intervention, and government social services agencies were required to take crisis referrals from all sources. More resources were appropriated for these changes in 1979, but then the early 1980s saw massive budget cuts.[76] Programs were not created and funded to meet the demands of families who could no longer ask the court to intervene. In recounting the inadequacy of the appropriations for voluntary services during this period, one researcher harkened back to New York judge Justine Wise Polier's opposition to enacting the *Noncriminal Misbehavior* standards. Judge Polier had warned that divesting the court of jurisdiction without adequately developing and funding voluntary services would harm children and families.[77]

There were some notable successes. Youth who once would have been charged with running away, in conflict with their families, violating curfew, and even truancy could no longer be detained. The fear of net-widening—that a greater number of youth would be involved in a less court-based system—also turned out to be unfounded. Approximately the same number of youth who had been charged as status offenders found themselves directed instead to social services.[78] Studies of

Washington State's new approach concluded nevertheless that decision-making discretion at each stage of the process still meant that many youth remained in the court system and experienced significant punishment. One reason was relabeling. Youth previously labeled "runaways" were being charged as "delinquents." The new legislation then subjected these youth to stricter sentencing guidelines on delinquent behavior. The second reason was that an appreciably larger component of the youth now being charged as delinquent were young people of color.[79]

The researchers who studied the reforms during their early phase concluded that removing status offense jurisdiction from the court and creating a more justice-based court system without also taking into account the ways that discretion influenced police, prosecutor, and judge decision-making diminished but did not eliminate the impact of court divestiture.[80] When judges followed the stricter guidelines for long-term institutionalization, there was less evidence of gender or racial bias.[81] The sentencing guidelines nevertheless allowed the judges "manifest discretion" to deviate from the guidelines to consider either mitigating or extenuating circumstances in some cases. Judges used that discretion to impose stricter sanctions on less serious offenders because of their concern that the youth needed treatment or was at risk and needed "help" or "control."[82] A history of running away—now no longer a basis for court intervention—was a strong predictor of a harsher sanction. The other predictor of a harsher sentence was being Black.[83] Despite these failings, researchers concluded that the system was getting fairer.

The Four D's: Deinstitutionalization, Diversion, Due Process, and Decriminalization

Other states began to reconsider their approaches to noncriminal misbehavior in the early 1970s even if they didn't go as far as Washington had. Three factors were crucial. First, the Supreme Court's mandate that delinquency proceedings adopt many due process protections had required states to consider whether they wanted to provide these protections in the "unruly children" cases. Second, federal legislation began to provide financial incentives to deinstitutionalize youth categorized as status offenders. And third, there was a renewed interest in programs to divert youth out of formal court proceedings. The sociologist Lamar

Empey labeled these factors—*due process, deinstitutionalization*, and *diversion*—as the "three D's."[84] They would soon be joined by a fourth— *decriminalization*—and would result in a reconfigured but still largely ineffective status offender system in a reinvigorated family court.

The passage of the federal Juvenile Justice and Delinquency Prevention Act (JJDPA) in 1974 is often cited as the turning point in addressing noncriminal misbehavior. Congress encouraged states to create plans that would preclude placing noncriminal status offenders in detention or correctional facilities with youth who had committed crimes in order to receive federal juvenile justice grants. This was the deinstitutionalization component, the *D* that reduced the power of the court to control these youth by taking away its most powerful weapon: locking them up. Referrals of status offenders to court decreased by 21 percent, and their detention decreased by half between 1974 and 1980.[85] The number of (noncriminal) misbehaving youth in secure facilities also dropped dramatically through the rest of the decade, reaching a point where researchers concluded that placement of status offenders in secure "large red-brick institutions" had been eliminated.[86] In fact, status offenders in all public and private facilities—from group homes to forestry camps to "semi-secure" institutions—also decreased steadily after the passage of the JJDPA. Between 1977 and 1991, the percentage of status offenders in these facilities dropped from 17 percent of the facility population to 5–7 percent—though this still left more than 7,000 youth categorized as status offenders in some form of custody.[87]

During the same decades, juvenile and family courts struggled to implement the Supreme Court due process mandates as states passed legislation defining what constituted "fair hearings" for minors. One solution was to divert many of the misbehaving youth out of court to avoid having to provide them with counsel or hold formal due process hearings. Instead, a diversion system would send them to programs that could provide specific services (education, job training, mental health) and keep an eye on them. Social service agencies, police authorities, probation departments, and sometimes court systems administered the programs. Nevertheless, most youth would remain subject to court jurisdiction if they did not comply with program requirements.[88] These court diversion systems are *not* radical nonintervention; diversion programs explicitly use court jurisdiction as coercive control. A social service or treatment program with all the same elements, staff, and resources using a nonintervention approach would impose no adverse consequences for noncompliance with the program. A court-connected diversion system could inflict significant penalties.

Studying this period of significant growth in diversion systems in the late 1970s and early 1980s, Professor Feld concluded that diversion for noncriminal misbehavior had resulted in a *worse* system for a greater number of youth. Research had shown that, with diversion programs in place, police and probation officers widened the net by using them for youth who previously might have been simply reprimanded and released. Youth who failed to comply with program rules or to attend the program as ordered could find themselves in court and subject to significant punishment, including being removed from their homes, without the protection of most due process protections. Feld concluded that "[diversion] reforms re-created elements of the pre-*Gault* juvenile court and provided a mechanism to coercively supervise minor deviants in an informal, standardless process without any procedural safeguards."[89]

Diversion programs also hid this supervision from the public's eye. Paul Nejelski, a former director of the Institute of Judicial Administration who reviewed diversion programs during the same period as Feld, noted that diversion programs reduce the visibility of coercive state action. When the public doesn't see the ways in which youth are screened for or treated in diversion programs, there is little incentive to consider fundamental systemic reform. As a result, this out-of-sight discretion can become increasingly arbitrary or discriminatory. Nejelski observed: "Diversion projects, like the juvenile court, may appear to prosper only if they enjoy very little public scrutiny."[90]

Diversion was only one means of sidestepping due process requirements in court. The fourth *D* was decriminalization. Instead of being defined as a "delinquent," a misbehaving youth was defined as a "status offender" or even a "neglected" or "dependent" child. Since the Supreme Court due process mandates applied only to youth charged with acts that would be crimes if committed by adults, redefining youth into other categories permitted states to avoid providing due process protections, as many states did. The federal fiscal incentives to remove misbehaving youth from being institutionalized with delinquents further spurred many states to reclassify misbehaving youth into a status offender cat-

egory. By the early 1980s, most states had created nondelinquent categories of youth "in need of supervision" like Maryland's JOINS (juvenile
offenders in need of supervision) or Massachusetts's CHINS (children in
need of supervision). New York had already created a separate category
of PINS (persons in need of supervision) as part of the unified Family
Court Act in 1962.[91] The statutory language used for PINS jurisdiction
was remarkably similar to the language of the original children's court
jurisdiction over delinquents: a child "who is an habitual truant or who
is incorrigible, ungovernable or habitually disobedient and beyond the
lawful control of parent or other lawful authority."[92]

And to the Four D's that spearheaded status offense jurisdiction
I would add a fifth: *decider* (for the judge). Juvenile and family court
judges during this period were fighting to keep control over as many
youth as possible. Barbara Flicker had written in her summary and analysis of the JJ Standards that everything but defining the boundaries of
court jurisdiction is "mere detail."[93] Judges certainly agreed with her;
their opinion was remarkably unambiguous. Following the decision in
Gault, the National Council of Juvenile Court Judges passed a resolution in 1967 reasserting the broad authority of the juvenile court over
children and outlining the philosophy and principles that should govern
positions taken by the NCJCJ. The introduction to that list of principles
included a not-so-subtle warning that if judges did not want to get side-
swiped by the Supreme Court again—as they had been in *Gault*—the
NCJCJ would need to adopt a set of principles to be cited in its amicus
briefs whenever issues related to the juvenile court were being litigated
in appellate courts. Those principles refuted the recent findings of the
Johnson Commission that had so thoughtfully rejected an unmediated
rehabilitative ideal. The specter that the juvenile court might become its
own obstacle to fundamental reform was manifest in the obstructionist
role adopted by the NCJCJ.[94]

The NCJCJ blamed "the pressures of urbanization and the upsurge of
interest in civil liberty and its constitutional safeguards" for misconstru-
ing the true nature of the juvenile court and potentially saddling it with
far too many due process protections. Since *Gault* had already declared
that juvenile delinquency proceedings required fundamental fairness,
the judges grudgingly acknowledged that several due process rights, like
the right to counsel, were necessary. But they were adamant that juvenile

delinquency proceedings were not criminal proceedings and not even adversarial proceedings in most instances. If certain due process protections were mandated for determining guilt or innocence, such protections need not extend to dispositional proceedings, where "the welfare of the child is the pole star which must guide the court's determination." This is true even though these dispositional proceedings could result in incarceration. The judges recommitted themselves to personalized justice for every child, regardless of why that child found herself in court, because the role of the court is not "to do something to a child because of something the child has done, but to do something of a constructive nature for the child, because of what it is, and what it needs, and according to the state of being in which it is found, whether that state be dependency, neglect, or delinquency."[95] This language corresponds almost word-for-word with the definition provided by Judge Edward F. Waite in 1921, when he wrote that the criminal court does "something *to* a child because of what he *has done*" while a juvenile court is "concerned only with doing something *for* a child because of what he *is* and *needs*."[96] Judicial discretion to determine what the child needed should remain the keystone of a court built on a therapeutic rehabilitative ideal.

The NCJCJ acknowledged that judges were not always successful in that effort, in part because—as their predecessors throughout the century had lamented—they didn't always get sufficient funding from the legislative and executive branches to provide the "solicitous care and regenerative treatment" needed. Judges were concerned with the child's right to custody, not to "unrestrained liberty." But the custody that the judges were protecting was not that of the child's own parent but of the court as *parens patriae*: "[C]ustody, care and discipline to which a child is entitled [from the court] should be as nearly as possible equivalent to that which wise parents give to their own children."[97] Just as Judge Paul Alexander had decried a decade earlier, to "deprive the court of its rightful status, [would] impair its intended effectiveness, [and would] deprive the child not merely of constitutional rights but of many invaluable rights regarded as the birthrights of every American child."[98]

Despite the vast research underlying the recommendations to reform the juvenile court issued by the Johnson Commission and cited by the Supreme Court that same year, the NCJCJ insisted "to prevent the destruction of the achievable benefits of the Juvenile Court system [we] require more extensive study and exploration than has been possible to date." Their bottom line was clear:

> BE IT FURTHER RESOLVED, that the National Council of Juvenile Court Judges is opposed to any narrowing of the jurisdiction of the juvenile court which would limit or eliminate any of the traditional jurisdictional grounds which generally are and have been found in the juvenile court statutes of the several states.[99]

The judges were not prepared to abandon a socialized, interventionist court in the face of either due process or a failed rehabilitation model. According to David Gilman, a former director of the JJ Standards Project, the NCJCJ was strongly opposed to most of the proposed JJ Standards but was insufficiently organized at the time to challenge the strong support within the ABA that was led by Livingston Hall, a legendary Harvard professor and chair of the ABA's criminal justice section.[100]

A decade later, the judges had organized. Their desire to maintain broad jurisdiction over families—and misbehaving youth in particular— was manifested during the process to reauthorize the JJDPA in 1980. By then the NCJCJ had been renamed the National Council of Juvenile and Family Court Judges (NCJFCJ), reflecting the rapid number of family courts that had been created in the interim. Testifying on behalf on the NCJFCJ at the House JJDPA reauthorization hearings, Judge John R. Milligan stated:

> The effect of the Juvenile Justice Act as it now exists is to allow a child ultimately to decide for himself whether he will go to school, whether he will live at home, whether he will continue to run, run, run, away from home or *whether he will even obey orders of your court.*[101]

The NCJFCJ successfully lobbied for an amendment to the JJDPA's prohibition against status offenders being institutionalized with delinquents in secure facilities if the status offender had violated a "valid court order (VCO)." A status offender placed on probation, for example, who violated the conditions of that probation, or one who had been placed by the court in a nonsecure facility and had run away, could now be held in contempt for violating the "orders of your court" and locked up with delinquent youth.[102] While not all states adopted the VCO exception, in the states that did, status offenses merged once again into delinquency; the court was back in control.

This was not good for the misbehaving youth who were caught. The formal separation of status offenses and delinquency during the 1970s did not result in better outcomes for all young people. Diversion efforts may have kept some youth out of formal court processing, but others were drawn further into the system through the net-widening practices of law enforcement and the court itself.[103] Decarceration efforts, which had dramatically decreased the number of securely institutionalized youth initially, saw those numbers begin to rebound, spurred by the bootstrapping results of violating a VCO.[104] At the same time, young people who might have been placed in the "big red buildings" were re-labeled "emotionally disturbed" or "otherwise psychiatrically impaired" and frequently admitted by their parents instead to psychiatric institu-tions for "treatment." During the 1980s, as status-offense institutional-ization decreased, psychiatric hospitalizations increased dramatically.[105] Status-offending misbehavior was further relabeled into "minor crimes" and "domestic violence" or "family offense" violations, which could re-sult in significant punishment.[106] At the same time, getting tough on crime began to be applied far more regularly and forcefully against younger and younger children. Some states lowered the age of criminal responsibility for certain crimes, especially crimes of violence, sending far more youth into adult criminal justice systems. Alternatively, states kept youth committing serious crimes in family court but significantly increased the length and security of incarcerations.[107] These changes, along with media hysteria about the coming wave of youth "super predators"—a mythical danger that was later disproved—affected the treatment of all misbehaving youth.[108]

Of course, all misbehaving youth were not treated equally. The flu-idity of categorizing misbehavior as a status offense, as a delinquent or criminal act, or as a basis for treatment confounds our ability to under-stand clearly what was happening to young people in trouble. In their award-winning examination of girls in the juvenile legal system, Meda Chesney-Lind and Randall Shelden concluded that misbehavior by boys and girls is more similar than different but that the system's response to such misbehavior differs significantly. Girls are more likely to be arrested and referred to court for traditional status offenses—running away, being incorrigible or ungovernable—as parents, schools, and police seek to enforce stereotypical female norms of obedience and modesty.[109] It is no accident that the case examples in this chapter are all girls. Whether Helen is getting drunk and meeting boys, Camille is disobeying her mother's rules, or Cindy is chaffing at her parent's restrictions, all of them represent a strong bias toward controlling girls' behavior historically and today. In the 1990s, behavior that used to be categorized as status offenses—particularly girls fighting at home or in school—now increasingly resulted in arrests for assault.[110] Parents frustrated with their daughter's conduct could use stricter enforcement of domestic violence or family offense policies to have their daughters arrested, and school districts enforcing zero-tolerance policies could do the same.[111] As the number of status-offending girls confined to training schools decreased under the JJDPA's decarceration mandate, an equal number of girls were being confined to institutions for minor delinquency charges.[112] Not only were girls more likely to be charged with status offenses; so were all children of color. The Johnson Commission had declared that "slum offenders are more likely than suburban offenders to be arrested and referred to juvenile court."[113] Youth of color continued to be disproportionately charged with status offenses (along with other, more serious offenses), adjudicated, and placed outside their homes.[114]

Professors Chesney-Lind and Shelton clearly established that society's impetus to control girls, especially any sexual or assertive behavior, had reinforced the interventionist policies to maintain and even strengthen status-offense jurisdiction. Ironically, the authors point out that these interventionist policies may further harm girls, who may be literally running away from abusive or miserable home lives and then are punished for defying court orders that fail to address the complexity of their experiences.[115] Those punishments increased as the backlash against deinstitutionalization grew. Unfortunately, juvenile and family court judges lamented their loss of authority far more than the failure of Congress and state legislatures to fund—and public agencies to implement—alternative and effective youth programs that would reduce punishment.

At a 1998 Senate Judiciary Committee hearing aptly titled "Fixing a Broken System: Preventing Crime Through Intervention," the juvenile court judge David Grossmann, speaking on behalf of the NCJFCJ, identified the deinstitutionalization movement as the main culprit in the court's inability to help children and families. According to Judge Grossmann, taking away the court's power to institutionalize young people in secure facilities in the first instance—and not just after the youth had defied a court order—rendered the courts impotent. The NCJFCJ's written testimony alleged that deinstitutionalization of status offenders (DSO) was as good as eliminating status offense jurisdiction and blamed the DSO movement for depriving the court of its ability to work with schools, community organizations, churches, and hospitals. Judge Grossmann declared that states that had "caved in to federal pressure and restricted [the] court's jurisdiction" had come to their senses and reasserted the court's authority.[116]

While the purpose of the Senate hearing was to consider the role of early intervention in preventing youth crime, Judge Grossmann was much more concerned with protecting "the juvenile and family courts [that] play a vital role in the health and welfare of our societies and communities [and] stand at the crossroads as guardians of the public safety and as enforcers and underpinning the actions of law enforcement, of schools, of parents."[117] The NCJFCJ's written submission similarly reaffirmed the centrality of the court's role, citing its recommendation, among others, that "[j]uvenile and family courts should maintain a role in serving children who are runaway, truant, drug dependent or beyond control. The court must have the clear authority to determine the need for services for these children and their families and to require that reasonable and necessary services be delivered."[118] Judge Grossmann's promise that the family court, with sufficient authority, would protect society is an example of creating "unrealistic and unrealizable expectations" that undermined public support for the court. As Professor Allen warned, too often friends of the court "have advanced insupportable claims as to the court's capabilities in the control of juvenile delinquency through the processes of treatment and supervision of delinquent children."[119] Too often, they have undermined more realistic and fundamental reforms. And too often they have won.

Becca Hedman: Giving up on Radical Nonintervention

The separation of delinquency and status offenses was mostly complete throughout the country by the 1990s. Washington State, which had championed nonintervention fifteen years earlier, was reversing that experiment. As with other retrenchment decisions, this one was also based on a small number of horrific exceptions.

Becca Hedman was an unlucky, traumatized child from birth. She was sexually abused when she was only six months old before being placed with her adoptive parents. Her adoptive brother sexually abused her at the age of five soon after her adoption was finalized. The sexual abuse haunted her relationships with other children, her sense of self-esteem, and her behavior in school. Becca began running away when she was twelve. Her parents placed her in a crisis residential center, after which she refused to return home. She bounced from the crisis center to a group home to foster care to a drug treatment residence. Most moves were characterized by deteriorating behavior—including drug use and prostitution—and exploitation on the street. One night Becca was brutally beaten and murdered by a john after she refused to give him back money after they had sex. She was thirteen.[120]

Becca's tragic murder prompted a wave of backlash against Washington's treatment of runaways. Her adoptive parents were outraged that she could not be held securely—being a runaway was not a crime. They worked with other angry parents of troubled youth to reinstate laws that would permit parents—or, if necessary, the state—to have their out-of-control children locked up. In 1995, the "Becca Bill" reinstated the full power of status-offense jurisdiction in Washington State.[121] The purpose of the law was not to punish young people for misbehaving but rather "to give tools to parents, courts, and law enforcement to keep families together and reunite them whenever possible."[122] Those tools included not only the assistance of "multidisciplinary teams" to provide services to children and families but also the ability to hold youth in secure facilities for longer periods of time. Separate provisions mandated strict enforcement of truancy laws.[123]

Five years earlier, the state had already begun reintroducing status-offense jurisdiction by creating "at-risk youth" (ARY) petitions, which allowed parents to bring their child to court for reconciliation services.[124] At-risk youths, like misbehaving youth before them, were alleged to be beyond their parents' control, have run away, are using drugs, or are otherwise placing themselves at risk to their own health, safety, or welfare.[125] It is not clear that the Becca's parents had ever tried to use an ARY petition. Moreover, most counties refused to hear ARY petitions because of scarce resources and overcrowded courts. The ARY law even contained an acknowledgement that its implementation was limited by the availability of funds.[126] The Becca Bill required that every ARY petition be heard in court; it further created a "children in need of services" (CHINS) category that permitted parents, the social services department, or even a child to file a petition in court seeking out-of-home placement.[127] Twenty years earlier in Washington, Cindy Snyder had asked to be declared incorrigible so she could be placed away from her parents. She and her parents then fought all the way to the Washington Supreme Court, where her parents were unable to persuade the court that Cindy should be returned to them. The court authority the Snyders had fought against was now reinstated.

No one knows whether the Becca Bill would have saved Becca. But Washington not only re-created a predominantly court-based, punitive response to noncriminal youth misbehavior; it adopted an even harsher regime. The state rejected the more moderate deinstitutionalization requirements of the federal JJDPA, forsaking federal funds to be able to lock up misbehaving youth. In the first two years after the Becca Bill was enacted, the number of petitions filed in Washington increased 600 percent.[128] From 1994 to 1997, the number of ARY petitions increased 500 percent (from 393 to 1,936), and the number of truancy petitions increased *from 91 to 15,627*. During those same years, the number of times judges imposed detention on status offenders increased 900 percent. The number of detention days ordered by courts rose from approximately 1,000 per year before the Becca Bill to more than 12,300 in 1997.[129] The counties were so overwhelmed by the expense that some began to charge parents for holding their runaway and truant children, and eighteen counties filed a lawsuit against the state for failing to fully fund the new laws.[130]

The Becca Bill was a response to several shocking tragedies in Washington; that is a dangerous, but not unprecedented, way legislation affecting children and families gets passed. The adage "hard cases make bad laws" is applicable here. In the decades that followed, Washington State not only faced numerous law suits challenging the lack of due process in the Becca Bill; it lost millions of dollars in federal funds because of its detention policies. From 2004–2007, the state reported being totally out of compliance with the JJDPA's basic mandate of not housing status offenders in secure facilities (even with the valid-court-order exception).[131] By 2011, Washington was locking up more status offenders—including truants—than any other state.[132] Even as the Washington Supreme Court upheld the juvenile court's inherent power to hold youth in contempt, the concurring opinion acknowledged that "numerous studies [indicate] that detention does not have an ameliorative effect on runaway behavior, and, in fact, often exacerbates the problem. The record in this case bears this out: repeated detention of these children did not stop them from running away."[133]

Despite all the evidence that misbehaving behavior did not belong in court, status-offense jurisdiction won out in the end. Maintaining the centrality of status-offense jurisdiction in family court was essential to maintaining the court itself. The court was able to recommit to its interventionist and discretionary authority not only in these cases but also in the wider range of family cases starting to flood the courts. Chapters 7 and 8 elucidate how the court's interventionist mandate was strengthened as the country became increasingly alarmed at child maltreatment. Soon the federal government would empower the court with even greater authority over families.

7

Creating a Family Court Industry

The 1970s was an extraordinary decade in the transformation of the family court. Following the Supreme Court's mandates to provide "fundamental fairness" in juvenile delinquency proceedings—especially the right to counsel—the juvenile court was tasked with creating hearings that reflected a greater semblance of due process. States also began to redefine "delinquency" to preclude youthful misbehavior; instead these youth were deemed "status offenders." Changing the label of the youth's misbehavior scarcely diminished the court's authority to determine whether these misbehaving youth were in need of "treatment, supervi-

Figure 7.1. New York County Family Court. Permission Jim.henderson, public domain, via Wikimedia Commons.

sion, or confinement." Young people charged with either delinquency or status offenses remained squarely under court dominion.

While the court was grappling with the impact of due process protections in delinquency cases and creating new procedures for status offenders, an even greater challenge surfaced. Changes initiated in child welfare practices in the 1950s and 1960s were aligning with new federal mandates in the 1970s to transfigure the court into a machine processing hundreds of thousands of cases each year. The traditional practice of a judge determining whether delinquent, destitute, or dependent children should be declared "wards of the court" and given services or sent away from home was reconstituted into a complex family regulation system. Federal and state initiatives shifted decision-making and problem-solving to the family court in an increasingly greater numbers of cases, spurring intended and unintended consequences for families, government agencies, and the court system itself and ultimately creating a veritable family court industry. In this chapter I address how that industry was created.

Child Welfare Becomes Foster Care

At the beginning of the twentieth century, the juvenile court had been tasked with providing mothers' aid to assist "suitable"—and almost exclusively—white women whose children were at risk of becoming dependent, destitute, or delinquent.[1] In the early years of the Great Depression, the juvenile court came to be seen as incapable of providing aid effectively to these families. The federal Children's Bureau began to advocate instead for counties and states to develop child welfare agencies able to provide an array of services for families in need. Katherine Lenroot, who in 1934 became the third director of the Children's Bureau, advocated for adding provisions to the 1935 Social Security Act to foster creation of statewide child welfare agencies; by 1939, every state had created agencies under plans approved by the Children's Bureau. The purpose of the child welfare program "was to establish, extend, and strengthen public-welfare services . . . for the protection and care of homeless, dependent, and neglected children, and children in danger of becoming delinquent."[2] Lenroot and her colleagues hoped to shift services out of juvenile court because these leaders had come to believe that the court was ineffective at its broad treatment goals and should content itself solely with adjudicating cases that had significant legal consequences. Increasingly they saw social work and mental health treatment as community-based, preventive measures to keep children out of court, not as components of the court's work. The court's reliance on punitive responses when therapeutic ones failed was especially worrisome to them.[3]

The public child welfare system created by the 1935 Social Security Act to provide financial support—first as Aid to Dependent Children (ADC) and eventually Aid to Families with Dependent Children (AFDC)—nevertheless remained rooted in the mothers' aid initiative that the early juvenile court had administered. Most of the white child-savers of the early era had been intent on transforming poor immigrant families into acceptable versions of white middle-class families. The meager aid distributed by the juvenile court was conditioned on "suitable home" requirements, ensuring that only mothers considered morally fit received support. Black mothers were excluded almost entirely.[4]

The creation of federal ADC was complicated by this history of oppressive racism toward Black mothers and children. While the federal government supplied a significant amount of the funding, states were permitted to set their own "suitability" standards for mothers applying for ADC. Relying on local white norms and prejudices, Black homes—particularly throughout the South—were considered immoral for having living arrangements that did not meet white middle-class standards. From 1955 until 1959, Southern states arbitrarily denied a majority of Black families any ADC without consequences from the federal government. In the wake of *Brown v. Board of Education* and other civil rights efforts, Southern states renewed suitable home rules to force Black families further into poverty with the explicit intention that they would flee the states and integration mandates would be minimized. In 1960, Louisiana tossed 23,000 Black children off the rolls because their parents were not married. This followed mass expulsions in other Southern states.[5]

The federal government finally responded with a rule requiring some greater definition of "unsuitable" and some services to these so-called unsuitable families. Known as the "Flemming Rule" (after Secretary of Health, Education, and Welfare Arthur Flemming, who served in President Dwight Eisenhower's cabinet), it was later incorporated into federal law. The rule shifted the focus away from the parent's unsuitability to considering whether, because she was applying for aid, the mother could not properly shelter, feed, and clothe her children. Parents could no longer just decide to withdraw their requests for ADC and keep their children at home. Now the child could be identified during the application process as neglected and then removed. Workers who were untrained or uninterested in providing services to these families instead increasingly removed the children and placed them in foster care.[6] Ultimately, tens of thousands of Black children were removed from their homes. As Professor Laura Briggs has written, this policy "transformed ADC and foster care from a system that ignored Black children to one that acted vigorously to take them."[7]

The control and distribution of ADC funds also engendered fights between the federal and state or local governments. The women in control of the Children's Bureau continued to champion a therapeutic casework approach to aid, wanting to anchor it to interventions that would not only provide material support but also continue to assist families in their march toward middle class self-reliance and well-being. States and localities, however, were more focused on drawing down federal moneys to substitute for the drain on public relief coffers and to minimize the cost of administering the programs. This led to hiring the least expensive workers to administer payments and not the trained social work professionals whose role was to find and assist families who needed not only material assistance but also therapeutic intervention.[8] Ironically, when states did hire trained social workers, they were often critical of the programs' focusing on eligibility and fraud, determining "suitable homes" standards, and requiring mothers to sue absent fathers for support.[9] Their administrative duties to monitor income requirements constrained their desire to provide more holistic assistance to families. Eventually, and with their collaboration, income supports under AFDC and other types of supportive social services were decoupled. AFDC remained an open-ended entitlement and the social services component of the program was capped, eventually losing half its value between the mid-1970s and early 1990s. Social workers no longer had to determine income eligibility but over time had fewer and fewer resources for the treatment and service programs they used to assist families, what one set of commentators called their "Faustian bargain."[10]

A further unintended consequence of this funding policy was that thousands of children across the country remained in foster care, since there were no federal rules governing foster care time limits and no financial incentives to return children home.[11] Public assistance was not constructed as a foster care program but only as a federal funding source for placement of children removed from parents who otherwise qualified for financial support. A policy to provide financial or other social service assistance to families so they could remain together never materialized.[12] The result came to be known as "foster care drift," with hundreds of thousands of children nationwide in the 1950s and 1960s spending years in foster care with no plan to return them home to their families. The highest percentage of children placed were from communities with the smallest public assistance grants.[13] One-fifth of these children were away from their parents for longer than six years; between 30–40 percent of children who entered foster care never returned home to their parents.[14] During this period, courts rarely terminated parental rights; children simply remained in the foster care system.[15] Attention to these languishing children was finally sparked in part by the country's increased concern with child abuse and with policies that would create a system of child protection that would soon be overseen by an immensely expanded family court.

Child Protection Mandates Start to Shape Family Court

The issue of child protection exploded on the national stage with the so-called discovery of child abuse by Dr. C. Henry Kempe in 1962. Dr. Kempe and his colleagues labeled the emerging documentation of physical abuse of children under three as "battered child syndrome" and provided an explanation for injuries that had previously been inadequately or inconsistently explained. The country was shocked by Kempe's findings, spurring the Children's Bureau to propose model child abuse reporting laws.[16] By 1966, only four years after Kempe's hospital study, all fifty states had adopted legislation to regulate child abuse; by 1968 all states had adopted mandatory child abuse reporting laws, first for physicians but soon expanding to teachers and other professionals working with children.[17]

When Kempe and his associates reported their findings about serious physical abuse, they intended to warn health professionals to be on the lookout for a small number of parents who were severely harming their children. They believed that these egregious cases numbered in the hundreds and that reporting to public authorities would keep this small number of children safe. The swift actions of states to promulgate reporting laws reflected the assumption that a limited number of children were involved, since only one state appropriated additional resources for the reporting system.[18] But Kempe was wrong. While fewer than 10,000 reports were filed in 1967, by 1979 almost a million reports were filed.[19] In 2019, 4.4 million reports were filed on approximately 7.9 million children.[20] Today, investigations have become commonplace in marginalized communities; poor, Black, and Native American families disproportionately come into contact with child protective services. Over one in three children nationwide—and over half of Black children—experience a child maltreatment investigation by age eighteen.[21] The vast majority of these reports are screened out and never result in further action or services, but at least half a million cases will eventually reach family courts.[22]

Equally pivotal to creating a family court industry was the passage in 1974 of the first federal child protection legislation: the Child Abuse Prevention and Treatment Act (CAPTA). CAPTA defined "child abuse and neglect" as "the physical or mental injury, sexual abuse, negligent treatment, or maltreatment of a child under the age of eighteen by a person who is responsible for the child's welfare under circumstances which indicate that the child's health or welfare is harmed or threatened thereby."[23] For states to receive federal funding to assist them with their burgeoning child protection systems, they had to adopt this broader definition. They all did.[24] Unlike physical injury, "mental injury, negligent treatment, or maltreatment" that harms or threatens to harm a child's welfare or health are far harder to define. The CAPTA definition required child protection systems and family courts to think about parents (and other guardians and caretakers) who were not abusive. This includes parents who could use corporal punishment legally as long as it wasn't excessive; parents who might not meet their basic parental responsibilities because of poverty, marginalization, mental illness, or substance use; and parents who tried but were unable to take sufficient care of their children, often for reasons far beyond their control.

It is important to pause a moment to consider the underlying meaning of child abuse, what we decide to label "child abuse or neglect," and who is held responsible. Scholars have long decried blaming parents for abusing and/or neglecting their children without acknowledging the larger political context.[25] Two years after CAPTA's passage, Professor David Gil—a leading researcher in violence against children—lambasted the definition of "abuse" that solely identified caretakers as responsible for child maltreatment. Instead, Gil posited that

> in a democratic, egalitarian society which we claim to be, every child ought to be deemed of intrinsically equal worth, and, hence entitled to equal social, economic, civil, and political rights, so that he or she may develop freely and fully in accordance with innate potential. When using this value position as frame of reference, child abuse means waste of a child's developmental potential, or interference with a child's development due to circumstances of living that are not conducive to optimal development, irrespective of who or what causes these deficits.[26]

Gil intended to explode the myth that most child abuse is the result of deliberate parental action and instead contextualize child abuse as a societal failure to maximize each child's potential by providing for the essential needs of families to raise their children. He found this structural child abuse in every aspect of national life: nutrition, shelter, employment, health, education, and the intervention of juvenile courts. The "stresses and strains" caused by this societal neglect is not just negligent but intentional, permitting the poverty and racism that permeate society to prevent children from reaching their potential and undermining what it means to grow up in a democratic and egalitarian society.[27] Fifty years later, Professor Nancy Dowd drew the same conclusion, identifying how children "face a reality of unfairness, inequality, differential valuing and potential risk of harm from the state" and calling for a New Deal for children "to ensure the maximum development of every child" based on proactive, affirmative, and egalitarian principles.[28]

This societal understanding and commitment to assisting all families to raise their children to their best potential was not the basis for CAPTA. Instead, CAPTA was enacted with the specific intention of denying that child abuse and neglect were related to poverty, racism, and other inequities and was presented instead as a "class-free, color-blind" approach that signified the personal responsibility of parents. This was done primarily by Senator Walter Mondale to gain bipartisan support and to ensure that President Richard Nixon would not veto the bill on the ground that yet another poverty program was being foisted upon the country. Despite testimony—including from Professor Gil—that linked child abuse to societal inequalities, poverty, and lack of educational opportunity, Mondale repeatedly sidestepped this narrative. Instead of CAPTA providing enhanced financial and material supports to struggling families, states would receive funding to fix defective families. Individual fault and failure would be emphasized rather than the more complex inequalities facing poor and marginalized families.[29]

Fixing defective families allowed the family court to hold on to its therapeutic roots even as it adjudicated specific causes of action against parents under CAPTA's "abuse and neglect" definitions. As Professor Leroy Pelton argued at the time, "the myth [of classlessness] permits many professionals to view child abuse and neglect as psychodynamic problems, in the context of a medical model of 'disease,' 'treatment,' and 'cure,' rather than as predominantly sociological and poverty-related problems."[30] Such a model of treatment and cure was deeply rooted in the family court, harkening back to the very beginning of the juvenile court when judges assumed roles as "doctor-counselors" or "judicial therapists" who "[are] specialists in the art of human relations."[31] The requirements under CAPTA rebooted this therapeutic impulse to fix families.

The Court Fights Back Against Limited Child Protection Jurisdiction

The year 1962 ushered in not only Dr. Kempe's findings but also a new unified family court in New York State, which would serve as a model for other courts around the country. As described in chapter 4, this new court was one of the first to consolidate most (but not all) of the situations where families needed to resolve problems in a court setting: delinquency and status offenses, child maltreatment and support, foster care and adoption, paternity, and nonmarital custody. This unified approach rekindled the early juvenile court's broad jurisdiction over children but differed in recognizing that these types of controversies had their own causes of action. Despite the recommendation that the divorce and marital custody jurisdiction of the New York Supreme Court (which despite the name is the state's trial court of general jurisdiction) be consolidated into the new family court, neither the supreme court judges nor the lawyers appearing before them wanted to remove that authority and cede financial power to the family court.[32] From the beginning, the new family court would supervise mostly families without money. As a *New York Times* reporter wrote only four years after the court was established: "It is a poor man's court. Lawyers are rare, courtrooms are bare. . . . Negro and Puerto Rican families predominate, and many regard the trappings of justice with bitterness and suspicion. Tears flow from their immobile faces."[33]

The New York family court, like others being created around the country, was intent on consolidating the issues not only to minimize the number of courts adjudicating overlapping issues but also to solidify control by the judge over the therapeutic interventions the court would provide, either through its own auxiliary services or in concert with other public and private agencies. These new family courts were a bulwark against the growing alarm that the juvenile court was incapable of fulfilling its therapeutic mission.

The movement to reinvigorate the court was led by Judge Paul Alexander, sitting in Toledo, Ohio. Juvenile and family court judges were fighting a three-front battle to maintain discretionary control over delinquent, misbehaving, and dependent children and their families. The first front was against critics who increasingly were troubled by the lack of due process protections for children charged as delinquent.[34] As I describe in chapter 5, their concerns would reach the U.S. Supreme Court, where, in a series of cases between 1966 and 1971, the Court would impose on the juvenile court "fundamental fairness" due process requirements that limited the court's discretionary power, particularly during the adjudicatory phase of proceedings. The second front was to maintain authority over status-offense cases, as they were severed from delinquency jurisdiction. As chapter 6 revealed, juvenile and family court judges, after losing the due process battle on the delinquency front, fought hard to retain their discretionary authority over status offenders, first in their rejection of the ABA/IJA Juvenile Justice Standards to eliminate status offenses entirely, and later in their attempts to preserve the ability to lock up status offenders who violated a court order. The third front was over children who had been labeled "dependent" in the original juvenile court.

The federal government strengthened and consolidated more authority over dependent and maltreated children by state and local governments' child protection agencies through the provision of AFDC for foster care, mandated reporting requirements, and eventually CAPTA. This led increasingly to questioning what types of dependency or maltreatment cases belonged before the court and what rights parents had to maintain control over their children. Scholars already dismayed with the ways delinquent youth were treated in court began challenging the poverty-based criteria for charging parents with maltreatment and allowing the court to decide that it would be in a child's best interests to be removed from her parents based on such criteria.[35] As with status offenses, the deepest investigation into the bases for the state to bring maltreatment allegations to the family court was conducted by the ABA/IJA Juvenile Justice Standards Project. The proposed *Abuse and Neglect* volume was controversial and was still being revised in committee when the overall project ended, losing the opportunity for final approval by the ABA House of Delegates.[36] Nevertheless, the volume and its proposals were hotly contested.

Like the *Noncriminal Misbehavior* volume concerning status offenses, the *Abuse and Neglect* volume at its core was about the extent to which the state intervenes in the life of a family. Barbara Flicker, executive editor of the project, described three aspects of overall intervention that the JJ Standards considered: the *grounds for intervention*, the *sources of intervention*, and the *nature of intervention*. In the context of abuse and neglect, the questions were: First, what is the basis for the state to identify and pursue parental conduct that places a child at risk of harm? Second, what agents of the state, including child protective investigators, attorneys, and judges, act on the identified conduct? And third, given the power to act, what can those actions consist of, including removing a child from home, providing or requiring services or treatment for the family, or even ending the parent-child relationship?

Flicker summarized the profundity of intervention by saying: "As a whole, the three factors indicated could be seen as constituting the single issue of jurisdiction, which fixes the power or authority of any entity to control an individual."[37] The fear of that authority drove the JJ Standards Project to conclude that "intervention, however benevolently intended, could be harmful and must be limited strictly to actions warranting official state coercion."[38] This conclusion was widely regarded as a loss of important discretion by state actors—especially judges—to protect children. The JJ Standards Project nevertheless chose to maintain its fidelity to limited state action and minimal discretion on the part of state actors.[39] The drafters believed intervention was doing more harm than good for most children and needed to be curtailed. The standards urged states to establish narrowly defined grounds for state intervention only when the child was suffering or at risk of imminently suffering serious physical, emotional, or sexual harm, lacked seriously needed medical treatment, or was being encouraged in delinquent behavior.[40] Vague standards of dependency or maltreatment that permitted intervention when a home was "unsuitable" or a child was not "adequately" being cared for led to arbitrary and intrusive decision-making by investigators, social workers, and judges.

Professor Michael Wald served as one of the reporters for the *Abuse and Neglect* volume. Two years after CAPTA's creation of broad categories for neglect in 1974, he wrote about the proposed abuse and neglect standards in an oft-cited law review article:

> Specific standards are more likely to be applied evenhandedly and without economic or cultural discrimination. Carefully drawn, specific standards also can present issues within a court's competence to decide. Current laws not only presume expertise that courts often lack, they also call upon courts to decide issues that cannot be easily adjudicated, such as what is a child's "best interest." Finally, vague standards require judges to make value judgments that are appropriately made only by legislators. The proposed standards place the responsibility of making value judgments at the legislative level, while leaving courts the still very difficult task of applying the standards in a given case.[41]

Specific, narrowly drawn standards were intended to shift the focus from holding parents responsible for their poverty or inability to conform to certain normative criteria to identifying the actual or likely harm to children of remaining with their parents. The issues were not only what trauma or insufficiency the child was experiencing at home but also what trauma would the child experience if the state intervened in the family's life. Except for those narrowly defined instances when court intervention was required, the JJ Standards recommended readily available, voluntary, community-based services without the need for court jurisdiction to access those services when families needed assistance. This was consistent with the type of services the JJ Standards had recommended in the *Noncriminal Misbehavior* volume. This recommendation was also consistent with efforts going back as far as 1914, when the sociologist Thomas Elliot began urging community-based voluntary services for families as an alternative to juvenile court intervention, and which would find its fullest realization in the Children's Bureau's support in the 1930s for shifting treatment and supervision away from the court and into community-oriented social welfare departments.[42]

While the *Abuse and Neglect* volume was not adopted before the project ended—and probably would have been rejected by the ABA's nationally representative House of Delegates—it is worth noting how vehemently the volume was opposed by family court judges. Justine Wise Polier, one of the most well-known family court judges in the country at the time, served as a member of the JJ Standards commission. Polier had been appointed to sit on the domestic relations court by Mayor Fiorello La Guardia in the 1930s and was a staunch supporter of integrating court-related services and processes and eradicating racism in the court. She also strongly believed in the therapeutic power of the family court and was dismissive of anyone characterizing the court as a coercive and ineffective instrument. Polier's dissenting statement in the *Abuse and Neglect* volume rejected what she considered to be the misplaced safeguarding of family autonomy over the child's best interests. She feared that leaving most children without court protection by more narrowly defining "endangerment" would result in far greater harm than bringing them into the court system. Polier was subscribing to the "safer course" approach that believed removing children from potentially unfit homes was less traumatic than the consequences of removal and placement in foster care. While later in the century the trauma of removal would come to inform judicial decisions more regularly, at the time Polier's position supporting court intervention was the norm. She believed that restricting court jurisdiction when insufficient attention and resources were available for voluntary use jeopardized children's well-being. Judge Polier also feared parents would not voluntarily seek what assistance was available in the community and that children would remain at risk without the court-mandated services. Remarkably, she blames the 1970s as a decade of "disillusionment, frustration, and increasing avoidance of concern for human problems" and for "lowering goals required to protect children." The family court with broad jurisdiction, she believed, was necessary to raise those goals.[43]

Another of Judge Polier's family court colleagues made similar charges against the *Abuse and Neglect* volume. Judge Nanette Dembitz, a cousin of Justice Louis Brandeis and a New York City family court judge appointed by Mayor John Lindsay, wrote about several aspects of the volume in the *Harvard Law Review*.[44] Judge Dembitz—before whom I fearfully appeared as a young lawyer soon after her article was published—can barely contain her anger at the suggestion of balancing the harms of intervention against the harms of no action. She believed that the *parens patriae* justification that underlay the original juvenile court remained as necessary for the court in 1978 as it had been in 1899. In her view, if some judges get it wrong some of the time or some cases smack of misplaced value judgments, the state must still be allowed to overcome parental autonomy to protect far more children than the JJ Standards would allow.

Judge Dembitz offered several of her own cases as examples of parental neglect that she believed would not meet the proposed standards. Her examples included a severely mentally ill mother verbally assaulting and beating her children with cords and sticks, and another repeatedly locking her child out of the house so he had to beg for food, not registering him in school, and allowing her paramours to beat him.[45] In fact, these conditions are exactly those contemplated in the JJ Standards definitions of "abuse" and "neglect" and would at a minimum generate an investigation into the child's safety and offers of assistance but, given their seriousness, would have triggered court jurisdiction. Judge Dembitz was as equally dismissive as Judge Polier of relying on voluntary services, but the ones she mentions as routinely being offered to parents before being charged in court were already known to be ineffective, especially casework counseling and referrals to other agencies for assistance.[46] As Professor Duncan Lindsey chronicled in his sweeping review of child protection, studies beginning in the early 1950s of agency interventions known as "casework" offered without concrete and material assistance were ineffective for children and families.[47] The voluntary services proposed by the JJ Standards, on the contrary, included day care, income maintenance, and health insurance—all services still unavailable for many families today.[48]

Judge Dembitz shared the opinion of most of her judicial colleagues that limiting the jurisdiction of the court and the discretion of judges would harm children, ignoring the harm that the CAPTA bases for jurisdiction did by sweeping far too many families into court who didn't need to be there and then mandating ineffective services.[49] She also ignored the harm children experienced in foster care, from living in "unsafe and unsanitary conditions, with poorly trained foster parents and without crucial mental health, medical, and education services [to being] abused and neglected at a greater rate than other children, and [having] an increased risk of delinquency and other behavioral problems."[50] Judge Dembitz and so many of her influential colleagues affirmatively rejected the evidence available at the time—from presidential commissions, Supreme Court cases, and reports about their own courts—that state intervention could or did cause harm.[51] Over the next decade, the federal laws that were strengthened to investigate and adjudicate child maltreatment largely affirmed her perspective. The JJ Standards recommendations to strictly limit intervention and provide community-based services and income supports were largely forgotten.

Children in Foster Care and the "Best Interest of the Child" Standard

The "foster care drift" described at the beginning of the chapter had left hundreds of thousands of children in foster care without any long-term planning for them to return to their families or find another home outside of foster care through adoption, guardianship, or custody. Their numbers continued to increase as CAPTA expanded the definitions of "abuse and neglect." Not surprisingly, as children lived longer and longer periods with foster families, they developed relationships that began to substitute for their biological family relationships. Foster parents began to assert that children had the right to remain with them because they were now part of their families. Biological parents, however, argued that no efforts had been made to help them maintain their relationships with their children or to have them returned home to them. To the contrary, foster parents were encouraged to become substitute parents while children were in their care.

What was best for the children stuck for years in limbo became highly contested and ultimately resulted in expanding court jurisdiction for longer periods of time and swelling court dockets. Consistent with the family court's mission to do good, judges conducting reviews of children's foster placements were tasked with deciding what was in the best interests of the child (BIOC). But how did they know whether the child protective agency's position was in the child's best interests or whether they should override that position? The state and federal legislative and judicial resolutions of this struggle during the 1970s were influenced greatly by the first two volumes of a popular trilogy by the psychologists Anna Freud and Albert Solnit and the lawyer Joseph Goldstein: *Beyond the Best Interests of the Child* (1973) and *Before the Best Interests of the Child* (1979). These books tried to define the concept of BIOC in psychological and legal terms. Since family court judges were applying the BIOC standard in most of their decisions, they had a large stake in the definition.

The *Beyond* volume proposed specific legal and psychological guidelines to give meaning to the overarching concept of BIOC whenever a child's placement was at issue.[52] These guidelines were intended to apply in private custody disputes being resolved by courts as well as child protection proceedings. *Beyond*'s guidelines were remarkably simple: once the state has intervened in the autonomy of the family unit, the child's needs become paramount and decision-making must be shaped by the child's sense of time and need for continuity in relationships. The authors warned decision makers in child protection proceedings that they lacked the ability to make long-term predictions on what is best for the child and, to the contrary, were really only determining the least detrimental alternative for the child. What was best—a stable family free from state intervention—had already been lost.[53]

Beyond recommended that lawmakers set a time limit for determining whether a child remained with a new caretaker (usually a foster parent) or be returned to the original caretaker (usually the birth parent) to highlight their psychological theory of continuity and stability of relationships and to give judges a rule to follow in determining what is best—or least bad—for a child separated from her parent.[54] Their recommendations became known as the "psychological parent theory." The centrality of continuity and stability for children and the need for specific guidance in custodial decisions struck a responsive chord for caseworkers and judges hungry to give definition to the BIOC concept that relied far too heavily on personal values and case-by-case decision-making.

Goldstein, Freud, and Solnit were not alone in their concerns about the indeterminacy of BIOC as a legal standard—whether in a private custody proceeding or when a child is placed in foster care. Scholars digesting their ideas became concerned, however, that *Beyond* had failed to distinguish between the private ordering inherent in most custody proceedings between parents and the enormous state power of agencies and judges in child protective proceedings. Professor Robert Mnookin, in a famous rebuttal to *Beyond* written in 1975—just after CAPTA was enacted—warned that states had failed to define clearly the circumstances to justify initial intervention in families, removal of children, and the appropriate bases for planning for a child once removed from parental care. Mnookin joined his Stanford colleague Michael Wald in recommending that child protection intervention be substantially limited to issues of physical health that can be determined clearly to present immediate or substantial risk to the child. Mnookin feared the power of the state to intervene in family autonomy for reasons more related to racial, cultural, and economic biases. He warned that using *Beyond*'s psychological parenting theory alone to define BIOC in a more determinate way failed to answer fundamental policy questions about the state's obligation to the family when the state removes children from their parents' care and has the power, ultimately, to terminate parental rights and give the child to a new family.[55]

One way to read *Before*, the second volume of the trilogy, is as a response to Mnookin's concerns. *Before* offers guidelines for the provision of reunification services for separated families and a specific time frame for when the state should stop attempting reunification and support the creation of another family for a child.[56] More fundamentally, *Before* is a powerful portrayal of families and of the state's power to destroy families. *Before* identifies three overlapping elements that emerge from the psychological, historical, and philosophical underpinnings of families: *parental autonomy to raise children; the children's right to have autonomous parents;* and *privacy for the family unit.* These elements form a core of "family integrity" that cannot be breached by state authorities except under two conditions. The first condition is when society as a whole has expectations for all children that individual families must obey, such as mandatory education, labor restrictions for minors, and vaccination policies. The second condition is when the state intervenes in the parenting decisions of individual families because those parents have failed to meet basic health and safety standards for children.[57]

Before prophetically warns of the difficulty in defining such an indeterminate standard as BIOC to intervene in families. The fear of state overreach narrows the acceptable bases for intervention considerably—and in ways similar to the soon-to-be-abandoned JJ Standards' *Abuse and Neglect* recommendations—by requiring a child's physical health to be at risk of impairment or impaired (whether through physical or sexual abuse or by neglect) before the state can intervene to protect the child. Grounds that rely on concepts of emotional neglect, actions of parents that can be interpreted through cultural biases, and conditions that spring predominantly from poverty should not fall within the state's power to intervene except through the provision of public benefits or voluntarily accepted services.[58] The authors note with dismay how the mandatory reporting laws that had been in place for little more than a decade had "contributed too little to protecting children" and instead had led to intrusive investigations of families needing "accessible and attractive services," not coercive intervention. The *Before* volume keeps the state at bay for all but the clearest provable examples of child maltreatment in order to limit intrusion into family privacy.[59] Nevertheless, once the intervention occurs and a child's placement is disturbed, Goldstein, Freud, and Solnit remained committed to the psychological theory developed in *Beyond*: the child's best interests are served by supporting whatever psychological parent-child relationship ensues, including a new parental relationship if the previous, usually biologically based, psychological relationship is irrevocably broken.

Before was also a response to the Supreme Court's 1977 decision in *Smith v. Organization of Foster Families for Equality and Reform* (*OFFER*). Relying in large part on the psychological parent theory developed in *Beyond*, a New York foster parent organization challenged city and state procedures for removing foster children from foster parents and placing them in another foster home or returning them to their birth parents. Unlike many other states at the time, New York's statutory and regulatory framework in child protection and foster care proceedings included specific procedures that a foster parent could invoke to challenge a proposed removal of a child from the foster home. In *OFFER*, the foster parents contended that, when a child lived with a foster family for a year or more, a "psychological family" was created that had a "liberty interest" to be protected similar to that of a biological family under the Fourteenth Amendment. They argued that the current process for removing children from their care did not sufficiently protect this liberty interest in the psychological family.[60] The authors of *Beyond* submitted an amicus brief supporting this position when the case reached the Supreme Court.[61]

In its decision, the Court was certainly solicitous of this foster relationship, noting: "No one would seriously dispute that a deeply loving and interdependent relationship between an adult and a child in his or her care may exist even in the absence of blood relationship" and rejecting the idea that a foster family is just a collection of unrelated individuals.[62] For that reason, the Court concluded that a foster family had some right to a fair procedure before children were removed from their care. But a relationship created by the state after involuntarily removing children from their biological families (or even voluntarily taking care of a child at the request of the parent) cannot be protected more than the biological relationship with a fit parent:

> It is one thing to say that individuals may acquire a liberty interest against arbitrary governmental interference in the family-like associations into which they have freely entered, even in the absence of biological connection or state-law recognition of the relationship. It is quite another to say that one may acquire such an interest in the face of another's constitutionally recognized liberty interest that derives from blood relationship, state-law sanction, and basic human right an interest the foster parent has

recognized by contract from the outset. *Whatever liberty interest might otherwise exist in the foster family as an institution, that interest must be substantially attenuated where the proposed removal from the foster family is to return the child to his natural parents.*[63]

New York's child protection law affirmatively protected the relationship between a child and a fit parent, even if the child is placed temporarily in foster care. The Court concluded that the central policy of the New York system is that "it is generally desirable for the child to remain with or be returned to the natural parent because the child's need for a normal family life will usually best be met in the natural home."[64] The Court was skeptical of an open-ended concept of "psychological parenting," noting that even Goldstein, Freud, and Solnit had not specifically identified the point at which a caretaker became a psychological parent.[65]

The authors offered an answer to the Court and to critics like Mnookin in their reply in *Before*: while there is a point when a child has the right to the new psychological relationship created by the state, that point cannot even be contemplated without first protecting the relationship of the biological family. The authors were aware—as the Court had been in *OFFER*—that the families being disrupted were poor and disproportionately families of color, far more likely to be deemed unfit by middle class professionals. Their goal was to diminish the indeterminacy of the BIOC standard by providing guidelines for decision-making to replace the value-laden, personal biases of the professionals involved with these families.[66] Limiting the grounds for removal and requiring readily available, voluntary services and assistance were essential elements to prevent family disruption. If a child had to be removed, a specific timeline must be established for returning a child home or recognizing the new psychological relationship. The foster care drift that had disrupted so many families and led to children spending years in limbo had also surfaced competing ideas about the best resolution of the dilemma. A new paradigm for child welfare and family court decision-making was emerging that would soon take form based on Goldstein, Freud, and Solnit's ideas about what to do with children at risk of or actually removed from their families. This paradigm would greatly expand the family court's supervision of families and child protection agencies.

The Adoption Assistance and Child Welfare Act and the Rise of Permanency

In 1977, the year *OFFER* was decided, nearly 500,000 children nationwide were languishing in foster care, spending a median of two and a half years in care and with 38 percent of all children staying in care over two years.[67] Congress began to realize that open-ended funding for foster care and dysfunctional state child welfare systems had condemned hundreds of thousands of children to living in state care with little hope of returning to their families. Goldstein, Freud, and Solnit had offered a new way to conceptualize BIOC in the child welfare realm: a child-centered way of thinking about supporting families to prevent foster care, quickly reuniting separated families, and supporting new psychological parents (essentially foster parents) when reunification efforts failed. This seemingly child-centered approach was consistent with the child investigation and protection system established by CAPTA in 1974. The result was a new law based on the concept of so-called *permanency planning*: the Adoption Assistance and Child Welfare Act (AACWA).[68] AACWA now required states to work for their federal foster care funding. Child welfare agencies would have to employ "reasonable efforts" to keep children safely at home with their parents and avoid unnecessary removals; if children could not remain safely at home, "reasonable efforts" were also required to try to reunify families. If a child remained in care for eighteen months, a family court review was mandated to determine a permanent resolution rather than permitting endless stays in foster care.[69]

To monitor these requirements, child welfare agencies were required to develop family case plans, and states had to conduct administrative or judicial reviews. Congress allocated funds to implement reasonable efforts for "preventive services" (to keep children at home) or "reunification services" (to return them there). Congress also included an "adoption incentive" to subsidize adoption if a child, despite reunification services, could not return home to her parents. The sad history of the AACWA is that the funds were never sufficiently allocated, state child welfare systems never fully embraced prevention and reunification, and the monitoring mechanisms—including the family court—never accomplished the law's goals.

To determine whether preventive and reunification services could indeed keep families together, appropriate funding was necessary to pay for those services and then evaluate them. Several promising "permanency planning" demonstration projects had indicated that a combination of decisive decision-making and effective services at every stage that a family was involved in in the child welfare system would result in fewer children being removed from their families, fewer children remaining in foster care, and permanency plans well-made if children could not return home. As Professor Duncan Lindsey concluded in his important analysis of this approach to permanency planning: "The studies demonstrated the potential of child welfare professionals using research-based knowledge to achieve more effective social service programs."[70]

Despite Congress initially allocating funds to implement reasonable efforts and the development of promising preventive programs, when the Ronald Reagan administration swept into office in 1981, support for major demonstration projects ended and significant reductions were imposed on federal spending on social programs.[71] The combined total federal funding for social services for children and families was scheduled to increase between FY 1981 and FY 1985 from \$3 billion to \$3.7 billion. Instead, by 1985, funding had been reduced to \$2.8 billion; only foster care remained an open-ended mandate for eligible children.[72] In anticipation of well-funded community support services for families under the AACWA, child protection workers had left children at home or began reuniting them with their parents. The foster care population plummeted by half from 1977 to 1983. When funding was cut and the families failed to get the anticipated assistance, "permanency planning became a revolving door," with children being placed in foster care, sent home, and then re-placed in foster care.[73] Without the services necessary to support parents in keeping their children well cared for at home, the investigatory and accusatory thrust of CAPTA became the dominant child welfare paradigm; placement became the primary response. Investigating a family and finding some evidence of maltreatment—especially maltreatment that was more about poverty and the stresses of parenting—were much easier than addressing the complex issues undermining the family's stability.

While the aspirations of "reasonable efforts" could never be achieved without funding, they correspondingly couldn't be achieved without definition. No federal administration ever promulgated regulations defining reasonable efforts under the AACWA.[74] This left child protection agencies and family courts struggling to define them. What, exactly, were "reasonable efforts" to keep a child safely at home or to reunify a family if there were few services to offer or if the services available did not match the needs of the families? What were reasonable efforts for a caseworker responsible for dozens if not hundreds of cases? What were reasonable efforts to engage families in figuring out what was wrong when the new federal law also included extensive paperwork obligations and multiple appearances at administrative and court reviews? Judges, with broad discretionary authority, were supposed to decide.

I began my career as a lawyer for children in delinquency and child welfare cases in 1980, the year that the AACWA became law. New York had already adopted its own child welfare reform legislation the year before, serving in part as a model for the AACWA. Everyone was reading Goldstein, Freud, and Solnit then, and we knew that caseworkers were supposed to be using the "psychological parent theory" in applying "reasonable efforts" to try to prevent children from being removed from their parents or to reunify them. If the children were lingering in foster care for too long, then the theory was supposed to be applied to the children's relationship with their new parents—that is, their foster parents. The monitoring provisions of both the New York law and the AACWA required administrative and court reviews of those efforts.

In New York, the family court was charged with determining whether reasonable efforts had been implemented at every stage of the process: at the point when a child might be removed from a parent (or had been removed in an emergency); if a parent had been found to neglect or abuse the child; at the dispositional hearing to determine if the child should be placed (or stay) in care or go home and what help the family may have needed for the child to stay home safely; and, if the child was in foster care, at any subsequent court hearing to determine whether the child would remain in care, return home, or even be freed for adoption. Given the purported priority of reunification before any other permanency plan under both state and federal law at the time, New York bestowed on these subsequent foster care hearings the ironic title of "extension of placement" hearings rather than "reunification hearings." The "reasonable efforts" determination was not only a legal requirement but also a fiscal one. If the judge did not find reasonable efforts on the part of the child welfare agency, federal funding was placed in jeopardy.[75] A "reasonable efforts made" check box was added to all the relevant court order forms to expedite court decision-making (but also to secure federal funds).

When I look back at those proceedings forty years ago, I am appalled and ashamed by my practice, the practice of my office, and the practice of the court. At the initial removal hearings, we focused solely on the children's safety, with the judge finding mostly that the children couldn't live safely at home. I doubt the words "reasonable efforts" were ever uttered (even if the judge checked off a box saying these efforts had been made). I rarely remember any discussion about whether there were services available so that the family could remain intact. If there weren't a grandmother or an aunt willing to take the child, foster care was the answer. This was the "safer course" that judges took: bringing the family under the court's therapeutic mantle to ensure the family received help and the child remained safe in the meantime. Because court dockets were so crowded, the fact-finding hearing to determine whether a parent had been neglectful or abusive generally was held many months after the child had been removed. During that period, it was very unusual for parents to receive any services that might have led to reunification. Often, they barely saw their children; official policy at the time permitted visits for as little as an hour every other week. Judges rarely ordered additional family time. Instead, children were supposed to settle into their foster homes and parents were supposed to contemplate their transgressions.

Once a fact-finding hearing was held to determine if the parents had, in fact, maltreated their children or, more likely, the parents "admitted" to some version of the charges against them—having conferred with their lawyers for a few minutes before entering the courtroom—several more months went by before a dispositional hearing was held to decide what should happen to the children. This period should have been the time when efforts were redoubled to see if the children could return home and what plan could keep them there safely. Instead, the time was routinely used for an "investigation-and-report," which usually provided all the reasons why the children were better off staying in care. A typical investigation-and-report case plan for the parents to get their children back included casework counseling, parenting classes, substance abuse testing, referrals to therapy, and that same paltry visiting schedule—which, if anyone had thought about it, added up to a total of two or three days of contact between parents and children in a year. These generic services rarely addressed the family's specific needs: Parents of teenagers were routinely sent to parenting classes for infants, and mothers were enrolled in substance abuse programs designed for single men. The parents' attorneys, usually court-assigned counsel with hundreds of clients, and the children's attorneys (then called "law guardians") seldom challenged the proposed plans. Once the dispositional hearing was over, I distinctly remember filing the case in the "closed" drawer in my office because the next hearing wasn't for eighteen months. Essentially, I had allowed the court to consign my young clients to a lengthy stay in foster care with no meaningful plan or services in place to reunify them with their family and, except in rare cases, to think about them again until a year and a half later. The therapeutic assistance contemplated by the court's discretionary power devolved into little more than rubber-stamping agency decisions on tens of thousands of cases moving along an assembly line.

And it gets worse. At the extension-of-placement hearing, the foster care agency routinely asked for an adjournment because the necessary reports were not ready. Other than hounding the agency for those reports, I rarely developed an independent proposal. My job was to interview my clients (who had not seen me in more than a year or maybe had never seen me because I inherited their case from someone else or they had been too young to interview) and see how they were doing in foster care. Sometimes they wanted to go home and I supported that; sometimes they wanted to stay in foster care and I supported that. Mostly I remember telling them that even if they wanted to go home—and my job was to tell the judge that—the judge wasn't likely to send them home because their parents weren't yet ready to take care of them. Of course, they weren't ready! Either no one had done the hard work necessary to identify the real problems facing the family and provide the right assistance or, even more commonly, the original problems that had been the basis for the removal had masked the far more complicated issues facing the family that had eventually come to light. So even if the parents had complied with the initial mediocre service plan, the underlying issues often remained unresolved, and neither the agency nor the judge (nor in many cases the child's attorney) could recommend the child returning home. Despite this scenario, judges hearing hundreds of cases every week routinely found that reasonable efforts at reunification had been made before extending the child's placement in foster care. That any of my clients ever returned to their families seems miraculous to me now.

The practices I just described were captured ten years later in a Vera Institute of Justice study of the family courts in Bronx and New York Counties. The study found that services were discussed in fewer than a quarter of the eighteen-month review cases and that judicial hearings held to determine whether a child should remain in foster care, return to her parents, or be freed for adoption—and what efforts were needed to accomplish the chosen goal—took five minutes on average in New York County and ten minutes in the Bronx.[76] This lack of meaningful judicial oversight combined with significant federal funding cuts resulted in an explosion of children in foster care. By 1997, the foster care numbers had shot back up to their pre-AACWA levels.[77]

New York was not alone in perpetuating this charade. During a congressional hearing in 1988, under questioning by Representative George Miller, a longtime child advocate in the House, Jane Burnley, the associate commissioner for the Children's Bureau, acknowledged that, in the federal case file reviews to determine whether reasonable efforts had been made by state child welfare agencies in individual cases, all her office could tell was that the form had been filled out by the judge, not that "reasonable efforts" had in fact been used to eliminate the need for placement.[78] The Office of the Inspector General of the Department of Health and Human Services came to a similar conclusion: "The [SSA] Title IV-E review process is often focused on whether certain forms are filled out appropriately rather than whether, in fact, the purpose of the law in preventing unnecessary placements is being met."[79] That Title IV-E review process was supposed to ensure that states were not being reimbursed for failing to comply with the provisions of the AACWA. However, even when states were found to be noncompliant during that period, Congress was reluctant to enforce disallowances, placing several moratoriums on planned fiscal sanctions with several explanations: confusion about the standards that states were supposed to meet; reviews that often applied to time periods long past; no mechanisms included for helping the states improve; and states sometimes being held responsible for circumstances beyond their control, like decisions and schedules of the courts.[80] My complicity in this farce was disgraceful, and the fact that it was being duplicated throughout the country does not diminish that disgrace. Without clear standards and regulations, sufficient funding, appropriate services, proper court supervision, and federal enforcement, the AACWA's goal of maintaining and reunifying families was doomed to fail.[81] While the AACWA's intent was for judges to take on a supervisory role of increasing responsibility, instead most judges found themselves making sure that the assembly line kept moving.

The decade and a half following the passage of the AACWA presented some of the most complicated challenges for families at risk of entering the child welfare system. The first was that funding specifically targeted for early intervention or prevention was reduced substantially. Those reductions were consistent, unfortunately, with the broader federal treatment of child welfare issues. Not only were final AACWA regulations never promulgated to guide states, the Department of Health and Human Services "could neither implement legislation adequately nor advise the Congress," as it had lost staff with expertise in foster care, adoption services, and training and ceased compiling essential data.[82] States did not step in to compensate for the failure of federal leadership:

> [Even] more disturbing is the realization that the child welfare "system" is no system at all. The federal leadership in promoting professional standards of practice and effective policy initiatives has permitted 50 different state "systems" to operate. . . . [As a result] the children's agencies in each state are overwhelmed by the number of cases, caseworkers are inadequately trained and responsible for too many children, and the resources for assisting families (such as public housing, prenatal care, and drug-treatment programs) are insufficient for the demand.[83]

Without adequate and flexible federal funding and professional guidance, social work professionals were increasingly frustrated with the limitations of their roles. Many states downgraded these positions to nonprofessional jobs that cost less and focused more on investigating than assisting families. The subsequent demoralized staff were caught between the AACWA's ideology of making efforts to keep children safely at home and the reality that the only fully funded service for families was placement in foster care.[84]

The families being investigated were in need of more assistance, not less. In his sweeping study *The Welfare of Children*, first published in 1994 with a second edition in 2004, Professor Duncan Lindsey rejected the residual approach of child welfare—waiting for a crisis before providing assistance—as unable to address the complex socioeconomic conditions of vulnerable families in the late twentieth century. Like other scholars before and after him, Lindsey persuasively centered poverty and its ensuing hardships as the central challenge of an effective child welfare system. During the first two decades of the AACWA, for example, the poorest families experienced a precipitous decline in their economic condition, with the poorest 20 percent of families living on less than $14,000 a year. By the 1980s, children were the poorest age group in America.[85] These children faced other indices of poverty: They were more likely to be raised by low-earning mothers; they were more likely to be children of color; if they were born to teenage mothers, they were at greater risk for health problems and poor cognitive functioning; and their parents had fewer educational and economic opportunities.[86] As remains true today, "no single fact about child abuse and neglect . . . has been better documented and established than their strong relationship to poverty and low income."[87]

This bleak economic reality was compounded by several other trends during the 1980s and 1990s. Many older children were being deinstitutionalized without adequate community supports for their mental health or behavioral issues. Deinstitutionalized status offenders did not receive the community-based services they needed; foster care placement became the default service instead. Homelessness, substance abuse addiction, and increasing numbers of babies born HIV-positive or with a positive toxicology for drugs or alcohol increased the severity of the issues facing these families, who had been further marginalized as the public provision of aid decreased.[88] A study by the economists Christopher A. Swann and Michelle Sheran Sylvester added that female incarceration—particularly the number of women imprisoned and their increased average length of sentence following the 1986 Anti-Drug Abuse Act—was the largest contributor to the sharp rise in foster care rates. Incarceration had a direct impact when the parent was in prison, but it also reflected the difficulty former inmates have in regaining custody of their children after being released.[89] In 1995, a Government Accountability Office report on foster care observed that the demands for child welfare services "grew not only because the number of foster children increased but also because families and children were more troubled and had more complex needs than in the past."[90] Families were washed away in the sea of troubles confronting them.

Family Court Holding On

In the meantime, the family court was consolidating its position after a rocky period of adjustment to the new delinquency due process requirements and the reconstitution of court authority over youthful noncriminal misbehavior. Rather than the proposed radical nonintervention that would have removed these youth from court jurisdiction entirely, the diversion systems created and funded to provide alternative supports for youth getting into trouble remained tethered to the court. Swelling numbers of youth and their families found the family court serving as the gatekeeper to diversion services. Whether the court suspended its authority while youth tried the services or the court used its authority to order them into those programs, the court remained central to dealing with these youth. As Professor Andrew Polsky noted in the early 1990s, judges had proved very resistant to their power being diminished. Using growing public sentiment about controlling youth behavior and enlisting allies in state legislatures that respected judicial authority, family court judges actually expanded the court's role. The court and its probation department secured federal funds to bring new programs under their direct control or indirectly used court authority to send youth into favored programs.[91]

Other scholars similarly noted the family court's expanding authority, pointing out that, whenever alternatives to the court were proposed, the court managed to retain its fallback position.[92] Judges regularly contributed to publications like *Juvenile Court Journal* and *Juvenile Justice* in support of the centrality and necessity of a vigorous family court, frequently overstating their cause with dire predictions of the consequences of a diminished court, including greater lawlessness and criminality.[93] At the same time, the AACWA mandates, which ostensibly were enacted to reduce the number of children in foster care, were instead clogging the court with greater numbers of cases that required decisions not only about parental fitness but also regarding what to do when children continued to remain in care. With the JJ Standards recommendations to limit court jurisdiction soundly rebuffed, the family court grew instead. The number of cases and the number of decisions it needed to make in each case soared, as did the number of collaborators it turned to for help, thereby swelling the size of the court and the costs of its operations.

The lack of federal guidance and knowledge following passage of the AACWA and the disorder in the state child protection systems became significant barriers to judges being able to make informed decisions. By the mid-1990s, twenty-one child welfare systems had been sued for being inadequate, with several foster care systems operating under federal supervision.[94] This impact litigation challenged myriad aspects of these systems: the inadequate way families were being investigated; the failure to provide preventive or reunification services to families; the limits on the agencies' ability to recruit and supervise foster parents, group homes, and residential facilities and train and supervise their personnel; the insufficiency in securing adoptive placements and finalizing adoptions; and the lack of post-permanency services to biological and adoptive families or assistance to youth as they aged out of care. In short, child welfare systems were being sued about every aspect of their work because they had failed in every component of their fundamental tasks to protect children and ensure that they were raised in safe, stable, and permanent families.[95]

The reduced financial support from the federal government and the disarray in federal child welfare knowledge not only reduced material assistance and support to families but also further diminished the professionalization of child welfare workers. To save money, states continued to reduce the expertise of their workers, relying increasingly on staff with minimal or no relevant education or experience. By the late 1970s, only 28 percent of public child welfare staff had any social work training, and of the 70–76 percent of the positions that required master of social work degrees, only 33 percent were filled by them. At the same time, states increasingly divided casework into specializations within child welfare, hoping to improve practice within a narrower specialty.

The result instead was even less overall child welfare knowledge—understanding the big picture of what was going on for children and families—and actually diminishing effective permanency outcomes as the number of workers involved in cases increased.[96]

The impact on the court was considerable. Caseworkers responsible for reporting to the court were often unprepared with reports or testimony, in part because of the number of cases but also because of their lack of training and experience. They also resented the haphazard scheduling of court cases. Court hearings often conflicted with their own mandated administrative proceedings, and there were long waits in court for a case to be called. They especially resented judges meddling in their case plans during the few minutes they appeared in court. Proceedings were increasingly considered "assembly line" justice without the time or expertise for anyone, including the judge, to make appropriate decisions.[97] Respect between judges and caseworkers was at a low, and judges began to look for other sources of expertise; but they did not look to lawyers to argue the law and improve outcomes for families.

Access to counsel remained elusive, especially for parents. In 1981, the Supreme Court held that parents facing termination of parental rights did not have an automatic right to counsel; instead, the trial court could make a case-by-case determination.[98] While the Court would hold the following year that termination cases required clear and convincing evidence, this was little solace if a parent didn't have a lawyer to substantiate that standard.[99] Moreover, there was no constitutional right to counsel in the initial child protection proceedings that determined parental unfitness or in the myriad reviews that followed, which mostly employed the vague best-interests-of-the-child standard that gave judges greater discretion. Even in states that provided a right to counsel to parents by statute or court rule in child protection hearings, states and counties have consistently underfunded these mandates, leaving parents without counsel at all or with counsel so overwhelmed and underpaid that provision of counsel becomes a "hollow right."[100] Courts also continued to cling to the promise of informalism in resolving cases—through mediation or case meetings—even as this approach expanded rather than contracted the number of proceedings that needed to be held and the number of participants crowding into the court.[101]

One of the provisions in the 1974 CAPTA law required states to provide *guardians ad litem* (*GALs*) to children in neglect and abuse proceedings to speak on the child's behalf and to provide additional information to the court. The CAPTA requirement provided neither funding nor standards for *GALs*. States implemented the provision in myriad ways, cobbling together combinations of paid and volunteer *GALs*, some of whom were lawyers, social workers, or trained volunteers. There was little uniformity from jurisdiction to jurisdiction or even from court to court on the role and expectations of *GALs*.[102] Nevertheless, the *GAL* provision meant that in most jurisdictions there was another opportunity for the court to secure information. Judges frustrated with local child protection services turned to this new source of assistance with the hope of reinvigorating their own inherent discretionary authority over families and agencies.

Most famously, in 1977, Judge David Soucup of Seattle began an experiment of using trained volunteers called "court appointed special advocates" (CASAs) in his court to serve as *GALs*. Whether or not he knew it, Judge Soucup was reaching back to the founding of the juvenile court for inspiration. The original court had relied on volunteers to staff the early support services like probation and detention homes that were considered essential features of a robust juvenile court. Many of these volunteers had been instrumental in creating the court in the first place. Women like Lucy Flowers in Chicago were "society women who generously supported the building of the city's charitable institutions" alongside their younger counterparts, who were the first generation of educated female child welfare experts.[103] Their work to fund and provide both paid and free assistance to the court established a pattern of turning to available volunteers when the court was especially under-resourced and overwhelmed.[104] Judge Soucup drew on this philanthropic tradition to provide what he believed he desperately needed: "[C]ommunity volunteers to independently investigate the cases, make recommendations, and speak up in court about what was in the best interest of the child."[105] This was so even though the child welfare agency presenting the case to the judge was already supposed to be representing the child's interest and that the "best interest of the child" was ultimately a judicial decision. The CASA programs spread so rapidly and effectively that a national

CASA organization was created only three years later.[106] By 1996, the national organization and its local programs had successfully lobbied for changes to CAPTA's *GAL* provision to permit a CASA to fulfill that role (along with lawyers and social workers who were already being appointed).[107] Many courts encouraged CASA programs to be developed because there were insufficient numbers of trained professionals to serve as *GALs* or judges were dissatisfied with the quality of their work.[108] Assigning a CASA to investigate and report to the court was a means to strengthen the judge's discretionary authority. Yet assigning a CASA also further diminished the professionalism of the voices in the courtroom while supposedly bringing in community voices.

However, as attorneys Amy Mulzer and Tara Urs have persuasively written, the rise of CASAs was not a victory for community participation in family court; it was the opposite. The overwhelmingly white, female, middle-class CASA volunteers have little knowledge or understanding of the communities from which most of the families in these proceedings come.[109] They are not trained professionals who are supposed to be educated in the core knowledge and values of their professions and be held accountable for their work or have any ethical standards for their role.[110] Like the volunteers at the beginning of the twentieth century— the so-called child-savers—these women have been given significant influence over families from cultures and neighborhoods often radically different than their own. The voices of these volunteers often drown out and substitute for the voices of the children or parents whose lives are at stake. Moreover, as Mulzer and Urs argue, because they are volunteers; their voices are imbued with a beneficence not granted to anyone else in the courtroom.[111] In some jurisdictions, like New York City, the role of a CASA is more limited; a CASA is generally providing information and assistance to the court and not recommending a solution to the judge based on their own analysis of "best interests." Even in this role, however, their presence calls into question why the system is so dysfunctional that lay volunteers with minimal training are necessary for the court to make effective decisions. In jurisdictions where a CASA is given far more authority, they can tell the judge what they think the judge should do about almost anything in the case. Should children be visiting their parents more or less? Should parents participate longer in reunification programs? Should children live with relatives or be adopted? This is a dangerous misapplication of the role of volunteers. The fact that judges felt the need to reach out to lay volunteers and give them such authority indicates how dysfunctional the child protection system had become, how little control the courts had over their proceedings, and how desperate judges were to recenter their therapeutic authority.

The ability to assert that authority effectively became increasingly elusive as state and federal policies as well as court administrators kept expanding the number of participants in child welfare proceedings, clogging the courtrooms and hallways of courthouses, making it almost impossible to set calendars dates when everyone could appear, and slowing any effort to reach permanent solutions for families. New York provides a sense of what a courtroom looked like in a child protection proceeding in the early 1990s (granted, a somewhat extreme example because of its commitment to legal representation for parties and its historical practice of contracting with nonprofit foster care agencies). A child protective services (CPS) attorney arrived to present the case with a CPS caseworker and maybe a supervisor; the parents were each entitled to an attorney, who at the time was appointed from a panel and likely was representing a hundred other clients; the child was assigned an attorney (and maybe a social worker) from the Juvenile Rights Division of Legal Aid. If the child had been in care for some time, the foster parent may have attended, occasionally with counsel. Depending on the stage of the proceeding, the private foster care agency caseworker—and maybe her supervisor and the agency attorney—would be there instead of or in addition to the CPS worker and attorney. There may have been a representative of a drug treatment program, a court-based mental health evaluator, a community-based agency involved with the family, or a CASA volunteer. In addition to the judge, there would be a clerk, court officers, the judge's court attorney, and, in some cases, a court reporter, a case coordinator, a social work intern, or another volunteer. Many of the court personnel came in and out of the courtroom. Sometimes other family members or friends attended. Twelve or even fifteen participants routinely filled the small space. The transformation from the judge and his trusty probation officer and the occasional volunteer into a multifarious organizational network that, in fact, extended far beyond the representatives in the courtroom was increasingly typical. The sheer complexity of the system only hints at the challenges of making the most informed and appropriate decisions on behalf of the families that found themselves in the court. Judges seeking solutions would soon be tasked with even greater authority, not only over the families but also over the CPS agencies bringing those families into family court. That additional authority would not, however, prove effective in addressing what by then was called a "national emergency" in child protection.

8

The Federal Family Court

The End of the Twentieth Century

The 1970s and 1980s had established a specific legal approach to child maltreatment that relied on reporting and investigating families and leading to the family court determining "whether legally cognizable abuse or neglect occurred, not to eliminate the situations that threaten children's safety."[1] The mandatory reporting laws had placed child protective services (CPS) caseworkers in the role of inquisitor, building a case against a parent that could result in a petition in family court charging neglect or abuse but rarely getting the family beneficial assistance. Professionals and neighbors had been socialized to call a hotline when they worried about a child, believing that they have done their duty to protect the child or get the family some help. A story recounted by Dr. Abraham Bergman captures this paradigm.

Dr. Bergman recalled giving a talk in 1984 at a national conference on abuse and neglect. His topic was "Does CPS Do More Harm than Good?" and his thesis was that, without proper skills or an ability to provide support, CPS workers are viewed as enemies of families. As he recounted, the audience was so angry that the editor of *Child Abuse and Neglect* (a friend of Bergman's) refused to publish the talk in the journal. Bergman had been deeply involved with child abuse as a hospital physician for decades when he gave that talk. He had observed nurses and social workers reporting every case of potential child maltreatment to the CPS agency, insisting that they were required by law to do so (even before they had sufficiently investigated the situation) or because reporting to CPS might get the family some services. Both misconceptions were dangerous and, as Bergman pointed out to them, wrong.[2] But they accurately reflected what the CPS system had become: a place where the country believed it had fulfilled its duty to keep children safe. That belief had investigated millions of families and helped to place close to a half-million children in foster care in the early 1990s.[3]

When the Child Abuse Prevention and Treatment Act (CAPTA) of 1974 was reauthorized in 1988, it established the U.S. Advisory Board on Child Abuse and Neglect (U.S. Advisory Board) to evaluate CAPTA. The U.S. Advisory Board determined its job instead was to evaluate whether the country was protecting children.[4] Two years later it began issuing a series of research and policy reports warning that "child abuse and neglect in the United States now represents a national emergency" and asking the federal government to replace "the existing child protection system with a new, national, child-centered, neighborhood-based child protection strategy [because] only such a strategy has any ultimate hope of eliminating this national scourge."[5] The reporting and investigating system costing billions of dollars had not kept children safe in large part because it lacked any ability to provide effective services that families needed. The U.S. Advisory Board determined that the emergency was so compelling that it issued an initial report just to stem the disaster. The ultimate goal was a radically different approach to child protection, one that centered on the human rights of children and that inescapably meant supporting their families and communities in raising them. This was a moral imperative on federal, state, and local officials to embrace and support how neighbors could help neighbors to create caring communities.[6]

The new administration under Bill Clinton began just as the U.S. Advisory Board was issuing its reports. The Clinton administration ignored these deeply studied and carefully documented recommendations of expansive material and preventive services woven into neighborhoods. Instead, it focused on "family preservation" programs, which were short-term, intensive casework services provided only to children at imminent risk of foster care placement. The effectiveness of these transitory casework-oriented types of family preservation programs had already been doubted. Nevertheless, in 1993 nearly $1 billion was appropriated over a five-year period for them. The programs proved disastrous, with many more children placed at risk and entering foster care.[7] The system had gotten worse, not better.

The Adoption and Safe Families Act

The U.S. Advisory Board's recommendations were still available for the Clinton administration to consider. But the administration and Congress rejected them again and chose instead a time-limiting remedy that accelerated the responsibility of everyone involved—child welfare agencies, parents, and family courts—to accomplish the goal of getting children out of foster care on an accelerated schedule and with far more emphasis on terminating parental rights. This was the Adoption and Safe Families Act (ASFA).[8] Since its enactment, ASFA has been characterized as having four broad goals: (1) Ensuring that child safety is paramount; (2) moving children promptly to permanent families; (3) making child well-being a central focus of child welfare agencies; and (4) improving innovation and accountability throughout the system.[9] The first two goals were and remain prevailing.

The central safety component of ASFA was the reconceptualization of the AACWA's "reasonable efforts" requirement. Under the AACWA, the federal government had failed to fund preventive and reunification services that would have supported the reasonable efforts mandates to keep families together or to reunify them, either leaving children at risk at home or at risk of entering and staying in foster care. Many in Congress feared that maintaining the reasonable efforts requirements in ASFA would continue to place children's safety at risk. The solution was to narrow the reasonable efforts requirements, exempting certain parents from having to receive any reasonable efforts to prevent foster care (mostly in extreme circumstances such as when a parent had previously killed a child) and enabling states to add other exceptions, which many states did.[10]

Shrinking reasonable efforts to keep families intact was compounded by the welfare reforms that were central to the Clinton administration's policies of moving mothers off welfare rolls to improve the lives of poor children. The social contract that had been in effect since the New Deal—though only more recently for BIPOC families—to provide basic income support to needy families was broken. The extension of Assistance to Families with Dependent Children (AFDC) during the administrations under John F. Kennedy and Lyndon Johnson resulted in a sharp drop in child poverty, including reducing the number of Black children living in poverty by a third. While the reductions leveled off, they still provided a safety net.[11] With Clinton's welfare reforms, most children affected would not move out of poverty; rather they would experience a net financial loss overall, with extreme poverty increasing for Black children.[12] The broad, community-based, easily accessible resources and supports advocated by the U.S. Advisory Board to reconceptualize child protection into a system to help families were increasingly at odds with the federal and state governments' unwillingness to support the most marginalized parents taking care of their children.

Nor did ASFA's permanency provisions support families whose children were at risk of or living in foster care. "Permanency" under ASFA meant first and foremost termination of parental rights (TPR) and adoption for thousands of children who had been living in foster care for much of their lives. ASFA required states to begin TPRs for children who had spent fifteen of the previous twenty-two months in foster care with limited exceptions.[13] The priority was not to return children home to their birth families. Reunification of children with their families began to drop prior to ASFA, but as a proportion of exits from care, the number of children being reunified with their parents decreased steadily from 60 percent to 52 percent by 2011, and the percentage of reunifications for Black children was even smaller.[14]

That the reasonable efforts language remained in the statute at all is undermined not only by the permanency requirements that accelerated the time by which parents had to be prepared to take their children out of foster care or risk losing their parental rights but also by the ways that resources were distributed. Adoption (and later guardianship) financial incentives were not matched by funding for family support programs. Federal SSA Title IV-E funding for qualified children placed in foster care remained an uncapped resource for the states, with federal disbursements providing 50–75 percent of the total state costs of foster care and adoption assistance for eligible children.[15] In 2001, Title IV-E funding to the states reached $7 billion, up from only $1 billion a decade earlier. Federal funding for reasonable efforts services to keep children safely at home—preventive services—remained capped, not even reaching the $1 billion mark by 2001.[16] ASFA's safety and permanency provisions, reinforced by federal funding choices, were sending children increasingly in one direction: away from their families. To get there, they and their families were spending more and more time in family court.

ASFA and the Family Court

ASFA completed the transformation of family court from an indepen-dent judicial body whose jurisdiction was to determine whether the state had rightly intervened in a family's life to protect a child—and, if so, to decide an appropriate disposition that was best for the child—into a willing partner in administering federal child welfare policy on a vast scale. This is because the obligations that ASFA placed on the court reoriented the court's decision-making around a particular ver-sion of permanency and safety and incorporated the federal meaning of those concepts into state law. Judges would still make case-by-case determinations about whether a parent had mistreated a child and whether that child would remain at home or be placed in foster care, but now they were under tremendous pressure to find that reasonable efforts were made to prevent removal or provide reunification services within shorter time frames and with a greater emphasis that children were at risk at home. ASFA further required judges to decide whether agencies had created effective "concurrent" permanency plans so that, if reunification with parents failed, plans that prioritized adoption would be implemented.[17] Judges would have to figure out how to incorporate these mandates into their decision-making while they hung on to their therapeutic aspirations.

Judges would be making these decisions knowing or being concerned about several things: that most of the families appearing before them were poor and disproportionately families of color, especially Black families; that broad societal supports for poor families raising children were increasingly limited; that the new Clinton "welfare reform" mea-sures promulgated in 1996 were yet unproven to advance the financial well-being of those families (which they ultimately did not); and that the targeted resources to keep children at home or reunify them re-mained unfunded or underfunded (and often unproven) and yet break-able families would be expected to utilize them in shorter and shorter periods of time.[18] Judges were also aware that federal Title IV-E Foster

Care and Eligibility Reviews and subsequent Child and Family Services Reviews—both of which determine whether state child and family service programs are in conformity with federal funding requirements—would be impacted by judicial decisions that found that no reasonable efforts were made to support families. Such findings could potentially have a significant fiscal impact on state child welfare services or stymie states' ability to fulfill their ASFA obligations to move children more rapidly toward permanency. The fact that few states were ever sanctioned for judges finding "no reasonable efforts" remained unknown for many years.[19]

Hidden in the ASFA framework is the central quandary for family court judges: Do the ASFA requirements impinge on the court's fundamental responsibility to protect the constitutional right of family integrity—for parents to raise their children and for children to be raised in their own families—as the court is facilitating ASFA's mandates of when and in what ways the state can intervene in family life? As an independent judicial authority, the court's role is to consider whether the state's intervention in family life is legally and factually justified. The statutory framework each state has created to define when and under what conditions the child protection agency can act is constrained by whether those definitions pass constitutional muster. In other words, do those state statutes, and the state judges who interpret them, protect "the fundamental right of parents to make decisions concerning the care, custody, and control of their children" as the Supreme Court has said is mandated by the Due Process Clause of the Fourteenth Amendment?[20] Is the judge compromised in this duty when, at the same time, she is being asked to supervise the sufficiency of the agency's efforts to comply with ASFA rather than with the agency's efforts to comply with what the judge deems the appropriate efforts to protect the constitutional rights of both the adult and child members of a family? Or is the judge's decision-making authority compromised when the judge's determinations could provide the federal government with reasons to penalize the state, including withholding federal funds? And from the perspective this book has raised: Has ASFA provided the family court with yet another opportunity to reinvent itself in order to use its significant discretion in ways that ultimately hurt families?

These questions are complicated by our increasingly sophisticated knowledge about how everyone—including judges—makes decisions. Professor Matthew Fraidin has posited that the ideology of the family court as a problem-solving court, coupled with judges' enormous discretionary power, must be analyzed through the behavioral theories that affect the way these judges make decisions. Fraidin notes: "Judges make decisions [in dependency cases] under the severe time pressures of large caseloads, with a paucity of reliable information, and themselves unavoidably influenced by the pervasive racial and economic disadvantage of the parties who appear before them."[21] These circumstances lead judges to use their intuitive faculties to take mental shortcuts as they plow through their cases, which bolster rather than diminish their cognitive biases.[22] The stress and pressure of limited time and information, coupled with their worries about making the wrong decision, elevates the likelihood that, as they rush through their cases, they will make mistakes based on behavioral biases. Examples include giving greater weight to the initial information presented, usually by the child protection agency, which then persists throughout the proceedings despite the introduction of other evidence that should engender reconsideration (the primacy effect); overattributing to poor parents and parents of color the narrative of the abusive monster intent on harming her child (fundamental attribution error); and the difficulty in changing one's mind and reconsidering new evidence after having repeatedly ruled otherwise (bolstering).[23] Additionally, since so many of their decisions are infused with the vague BIOC standard, judges are constantly having to predict what may happen in the future.[24] These cognitive limitations, married with the intense expectations of ASFA and the fiscal realities of state and local funding, increasingly undermined the ability of judges to uphold constitutional principles established to protect family integrity.

Discretion and Interpreting the Meaning of "Reasonable Efforts"

ASFA's permanency and safety requirements have affected how family courts weigh state intervention into family life. The statutory "reasonable efforts" requirement created by the AACWA represented an attempt to narrow the scope of state intervention unless absolutely necessary. ASFA relieved agencies and courts from the principle that reasonable efforts to prevent children from being removed from their families required a concerted effort to preserve the family. Child safety under ASFA was interpreted as diminishing the need to work diligently to keep children at home or to reunify them with their parents. Several high-profile cases of horrific abuse were used by ASFA lawmakers to justify limiting the use of preventive services before removing children from their homes. Stories of children being starved and tortured by parents were interpreted to mean that child safety would now triumph over the rights of biological parents to raise their children, even though abuse was not the triggering factor in the vast majority of families eligible for preventive assistance. Several state supreme courts soon identified this transformative effect on state child welfare policy as an historic shift in the definition of "reasonable."[25] "Reasonable" no longer meant "diligent"; reasonable required much less time and effort.

ASFA's clarification that reasonable efforts required agencies to spend less time and effort trying to maintain or reunify families not only changed courts' interpretations of reasonable efforts; it fundamentally changed the *focus* of courts' decision-making. Legal scholars who closely examined TPR decisions soon after ASFA's passage found a profound influence on the way trial and appellate courts across the country interpreted "reasonable efforts" even if the impact could not be gauged in every individual decision.[26] As some state supreme courts have acknowledged, ASFA, like the AACWA before it, may be a federal appropriations law requiring states to conform to its mandates to receive funding, but it has nevertheless deeply altered agency and court decision-making.[27] Courts were now interpreting the meaning of ASFA during TPR proceedings rather than determining whether sufficient evidence existed to sever the constitutionally protected child–parent bonds. The language in an Iowa appellate court case, *In re N.J.*, a few years after ASFA's enactment illustrates this profound effect.[28]

A young girl, Nicole, had been sexually abused by one of her older brothers. Her mother, Sherry (as she was referred to in the court case), was advised not to allow Nicole to play unsupervised with her brothers. Sherry allowed them to play together outside their home, and while Nicole wasn't abused again, the children were removed from Sherry's and her husband's care. When Nicole was later returned home, a female babysitter also sexually abused Nicole; neither Sherry nor her husband were ever accused of sexual abuse or of knowing that the babysitter was a sexual predator. When Nicole was replaced in foster care, Sherry attended twice-weekly supervised visits with Nicole and underwent a psychological evaluation and counseling along with her children. Nevertheless, CPS filed a TPR, believing that Sherry could not keep Nicole safe and relying on ASFA's mandate to begin termination proceedings more quickly. The juvenile court terminated Sherry's rights; she appealed, arguing that the agency had not made reasonable efforts to return Nicole home and that it was in Nicole's best interests to be reunited with her mother. In upholding the TPR, the appellate court practically scolded Sherry for not understanding how ASFA had changed the agency's and the juvenile court's decision-making processes:

> What Sherry ignores is the shift in priorities mandated by [ASFA]. . . . Long-term efforts at family reunification are no longer required or even recommended. . . . [T]he law focuses [instead] on "time-limited reunification services" . . . [where] the new law places "greater emphasis on the health and safety of the child, and mandates a permanent home for a child as early as possible."[29]

Nicole's safety was considered endangered from her youngest brother, Brandon, still living at home. Brandon had never sexually abused Nicole, but he had also engaged in sexual misconduct. Since CPS did not trust Sherry or her husband to supervise Nicole sufficiently to protect her from Brandon's potential misconduct, the juvenile court relieved CPS of making further efforts toward reunification. But was this in Nicole's best interests?

Everyone agreed Nicole and Sherry had a close bond. Sherry regularly visited and had used parent counseling to improve her parenting skills since Nicole's second placement, making "great strides in managing Nicole's behavior during supervised visits. She was asserting her role as parent and Nicole was responding positively."[30] The concerns expressed by a psychologist about Sherry's parenting abilities soon after Nicole was re-placed in care were being addressed successfully. The only evidence cited by the appellate court that Sherry couldn't keep Nicole safe occurred *before* Nicole's second placement and *before* Sherry had been provided with parent counseling and guidance. Given this progress and the strong bond between mother and child, why couldn't—indeed, why wouldn't—the agency continue to try to reunify Sherry and Nicole, thereby maintaining its successful efforts to improve Sherry's parenting and Nicole's safety?

The juvenile court rejected the recommendation of Nicole's *guardian ad litem* of a continued stay in foster care with increased family visiting—and the potential of Nicole returning home—because that would violate ASFA's permanency requirement. The judge noted instead that adoption would give Nicole the stability she needed. But Nicole was living in a foster family unwilling to adopt her. She would have to be moved at least once more, losing both her biological mother and her foster family in the name of permanency and stability. Neither Sherry's right to raise her child nor Nicole's right to be raised by her mother were protected by this decision. Neither was the decision in Nicole's best interest—severing the one parental bond she had for a yet-unidentified new parent. Based on nothing more than aspiration, the juvenile court found, and the appellate court agreed, that Nicole "will ultimately be happier with the stability and permanency of adoptive parents as opposed to having a biological mother whom she sees only occasionally."[31] The Iowa courts holding this young girl's fate in their hands had followed ASFA's mandates, regardless of whether they actually provided "permanency, safety and well-being," or were in Nicole's best interests, or whether—crucially—they had protected a daughter's right to be raised by her mother.

Iowa courts may have made the same determination about Nicole pre-ASFA, but Professor Kathleen Bean, in her sweeping review of case law a few years after ASFA had been established in state policies and practices, found state courts had shifted their analyses to give greater weight to the health and safety of the child and had redefined "reasonable efforts" to reduce both the length and nature of those efforts.[32] Well-intentioned parents had less time to reunify with their children with the same or fewer services; parents were now expected to resolve their difficulties more quickly, even if agency efforts to assist them were delayed or reduced.

Family courts issue far fewer opinions on the reasonableness of agency work with parents when children are at risk of being removed from their parents' care or soon after they've been placed in foster care.[33] Instead, case law addressing reasonable efforts usually tells the story at the end of the journey, when the question before the court is whether parental rights should be terminated. As they review agency efforts, courts may admonish agencies for their failure to provide timely services, but because these admonitions occur when the court is more focused on the child's time in foster care, such failures are less likely to stop a TPR.[34] Worried about timeliness after the passage of ASFA, courts allowed for shorter and shorter periods of time for parents to benefit from assistance, justifying even just several months as enough time to comply with agency case plans.[35] For parents who seemed unable or unwilling to change, a sense of futility tinges the courts' discussions of reunification efforts, often excusing or shortening the agencies' responsibilities.[36] This is particularly disturbing when futility is used to justify clear failure on the part of agencies to assist in reunifying families and instead becomes an excuse for finding that reasonable efforts were made. While Professor Bean found closer scrutiny of both parents and agencies in the post-ASFA decisions she cites, agencies far more than parents seem to receive the benefit of the doubt. Post-ASFA courts used the language of "reasonable efforts" for parents as well as the state, although this is a requirement imposed on the state, not on the parent.[37] Of course, parents have an obligation to work toward reunification, but the means to do so is often hampered by the very problems that led to placement in the first place—and for which many families received little or no assistance before the child was removed. Even today, many families investigated don't receive services during an investigation or after substantiating some evidence of maltreatment.[38]

Once a child is removed, whether a family receives the right services or uses them effectively is not always a measure of the child's safety. Nevertheless, if parents don't show quick improvement, courts are far more willing to excuse agency mistakes, lapses in services, and half-hearted efforts in the post-ASFA world.[39] Bean found that courts generally take for granted "the State's ability to provide adequate services is constrained by its staff and dollar limitations," while sometimes the court even explicitly notes that in tough economic times the "state has a legitimate interest in making the best use of its limited resource."[40] Courts today continue to excuse states because of fiscal constraints.[41]

State Resources, Reasonable Efforts, and Court Decisions

But do states make the best use of their limited resources? What if the way those resources are used don't keep children safe or secure their permanency? Mandated reporting procedures are only one example of how state child protection systems have failed to keep most children safe. If a state chooses to employ its resources for ineffective systems, what is the impact on the family court when it must make crucial decisions to protect children and ensure the integrity of families? Is the family court relieved from requiring the state to provide the appropriate assistance to families either under state law or within the mandates ASFA requires because the state has made a bad choice in how to structure and fund its child welfare system? More fundamentally: Does it relieve the court from its duty to determine when the state may properly intervene in family life or ensure that the state is actually protecting a child?

In the years preceding ASFA's passage, twenty-one child welfare systems had been sued for being inadequate, leading to several foster care systems being operated under federal supervision in the mid-1990s.[42] In the decades since, impact litigation continued to be filed, both by advocates within states and by national organizations, particularly Children's Rights, Inc. (CRI), whose docket includes states in every part of the country. These suits have challenged the inadequate way that state child welfare systems protect children being investigated; provide preventive or reunification services to families; recruit and supervise foster parents, group homes, and residential facilities; train and supervise their personnel; secure adoptive placements and finalize adoptions; and provide post-permanency services to biological and adoptive families or assist youth as they age out of care. In short, child welfare systems have been sued about every aspect of their work because they have failed in every component of their fundamental tasks to protect children and ensure that they remain with their families or are raised in safe, stable, and permanent families. In 2014 alone, federal courts were monitoring judgments or settlements in Connecticut, Georgia, Michigan, Mississippi, New Jersey, Oklahoma, Tennessee, Washington, D.C, and Wisconsin.[43]

A case filed by CRI in 2015 against Arizona state officials provides a representative example of the problem. While making reasonable efforts to place children with their siblings is mandated, CRI identified that, at least a third of the time, children were placed apart from their siblings and about a third of the time out of their zip codes, meaning out of their neighborhoods and communities. In September 2014, Arizona had only 5,669 spaces in licensed foster homes available for 9,418 foster children who were not being placed with relatives. When homes are not available, children may sleep in agency offices. There are also insufficient therapeutic foster homes for hundreds of children clinically diagnosed as emotionally disturbed. Arizona had also failed to investigate in a timely manner over a thousand reports of children being *mistreated while in state care* during almost three years beginning in 2010.[44]

Such representative failures are well known to family court judges as they determine whether the child welfare system is working on behalf of any individual family. These judges read the local newspapers and watch the evening news. More than the general public, they follow the fiscal tribulations of their state governments struggling to stretch limited dollars. But these judges have a different job than federal judges being asked to determine whether the system as a whole has failed so badly that it falls below constitutionally permissible standards of state action and has to be fixed. These judges also have a different job than the lawmakers deciding where to spend tax revenues. Family court judges—and the appellate judges reviewing decisions—have to decide whether the state intervened to protect a particular child and assist a particular family in a manner that conforms with our understanding of when the state can intervene appropriately in a family's' life. As the Supreme Court observed when determining that the standard of proof in a TPR case required clear and convincing evidence: "In appraising the nature and quality of a complex series of encounters among the agency, the parents, and the child, the court possesses unusual discretion to underweigh probative facts that might favor the parent. Because parents subject to termination proceedings are often poor, uneducated, or members of minority groups, such proceedings are often vulnerable to judgments based on cultural or class bias."[45]

Judges thus have a duty to be particularly diligent when weighing the state's efforts to assist families before permanently severing legal bonds. These judges should not be in the business of excusing the state for not doing its job well or spending its money wisely if that standard isn't met. Neither is the family court a child protection agency that makes choices about where to spend its resources. If the state and local child welfare systems make the wrong choices, the court should not be empowered to condone those choices but instead has the duty to protect the legal interests of the child or family affected by any mistakes.

Court Supervision of Child Welfare Agencies

Many believed that ASFA gave the family court the independent duty just described by expanding the court's supervision in individual cases and by inserting itself more fully into determining whether the plans developed to keep the child safe, move the child toward permanency, and protect the child's well-being are the right plans. The AACWA, as discussed in chapter 7, had had a similar goal. To eliminate "foster care drift," the AACWA required the court to review the child's placement after eighteen months and make a decision about whether the child should remain in foster care after determining whether "reasonable efforts" had been made toward reunification or another placement goal. The court failed miserably in achieving that goal.

Despite the family court's inability to enforce AACWA's reasonable efforts requirements, ASFA mandated even more heightened court involvement. Family courts would now be expected to hold review hearings—renamed "permanency hearings"—within twelve months of placement. If reasonable efforts are suspended under one of ASFA's exceptions, a court can hold a permanency hearing as early as thirty days after a child has been removed from her family to begin a process toward adoption or another permanency goal other than reunification.[46] ASFA's permanency requirements became a death knell for families. While exact figures are hard to obtain for the number of children whose parental rights have been terminated since ASFA's enaction, over two million is a fair estimation.[47] By last count, over 71,000 children were awaiting adoption after termination of their parents' rights.[48] Like Nicole, whose story was told earlier, many children have a goal of adoption but have no adoptive parents. In most years, twice as many children wait to be adopted as are adopted; children wait for a new family on average for two years.[49] This wait and the likelihood and time to adoption have all fallen disproportionately harder on Black children. Since 2000, their adoption rate has fallen dramatically as a percentage of the foster care population.[50]

ASFA and its implementing federal regulations added judicial supervisory requirements with no additional resources for the court to do this
job; without shifting federal funding toward preventive and reunification
services that would have eliminated or reduced the number of children
entering or remaining in foster care; and with no effective federal monitoring system to measure whether either the child welfare systems or
the courts were, in fact, making timely and appropriate decisions.[51] One
step aimed to remedy this burden was the Strengthening Neglect and
Abuse Courts Act of 2000 (SANCA), which funded some jurisdictions
through competitive grants to develop data collection and case-tracking
systems to improve court processing of ASFA-related cases.[52] Congress
was beginning to acknowledge that its enactment of ASFA had greatly expanded the courts' work by increasing the complexity of its decisions and
expanding the number of hearings to be held, but also by changing its
job to include significant monitoring of state child welfare systems.[53] The
one role of the court explicitly required by ASFA, however, is not listed
in SANCA's list of "findings" about the centrality of a well-functioning
court system to administer the goals of ASFA; that is, the goal that the
court is required to determine whether reasonable efforts were made to
prevent a child from entering foster care. SANCA's sponsors abandoned
even a pretense that the court's role included this fundamental decision,
continuing to shift the meaning of "safety and permanency" away from
keeping children safely and permanently at home.

The Price of Collaboration on Families

SANCA's efforts to improve court functioning was intended to reinforce
ASFA's ambition for child welfare systems and courts to collaborate to
make the law work through a new monitoring system. In 2000, the Children's Bureau began to implement a federal review system to measure
state compliance with Title IV-B and IV-E funding mandates. The Child
and Family Services Reviews (CFSRs) were intended to assess state conformity with federal requirements related to their child welfare systems,
in particular ASFA's goals of safety, permanency, and well-being.[54] In the
first round of CFSRs, no state was in substantial conformity with all the
requirements, and no state achieved substantial conformity in the area
where courts are seen to most directly impact the child welfare system:

permanency and stability.[55] In other words, too many children were being moved in and out of foster care or from placement to placement within foster care, and too few were finding permanent homes by being returned to their parents or being adopted.[56] To remedy this failure, the Children's Bureau mandated that the family court (and other stakeholders in the child welfare system) participate in the CFSR process and the subsequent development of a Program Improvement Plan to respond to the areas where the state had failed the review.[57]

On the one hand, including a broader swath of the child welfare system—including representatives from other agencies, attorneys and other advocates, parents, and tribal representatives—has the potential for including more voices and ideas into improving child welfare and diminishing many of the cultural, racial, and economic inequalities the system creates or heightens. On the other, it creates a "we're all in this together" sense that obscures the inequalities that exist among the various participants and blurs professional roles, especially of advocates and judges. Courts are being mandated by the federal government to collaborate on systemic reform to achieve the exact outcomes that judges are being asked to evaluate in individual cases. Below is an example of how this collaboration is not value neutral.

The New York Permanent Judicial Commission on Justice for Children is a statewide commission whose responsibilities include helping to ensure collaboration among state and local stakeholders in the child welfare system. I was a member of the Commission for twenty-seven years. When ASFA was first being implemented in New York, the Commission embraced Adoption Celebration Days to help finalize adoptions that had been lingering for far too long. Judges and other court personnel often volunteered to work weekends to complete these adoptions and participate in the celebrations. Thousands of children were finally legally part of a family they had been living with in foster care, most of them for many, many years. The celebrations were wonderful, and everyone felt inspired.

No parallel efforts and celebrations were planned for children being reunified with their parents—an issue that I raised at several Commission meetings over the years—even though thousands of children also lingered in foster care because their reunification plans were not finalized. "Reunification Days" would have been just as wonderful—

returning children to their families and homes when they no longer needed to live in foster care. Orders for post–foster care assistance could have been finalized, and donations that might have made the transition home easier—new beds, toys, or clothes—could have been secured. But they weren't. All that collaborative effort went only one way—toward adoption. The purpose of this story is not to diminish the work done on behalf of the children being adopted. It is instead to point out that the ASFA adoption directive was reinforced by a systemic collaboration that wasn't replicated on behalf of children going home. Adoption was in the air and in our hearts. How could this not affect a judge's thinking about the meaning of permanency when making a decision whether to consider reunification of a family or terminate parental rights? It did.

In New York and around the country, the pressure to collaborate as a CFSR "stakeholder" in the child welfare system's interpretation and application of ASFA was pervasive. In case the federal directives were not sufficiently clear to every family court judge, in July 2004 the National Council of Juvenile and Family Court Judges (NCJFCJ) sought a seat at the table for judges during the development of the CFSR Program Improvement Plan because ASFA "has strongly designated the Courts as the monitor for the permanency, safety, well-being and outcomes for children." The Conferences of Chief Justices and State Court Administrators issued a resolution the following week, expanding the NCJFCJ's "monitoring" role well beyond ASFA's intention and declaring that "Congress charged the state courts with oversight responsibilities for the state child welfare systems and, as such, state courts are critical stakeholders in these systems." The chief judges chided state court systems that had not collaborated on the first CFSR and urged every state court system to participate in every phase of the federal reviews. In case some state court judges *hadn't gotten the memo*, the chief judges resolved that the Children's Bureau should communicate with the chief state court administrators directly to ensure that there was judicial participation in the federal reviews.[58] Systemic collaboration was also paired with court reform money, providing state court systems with grants that eventually were contingent on implementing ASFA and CFSR participation.[59] Judges in their courtrooms were not immune from the expectations of implementing ASFA in collaboration with the very agencies charged with proving to them that they had met ASFA's safety, permanency, and well-being requirements.

This point is reinforced by two lessons about the role and meaning of judicial leadership, a kind of leadership that has always characterized family courts and which has been questioned throughout this book. The first is a concern raised by Professor Melissa Breger about the way the culture of the family court is especially conducive to a "groupthink" mentality.[60] In the context of child welfare, many stakeholders interact over a long period of time. They are the CPS and foster care agency caseworkers, supervisors, and attorneys; the CASA volunteers; the parents' and children's attorneys or *guardian ad litem*; the court personnel and the auxiliary services (like mental health evaluators or substance abuse testers); and the judges themselves. In jurisdictions of all sizes, these participants may work together on multiple cases. A way of doing things develops that places tremendous pressure on the various players to reach consensus, not to challenge court norms, and to keep the leader of the group happy, that leader being the judge. If a particular judge, for example, is collaborating on a state project with the other stakeholders to improve the timeliness of decisions to meet ASFA deadlines, every other stakeholder's behavior may change. The parent's attorney may be reluctant to file a motion to challenge the accuracy of a drug test, request a second opinion on a bone fracture, or urge unsupervised home visits. The caseworker may keep quiet about a new parenting program that might work for this family but is likely to take several more weeks to open. The CASA volunteer may downplay a child's ambivalence about being adopted. The mental health evaluator may not bother asking for the opportunity to observe one more visit between a parent and child before deciding whether to recommend reunification or termination of parental rights. Even the judge may find reason to deny a legitimate adjournment request. They are collaborating on a timeliness project— whether embedded in their subconscious or purposefully on their minds. This may be a very good systemic idea, but it can undermine their independent professional obligations. There is good reason that the word "collaboration" has both positive and negative connotations.

The second lesson on judicial leadership is that the collaboration mandated by the Children's Bureau to implement ASFA is focused on improving the current child welfare system, not creating a new one. The current crisis-oriented system is structured and funded to prioritize reporting and investigations, removals and placements, and court-driven decisions. This system has yet to succeed in keeping children safe, stable, and well. An alternative system would be structured and funded to prioritize family integrity supported in multiple ways: through income maintenance and primary preventive services like child and health care; with community-based assistance and targeted and proven prevention and reunification efforts; and by strictly limited court intervention. Such an alternative system does not centralize the court in decision-making, services, or collaborative ventures. Instead, the court is used only when these other systems cannot keep a child safe. That alternative system does not glorify judicial leadership of a stakeholder team but judicial constraint, a lesser and less glamorous role but one far more consistent with constitutional principles and separation of powers. ASFA reinvigorated the family court in its central leadership role as a problem-solving court intent on doing good and emboldened judges to collaborate on improving the current, failing family regulation system. The result has been the continued destruction of families.

In the Wake of ASFA: Faux Permanency

Earlier in this chapter, we read that nine-year-old Nicole lost the opportunity to be reunited with her mother, Sherry, when an Iowa court determined that ASFA's emphasis on permanency and stability decreed that, despite their close relationship, Sherry's parental rights be terminated and Nicole placed for adoption whenever adoptive parents could be found. Nicole received neither permanency nor stability as a result of that decision; she lost both her birth mother and then her foster parents (who were unwilling to adopt her). The Iowa courts understood that ASFA's mandate for "a permanent home for a child" prioritized terminating parental rights and finding an adoptive home for Nicole over ensuring that Nicole had a long-term, stable, loving family. This is an example of how ASFA transformed the meaning of "permanence." According to social work professor Mark Testa, "permanence" as defined by current law means "binding" rather than "lasting." *Lasting permanence* arises out of an enduring relationship and a sense of belonging; *binding permanence* legally cements an enduring commitment.[61] By choosing to make Nicole a legal orphan (she had no legal parent after her mother's parental rights were terminated) while betting that she

Figure 8.1. *Represent*: "The Search for Home". Courtesy of Youth Communications.

would eventually be placed in an adoptive family, the courts overseeing her well-being prioritized the prospect of *binding* permanence over the likelihood of *lasting* permanence.

Nicole is not alone. ASFA has a specific pecking order of permanency. Even if reunification is the first priority for the overwhelming number of children entering foster care, only about half the children eventually return home.[62] Between 1998, when ASFA's effect began to be felt, and 2011, the number of children being reunified with parents decreased steadily from 60 percent to 52 present, and the percentage for African

American children was even smaller.[63] In 2019, only 47 percent of children left foster care to be reunited with their parents.[64] Neither financial nor policy incentives favored reunification with parents. Courts understood that point as they downshifted their expectations of what "reasonable efforts" were required of agencies to assist parents in preparing to bring their children home. For some children, like Nicole, the courts applied ASFA's time-limited reunification mandates so narrowly as to choose adoption (without available adoptive parents) over reunification with her mother.

ASFA's other permanency options include legal guardianship; permanent placement with a fit and willing relative; and "another planned permanent living arrangement." A central barrier to pursuing these permanency options, however, is that adoption must be ruled out first. Adoption—the legally binding permanency option under ASFA—is considered more likely to succeed than the alternative permanency options that Testa has defined as "lasting" permanency.[65] This myopia about adoption has had significant negative consequences for many children, particularly older youth, and it has further distorted the family court's decision-making duties.

Professor Cynthia Godsoe believes that the ASFA permanency framework has clung to an idealized vision of the "happy ending" of a child being adopted out of foster care—like the adoption celebration days noted earlier—at the price of leaving many children without realistic alternatives of lasting connections with relatives and other important people in their lives. Godsoe draws on evidence Testa, and others have identified about the stability of strong kin relationships in guardianship placements to recommend that adoption does not have to be ruled out before other permanency options are explored. This is to counter the idea that only in adoption will children and caretakers experience permanence.[66] She warns that requiring kin caregivers to choose adoption imposes a false legal relationship upon both kin caregiver and child, thereby undermining the ties of extended families and forcing an unnecessary legal choice when alternative permanency options are readily available.[67] Stories abound of relative caretakers—grandmothers, aunts, cousins—being threatened with children being removed from their care unless they agree to adoption. This undermines what we know about children placed in care with relatives rather than strangers: they have better outcomes overall than other children in foster care; they experience fewer placement changes; they have fewer behavioral problems; and more siblings are placed together.[68] Enforcing the "first rule out adoption" policy only places these children unnecessarily at risk of harm by endangering their stable kin placements.

Professor Godsoe also questions why these families have to be fit into this idealized type of binding permanency. After all, she points out, families look very different than they used to. Many more adults take on the role of parent today than in conventional nuclear families. We are increasingly used to blended families with shared adult decision-making, where children are expected to do just fine. Godsoe believes that lawmakers, caseworkers, and judges are simply unable to envision an extended family *parens patriae* caught up in the family regulation system in the same way as these other blended families in our society.[69] The result of remaining enamored of adoption has, in fact, had a profound and terrible impact.

Legal Orphans, Broken Adoptions, and Restored Parental Rights

The young people who leave foster care after parental rights have been terminated are now called "legal orphans" by the system that created them. Many will linger in foster care for years, eventually becoming part of about 8–10 percent of the foster care population that ages out every year—over 20,000 young people—with no permanent homes.[70] If Nicole was one of them, she may have found her way back to Sherry, as many young people do. One study found that over a quarter of the youth without a legal relationship to their birth parents return to them after they age out of foster care.[71] So do many young people who have been adopted by other parents. While most states and localities have not tracked what some advocates have called "broken" adoptions, and while the research has been difficult to quantify, there is growing consensus of the human and fiscal costs of ignoring the problem of failed adoptions.[72]

The false hierarchy of "binding" permanency has led to one of the most bizarre responses by states and judges: re-creating parental rights. As of 2017, nearly half the states have enacted statutes to reinstate or restore parental rights when a child has never been placed for adoption, an adoption has never been finalized, or an adoption has failed.[73] These statutes struggle to balance the correctness of the earlier judicial decision to sever the legal relationship between parent and child with the current petition to re-create that same family. Termination of parental rights is the most serious civil consequence to befall a family, requiring proof by clear and convincing evidence and often subject to appellate review before being finalized. To have to re-create such a family—to eliminate what has come to be called the "family death penalty"—underscores ASFA's destructive impact.[74]

Even before these statutory remedies started to be drafted, judges began to entertain petitions from birth parents to vacate termination orders, to grant parental custody, and even to allow these parents to adopt their own children.[75] Yet undoing such a momentous decision will neither solve the problems of thousands of legal orphans nor create trust in the court processes. Weighing in on the problem in 2012, the NCJFCJ passed a resolution urging judges to take various steps to reduce the risk of legal orphans aging out of foster care. Their recommendations included consideration of reinstating parental rights as well as not making "reasonable efforts" findings if agencies were not actively trying to secure a permanent place for a legal orphan with a safe and caring adult.[76] What was missing from the NCJFCJ's resolution was a call for judges to refuse to make reasonable efforts findings unless specific and ongoing efforts were being made to reunify the child with her parents *before* a termination proceeding. That judicial determination would likely have far more impact on preventing legal orphans.

Another back-end response to having created legal orphans has been to keep youth in care longer or to permit them to reenter foster care if their permanency plan fails. Through the federal Fostering Connections to Success and Increased Adoptions Act of 2008, states can receive Title IV-E reimbursement for youth staying in care until twenty-one. Some states have used this support to provide more services and assistance to youth for longer periods before they are left on their own; some, like New York, have even passed laws permitting youth to return to care after they have turned eighteen if the young person can show that she has no viable alternative.[77] In vast numbers, these "aged-out" youth are homeless, jobless, without higher education or training, suffer from mental illness, or likely have had contact with the criminal legal system.[78] Paradoxically, while these catastrophic outcomes for aged-out youth have led states to allow them to reenter foster care, remaining in or reentering care for those extra years at the end is worthwhile if the alternative is being on their own.[79]

Professor Randi Mandelbaum has recently argued that what is really needed is to abandon the very concept of permanency for these older youth and replace it with far more concrete planning for their stability and emotional connections to supportive adults as they leave foster care. This is what youth say they want, and it will also free judges to craft orders more likely to achieve goals prioritizing Testa's "lasting" permanency by paying attention to the caring adults in the youth's life. The federal reporting and investigation regime that began under CAPTA, and the permanency hierarchy solidified under ASFA, have yet to grapple with the consequences of removing millions of children from their families without the resources or commitment to try to prevent those disruptions in the first place or to reunify those families before doing anything else. Lawmakers have failed to grapple with the heartbreaking complexities of attachment, trauma, and grief these children experience.[80]

The current efforts to undo the damage reflect this bias. There are calls for more efforts to prepare willing youth and adults for the transition to adoption or guardianship; for more postadoption services to support these new families; and for more money to pay for these efforts.[81] Child welfare systems, in collaboration with courts, are holding trainings on trauma to help caseworkers and judges understand what children have experienced both before and during foster care to help them transition into more successful lives.[82] And there are studies to understand how to prevent broken adoptions.[83] These are not unworthy efforts; they just reinforce a system built on removing a vast number of children from their families and expecting an ever smaller number of them to return home.

The Ultimate Impact of Federal Mandates on Family Court Judges

This chapter and chapter 7 have identified many of the ways in which federalization has impacted how family court adjudicates child protection proceedings. The court's centrality has been reinvigorated by providing judges with far greater authority to monitor families and child welfare agencies, harkening back to the original managerial role of the juvenile court judge. The court's historic approach to finding children "dependent" based on poverty has been reinforced by federal definitions of "dependency" that equate poverty and the impacts of inequality with neglect. At the same time, federal laws, especially ASFA, have distorted the court's mandate to protect the legal or best interests of the child by imposing specific directives that have prioritized definitions of "safety" and "permanency" that do not support families raising their own children. While these directives have limited some of the court's ultimate discretion, judges retain extraordinary discretion in the thousands of orders they issue on parental behavior, parenting time with children, treatment obligations, and services requirements. They remain empowered to do whatever good they think they are doing.

III

The Road to Abolition

9

The Failure of Reform

Maintaining the Court's Centrality

Even as the family court reinvented itself throughout the twentieth century to remain relevant, the Great Idea of a court created to do good by intervening in family life remained its central purpose. Despite layering on some formal and adversarial processes, the court retained its role as a place to help families resolve their problems, and the judge continued to assume the role of judicial leader. As Judge Leonard Edwards said in 2004, the family court judge is "an administrator, a collaborator, a convenor, and an advocate."[1] These multifaceted jobs permit the court to intervene dramatically once families enter the court.[2] Yet the core question remains: Should the judge be given such a wide range of discretionary power and authority?

If a state is exercising state control over individuals and families, a determination has to be made about *where* that control is situated. The question presented here is whether there is a need for a separate, specialized court to exercise control, or whether legal remedies of any form are the most effective means to resolve family problems and provide family support. In 1982, Professor Edward Mulvey asked whether it was possible that a unified family court system could withstand "later claims of misdirected idealism" and would "provide a more realistic appraisal of the judiciary's role in the regulation of family problems." Mulvey noted that "considerations regarding the expected effectiveness of the court in regulating family dysfunction have never been adequately resolved" and that "the question of whether the court's attempt [to resolve family problems] will produce gain far outweighing harm is unanswered although often assumed."[3] In this book I have tried to answer this core question about the assumption that family court does more good than harm, as well as interrogating other critical assumptions: that bringing children and families to court will assist them; that a court built on a therapeutic approach is a good place to solve family problems; that specialized judges leading a problem-solving team is effective; and that reduced adversarialism and minimal due process are more appropriate for family-related legal issues. All of those assumptions have underlain most reform efforts historically and today without sufficient interrogation into their validity.

The importance of this analysis is amplified by the most recent family court reforms that harken back to several of the earliest configurations of the court. There is not only a call for specialized parts to address specific issues—like drug treatment—but also a call for all family-related issues to be unified within the broad jurisdiction of the family court.[4] Specialization and expanded unification efforts center the judge to supervise and monitor the families and agencies before the court. There is also a continued belief that informalism as a method to resolve family issues—in court proceedings and as a complimentary but mandated part of court processes—is an effective, even essential court tool. As the court's jurisdictional power has continued to expand and diversify, the alternatives of less intervention or even nonintervention, reduced jurisdiction over families, and heightened due process have become more elusive. These alternatives rest on a very different set of assumptions: that intervention has not proven to do more good than harm; that courts are not the best place to solve family problems; that most families would be better served with voluntary, community-based, noncoercive, and nonpunitive assistance; and that judges are not best suited to be leaders of problem-solving teams. These assumptions construct a different court, a court whose mandate is not to do good. In this court, children and families would find themselves there under very limited circumstances—when a child is alleged to have committed specific, very serious crimes, or a parent is alleged to have seriously mistreated a child—and no alternative system but a court can provide the due process protections necessary for state intervention. In this court, the judge is an impartial jurist, applying procedural and substantive law to ensure constitutional protections and whose first determination is whether the court's jurisdiction is even necessary. If the judge finds legal accountability, the court then has the responsibility to craft the least intrusive and detrimental alternative for children and to maximize family integrity and autonomy.

The constraints on creating a court adjudicating family issues that embraces this narrower mandate, or shrinking the current court sufficiently to justify shifting its authority to other civil and criminal courts, are monumental. Each chapter has presented examples of judges' and judicial organizations' firm rejection of less or no intervention even in the face of significant evidence that intervention was harming children and families. The Supreme Court's 1971 decision in *McKeiver* gave the juvenile court another chance to prove that it could be an effective helping court. That chance was provided despite the Court's own earlier decisions in *Kent* and *Gault*, which were highly critical of the court's arbitrariness and lack of due process. Similarly, the later call for far narrower jurisdiction in abuse and neglect cases and virtually no jurisdiction in noncriminal misbehavior (status offense) cases in the proposed Juvenile Justice Standards was rejected by prominent judges as no more than a reflection of the 1970s culture in its "current distrust of altruism and paternalism and the resulting disparagement of the *parens patriae* function of the state in protecting and aiding children."[5]

In 1980, Judge John R. Milligan, on behalf of the National Council of Juvenile and Family Court Judges, castigated Congress for having stripped judges of their power to lock up status offenders with delinquents, lamenting that "[the] effect of the Juvenile Justice Act as it now exists is to allow a child ultimately to decide for himself whether he will go to school, whether he will live at home, whether he will continue to run, run, run, away from home or whether he will even obey orders of your court."[6] Even resolutions from the NCJFCJ, the Conference of State Court Administrators, and the Conference of Chief Judges concerning juvenile and family courts consistently center the solutions for improvement around judicial leadership in problem-solving and less adversarial courts in collaboration with the other branches of government. Within the judicial hierarchy, there remains great support for maintaining family court and improving it incrementally.[7]

To understand the limits and failures of incremental reform, this chapter first considers the enduring myth of a socialized, informal court able to do good before considering how most reforms respond to crises rather than to the fundamental structure of the court. The chapter then turns to examples of how judges are able to abuse their discretionary power despite reforms enacted to limit that power. Finally, the chapter considers how reforms intended to improve the court are limited and fail because they continue to rely on the belief that inspired judicial leadership will be sufficient to secure meaningful reform.

The Enduring Myth of a Socialized and Informal Court

The original juvenile court and its prodigy were built on the belief that *socialized* courts implemented with informal processes were better in family-related cases. This remains a driving force not only in family court but also in the newest renditions of problem-solving courts developed at the end of the twentieth century. What problem-solving courts then and now offer is a form of therapeutic conflict resolution and rehabilitation for the individual that sidesteps the underlying structural reasons for the disputes. As Professor Christina Harrington observed: "The origins of these disputes are depoliticized or ignored, and the resolutions are internalized by the individualized form of participation. Conflict in this setting is absorbed into a rehabilitative model of minor dispute resolution."[8]

"Informalism," or informal justice as a process, has often been hailed as expanding the disputants' participation and equalizing power, but it must also be understood as a mechanism expanding state control. When the original juvenile court judges brought children into "a room with a table and two chairs . . . where in a more or less formal way the whole story may be talked over" or when, fifty years later, Judge Paul Alexander urged lawyers to tell their clients "[y]ou just go over there and tell [the judge] the whole story," the informality of those practices cloaked the judge's power. Coercion is disguised in informal court and court-related proceedings, sometimes by diminished or altered punishment—substance abuse treatment rather than incarceration or removal of children—and sometimes by expanding what constitutes legitimate state intervention.[9] The development of robust court diversion programs for status offenders, discussed in chapter 6, often meant that youth who might have simply been left alone were drawn into diversion programs and faced judicial consequences if they weren't sufficiently reformed.[10]

In family court child protective proceedings, not only are proceedings often informal and frequently bereft of adequate due process protections; there has also been a steady rise of administrative and court-based case conferences since the implementation of the Adoption and Safe Families Act of 1996. Hailed as a way for families to participate in decision-making prior to or in conjunction with court proceedings, these conferences are also supposed to help resolve issues that would otherwise take up court time.[11] What is rarely acknowledged is that the promise of informal processes—especially avoiding court and receiving needed help—is a form of coercion that "serves to *persuade* parties to submit to informal justice, to *agree* to the outcome, and to *comply* with it."[12] These processes also expand overall surveillance of families, often without assistance of counsel and the imposition of evidentiary rules, both of which would offer some defense against open-ended discussions that may jeopardize the participant's position, including later in court. Instead, since these conferences are "informal" and give a parent or youth the opportunity to have their "voices heard," they are viewed as supportive and problem-solving.[13]

Greater authority to supervise families, and piling on multiple informal processes to fix families, have also grown in the private family dispute resolution cases since the 1990s. As Professors Jane Murphy and Jana Singer identify in their exploration of private family dispute resolution, this leads to expanding family court intervention and supervision to problem-solve rather than resolve legal disputes with legal due process protections in place.[14] Many of the litigants in family dispute resolution cases are low-income and nonmarital. They are subject to heightened surveillance and intrusion through the informal processes without their procedural rights being protected or their substantive needs being served.[15] Moreover, they find themselves at risk of endless court supervision, like the families in cases of state intervention.[16]

The contradictions of informalism in family court are confounding, yet they remain central to determining whether the court is capable of being reformed. This is because, as Professor Richard Abel has explained: "[Informal justice] appears to be simultaneously more and less coercive than formal law, to represent both an expansion of the state apparatus and a contraction. For the same reason it is peculiarly resistant to criticism: When accused of being manipulative it can show its non-coercive face; when charged with abandoning the disadvantaged it can point to ways in which informal justice extends state paternalism."[17] This chameleonic ability has allowed the court to sustain its basic structure and approach and avoid any significant challenges to its continued existence. Even in response to periodic crises, the reforms are never fundamental.

Framing Reform Around Crises

By the early 2000s, family courts were processing hundreds of thousands of cases each year, often carrying the heaviest judicial caseloads in their states.[18] In those cases where the state is actively intervening in families' lives—in child welfare, status offenses, and juvenile cases—the numbers grew enormously in the last quarter of the twentieth century before leveling off and even decreasing in some instances. On the private law side, particularly in cases of custody and financial responsibility for children between parents or other caretaking adults, the numbers were even larger, overwhelming the courts not only with initial custody and support decisions but also with subsequent petitions to modify those determinations.[19] Those caseload numbers are a contributing factor to the court's inability to do its job, but what is far more important is how we think about and respond to those numbers.

Family court reform is invariably framed as a response to crisis. In the early 2000s, one report on the New York Family Court was titled "A Call to Action: A Crisis in Family Court," while another began its executive summary section with the heading "The Crisis in New York's Family Court."[20] Court systems in general suffer from this crisis mentality, lamenting the volume of cases, congestion, and delay. In a sweeping study of the California court system from 1960 to 1990, Professor Harry Scheiber concluded that court systems will forever be under-resourced, only sometimes more so than others. The procedural reforms usually instituted to address the caseload or resource crisis of the moment— what Scheiber called "adjustments" rather than "reforms"—generally have limited, short-term effects on making the court work better.[21] That doesn't argue against identifying what isn't working and instituting better processes to address the problem but rather understanding the limitations of those adjustments, especially if they are inconsistent with more fundamental values that the court is trying to achieve.

When Professor Malcolm Feeley studied several late twentieth-century criminal court reforms, he identified the dominant approach to reform as being administrative. Administrative reform seeks to improve the court through greater coordination among the system participants and better management of the overall system. This approach is consistent with many of the family court reforms proposed and implemented since its inception. The challenge to this approach rests in the system itself, whose complexity and fragmentation eschews such organization. An administrative approach often relies on a formal description of the court system process "as a basis for diagnosing problems and constructing remedies" but without adequately reflecting the day-to-day practices that will impact those remedies. Feeley called this the "fallacy of formalism," and he used, among other examples, the persistent call for more resources to reduce court delays as if court delays were a discrete problem rather than created by multiple factors, including the targeted use of delay by defense counsel in criminal proceedings.[22] When the arrest rate almost doubled between 1960 and 1970, New York and Washington, D.C., both responded by increasing the number of judges to address backlogs and delays; several studies later found that merely increasing the number of judges was not effective in reducing either.[23] Those studies did not stop calls for more judges as a solution, in part because adding more judges is a simple idea that can be easily sold even if it's wrong: it is a fallacy of formalism.

The fallacy of formalism also reflects a comfort with certain solutions. Family court reform begins invariably with the goal of making the court more efficient, in large part to address caseloads. As with reform efforts in every other type of court, getting a handle on what is not working in the court—too many adjournments or too few adoptions—generally is met first by a proposal for more resources, especially more judges. Explaining the court's problems as a lack of resources places the blame on a problem that does not implicate the players in the system, diminishing the necessity to search for other causes that may disrupt relationships or change the way things are done.[24] Even if there is some disagreement as to where court reform money should be spent, obtaining more money almost universally is seen as necessary to reform the court. While the frame of resources fits our conventional understanding of what is wrong, this framework blinds us from considering alternative solutions. And then, if resources disappear, we have not created sustainable reform.[25]

In 2008, at the direction of the New York state legislature, the Office of Court Administration was tasked with setting a cap on the number of cases that children's lawyers handling child protective and delinquency cases are responsible for at one time.[26] This reform was hailed as a major accomplishment. Child advocates across the country have always lamented an inability to represent their clients effectively because of heavy caseloads. In the mid-1990s, I served as the attorney in charge of the Juvenile Rights Division of the Legal Aid Society, which represents most of the children subject to the child welfare and delinquency systems in New York City. At the time, we represented over 40,000 children in a year. Each of my budget requests to the state sought more money to hire more lawyers to lighten their caseloads. There was no question that the lawyers could not reach the standards of representation they sought to provide to all the clients on their docket; the numbers were too high. But even as I wrote those budget requests, I knew that caseload management skills varied among the lawyers. Some lawyers could manage high caseloads well; some could not. Some were willing to learn innovative case management techniques; some were not. Some were able to draw on available resources like social workers and investigators; some were not. Focusing on the numbers alone masked deeper problems in our practice and conveniently allowed us to frame most issues in terms of "resources."

The implicit consequence of limiting caseloads is that children will receive better representation. With more time, the lawyers will learn new skills, try different strategies, become better at their jobs, and be less traumatized by the work. Several years after I left my position at Legal Aid to return to teaching, I was asked to co-facilitate a meeting of child advocates from around the state to discuss the potential of caseload caps on lawyers' work before the case-cap restrictions were implemented. The discussion was framed around "workload" rather than "caseload" to encourage the participants to use the new financial resources the case-cap restrictions would generate to reconsider their practices. We were concerned that the unanticipated consequences of case caps—including that the representation would be easier but not better, that the outcomes for children may not improve, or that the reform would fail to consider the impact on the rest of the court system—could squander the opportunity the case caps provided.

The chief administrative judge was tasked with reporting the case caps' impact by the end of 2010, two years after the restrictions were implemented; as far as I can tell, that study was never completed.[27] In his work, Feeley concluded that among the reasons that reforms are not evaluated is that the reform proponents often have little incentive to evaluate because they know their idea is good.[28] Who doesn't think that case caps are a good idea? Who wants to know that capping the number of cases hasn't produced the intended results? Not the advocates who pressed for the caps, not the legislators who thought it was a worthy reform, and not the court administrators who implemented the reform and have moved on to other issues. After all, each lawyer still has fewer cases, at least until there is a budget crisis and no one bothered to prove that the case caps really made a difference.

The administrative imperative that champions funding efficiency and organization is perhaps most challenged by the very nature of court systems themselves. Feeley found that the adversarial nature of courts significantly impacts enacting reform. While family court is heralded as a problem-solving alternative to a strictly adversarial system, ultimately cases are filed, litigants appear, and judges make decisions. The industry that family court has become creates vested interests as well as local and broader sets of expectations that are reinforced by financial incentives and/or fiscal constraints. The complexity of the current system entails a diversity of cases; multiple parties; public and private agencies; professional and system personnel; powerful unions; court and community-based services; volunteers; and policy makers, foundation funders; and academic hangers-on. This multifaceted system is not easily harnessed by broad administrative efforts to impose order. Resistance to new ideas, resentment of those ideas being imposed by "outsiders," and the inclination to change incrementally are compounded by the specific challenges of implementation inherent in the adversarial system: too many players have different values or goals; ideas about how to go about implementation vary; and no one wants to be evaluated.[29] Feeley identified a concern with administrative reforms that this book has also raised: that "the greatest danger in the administrative strategy is that it will work, that it will transform a contentious and embattled group of professionals into cooperative bureaucrats," ultimately blunting a rights-based strategy for change.[30]

A cooperative bureaucracy is enhanced by family court unification. The "one family/one judge" reform proposal, which has been resurrected as part of the current family court unification movement, has, among other goals, an administrative impetus for consolidating all cases related to a family before a single judge to make the system more efficient. A judicial forum with broad jurisdiction that centralizes court activities and minimizes the need for litigants to appear in multiple proceedings in multiple fora is seen not only as efficient but also as effective for litigants.[31] Such consolidation may be very desirable in the case of divorce, custody, and support, since they are so inextricably linked. But it may undermine the rights or interests of other litigants. For example, when a youth is being charged with delinquency and his mother has brought a separate domestic violence case against her partner, whether the judge detains the youth may be based on whether the judge is worried the youth will witness domestic violence or live in a home with a lesbian mother and her partner, two reasons for taking away the youth's liberty that may be irrelevant to the issue of parole. A mother may even be reluctant to file the case against her partner for fear that the judge will use it against her when she asks for her child to be sent home. Consolidation may work against the mother's right to be protected and the youth's right to be paroled.

Efforts to reform courts cannot be separated from the laws and policies governing what makes a case justiciable and how much discretion the court is given to resolve the case. In the three areas of jurisdiction that have been examined in this book—juvenile delinquency, status offenses, and child welfare/family regulation—reforms to those systems in the last hundred years have been unable to significantly limit court jurisdiction or have actually expanded it.

Even when the court has been more constrained by legal mandates, the judge retains significant discretion in implementing court processes and crafting outcomes and may even abuse that discretion in the guise of judicial authority. Examining the limits of reform in these three realms reinforces the argument that this broad discretion—allegedly to do good by whatever means the court chooses, including punitive and coercive ones—routinely hampers reforms that range from implementing due process decrees to keeping misbehaving youth out of court to protecting family integrity. The next section looks at how judges continue to thwart due process mandates by claiming and executing excessive judicial discretion.

Due Process Mandates Fail to Stop Judicial Autocracy

The United States Department of Justice (DOJ) has been empowered since the mid-1990s to investigate systematic violations of children's civil rights in juvenile legal systems. Their work most often focuses on the conditions of confinement in juvenile detention and institutional facilities run by, or on behalf of, state or local governments. These conditions include the lack of proper medical care, inadequate mental health services, and insufficient or nonexistent educational opportunities as well as protection from physical and sexual abuse by staff and other inmates and unequal treatment for youth because of race or ethnicity. Their investigations usually result in reform plans for facilities to address sometimes dire and life-threatening conditions as well as proposals for alternatives to detention and incarceration.

Recent investigations have implicated facilities or systems in sixteen states.[32] Most relevant here were the DOJ's unprecedented investigations under the Barack Obama administration into the systemic lack of due process and equal protection in juvenile courts.[33] These investigations touched on four of the key issues explored in Part I of this book: lack of due process in juvenile court; excessive judicial discretion; punishment rather than or as treatment; and the disparate impact of the court's work on Black children.

The struggle for all juvenile courts since *Gault* has been to balance the due process protections that are essential for a fair and regularized process while addressing the special needs of children for preventive and rehabilitative help. As the Court in *Gault* emphasized, providing due process protections was not meant to replace "the conception of the kindly juvenile judge . . . by its opposite."[34] But it is not kindliness that has given rise to the failure of juvenile courts to protect children; it is discretion. Discretionary misuse of power is at the core of every recent DOJ investigation into the court's processes, uncovering what the DOJ has described as pre–*Gault* era practices.[35]

In 2009, when the DOJ began its investigation into the Juvenile Court of Memphis and Shelby County, Tennessee, children were being detained and sent to trial without knowing the charges against them. During pretrial probation conferences, children were not warned against self-incrimination; they were detained without timely probable cause hearings; and they were waived to adult court without adequate hearings. These pervasive due process violations stemmed in large part from a pre-*Gault* perspective on the role of the court and counsel half a century after *Gault* had been decided. Court officials spurned interjecting these protections into the court process, worrying that a more adversarial process would diminish civility among court personnel and youth. Juvenile defense lawyers failed to properly represent their clients with the judges' imprimatur: they permitted their clients to incriminate themselves; admitted to their clients' guilt during court colloquies; failed to request discovery; failed to challenge probable cause; and failed to file due process motions or appeals.[36]

Several years later while investigating the St. Louis County Family Court in Missouri, and issuing a "Statement of Interest" in a suit against the Superior Court of Fulton County, Georgia, the DOJ found similar systemic infractions in both jurisdictions. These investigations uncovered the failure to provide zealous counsel at every stage of a delinquency proceeding as well as the practice of judges routinely permitting children to waive the right to counsel without first consulting a lawyer.[37] How do courts today fail to incorporate these basic principles into their practices fifty years after *Gault*? St. Louis County had *one* full-time juvenile public defender. There was no uniform financial eligibility standard to determine indigency in order to have counsel appointed. If the court determined the child did not qualify for assigned counsel but the parent could not pay, the court required parents to pay a retainer against legal fees. Court files contained liens against parents unable to pay. The few private attorneys on the judges' "lists" who were assigned to represent children were not required to meet any special training or experience criteria.[38] Similarly, in Shelby County, Tennessee, a central condition of the ultimate settlement between the DOJ and the county was remedying the lack of sufficient dedicated lawyers with training and experience in juvenile practice.[39] But securing an adequate number of attorneys will not be sufficient. In every one of these DOJ investigations, judges and other court officials flouted the law by disregarding juveniles' basic constitutional rights.

When Justice Fortas in *Gault* declared that "the condition of being a boy does not justify a kangaroo court" and reminded juvenile court judges that "the admonition to function in a parental relationship is not an invitation to procedural arbitrariness," the procedural protections the Court was requiring were intended to prevent the harsh and disproportionate detentions and punishments that juveniles were then receiving routinely.[40] That harsh treatment nevertheless remained. In Memphis, children detained were subject to extreme restraints, including three shackling "restraint" chairs, an isolation room, and "dangerous and unconventional pressure point control tactics," which, while never justified, were often used when no threatening behavior was apparent. Bond was frequently set in detention hearings, often at excessively and sometimes unconstitutionally high levels.[41] Detention conditions—as well as postadjudication dispositions—fell disproportionately on Black children.

In the Shelby County juvenile court investigation, Black children were disproportionately represented in almost every phase of the juvenile legal process. Black children were only a third as likely to receive a warning than to be referred to court; twice as likely to be detained; twice as likely to be transferred to criminal court; about half as likely to receive a lesser sanction like a fine or community service; and one and a half times more likely to be confined in a juvenile corrections facility.[42]

In Meridian, Mississippi, the DOJ actually filed a "school to prison pipeline" complaint against the school system, the city, the county, and even the youth court and its judges for establishing an unconstitutional system of automatically arresting children suspended from school and sending them to the youth court, where they were placed on probation and required to serve their school suspensions in juvenile detention.[43] Between 2006 and 2009, all of the students referred to law enforcement under these policies were Black; all of the students expelled were Black; and 96 percent of the students suspended were Black.[44] Race mattered, again and again, at every point.

What ties together these investigations is how unlawfully judges—mostly under the public's radar—managed their courtrooms. Judge William Skinner II, in Hinds County, Georgia, defied a federal court consent decree for several years, continuing to handcuff youth waiting to appear before him regardless of their offense. Skinner claimed he was not a party to the decree and could continue his own courtroom policies, not only handcuffing but also detaining youth beyond the terms of the consent decree. Judge Skinner sued the county for shifting money away from the court so as to bring the county youth facility into compli ance with the decree; that suit was dismissed. After four years, Skinner finally participated in negotiating a new memorandum of understanding limiting his freewheeling ways.[45]

Judge Skinner could be dismissed as an errant example of misusing judicial power if the history of such misuse in family court were just history. But the practice of abusing judicial discretion remains far too prevalent to ignore. Florida provides another troubling example. The Florida Department of Juvenile Justice (FDJJ) has on its website a section titled "Myths vs. Facts" to dispel commonly believed myths about the state's juvenile legal system. One of those myths is about the most effective way to reduce recidivism. An important role of the FDJJ is to provide a comprehensive predisposition report and recommendation to the court prior to the judge determining whether and where to commit a youth. Such a report represents one of the core reasons for maintaining a separate court for children: that a detailed understanding of a young person will result in a disposition that will move the youth toward a productive adult life. Yet Florida's family court judges regularly bypass this report process on felonies and even misdemeanors—especially when they believe the FDJJ will not recommend residential commitment—and order the youth into a facility. These judges are perpetuating the myth that they know what is best to reduce crime. The "facts" are, however, that these "direct or bench" placements have 8 percent higher recidivism rates than identically matched youth who received probation. And lower-risk youth of color are more likely to be committed without the FDJJ report and recommendation—putting them at higher risk of recidivism.[46]

In 2009, the Florida Supreme Court chastised family court judges for not embracing the intent of the legislature for the courts to work with FDJJ "to provide juvenile offenders with dispositions that adequately and individually address their particular needs and risk levels."[47] The specific issue in E.A.R. v. State of Florida, was a family court judge's failure to identify the evidence and state the basis for disregarding FDJJ's recommendation for E.A.R. (the boy in question) to be placed in a moderately secure facility and instead committing him to the most restrictive and secure facility where his treatment and rehabilitation were likely to be compromised.[48] The larger issue was the family court judge's failure to recognize that "a disposition hearing is actually the culmination of a more extensive process, which the Legislature constructed to provide adjudicated juvenile offenders 'the most appropriate dispositional services in the least restrictive available setting' while also protecting the public from further acts of delinquency."[49] In other words, understanding that the entire purpose of creating an alternative juvenile legal system was to treat and rehabilitate young people so they stop committing crimes.

The most egregious example of abuse of judicial power occurred in Lucerne County, Pennsylvania, over the course of five years, from 2003 to 2008, when Judge Mark Ciavarella, presiding over juvenile proceedings involving more that 6,000 cases and 2,500 children, removed more than 60 percent of the children from their homes. Over 50 percent of the children who appeared before Ciavarella did so without counsel.[50] While the story is mostly known because Ciavarella received millions of dollars in kickbacks for sending children to a privately developed but county-run juvenile corrections facility, that corruption was facilitated by the judge's ability to run the court as he saw fit. In the final report of the state commission tasked with investigating the scandal, Ciavarella was described as a "zero tolerance" judge who took a hard line on crime, especially in schools; routinely broke court rules, including the provision of counsel; and frequently sent youth away from home when they got into trouble, especially in school. The report highlighted: "Juvenile court was Ciavarella's domain. He ruled there supreme . . . [and the] records show, his manner was harsh, autocratic and arbitrary. He judged by formula rather than by individual evaluation."[51] His misdeeds were uncovered when the Juvenile Law Center of Philadelphia (JLC) was alerted that children were being railroaded through the court and began investigating the allegations. JLC filed a petition in the Pennsylvania Supreme Court contending that children were not represented by counsel or were not lawfully waiving their right to counsel.[52] That original petition was denied, but as the corruption scandal emerged and the United States Attorney filed criminal charges against Ciavarella, the JLC returned to the Pennsylvania high court and renewed its request. Eventually, under a special magistrate, all the cases adjudicated by Ciavarella were vacated, and the records of those 2,251 children were expunged.[53] The JLC continued its advocacy, which resulted in new court rules requiring all juveniles under fourteen years of age to have lawyers at all delinquency proceedings; providing that youth fourteen years and older may waive their right to counsel only in limited circumstances and only if the court is satisfied that the juvenile made a knowing, intelligent, and voluntary waiver of that right; deeming all juveniles indigent and entitled to an attorney if they appear without one in a delinquency matter; and strictly limiting physical restraints on children appearing in court. Soon afterward, these rules were enacted into state law.[54] They should—but may not—curb judicial discretion in a court that glorifies judicial authority.

Family Court and Status Offenses: Still Not Letting Go of Misbehavior

In the first few years of the twenty-first century, over 200,000 children each year were charged with status offenses with around 16,000 of them being detained at some point in the proceedings and close to 15,000 children being placed out of their homes as a final disposition.[55] The good news is that those numbers have dropped steadily. Petitions were halved to just under 100,000 in 2018, and fewer than 5,000 children were detained and 2,300 children were placed out of their homes that year.[56] Despite the overall numbers dropping, between 2005 and 2018 the proportion of petitioned status offense cases involving Black and Hispanic youth increased. The total petitioned status-case rates for Native American youth and Black youth were consistently higher than case rates for all other racial categories.[57] These are not just statistics but children's lives. Given what we know about the poor outcomes for youth processed through the family court—particularly when they are removed from home—continuing to prosecute youth for behavior that is not a crime and removing them from their homes must be stopped. The downward trend is not accidental; there has been a revived recognition that coercive action for status offenders is ineffective and costly.[58] Yet a recent case from a rural county in Tennessee, described below, exemplifies the long-standing, pervasive, and continuing abuses of court jurisdiction over status offenses, which continue mostly to be hidden from public scrutiny.

John was a victim of bullying in his freshman year of high school. He had been diagnosed in third grade with ADHD, major depression, and anxiety and suffered from problems with his physical motor skills. John's school identified him as a student with a disability eligible for special education supports and services. In November during his freshman year, John attempted suicide after repeated bullying. A psychiatrist and therapist recommended that John receive homebound education while he was adjusting to his medication and recovering from his emotional trauma. His family expected the school administration to respond appropriately to the hostile environment John experienced before his return to school. John's doctor's orders covered his absences from school through Christmas break. On his first morning back at school in early January, John was called to the principal's office over the school's public intercom.

When he arrived at the office, he was confronted by a city police officer who told him that he was under arrest for truancy and would be taken to the juvenile detention center. He was arrested in front of the entire school during a class change, placed in the back of a police car, and driven to the juvenile detention center. There he was told to strip naked, ordered to shower, and given an orange jumpsuit, white socks, and orange flip-flops. He was bombarded with questions—Have you had sex? Do you have any sexually transmitted diseases? Do you use drugs?—before being compelled to give a urine sample (which tested clean). John was allowed one phone call to his mother at the end of the day. His mother found out about his arrest around the time that he should have been getting home from school. John spent the night in a locked cell, where he was housed with other juveniles who were charged with drug offenses and robbery and with one youth who was set to be tried in adult criminal court. The next morning John appeared in juvenile court still wearing the orange jumpsuit but now also handcuffed and in shackles. When his case was finally called before a packed courtroom, the judge did not allow either John or his family to speak. He was not represented by an attorney. The judge told John that if he didn't go to school he would be placed in a foster home. The judge then ordered the child welfare authorities to investigate John's family home. Afraid of disobeying the court, his family took John back to school for the rest of the day.[59]

John's experience was especially traumatic and disgraceful, but status offense petitions for truancy and subsequent detention are not exceptional. In 2016, 57 percent of status-offense petitions in the country were based on truancy.[60] In Colorado, an investigation of status offenses for truancy found that nearly half of youth found to be truant also received public mental health services and that those youth with serious mental health concerns were three times more likely to be detained for truancy. Youth detained for truancy are nearly two times less likely to graduate from high school and are nearly twice as likely to have subsequent delinquency compared to other youth found to be truant. These types of findings are finally having an impact. Following the investigation, laws and practices in Colorado were changed, leading to a drop in the number of status offenses for truancy of approximately 40 percent from 2010 to 2017, with the number of detained youth dropping from a high of 482 to a low of fifteen.[61]

In 2007, for the first time since the end of its Juvenile Justice Standards Project in the early 1980s, the American Bar Association (ABA) officially reconsidered status offenses, adopting a recommendation urging state, local, and tribal governments to mandate "the development and implementation of targeted evidence-based programs that provide juvenile, family-focused, and strength-based early intervention and pre-court prevention services and treatment to alleged juvenile status offenders and their families." The resolution called for more gender-responsive programming and urged Congress to tie federal funding to these community-based, preventive, family-friendly proposals.[62] Invoking the earlier JJ Standards Project, the ABA's House of Delegates noted that the ABA had always been a voice for progressive youth policy (even though the *Noncriminal Misbehavior* volume had been tabled for being too radical). The policies they were now heralding made "helping families resolve their problems internally" a more effective approach by shifting responsibility for diversion and prevention to social services systems and away from juvenile legal or probation agencies that traditionally address criminal or delinquent behavior. The resolution promotes community-based alternatives, including respite care, to any out-of-home placements, especially as an alternative to secure settings: "Research shows that punitive approaches, such as secure detention, are ineffective at reducing recidivism, stigmatize youth, and cost significantly more than pre-court diversion services, the latter of which results in better outcomes for youth and families."[63] The resolution warns that detention and placement imply wrongdoing and delinquent behavior and "carries the stigma of being a 'bad seed'"—a clear throwback to the concerns about labeling that the JJ Standards Project emphasized decades earlier. The ABA urged Congress to amend federal law to preclude judges from locking up status offenders by eliminating the valid court order (VCO) exception, which allows judges to commit a youth to a secure facility if the youth violates a direct order of the court. The ABA's resolution also advocated for clearer and higher prevention standards for the states to meet "to avoid unnecessary judicial and state child protection or juvenile justice agency involvement that could stigmatize youth unnecessarily."[64] Three years later in 2010, for the first time in its history, the National Council of Juvenile and Family Court Judges similarly supported VCO repeal.[65] Neither organization's advocacy was sufficient to eliminate locking up status offenders.

Reforming but Not Repealing the VCO

In December 2018, Congress reauthorized and revised the Juvenile Justice and Delinquency Prevention Act (JJDPA). The most contentious aspect of the law continued to be the power of judges to commit a status offender to a secure detention or correction facility if the youth violated a valid court order. Prior to the reauthorization, in FY 2016, twenty-five states (and all U.S. territories) reported no VCO use. Nevertheless, in the states that continued to use VCOs, they could number in the hundreds.[66] A 2015 report found that almost 20 percent of detained status offenders and other nonoffenders were placed in living quarters with youth who have committed murder or manslaughter, and 25 percent were placed in units with felony sex offenders. Detained youth are often held in overcrowded, understaffed facilities that, the report noted, can breed violence and exacerbate unmet needs.[67] Family court judges invoking their VCO authority know all too well about the local conditions.

Senator Tom Cotton of Arkansas—a state that used the VCO 832 times in 2016—single-handedly stopped full repeal of the VCO. The compromise was a set of rules that judges must follow if they want to use the provision and limiting the length of incarceration. States continuing to permit the VCO must create plans to ensure the timely release of youth held in a secure detention or correctional facility; identify specific reentry procedures for released youth; and create alternatives to secure detention.[68]

While these restrictions will certainly continue to reduce the use of lockups for status offenders and keep them out of dangerous facilities, the VCO is only the worse aspect of charging a young person with a status offense. Being charged as a status offender is a stigmatizing, humiliating, ineffective, and punitive way to address complex family and community problems. Youth are blamed by their parents, their school, or the police and then fight these authority figures in court to challenge the allegations or try to exonerate themselves. This is bad for families. The *Noncriminal Misbehaving* volume of the JJ Standards Project that was tabled succinctly summarized the dangers of status-offense proceedings:

> Allowing formalized coercive intervention . . . in unruly child cases undermines family autonomy, isolates the child, polarizes parents and children, encourages parents to abdicate their functions and roles to the court, may blunt the effectiveness of any ameliorative services that are provided, and cuts against the development of controls and means within the family for the resolution of conflicts.[69]

Yet even when judges understand this analysis, they use their power to improve the process, not eliminate it.

Enlightened Judicial Leadership Isn't the Solution

Many judges work diligently to keep youth in the community and out of intrusive court processes. A 2012 report on nine judges around the country titled *Positive Power: Exercising Judicial Leadership to Prevent Court Involvement and Incarceration of Non-Delinquent Youth* highlighted judicial work that was driven by four concepts: demand for the best available information of what produces good outcomes for youth, families, and communities; balancing effective alternatives to detention while protecting community safety; partnering with all segments of the system to produce community-based solutions; and using judicial leadership to help reach solutions.[70] These goals will again lead to fewer status offenders penetrating deeper into the system, as they have every time a court system or legislative mandate has combined well-funded, community-based services and assistance with curtailed court jurisdiction.

These goals nevertheless raise the most profound, if unintended, consequence of the court system, as the Johnson Commission noted in 1967: "[The] most informed and benign official treatment of the child . . . contains within it the seeds of its own frustration and itself may often feed the very disorder it is designed to cure."[71] Two of the goals included in the 2012 *Positive Power* report will do that—the one that balances community safety with effective alternatives to detention, and the one that urges judicial leadership in reaching solutions. If these youth are not committing crimes, then what is the community safety that needs to be balanced? As one of the judges in the report, Judge Karen Ashby of Denver, found, most status offenders ordered into locked detention "were at risk to no one but themselves."[72] Judge Steve Teske of Georgia put it more bluntly: "Adolescents sometimes do stupid things, and I did plenty of stupid things as a teenager. But I was never arrested or referred to juvenile court, and today I am a judge."[73] Adolescents doing stupid—but not criminal—things don't belong in court. Judges Ashby and Teske, along with the other judges highlighted in *Positive Power*, have worked to diminish detention while developing promising diversion practices for status offenders. Regardless of that promise, however, if we define youthful misbehavior as behavior that impinges on community safety, the court's "seeds of its own frustration" have cyclically led to abandoning noncoercive, community-oriented solutions for punitive ones.

And we continue not to treat all misbehaving youth equally. I am sure Judge Teske realizes that part of the reason he wasn't arrested for his youthful misbehavior was personal demographics—including his race—that made him less likely to come to the attention of the police and courts. Throughout the history of defining and bringing misbehaving youth to court, the juvenile legal and status offense systems have repeatedly treated youth exhibiting the same behavior differently by race, gender, economic status, and community. Judge Frances Doherty of Nevada discovered that girls were detained for less serious offenses and remained on probation for longer periods of time than boys.[74] That finding would not surprise Helen Geddes, Camille Sippy, or Cindy Snyder, all depicted in chapter 6, or the researchers who have drawn the same conclusions for decades. Does the phantom of "community safety" really outweigh the harm applied disproportionately to these youth?

The *Positive Power* report also resurfaces the historical meaning of "judicial leadership" in family court. As it applies directly to status offenses, two points are worth repeating. First, any court project that is built around the practices of individual judges rather than laws and rules intended to restrain judicial discretion are only as good as those judges. Judge Joan Byer, featured in *Positive Power* for her development of the Louisville, Kentucky, truancy diversion project, warns that not any judge should be involved with this project but rather only ones with the right judicial temperament: "A disciplinarian who is inclined to focus on failure is not the right person for this job. A combination of firmness and warmth, coupled with seriousness and an emphasis on success and strength, is essential."[75] That is exactly the same point that Walter Gellhorn made when he studied the New York City Children's Court in 1954. While Gellhorn was advocating for a unified family court, he nevertheless recommended that the "school part" for truants not be consolidated because the "school part" judges "seem not in general to arouse fears, resentments, and emotional blockades to the acceptance of treatment," unlike the experiences in other parts of the court.[76] Like the juvenile court's founders, Gellhorn and Judge Byer *should* expect every family court judge to have these attributes. But their warnings then and now remind us that most judges don't have those attributes and never did. As Justice Blackmun wrote in *McKeiver*: "Too often the juvenile court judge falls far short of that stalwart, protective, and communicating figure the system envisaged."[77]

The second point is that all the judges acclaimed in *Positive Power* are committed to ending the harms caused by treating youth as status offenders. If they truly want to end that harm, then they should be advocating for the elimination of court jurisdiction in these cases and urging state and local officials to use all the resulting funds for the interventions that have been shown to help these youth and their families. What we know from the last 120 years of court history is that dragging misbehaving youth through the court system is ineffective, discriminatory, expensive, and harmful for them, for their families, and for their communities. The work the *Positive Power* judges are doing to limit harm and do good for the youth they oversee may be admirable judicial leadership. But giving up that power would be inspired judicial leadership.

Maintaining the Centrality of Judges in Family Regulation: Court Improvement Projects and Model Courts

Judicial leadership also continues to animate reforms in child protection and dependency court proceedings. The fourth National Summit on Judicial Leadership in Child Welfare was held in Minnesota in 2019, almost fifteen years after the first summit was convened there. In the opening session, Jerry Milner, head of the federal Children's Bureau at the time, denounced the failure of the entire apparatus of child welfare—including courts—to support families and keep children safe. He asserted that no one in the audience should be comfortable with this critique and should instead despair, along with Milner himself, their collective failure. He nevertheless found reason to hope. If family court judges would lead the change by supporting families with kindness and compassion, providing them with due process and legal representation, and ensuring that the assistance that families need to remain together were available long before they found themselves in court, then only those children who absolutely needed to be removed from their families would be. These exhortations were consistent with the principles intended to be used as a guiding vision during the summit and after participants returned to their courthouses: first, courts create a culture that values all families; second, courts ensure that children and families involved with child welfare experience a legal system in which they have meaningful access to justice and their rights are protected; and third, courts lead collaborative efforts to help families and strengthen communities.[78]

What sets Millner's remarks and these principles apart is their focus on keeping families together, listening to families' concerns, and supporting them before they reach a crisis. As in some of Millner's other speeches and writings, this is a rebuke and a rejection of the precepts of the Adoption and Safe Families Act (ASFA) that resulted in tearing millions of children away from their families, often forever. Millner's call to action is brave and heartfelt and important. He nevertheless relies on judicial leadership to mobilize this change, just as judges have been called on to lead reform since the juvenile court was established. Millner also does what so many before him have done: he points to an outstanding judge as an exemplar to follow, in this instance Judge Trent Farve, who in only two years significantly reduced the number of children in foster care in Hancock County, Mississippi. Judge Farve follows in the footsteps of those judges who are capable of that leadership and somehow make vast improvements, often until they move on to other positions and their successors don't have the same skill or interest or perspective to continue their predecessor's work.[79]

The context of Millner's speech is also important. The late twentieth-century movement to unify and reform family court just predates ASFA but eventually becomes fully entangled in ASFA's safety, permanency, and well-being mandates and the enhanced obligations that the court work collaboratively with child welfare agencies to ensure ASFA's implementation. Federal and foundation funding for court reform developed a complicated combination of reform efforts that engaged not only state and local child welfare agencies and the family courts but also the Conferences of Chief Judges and Chief Administrative Judges, the National Council of Juvenile and Family Court Judges (NCJFCJ), the National Center for State Courts, the American Bar Association's Center on Children and the Law, and myriad contracted consultants, including think tanks and academics, to create materials and trainings and to study the reform efforts and issue reports.[80]

Two key court reform projects emerged. The first was the Model Courts program spearheaded in 1980 by the NCJFCJ and funded initially by the Edna McConnell Clark Foundation and later by the U.S. Department of Justice.[81] Model court judges are supposed to lead by example for their colleagues locally and nationally. Forty years later, leading by example remains a key component in model court judicial leadership. One of the most recent NCJFCJ model court publications declares: "[These] national judicial leaders have considerable experience leading system-wide collaborative stakeholder teams to design and implement program, practice, and policy changes to improve outcomes for children and families involved in the foster care system."[82]

Model courts do, in fact, model best practices for judges and over time have shifted their focus from merely getting the court to work more efficiently to paying far closer attention to the impact the court has on families. What the model courts have in common with earlier claims of the court's remarkable achievements is that they haven't proven that the modeling itself has made the difference. Publications about model courts craft language very carefully not to claim cause and effect, but they nevertheless give the impression that, because a court has become a model court, important outcomes have resulted. These claims include a reduction in the number of children in foster care; an increase in adoptions; timelier hearings; greater focus on foster children's education; reduced time between hearings; and more use of alternative dispute resolution to eliminate the need for additional court hearings.[83] What we don't know for most of these accomplishments is whether the reason is the special funding and technical assistance the model court received; the quality of the judge in the model court; the greater availability of targeted resources; or, crucially, whether these changes happened for reasons entirely beyond the control of the model court. Neither do we know whether these models are scalable. In just one example, the New York City family court, as a model court, is credited with greatly reducing the number of children in foster care. The model-court status may have contributed to the drop in foster care numbers, but there are myriad reasons far beyond the court as a model court, including positive ones—like the creation of institutional family defense practices—and ones that haven't yet been analyzed but are worrisome—like placing children under court supervision with their parents or another caretaker instead of formal foster care. It is, of course, very difficult to measure the cause of a change in outcomes, and the attempts that have been made have not yielded definitive results beyond recommended but unproven best practices.

The second and most significant attempt by the federal government to support and analyze family court reform occurred in the 2000s. The federal government had been funding the Court Improvement Project (CIP) since the early 1990s and began a series of evaluations of CIP. The first study acknowledged that the CIP was still in its infancy but appeared to be a catalyst for getting disparate parts of the court system to work together.[84] Those involved in the initial efforts agreed that suddenly it felt like all parts of the system were collaborating to accomplish change and that there was finally a meaningful opportunity to fix a very broken system.[85] Nevertheless, even in this early study, the authors warned that states needed to document their efforts and the outcomes if they were going to be able to replicate successes and address challenges.[86] Two years later, the same authors were asked to determine whether the states' CIP efforts were even capable of being evaluated. Their 2003 feasibility report provided the first real insight into how difficult it would be to assess reform efforts: CIP funding had let a thousand flowers bloom without asking states to keep track of the outcomes in any rigorous fashion. A range of creative and perhaps effective projects were being piloted with almost no way to measure whether they were working or whether they could be replicated. After almost ten years of court reform funding, this 2003 report was the first serious attempt to generate systematic knowledge about CIP. The 2003 feasibility study concluded that having a review of state projects at certain moments in time would provide a broader context for the more in-depth evaluations that were proposed.[87] In 2007, that "snapshot" review was published. Emily Cooke, who was then the CIP project officer, cautioned that the snapshot was *not* intended to "assess the quality or impact of CIP reforms." Yet the report culminates in a chapter titled "Successes Attributable to State CIP Programs." The authors then list a surprising number of accomplishments that state CIP coordinators *attribute* to CIP, including improved representation of parties, enhanced collaboration among stakeholders in the system, and improved quality of hearings.[88] This was attribution without proof.

The final CIP evaluation was completed in 2010 but is not currently (and never was) easily available; I secured it in 2012 through the graciousness of David Kelly at the Children's Bureau. Not surprisingly, the final evaluation essentially captured Malcolm Feeley's findings that courts—in this case in collaboration with child welfare agencies—are mostly working toward greater coordination and better system management. As Feeley also noted, this administrative approach can be a dangerous endeavor that leads to collaborations that can actually *undermine* the rights of the various parties. What is the clearest lesson from the final evaluation, however, is that it is impossible to evaluate how a particular reform funded pursuant to CIP implicates the overall workings of the court. As the evaluation noted:

Dependency court reform is an [ongoing] and evolutionary process [undertaken at all levels of government, and given] dependency court reform's evolving nature, and the fact that CIP is generally used by States in a flexible manner to fund systemic reform, it is challenging to implement rigorous evaluation strategies to measure the program's impact. Within the study sites, we found much progress and movement largely consistent with Federal and site intent. However, it was difficult to consistently attribute these changes solely to CIP given the existence of many other reforms and factors. Still, the data and perceptions on the ground indicate that CIP played a key role as a facilitator of reform, consistent with the program's intent.[89]

Perhaps the CIP funding did move courts in the direction the federal government and local CIP sites intended. But what we know about the overall contributions of family courts to implement improvements to the child welfare systems in the subsequent years, and to our understanding of the sheer numbers of children impacted by these systems, Millner's remarks of despair in 2019 more accurately represents what happened.

As chapter 8 outlined, in 2000 the Children's Bureau created the Child and Family Services Review (CFSR) process to measure state compliance with federal funding mandates to support positive child safety, permanency, and well-being outcomes. Starting with the second review begun in 2007, family courts were required to participate in the process, including in the Program Improvement Plan (PIP), to respond to areas where the state had not achieved compliance. There have now been three reviews, and a fourth has begun. The CFSR aggregate report for the third round, which was conducted between 2015–2019, concluded: "The 51 states reviewed in Round 3 met few of the performance standards established by the Children's Bureau for the 7 [measured] outcomes."[90] The Children's Bureau issued a separate report on the extent to which the "legal and judicial communities" were in substantial compliance on the factors most related to their work: achieving timely permanency; promoting and maintaining family relationships and connections; meaningfully engaging families; and keeping families together. Since the reviews are based largely on a limited number of case samples during the finite review period, they "cannot be considered fully representative of national characteristics of the child welfare system. . . . [However,] the results help to illuminate areas of practice and systemic strengths, challenges, and opportunities for targeted improvement activities."[91] Their illumination is dismal. While there are some positive outcomes within specific categories in every measure, no state achieved substantial conformity across the combined measures most closely associated with judicial involvement. Tellingly, the lowest-performing of the CFSR outcomes is permanency and stability—key mandates for courts—and one of the lowest performing systemic factors is the case review system, which focuses on the court process.[92]

Describing this CFSR story from a national numerical perspective reveals little overall change in official numbers. Between FY 2012 and FY 2017, the number of children in foster care on the last day of the fiscal year increased from 392,000 to 437,000, before dropping to 407,000 in FY 2020, the lowest number in care since 2014. Entries into foster care fluctuated around 250,000 during the same period, except for 2020, which saw a substantial decrease (and which may ultimately be attributed to the COVID-19 pandemic). The number of children awaiting adoption fluctuated between 102,000 and 126,000, remaining between 26–29 percent of the children in care for the previous decade. The percentage of those children whose parental rights had already been terminated fluctuated during the previous decade but was always more than 50 percent. The percentage of children exiting care having been adopted has increased since 2014, reaching a high of 26 percent in FY 2019 and FY 2020.[93] These numbers and the outcomes specifically attributed to the court defy any semblance of improvement.

The official numbers, however, don't even tell the whole story. While the overall numbers of children in foster care remained above 400,000 in the previous decade—in and of itself an outrageous number of children as wards of the state—we now know that most states also operate hidden foster care systems "that make profound decisions without court involvement or oversight, or any meaningful checks and balances [by changing] custody of children (sometimes permanently), [remove] legal obligations for the agency to help reunify parents and children or to supervise children to ensure their safety and well-being, and fail[] to provide kinship caregivers with supports comparable to those in formal foster care."[94] Notably, as Professor Josh Gupta-Kagan has brought to light, this practice of child protective agencies largely coerces parents who are being investigated for potential neglect or abuse into signing "safety plans" that place their children with family or friends (or sometimes even strangers) without any of the attendant protections or assistance that the formal system is obligated to provide. This practice enables states to sidestep the costs and requirements of court processes and foster care altogether while potentially leaving many children and families unserved and unprotected. While many times an informal agreement to change custody is beneficial—especially when a relative or friend is available for a short respite while a parent resolves a particular issue and the family avoids the stress and disruption of state intervention and court adjudication—the widespread use of this coercive practice intimates more nefarious reasons. Gupta-Kagan found that federal funding sources under the Kinship Navigator Program and the Families First Prevention Services Act provide unintended financial incentives for states to use hidden foster care in the guise of preventing children from entering foster care. The Kinship Navigator Program is not income-based, so the state can draw down more funds with fewer eligibility requirements. States that use these funds to support the transfer of children through unregulated safety plans can provide some income support to these kin but are freed from other regulatory obligations to ensure the appropriateness and safety of the children's care or to work toward reunification of the parents and children. Similarly, funds available under Families First to prevent children from entering care can be used to sidestep regulation and reporting requirements. The statutory language of Families First is aimed at preventing children from entering care, not preventing them from being separated from their parents. The law encourages a child to be placed with kin but without meeting any particular legal standard or the provision of any due process protections to the family. The subsequent reporting requirements ask only if the state kept a child out of care, not if the state kept parents and children together—again providing an incentive to utilize hidden foster care.[95]

There is no known count of the number of children in hidden foster care, but Gupta-Kagan estimates there is strong evidence that the numbers are very high, possibly equal to the number of children in formal foster care.[96] And while this book has asserted that the family court collaborating with and monitoring child protection agencies has failed to ensure family integrity or keep children safe and well, this hidden system reveals an even starker truth. While model programs and best practices were being developed to improve the family regulation and court systems, states were creating a shadow system to sidestep what were supposed to be meaningful and lasting reforms.

Reform Has Failed

The time has come to stop trying to reform the family court. Let's move from endless reports declaring the "crisis" in family court, always accompanied by the same recommendations—more resources and more judges—to make the court work better. Let's acknowledge that the court is never going to be in "substantial compliance" with statutory mandates to keep families together and stable or to find children permanency. We need to stop reforming around the edges of what we know. The Great Idea has failed. It is time for a new vision.

10

Abolition

In the spring of 2020, family regulation reforms began to sweep the country. The state of New York eliminated the term "incorrigible" from its status offenses statute, encouraged by the Brooklyn-based Girls for Gender Equity, which lobbied the legislature under the banner "Encourageable not Incorrigible."[1] Community activists also spurred New York to amend its child abuse and neglect reporting law, raising the standard of evidence from "some credible evidence" to "a fair preponderance of evidence" to initiate a court petition for child maltreatment and reducing the impact of "hotline report" records.[2] During that same spring, Illinois governor J. B. Pritzker announced a plan to close five state juvenile detention centers that were "too punitive and too ineffective . . . exacerbate [the] trauma . . . [and create] a culture of instability and violence." Instead of large detention facilities "rife with racism," in Pritzker's words, juveniles would be sent to residential treatment centers, with dormlike accommodations and wraparound services.[3] California governor Gavin Newsom adopted a similar plan, moving to close all state juvenile prisons and keeping youth closer to home in county facilities by July 2021.[4] And in reaction to staff abuses in Philadelphia's youth residential and group home facilities, a new youth ombudsperson office was created to investigate complaints.[5]

While these changes are likely to reduce the harm to some youth and families, they are essentially back-end reforms, leaving in place the structures that have regulated marginalized families for more than a hundred years. Not labeling a youth "incorrigible" without eliminating status-offense jurisdiction altogether fails to address why truant, runaway, or "misbehaving" youth who haven't broken the law are brought to court at all. Closing juvenile jails and prisons yet sending youth to other institutions doesn't reckon with whether most of the young people held should *ever* be prosecuted or placed away from home, even with an appointed ombudsperson (and additional bureaucracy) to investigate any maltreatment. And providing for a fairer system of sealing records is a very small step to confront the needless investigation of millions of families yearly through a mandatory and often anonymous reporting system. Why should thousands of these families still find themselves in family court and hundreds of thousands of their children be placed in foster care?[6] The reforms are not intended or designed to dismantle the deeply embedded and failed approaches to "helping" families through the family court. And they certainly don't question whether family court should continue to exist as a mechanism to manage families.

Why and How to Abolish Family Court

This final chapter provides a road map to shrinking the systems that send families and children into family court, shrinking the family court, and ultimately abolishing it. This process draws from abolitionist theory and practices confronting the criminal legal system, albeit understood and applied differently in the context of family court. Creating mechanisms to reduce the number of families who reach the court are steps to shrink the system, or what some scholars call "minimalism."[7] But the reason that minimalism alone won't remedy the failures of family court is that it won't eliminate the persistence of the court's fundamental purpose, which is to "do good." The Great Idea of creating a therapeutic court with beneficent judges who will solve the problems of families remains its foundational premise no matter how big or small that court is. Neither multiple reinventions over the past century nor layering procedural protections atop its hearings have diminished the interventionist spirit of such a court to save children and, if they can't be saved, to punish them or their families through extreme intrusion, surveillance, separation, or incarceration. At the same time, the family court has neither the authority nor the inclination to confront the structural barriers that bedevil the marginalized families appearing there. It focuses instead on the specific child, youth, or parent before it as the problem to be fixed, reinforcing the belief that the court, by fixing the person, will fix the larger systemic problem. The history of this court, as illustrated throughout this book, has demonstrated how that approach has failed.

An abolitionist approach, in contrast, embraces different premises about family court. The first is that a court is not the place to solve problems but instead—and only when necessary—is the forum to adjudicate disputes. The idea of a therapeutic court has blurred the distinction between actual legal controversies and the social problems families face—like poverty and systemic marginalization—that cannot be addressed by a court process. Yet massive surveillance and regulatory systems are primed to send families into court not because there is an adversarial legal dispute but because the court has been designated as the place to manage marginalized families and their problems.

Second, an abolitionist approach rejects trying to improve this kind of court. The family court has been "reformed"—or, more honestly, reinvented and readjusted—repeatedly since its birth as the juvenile court. Yet those adjustments have failed to improve either the processes or the outcomes for most of the litigants and have instead caused significant harm.[8] The U.S. Second Circuit Court of Appeals once cautioned against using the "best interests of the child" standard as a justification for inappropriately intervening in family life. The court feared that the "best interests" standard glorified doing good while ignoring C. S. Lewis's warning that "[o]f all tyrannies a tyranny sincerely exercised for the good of its victims may be the most oppressive. . . . [T]hose who torment us for our own good will torment us without end for they do so with the approval of their own conscience."[9] The family court's belief in its ability to do good has salved its conscience and prevented it from confronting the harm that even well-intentioned do-gooding has caused.

The mission to do good has also thwarted the court from recognizing how it has helped to drain resources out of communities and into the court or the government agencies that report to the court. The effect is twofold: Communities in great need are underserviced by trusted supports and the structural inequities that might be at least partially addressed by those community resources are ignored. Court observers have identified this problem since the court's founding. Worse still, those inequities are transformed into questions of individual responsibility. The effect here is even greater. By structuring responses to marginalized families around court processes that focus on blame and intervention, the grossest inequalities that propel those families into court are ignored.

My colleague Professor Kendall Thomas once said that "abolition is looking at problems from the perspective of the governed." From the perspective of children and families who find themselves in family court, they want a different solution to the issues that got them there. Embracing their voices is an integral part of the solutions this chapter offers. I draw on Professors Lani Guanier and Gerald Torres's conception of *demosprudence*, which emphasizes "the role of culture shifting, not just rule shifting, in producing durable social change"; demosprudence "represents a philosophical commitment to the lawmaking force of meaningful participatory democracy."[10] Thus the goal of abolishing the family court must be consonant with the experiences and agendas of those most deeply harmed. I doubt we would even be talking about abolition of the family court without the truth-reckoning brought about by impacted youth and parents. This culture-shifting has meant that, rather than relying on traditional advocates and action-oriented academics—like myself—to lead, impacted youth and parents "integrate lawyers not as leaders but as fellow advocates . . . in producing durable social and legal change."[11] Many of the solutions I propose for change have been built on the advocacy of those activists.

An abolitionist mindset requires us to let go of our historical beliefs. Each time proposals to move significant authority out of the court have been proposed, judges have warned of the dangers to families of diminishing judicial power. When various reformists and policy makers recommend replacing judicial authority and jurisdiction—especially with the development of community-based, voluntary, and comprehensive supports—family court judges have obstinately responded with "we may not always get it right and we might do some harm but we're better than any other alternative."[12] Professor Brendan Roediger points out how this is "a defensive idealism or reformism [that] demands its own replication," and if "we are serious about disrupting the generational reproduction of the racial social order," then we must liberate ourselves from our allegiance to the governing structures we know, including these courts.[13] This call is eerily similar to Professor Francis Allen's 1964 admonition that fundamental solutions were not to be found in the juvenile court but "in the direction of integrating our alienated populations into full participation in the social, economic, political and cultural life of our communities."[14]

Finally, an abolitionist mindset allows for interim measures that are not "reformist" in nature—those intended to strengthen and improve the current system—but represent steps necessary for the *deconstruc-*

tion of the regime. Every step in the process has to be scrutinized to see if in fact it reduces surveillance, investigation, and intervention. This vigilance is essential because, as Roediger notes: "Reforms, no matter how serious or how imaginative, can never change the nature of the arrangement, which is control."[15] To recognize the depth of that control, to be consonant with the experiences and agendas of those children and families most deeply impacted, it is not possible to replace the court with a new, better version. Instead, we must use a radical imagination first to shrink and then to abolish the court. And then we must use a radical imagination to consider how to support children and families without controlling them so they achieve full democratic participation.

This chapter presents a framework for abolition and reinvention in three parts. Under the overarching idea of radical nonintervention, the initial discussion differentiates between the need to treat children differently from adults and the need for a specialized court that adjudicates those children and extensively intervenes in families' lives. The socialized family court that intrudes especially in the lives of marginalized families and tries to "fix" them needs to be replaced by a system of supports that reduce greatly the need for any court intervention. The second part recommends steps to close the door to the court by narrowing significantly the court's jurisdiction over children and families. For the far smaller number of people finding themselves in court, additional due process protections and statutory changes will replace discretionary authority to "do good" and further diminish the need for a separate socialized court. The last section embraces a political agenda that relies on those communities most deeply affected by the current family court regime to lead us toward a system of supporting children and families to reach their fullest potential.

Radical Nonintervention

The first step in diminishing the role of the court in people's lives is determining what activities, actions, or people don't belong in the family court process. This is complicated by the multiple systems that send children and parents into the court. I have focused primarily on the three areas of state intervention that motivated the creation of the original juvenile court: *delinquency*, *status offenses*, and *child dependency*.

Because these three areas have the greatest impact on individual liberty and family integrity, they represent not only the greatest power that the court can exert over families but also the greatest harm it can cause. At the same time, deciding who or what does not belong in court raises the question of where it does belong or whether it belongs anywhere at all.

Historically, the central animating purpose of creating and maintaining a separate court for children was to divert children and youth out of the adult criminal justice system. And the court did succeed in this goal.[16] As Franklin Zimring noted in his 1999 contribution to a one-hundredth anniversary volume, *A Century of Juvenile Justice*, we *should* rightly celebrate treating children differently from adults when they get into trouble, and we should maintain our commitment to "a jurisprudence of patience and restraint, an institutional commitment to do less harm than the criminal courts did to young offenders."[17] While the latest neuroscience and developmental psychology research reconfirms the justification for treating children accused of crimes differently from adults,[18] the treatment that most children *currently* experience in the court is not "a jurisprudence of patience and restraint." Neither is "less harm" necessarily done to young offenders by the juvenile legal system. This is because the other animating purpose of the court was to fix children (and later families), which has failed. This reality allows us to ask whether what is needed is not a separate court but a greater commitment to treating children differently than adults. Instead of trying to fix children and families, we need to create ways to support them. Let's look at the first aspect: what it means to treat children differently.

What Treating Children Differently Means

Since the beginning of the twenty-first century, the Supreme Court has issued several "children are different" cases involving youth tried in adult court for serious violent crimes. In the first, *Roper v. Simmons* (2005), the Supreme Court reversed its long-standing position permitting the state execution of children. It held instead that the juvenile death penalty violated the Eighth Amendment's prohibition against cruel and unusual punishment.[19] This result was brought about in part by Justice Anthony Kennedy's identification of three features that distinguish children from adults in criminal cases: their immaturity and impulsivity in decision-making; their susceptibility to peer pressure; and the transitory nature of adolescent personality development, which constrains a determination that a particular adolescent is truly depraved and thus deserves the ultimate punishment. The Court also found that these characteristics made children less susceptible to the intended deterrence of a death sentence dangling before them; as Justice Kennedy explained, "it is evident that the penological justifications for the death penalty apply to [children] with lesser force than to adults."[20]

Several years later, in *Graham v. Florida* (2010), Justice Kennedy applied the same categorical analysis about how children meaningfully differ from adults to conclude that sentencing juvenile offenders who have *not* murdered to life without parole is disproportionate to the juvenile's culpability and therefore is also barred by the Eighth Amendment.[21] In applying this "children are different" analysis to a non–death penalty case, Justice Kennedy determined not only that juveniles are categorically less culpable than adults (especially when they have not killed) but also that they are categorically less deserving of a sentence of life without parole—a sentence as severe as death for a young person.[22]

This led, only two years later, to Justice Elena Kagan's opinion in *Miller v. Alabama* (2012), where the Court was asked to apply this categorical restriction against mandatory life without the possibility of parole to *all* juvenile punishments, including killing. Justice Kagan agreed that mandatory life without the possibility of parole was unconstitutional, but she stopped short of holding that a life sentence without the possibility of parole could *never* be imposed; instead, the hallmark features of chronological age, family life, the type and extent of participation in the crime, and the ability of a young person to utilize due process protections all factored into the sentencing decision.[23]

Finally, the Court's most recent decision to consider extreme sentences for young people, *Jones v. Mississippi* (2021), does not require a judge to find a youth "permanently incorrigible" in order to impose a sentence of life without parole; even with this setback, the basic framework accepting that children are not, as Justice Kagan wrote, just "miniature adults" remains.[24]

In its only application of "children are different" directly to *juvenile* court, the Supreme Court considered the differences between adults and children more broadly in *J.D.B. v. North Carolina* (2011).[25] J.D.B. (or

"Jake," as the North Carolina appellate court called him) was charged with two counts of delinquency for breaking and entering and larceny after he confessed to the crimes. His confession followed an interrogation at his middle school by two police officers and two school personnel, including the assistant principal. The North Carolina Supreme Court decided that it did not have to consider Jake's age when deciding whether he was in custody when he confessed during the interrogation in school.

The U.S. Supreme Court thought differently.[26] Justice Sonia Sotomayor focused on whether a reasonable person in Jake's situation would understand that he was not required to answer the questions and that he was free to leave. Justice Sotomayor said the proper standard to determine whether Jake understood what was happening to him had to include consideration of his age. Jake, a thirteen-year-old special education student, had been removed from his social studies class by a uniformed "school resource officer," taken to a closed conference room, met with four adults, including the assistant principal, and was warned by the police investigator that he could be separated from his custodial grandmother and detained until a court hearing.[27] Justice Sotomayor found that a reasonable youth in Jake's situation would believe he was in custody and noted that the science bore out "the settled understanding that the differentiating characteristics of youth are universal."[28] Jake's case was remanded for the North Carolina courts to apply this new juvenile standard.

These constitutional "children are different" cases justify rethinking many of the ways that youth are treated in a juvenile or criminal legal context. If Jake had committed a more serious crime, perhaps landing him in adult court, he would still be thirteen, and whether he was in custody during his interrogation would still require consideration of his age.

This jurisprudence does not turn on the court involved but on the fact of being a minor. While the original purpose of the juvenile court incorporated the belief that children are different and should be treated differently, it was equally convinced that the kindly juvenile court judge knew how to treat the child based on his own subjective beliefs about the child's needs. Recall that Judge McGhee thought Gerald Gault should be committed to a state institution for six years for making a lewd phone call and that Judge Gutowicz declared Joseph McKeiver delinquent and placed him on probation on totally unsubstantiated evidence. Separating the two purposes of the court—not treating children as adults and fixing the child—allows us to reimagine that a separate court is not what is necessary to consistently treat children as children.

Letting Go of the Family Court as a Socialized Court

The second animating purpose of the court was to intervene to do good. That purpose has been offered frequently to maintain broad court jurisdiction over children and families to ensure that they get the help they need. Judges have long argued that families, without compulsory orders and court supervision, will fail to access assistance or treatment or the state will fail to provide it. The inability of the Juvenile Justice Standards in the 1970s to limit court jurisdiction in child protection cases or to remove status offenses entirely from court jurisdiction can be traced to the strong opposition of nationally known family court judges at the time, such as Justine Wise Polier. Judge Polier, a commission member of the Juvenile Justice Standards Project, dissented from the recommendation to eliminate status offenses. She acknowledged that voluntary services "accepted by both children and families will prove more effective than when they are coerced by a court," but she insisted that ensuring such services were available without court intervention was an unrealistic and romantic notion.[29] After the decision in *Gault*, Judge Polier had written that it was the failure of legislatures and policy makers to provide for assistance outside of court that required the court to remain a sentinel for protecting children. While the judge readily acknowledged that the court was unable "to correct the environmental deprivations and injuries which increasingly oppress the children of the urban poor [and] to create compensatory services for children denied an adequate standard of living, health services, decent homes or good schooling . . . [and] the denigration and hurts imposed on children . . . through ongoing discrimination by reason of color or race," she saw little possibility for society as a whole to take on those responsibilities. She insisted instead that the dispositional authority of the "social" family court must continue to be integrated into services for the subject families.[30] This belief that what families need is never going to be created outside the court has sustained the opposition to "dejudicialization" throughout the court's history, reinforcing the belief that the court has an essential role in family well-being.

Radical nonintervention asks us to let go of the role of the court as a social court and to look at each practice that sends or draws families into court and ask how that practice can be shrunken and eventually eliminated. When the sociologist Edwin Schur proposed this concept in 1973, he moved beyond diverting children from court and opposed almost all forms of intervention by courts and social agencies. He insisted that "if the choice is between changing youth and changing the society . . . the radical noninterventionist opts for changing society."[31] Schur identified that radical nonintervention implied "policies that accommodate to the widest possible diversity of behaviors and attitudes," and he anticipated abolitionist theory by recognizing that a just juvenile legal system cannot be constructed inside an unjust society. At the same time, Schur acknowledged that, for a narrowly defined set of actions, a court of law remains necessary—but not a social court.[32]

Letting go of the family court as a social court resets its purpose. In 1967, the sociologist Edwin Lemert called for "judicious nonintervention" (a precursor to Schur's radical nonintervention) as a way to shrink the matters that should reach a juvenile or family court. The most obvious were status offenses, but he went further, urging that cases "treating a profusion of child and parental problems" had overwhelmed the court and didn't belong there. Only cases that have exhausted all other solutions should be brought to a court of law for a legal judgment. Lemert wrote: "Law operates by punishment, injunction against specific acts, specific redress, and substitutional redress. It cannot by such means make a father good, a mother moral, a child obedient, or a youth respectful of authority."[33] Trusting in the court's magic to pull off these wonders had already been disproven repeatedly.

The Precarity of Families in Family Court

Steps to implement a radical nonintervention theory are informed by the current precarity of families who most frequently find themselves enmeshed in the systems that lead them to the court. If these families are going to be the engines of change, the systemic barriers that habitually undermine their ability to participate fully in all aspects of the polity must be acknowledged and addressed. These families are overwhelmingly multigeneration poor; they are disproportionately people of color, especially Black and Native Americans; their history of marginalization from universal access to societal benefits is pervasive; the traumas they experience are imprinted across generations; and their children's developmental potential has been thwarted from long before they are born. Superimposed on these conditions is surveillance so pervasive that it extinguishes traditional ideals of privacy rights.[34]

A framework of precarity works best to reimagine an approach to embracing all families. "Precariousness" is the generalized exposure to risk or harm we all share; "precarity" is the heightened and differential exposure to precariousness that is politically produced "in which certain populations suffer from failing social and economic networks of support and become differentially exposed to injury, violence or death."[35] These risks and exposures are politically created by the state. The counter-strength of those caught in this precarity is not their individual resilience to adjust to or overcome such adversity; it is their collective resistance to conditions that prevent them from living their lives fully.[36] As the parent leaders and activists at the family advocacy organization RISE recently wrote:

> The expertise and leadership of parents and youth with lived experience of family policing belongs at the center of the movement to abolish the system. . . . [Those] personally impacted and affected by a system should be the lead and face of advocacy, using their first-hand experience to lead the movement in the direction they choose. . . . [They] must be the architects of their own activism and political agenda.[37]

The specific recommendations I offer to shrink and then abolish the family court reflect the knowledge that I have gained as an ally and advocate with parents and youth.

Barring Who Walks Through the Door of the Court

Today's family regulation system includes not only the child protection/child welfare system but also the juvenile legal and status offense systems. The founders of the juvenile court understood the interconnectedness of these areas regardless of whether their practices were sound. This interrelationship leads to considering two approaches to reimagining the systems that enmesh families. The first is finding those places where specific actions can have immediate, jurisdictional effects, like eliminating status offenses and narrowing the definitions of "neglect." The second approach advocates for far more sweeping, holistic change in society to address the central issues of poverty, racism, inequality, and precarity that determine which families are controlled by the family regulation regime. While these two approaches are intertwined, the work they are doing is easier to contemplate separately so that short- and long-term goals can be pursued concurrently. The changes in jurisdictional and discretionary authority will be discussed first, as that authority reinforces and exacerbates the inequities; that leaves a clearer path to shifting fiscal resources from a shrunken family court system to the primary prevention and targeted resources that are desperately needed.

Eliminate Status Offenses

Eliminating status offenses from court jurisdiction entirely is perhaps the clearest and easiest step to shrink the family court. The number of petitioned status offense cases peaked at over 200,000 at the beginning of the twenty-first century and dropped by over half by 2018, with the largest proportion of cases now involving truancy. The other categories—runaways, curfews, ungovernability, and liquor law violations—all decreased. While the numbers of cases for both male and female youth decreased by 2018, females still accounted for a substantially larger proportion of the petitions. And the proportion of cases involving Black and Native American youth increased.[38] Youth who identify as LGBTQ+ are more likely to be stopped by police, arrested, and convicted for engaging in the same behaviors as their cisgender peers, increasing their likelihood of being dealt with as a status offender.[39] Despite the persistent disproportionality by gender and race, the decrease in absolute numbers signals an opportunity to build on this trend. Starting with the Johnson Commission's 1967 report (*The Challenge of Crime in a Free Society*), there have been repeated calls for getting noncriminal misbehaving youth out of court. Research has consistently identified the harms of court involvement, including the stigma of going to court, the greater likelihood of later criminal behavior, and the overall disruption in education. Research has also identified the advantages of community-based programs that reduce reoffending; improve educational attainment, skills building, and behavioral health; and strengthen family functioning. The consequences of detention and incarceration for status offense behavior is even more dire, with family, school, and community connections broken and a greater likelihood of violence and harm in these institutions.[40]

Given that truancy is currently the most common reason for status-offense petitions, eliminating status-offense jurisdiction will diminish the availability of schools to use courts to punish youth for truancy while also diminishing the likelihood of those youth penetrating deeper into the juvenile legal system. The majority of youth who find themselves somewhere in the juvenile legal system have had their schooling disrupted by suspensions or expulsions. Youth of color, especially Black students, are suspended and expelled at higher rates than white students and are more likely to be involved in law enforcement actions within schools. Black students represent 16 percent of student enrollment but represent 27 percent of students referred to law enforcement and 31 percent of students subjected to a school-related arrest. Youth within juvenile detention facilities who are most likely to have school discipline histories are LGBTQ+ and gender-nonconforming girls of color.[41] Truancy often results from the unmet needs of youth with an unknown, underdiagnosed, or mistreated disability.[42]

Chapter 9 noted the work of a group of judicial leaders to divert youth out of court for status offenses through community-based efforts instead of formal adjudication.[43] The logical next step is to eliminate the jurisdiction entirely. No court should be given authority over this type of youthful misbehavior. Many states also permit municipal courts to regulate age-specific misbehavior like violating curfews or possession or consumption of alcohol or tobacco.[44] This jurisdiction should also be abolished so that the only consequence for these youth is the offer of voluntary services or assistance. Eliminating status-offense jurisdiction will also eliminate any opportunity for judges to incarcerate these youth under the violation-of-court-order exception, as thousands of misbehaving youth continue to be. Moreover, ending status-offense jurisdiction will free up millions of dollars in savings to invest in the creative, meaningful, and destigmatized community-based resources desperately needed.

Create a Much Smaller Juvenile Legal System

The 1967 Johnson Commission report called for keeping as many children as possible out of the formal juvenile court system. Stopping them from coming in the front door would diminish all the harms likely to follow. Instead, millions of children were funneled through juvenile (and adult) courts in subsequent decades.

As chapter 5 expounded, prosecution in the juvenile court became harsher and more extensive, and youth were more likely to be subject to transfer to adult court or receive blended juvenile and adult sentences. The promising due process protections layered onto juvenile proceedings did not protect many of the youth in these increasingly retributive courts. On the contrary, as chapter 9 revealed, investigations throughout the country in the 2000s uncovered systemic violations of every due process right available for youth, especially the right to counsel. Yet in the aftermath of the get-tough "scared straight" period of the 1980s and 1990s and the nonexistent "super predator" myth in the media, youth crime fell, especially violent crime. As Professor Feld argues, the passing of the moral panic gives us the opportunity to create more sensible youth policies.[45]

In 1999, Feld wrote *Bad Kids and the Transformation of Juvenile Court*, leading him to recommend abolishing juvenile court, a reflection of his "despair over the unalloyed punitiveness and racism of delinquency sanctions, the limited efficacy of treatment, and the juvenile courts' procedural deficiencies."[46] In his more recent work, however, Feld pulls back from abolition to reconsider the potential for the juvenile court's diversionary mission, relying in part on the newest "children are different" research that the Supreme Court has recognized. I disagree with Feld not in the objective of his proposals but in his renewed belief that juvenile court or family court can achieve them. I think, instead, that the changes that will reduce the court's harm will lead to its demise. What will be left are those significantly smaller number of serious cases that can be adjudicated in a "youth part" of an adult court that applies what Feld calls a "youth discount" to sentencing, separate facilities, re-cordkeeping, and rehabilitation.[47] The way to accomplish reductions is outlined next.

Raise the Minimum Age of Responsibility

The assessment of juvenile legal responsibility has both a *minimum* age and a *maximum* age. The minimum asks how young can a child be to be held responsible for acts that would be criminal if committed by an adult. Both the Committee on the Rights of the Child, which monitors the implementation of the United Nations Convention on the Rights of the Child, and the United Nations Global Study on Children Deprived of Liberty have called on countries to set the minimum age of prosecu-tion at fourteen years old, which is the most common minimum age internationally.[48] In the United States, no state aligns with this minimum age standard; twenty-eight states have no minimum at all, and the others are as low as six to eleven. New York and Connecticut joined Califor-nia, Massachusetts, and Utah in raising the age to twelve.[49] Arrests of children age twelve and under decreased in recent decades, but between 2013–2018 over 30,000 children under ten were arrested and 266,321 children ages ten to twelve were arrested. In 2020, over 60,000 children age twelve and under found themselves in juvenile or family court.[50]

Whether *very* young children are considered competent to participate in a court proceeding is governed in each state by a range of laws and cases, relying extensively on court discretion. Consistent with the entire juvenile legal system, Black children and Native American children age twelve and under disproportionately find themselves in court proceed-ings. Some of these children will be removed from their homes and de-tained or incarcerated, disrupting their development, family ties, and education while exposing them to higher risks of violence in institutions and poor physical and mental health as adults.[51]

An example of this judicial treatment of young children was recently reported by Pro Publica. In 2003, the juvenile court judge Donna Dav-enport of Rutherford County, Tennessee, issued her own rules requir-ing all children arrested to be taken to the detention facility. She later gave the director of the facility complete discretion to hold children. Davenport described her work as a calling. "I'm here on a mission. It's not a job. It's God's mission," she told a local newspaper. She calls the children in her courtroom *hers* ("I'm seeing a lot of aggression in my 9- and 10-year-olds"). She said she only locked up one seven-year-old but lots of eight- and nine-year-olds. Judge Davenport sometimes refers to herself publicly as the "mother of the county." Most of these children are Black; Davenport is white. In 2016, ten young Black children (the youngest was eight years old) were arrested for watching a fight between other elementary-school children. The four girls were eventually released, but the six boys were sent to detention, and one twelve-year-old was put in solitary confinement—*for watching a fight!* After a public outcry, the charges were dropped, but the children arrested suffered trauma in the following years. In June 2021, the county settled a class action lawsuit for $11 million for the detention practices of the judge and the facility.[52]

Such abuse of judicial discretion on young children could not happen if the minimum age were raised to fourteen. While the exact number is difficult to ascertain, 54 percent of the cases processed in court in 2018 were youth fifteen and younger. That is more than 200,000 youth.[53] Even with the likelihood that many of those cases involved fifteen-year-olds, tens of thousands of children would not have found themselves in any court. As in many other countries with a higher minimum age, they would instead receive services and supports consistent with their needs.[54]

The Maximum Age of Juvenile Legal Responsibility

At the other end of the spectrum is the maximum age for juvenile rather than criminal adjudication. Currently forty-seven states set the maximum age at eighteen. As lawmakers become increasingly aware of the research on adolescent psychology and brain development, there is greater attention to the effect on criminal responsibility and sanctions.[55] Like younger adolescents, older youth and young adults (eighteen to twenty-one) take more risks and engage in more sensation-seeking behavior; they respond more to immediate outcomes and are less likely to delay gratification; they are more responsive to peer involvement and are more swayed by adult coercion.[56] These risk factors should also apply when a youth can be transferred to adult court or a judge can impose a greater juvenile sentence or a juvenile/adult blended sentence. From the late 1970s through the 1990s, states became increasingly punitive, lowering the transfer age for a greater number of crimes and increasing the use of harsher sentences.[57] In 2018, in a small step forward, California became the first state in the country to limit transfer eligibility exclusively to sixteen- and seventeen-year-olds.[58]

How is raising the maximum age and limiting transfers consistent with abolishing family court? What is essential is understanding how adolescents are different than adults and treating them accordingly. A "youth part" in an adult court can incorporate the scientific principles that distinguish adolescents from adults and strictly apply due process protections that accommodate adolescent development. It can seal youth records or otherwise mitigate the collateral consequences of an adult conviction and create dispositional alternatives that build on restorative and rehabilitative principles. Both techniques are more likely to provide the best outcome for the young person and for society. What is important to recognize is that being an adolescent or young adult impacts how someone interacts with law enforcement; decides to waive the right to remain silent or the right to counsel; provides false confessions; doesn't understand the consequences of plea bargaining or going to trial; and generally affects the ability to work effectively with counsel.[59] A "youth part" adjudicating young people at least fourteen years old and extending to anywhere between eighteen and twenty-one years old can establish patterns of practices that accommodate the limitations of this specific age range, taking into consideration the capacity distinctions between the youngest and the oldest youth.

Specialized public defender practices have already been created for adolescents who have been transferred to adult court. These practices consider how to represent an adolescent effectively, especially those youth most likely to find themselves in court: youth of color and poor youth from marginalized communities. For example, the Adolescent Intervention and Diversion Project of the New York City Legal Aid Society combines high-quality and interdisciplinary litigation defense with a focus on the educational, social, and treatment needs of a youth in order to provide advocacy both inside and outside the courtroom. The team examines the young person's life as soon as possible to allow for targeted service plans that can facilitate dismissals, better plea agreements, and more rehabilitative sentences. Case outcomes using this specialized practice resulted in fewer convictions and less incarceration and already offer a template for representing fourteen to twenty-one-year-olds in a "youth part."[60]

Limit Crimes That Bring Youth to Court

Along with limiting which youth can be arrested and charged, the next step is to eliminate some of the crimes that currently bring youth to court in the first place. These are mostly nonviolent crimes—often the same acts that are defined as status offenses but are in the criminal code, like drug possession, minor traffic offenses, trespassing, and damaging property at school. Treating these types of actions for what they are— behaviors that most adolescents engage in but only a targeted number find themselves in court for—would put fewer young people at risk of having their lives derailed as they are thrust deeper into the juvenile or criminal legal systems. Alternatively, if these actions are not decriminalized, the consequences should not result in any form of criminal penalty beyond restorative ones, like formal apologies, community service, or participation in community-based programs that emphasize opportunities for youth engagement. Records of these types of cases should be sealed. And while the imposition of civil fees as an alternative to criminal penalties has often been suggested, fees for many families are beyond their financial capacities and should not be imposed.

Improving Due Process Protections

The holistic principles of adolescent representation described above are grounded in heightened levels of due process protections. Professor Mae Quinn has suggested that the entire theory of "fundamental fairness" due process, which Gault required in juvenile court proceedings, can be reimagined under the "children are different" cases to expand rather than contract juvenile rights.[61] For example, if due process requires the "guiding hand of counsel" to protect young defendants, and these defendants are categorically different than adults, then they need counsel at points that the Supreme Court has not deemed necessary for adults, such as during pre-petition meetings with probation officers or post-disposition to ensure that correctional facilities are providing appropriate education. Quinn builds on other commentators to recommend that juvenile advocates resist calling for more rights like adults have and instead define the meaning of "fundamental fairness" to reflect a more expansive view of due process that is "fundamentally fair to youth in light of their limited capacities, their specific needs, and the nature of proceedings in which they may find themselves in conflict with the state."[62] Quinn situates her recommendations in the context of juvenile court, in part to critique the analysis that due process is more likely to be found currently in adult court, and in part to identify how juvenile court itself is more complicated than adult court and thus needs more nuanced interpretations of due process rights such as competent representation. She notes how several states today are providing counsel for children in juvenile court before formal proceedings begin or after they are concluded.[63] The expansive availability of counsel for young defendants builds on other key due process enhancements. Arrested young people should never be questioned by the police without a parent or trusted adult present; those adults should then share in the youth's confidentiality protections. Young people should not be able to waive their right to counsel except in extraordinary circumstances—and never without having consulted with counsel first. Crucially, youth should have the right to a jury trial.

There were few calls to provide jury trials for youth in the forty years following the *McKeiver* decision denying that right. The few state courts that had considered the issue relied on *McKeiver* or held that their state constitutions did not require jury trials for youth despite the sharp punitive trend in juvenile courts in the final decades of the twentieth century.[64] Then in 2008, the Kansas Supreme Court reversed a decision it had made twenty-four years earlier denying youth the right to trial by jury. This time the court held that the sweeping changes to the Kansas laws governing delinquency compelled a reversal. The court noted that the purposes clause of the juvenile code "[had] shifted to protecting the public, holding juveniles accountable for their behavior and choices, and making juveniles more productive and responsible members of society . . . [which is] more aligned with the legislative intent for the adult sentencing statutes."[65] Language used in Kansas's juvenile statutes was now more similar to the language used in criminal laws, including using the term "sentence" rather than "placement." Youth were now incarcerated in "juvenile corrections facilities" according to a sentencing grid that was based on the level of the offense committed. And the judge was permitted to consider aggravating circumstances to go "off the grid" to impose *greater* punishment. Traditional protections of the juvenile court that *McKeiver* had cited—especially the confidentiality of records and hearings—had been largely abandoned.[66] The Kansas Supreme Court concluded that the *parens patriae* characteristics identified in *McKeiver* of "fairness, concern, sympathy, and paternal attention" no longer distinguished the Kansas juvenile court from its adult counterpart. Children were therefore entitled to jury trials.[67] Several other states agreed, either amending their juvenile codes or through high court decisions, acknowledging (as the Kansas court did) that the line between adult and child proceedings and punishments had blurred.[68]

The recommendation here for a jury trial is not just because those lines had blurred. It is because juvenile proceedings historically and today in and of themselves unfairly adjudicate and punish children. Any juvenile legal proceeding that takes away a child's liberty—through the imposition of probation or treatment or in the form of placement or incarceration— should provide for the opportunity of a jury trial. Jury trials should not be seen—as the Kansas Supreme Court saw them—as an inevitable result of treating children as adults. Instead, they should be seen as part of the package of due process rights that protect children as children.

There are many other reforms to the juvenile legal system that would improve the outcomes for youth but don't directly address shrinking the court, in particular reducing punishments that include detention and incarceration. To the extent such changes will improve the overall well-being of youth caught in these systems, they will be discussed in the last section of this chapter.

Reimagining Child Welfare: Barring the Door Again

The failed approach to keeping children safe and flourishing through state intervention has been chronicled throughout this book. As I have contended, our current system of surveillance, reporting, and investigations followed by removal, supervision, and often permanent destruction of families has disproportionately inflicted significant harm on the most marginalized and disadvantaged families in our country without fulfilling the promise to protect children and support parents in raising their children. While there have always been some scholars, practitioners, and impacted people who have pleaded for a more effective and humane system, that call since the turn of the century has been amplified by the advocacy of parents and youth and by the slow but growing acknowledgement by a greater number of professionals that their job is to ally with that advocacy.

End the Current System of Child Protection Reporting

The child protection services (CPS) reporting system has become so pervasive that for many people it *is* child protection: "If you see something, say something." Everyone knows there's a child abuse hotline to call. Almost every person who interacts with minor children is now a mandated reporter, and the general public is encouraged to voluntarily report concerns. Many states allow anonymous reporting. Millions of families are disrupted by investigations that result from reporting, most of which do not to lead to substantiation that maltreatment occurred or to the provision of services. The U.S. Advisory Board on Child Abuse and Neglect identified this disconnect between the reporting system and protecting children when it wrote in the early 1990s that "it has become far easier to pick up the telephone to report one's neighbor for child abuse than it is for that neighbor to pick up the telephone and receive help before the abuse happens."[69] The practice has only grown since then: one in three children and one in two Black children are investigated today by the time they reach eighteen years old.[70]

The current system of reporting is ineffective, expensive, and harmful. As the legal scholar Dale Margolin Cecka found, reporting practices vary greatly state to state, with disparate standards for when to screen in calls or investigate families. Hotline screeners may not have adequate qualifications or training, their judgment is subject to considerable error, and a decision to investigate a family may be made by a single person. The public is not educated in what to report and makes baseless calls; the practice in every state is to err on the side of overreporting. Moreover, intentional and false reporting, especially from anonymous callers, is extensive. All this is not only a terrible drain of resources from supports that actually assist families; it can lead to disrupting and harming families even if no further action is taken.[71]

Mandated reporting is not the solution. Ending mandated reporting is an essential step toward creating trust with service providers and an alternative system to assist families. Instead of mandated reporters receiving training on how to report, they need training on how to connect that family to assistance.[72] Schools—which are misleadingly considered to be the most reliable reporting source—are the largest category of reporters, but their reports are less likely to be substantiated or result in services being provided.[73] Parents lose trust not only in schools but in all the other mandated reporters like therapists, doctors, and other treatment providers.[74] Freed from mandated reporting, the professionals that families interact with can be part of a system of care, which I detail more fully at the end of the chapter.

For the far smaller voluntary system of reporting that remains, the criteria for what constitutes neglect or abuse must be clearly understood and communicated to any caller. The hotline must also provide those callers with community service alternatives to contact. For those calls that justify further investigation, strict criteria must be followed, including providing parents with a clear understanding of their rights when they are subject to an investigation.[75] Reduced reporting will also reduce the negative impact that registries have where millions of parents are listed as having a report substantiated even if this report has not resulted in further agency or court action.

Change the Definitions of "Neglect" and "Abuse"

The definition of "child maltreatment" pursuant to the Child Abuse Prevention and Treatment Act (CAPTA) and incorporated into state law definitions is vastly overinclusive. As Professor Michael Wald has argued for many decades, jurisdiction should be based on defined harms to children: inflicting physical injury; consistently exposing children to conditions that carry substantial risk of physical injury or serious threat to a child's health; engaging in or exposing a child substantial risk of sexual abuse; and failing to provide essential medical care.[76] These serious harms affect at most between 10–20 percent of the 3.5 million children investigated; only half of the overall cases are later substantiated, and many of the rest may or may not receive additional supervision or services.[77] These serious allegations are the only causes of action that belong in court. The vast remainder of families need support, assistance, and services that neither CPS nor the court is able to provide. Wald argues that the use of differential response—with CPS providing assistance for cases substantiated but not sent on to court—and the current regime of preventive services are either ineffectual or do not reach the families who most need the targeted assistance.[78] These are the families with chronic and complex problems for whom a vast system of primary prevention and voluntary secondary prevention is essential to support them in raising their children.

What will most effectively close the door to court for children and families is twofold. In the short term are the targeted community-based and voluntary supports and services that prevent family dislocation. The long-term goal is the transformation to a different economic and political system that understands the needs for families to raise children well. They will both be discussed in the last section of the chapter addressing how we reimagine strong and vibrant communities for and with families.

Change What Happens If a Family Is Brought to Court

When the safety of a child must be determined through a formal court proceeding, the due process protections that reflect the seriousness of legal intervention in family life must be provided. These protections—at a minimum—must include robust counsel for parents, strict judicial application of legal mandates, and permitting only lawyers to represent children pursuant to federal *guardian ad litem* requirements.

ASSURE THE RIGHT TO DUE PROCESS: PROVIDE LAWYERS

In 1981, the Supreme Court in *Lassiter v. Department of Social Services* held that parents in termination of parental rights (TPR) cases did not have an absolute right to counsel but only a case-by-case determination. In his dissent, Justice Blackmun found "virtually incredible the Court's conclusion today that [this] termination proceeding was fundamentally fair. . . . [T]he Court simply ignores the defendant's obvious inability to speak effectively for herself."[79] Fortunately, in the years since, forty-five states and the District of Columbia have provided indigent parents with a categorical right to counsel in TPR proceedings, and many states have also expanded the right to counsel to other child protection proceedings in the family court. Yet acknowledging the role of counsel in protecting the fundamental right of family integrity has not resulted in effective representation nationally. Serious limitations exist on the actual provision and assistance of counsel for parents in child maltreatment and TPR proceedings nationwide. Attorneys may not be appointed for all stages of the proceedings; they may be appointed after critical preliminary processes have begun; they may not be properly compensated.[80] This severely limits protecting the due process rights of parents in these cases.

The development of multidisciplinary, holistic law offices for indigent parent defense in several states in this century has marked a turning point in our understanding of effective lawyering for parents. These offices, which include social work and parent peer advocates, have been shown to dramatically increase the safe return of children during their first year in care and reduce the time spent in care without children suffering a subsequent substantiated report of maltreatment.[81] Advocacy teams address many of the out-of-court challenges parents face, including having an advocate at case conferences or to accompany a parent to secure benefits or services, and especially helping a parent to feel empowered to directly and fully participate in her representation. Reflecting the success of these offices, the federal government in 2018 began allowing states to seek federal reimbursement under SSA Title IV-E for the cost of providing legal representation to eligible parents (and children), and in 2020 it specifically clarified that the funds could be claimed for multidisciplinary advocacy teams. States now have the capacity to create or greatly expand effective representation with significant federal funding.[82] In a court that has reluctantly and inconsistently applied due process protections, having counsel available at every stage of the proceedings—and even prior to a petition being filed—could significantly reduce the time and destructive impacts of these proceedings.

APPLY THE LAW

Having representation in a court proceeding is going to increase the possibility of a fair outcome. But equally important is having judges who embrace their role to protect the integrity of families by applying the law and ensuring that the state intervenes to protect children only when their safety is actually at risk. This has not been the traditional role of the family court judge—or even the role that is championed today. Instead, the role of the judge as a problem-solver who applies therapeutic principles in a social court continues to tether judges to their historical roots. As chapters 8 and 9 detailed, judicial leadership and collaboration were concretized into federal policy, requiring judges and child welfare agencies "to demonstrate meaningful and ongoing collaboration" and "to work toward shared goals and activities."[83] The danger of this approach cannot be overstated: collaborating judges will not hold their agency collaborators to the legal standards required.

What happens when judges stop collaborating and instead consistently apply the law? In 2020, Casey Family Programs funded a study of Judge Ernestine Gray's juvenile court protocols in Orleans Parish, Louisiana. During the final decade of her long judicial career, Judge Gray instituted a system of court proceedings for her and her judicial colleagues during the pre-adjudication period to determine if a child should be removed from home; whether, if removed, kin care was investigated and used; and if the child could safely return home after removal. Fourteen days after the first custody decision, Judge Gray held a second hearing to see if the agency was timely filing a maltreatment petition and whether a removed child could return home. She enforced the legal standard for removal and/or return and required the agency to meet that standard with admissible evidence and not suggestions, hunches, or inadmissible hearsay. She held everyone to the legal standards justifying state intervention and removal and expected everyone to be prepared to go forward. The result was miraculous. There were over 200 children in foster care in Orleans Parish in 2011; by March 2017 there were twenty. This was the lowest number in the state; Orleans Parish had 2.5 children in foster care per 10,000, while the national rate was 58.5 per 10,000. If a child was removed, she was likely to return home after the second hearing. The recurrence of reported maltreatment was comparable to the state rates at the time—not higher—despite leaving children home or returning them there quickly.[84]

When children are removed from their parents, ASFA requires the judge to determine first that "reasonable efforts" were made to keep the children safely at home, a finding that then triggers federal funding. Judge Gray made those findings in thorough legal hearings. Studies of reasonable efforts findings indicate that most judges just check the box on the form saying reasonable efforts were made, even if they don't believe it. A common reason is that judges are unwilling to rule on the failures of the agency and cut off the funding, further depleting resources.[85] Of course this is a vicious cycle that ultimately does the most harm to the families disrupted, not the state agencies. Judge Gray's system broke that cycle, keeping more children safely at home, saving costs for foster care, and holding the state responsible to the law.

PROVIDE LAWYERS, NOT HELPERS

The industry that family court has become is still tied to the concept of the *child's best interests*. This is manifest in CAPTA's provisions that allow a child's interests to be represented by a *guardian ad litem*, who does not have to be a lawyer and can be a lay volunteer.[86] As chapter 7 noted, as the family court exploded with child protection proceedings in the late 1970s, judges turned to lay volunteers—especially court-appointed special advocates, or "CASAs"—to provide them with information and recommendations on what was best for the child, harkening back to the earliest child-savers who founded the juvenile court. CASAs are predominantly white and middle-class and are unlikely to be trained in law, social work, or other relevant disciplines. Their charge is to recommend what is best for a child, even if they are unfamiliar with the child's family and community. Research has shown that CASAs spend less time with Black children; conferred more often with agency case workers than with family members; and overwhelmingly agreed with agency recommendations on visiting, permanency planning, and services—all serving to amplify agency power in the courtroom. One study found judges agreeing with CASA recommendations 71 percent of the time.[87] Lay volunteers like CASAs should not be part of the court. There are myriad opportunities to volunteer to enhance the strength of families in their own communities rather than enhance the state's power to intervene in those families.

CAPTA should be amended to permit only lawyers to represent children. In recent years, there has been a growing embrace of attorneys for children who are child-directed or, if the child is too young, to represent the child's *legal* interests rather than their "best interests." Great efforts have been made on the national and state levels to set higher standards for representation, improve the quality of training, and push states that have not yet ensured representation to do so.[88] Initial studies indicate that high-quality legal representation—especially multidisciplinary teams—resulted in less time in care and more family preservation.[89] The federal policies that now allow Title IV-E funding for parent and child attorneys is an incentive for states to eliminate *GAL* best-interest representation. What may be the most important change, however, is the mindset of child advocates today. There has been a reckoning that too many children's attorneys were child-savers and that not enough of them understood their primary role as protecting children's rights and their desires to live with their own families in their own communities and to ensure that the state intervenes in families' lives only when legally necessary.[90]

Change the Law That Should Apply in Court

The Adoption and Safe Families Act (ASFA) is now understood to be part of the destructive and racist policies that were incorporated into the Anti-Drug Abuse Act of 1986, the Crime Bill of 1994, and the Personal Responsibility and Work Opportunity Reconciliation Act of 1996.[91] The wars on drugs, crime, and welfare became a war on families—most especially BIPOC and impoverished families—with ASFA leaving at least two million families destroyed since its implementation in 1997 and with an average of over 20,000 young people "aging out" of foster care each year, most of them legal orphans with no legal ties to any parent.[92]

Repeal ASFA

A groundswell to repeal ASFA began through the organizational work of impacted mothers, community organizations, and allied advocates to situate ASFA squarely in the oppressive, racist history of family separation. This "repeal ASFA" movement stresses that, at a time when nearly half the children in the family regulation system were Black and most were poor, sponsors of ASFA legislation, like Senator John Chafee, were denigrating these families by saying: "It's time we recognize that some families simply cannot and should not be kept together."[93] This attack on BIPOC and impoverished families persists; the damage it has caused spurred the repeal movement. Judges, government officials, academics, policy makers, and advocates now recognize the vast harms that ASFA has caused for decades.[94]

A recitation of numbers can't capture the personal traumas and injuries experienced by parents and children torn apart. They live with the compounded stresses and anxieties of displacement, rejection, shame, and grief. Young people suffer from "ambiguous loss" after losing parents, impacting their sense of identity and belonging. After parents lose children, they experience heightened mental illness, fall into substance use and abuse to numb the pain, engage in increased reckless behaviors, and suffer "structural vulnerability" in their housing and relationships.[95] Moreover, the outcomes for youth leaving foster care are terrible: "Across a wide range of outcome measures, including postsecondary educational attainment, employment, housing stability, public assistance receipt, and criminal justice system involvement, these former foster youth are faring poorly as a group."[96]

ASFA's repeal will reorient intervention into families by prioritizing *prevention* upstream and *reunification* of families downstream rather than adoption or any other permanency goal. The time frame for instituting a TPR petition ("fifteen out of twenty-two months") and "concurrent planning," which undermine reunification efforts, would be eliminated. The requirement to rule out adoption before considering other permanency plans would increase kin guardianship. The federal government can recalibrate financial incentives to reward states for preventing removal or achieving reunification rather than for encouraging adoptions. The lackluster approach of "reasonable efforts" can be reconfigured into "active efforts" to keep families intact. This higher standard already is part of the Indian Child Welfare Act (ICWA). ICWA's active efforts include "the provision of financial assistance, food, housing, health care, and transportation, and if an out-of-home placement is warranted, visitation with parents and extended family quickly, often, and throughout placement."[97] For families that do reach the court, each of these steps will reorient judges to prioritize family integrity, promote greater safety and well-being for children, and hold agencies to a high standard of providing the assistance families actually need.

Affirmatively Reorient the Meaning of "Permanency"

Building on Professor Mark Testa's distinction between *lasting* and *binding* permanency, discussed in chapter 8, permanency outcomes for children must respect the centrality of children's relationships with their families and communities. Relative and fictive-kin guardianship should always be the preferred placement for children if they have to be removed from their parents. "We know now that it is better to sleep on your grandmother's floor than in a princess bed in the home of a stranger, or more likely, the homes of more than eight strangers which is the average number of moves a child in foster care experiences."[98] These kin guardians should have equalized placement rates while the regulations that are placed on stranger foster homes should be minimized for kin. If children cannot return to their parents full-time, agencies and judges should respect family and community values for determining what permanency arrangement will strengthen the child's well-being; this is also a step toward rebuilding community trust in government agents. As Testa has observed, there is little difference in outcomes between the *lasting* permanency of relative guardianship and the *binding* permanency of relative adoption.[99]

There are also calls for eliminating TPRs and adoption out of foster care entirely, challenging the ideal of the adoptive family, which masks the true harmful impact of severing familial bonds for a purported (and unrealistic) permanent solution.[100] This proposal is consistent with Native American tribal courts employing customary adoption that suspends rather than terminates parental rights. After years of advocacy, the Children's Bureau now permits SSA Title VI-E funding to support customary adoption in tribal courts; this should be an option for all courts.[101]

In summary, the proposals I recommend for substantially shrinking the family court and then shifting the remaining proceedings to other dispute resolution courts include the following key steps:

1. Eliminating status-offense jurisdiction
2. Creating a smaller juvenile legal system by:
    a. raising the minimum age of jurisdiction to fourteen;
    b. raising the maximum age of applying "children are different" rules to age twenty-one;

    c. reducing crimes subject to court processes and/or changing the dispositions for these crimes to emphasize youth engagement and services; and

    d. expanding and applying strict due process protections that acknowledge how children are different than adults in legal proceedings.

3. Reimagining child welfare/family regulation systems by:

    a. ending the current system of mandated and voluntary reporting;

    b. revising and limiting the definitions of neglect and abuse;

    c. assuring full due process protections for parents and children, including the right to counsel;

    d. rigorously applying the law to diminish "best interest" discretion;

    e. eliminating *GAL* representation for children and eliminating the role of "best interest" volunteers in court;

    f. repealing ASFA; and

    g. reorienting the meaning of permanency for children.

These steps to limit who is brought to court, what jurisdictional authority the court should have, and what process is fair lead to a far smaller court, one that could far more easily be absorbed into the criminal and civil court systems without retaining its historical therapeutic role. In short, it would become a court of law and not a social court. Even if a court of general jurisdiction chose to create specialized parts, specialization does not mandate therapeutic intervention. Moreover, a court of general jurisdiction may also have greater authority over executive agencies, like housing and benefits agencies, to protect or secure a family's entitlements. The remaining work force could be retrained and redeployed to support families and communities. Bureaucracies could be shrunk; the billions of dollars spent on systems of detention, incarceration, and foster care could be redistributed.

Reimagining a World without Family Regulation and Family Court

In the spring of 2020, to honor the twentieth anniversary of Dorothy Roberts's book *Shattered Bonds*, Professor Nancy Polikoff and I organized a symposium with the *Columbia Journal of Race and Law* titled "Strengthened Bonds: Abolishing the Child Welfare System and Re-imagining Child Well-Being." Roberts's book, written soon after the excessive punitive turn of the Clinton era that included ASFA, catalogued for a new generation the racist capitalism and white supremacy at the heart of destroying families we do not believe can raise their children well: Black and Native American families, impoverished and traumatized families, and families punished for their state-created precarity and otherness. In the two decades that followed the publication of *Shattered Bonds*, reform efforts to improve family regulation and the family court continued, but increasingly so did efforts to look outside of these systems for ways to support families. The narrative and the narrators began to change. Calls for incremental and mostly ineffective reform were no longer enough. The voices of parents and youth stopped being anecdotes included in speeches or opening paragraphs of articles by journalists and academics. Instead, they became the impetus for a movement to dismantle rather than reform the destructive structures of this system and to create the spaces and beliefs for "envisioning and embodying change."[102]

What makes this movement so strikingly different from the dismantling proposals of earlier generations of policy makers, scholars, and practitioners is the growing centrality of the affected families and the willingness of so-called experts to become allies, recognizing at long last that the families they advocate, treat, or provide services for are the experts and bearers of their lives.[103] It is not easy for people like me to step back and make room, to recognize the harm I may have caused in my professional work, to acknowledge my mistakes, and to understand it isn't just about doing my job better. Even in the "Shattered Bonds" symposium—where the presenters and writers included many parents and youth who are part of this movement—two academics made the choices and organized the gathering. This also has to change.

"If It Was Your Family"

The current moment reflects the evolution of affected youth, parents, and communities into warriors for change. Youth have often insisted "nothing about us without us" but lacked the organizational and financial capacity to sit at the table to secure those demands. That is also changing. Youth who collaborated on a contribution to the symposium interrogated their complex and differing experiences with the family regulation system for ten months to consider their recommendations. "[They] spoke freely about the trauma of being 'relocated' to a foster home, feeling commodified during their time in care, experiencing a disjointed and non-participatory judicial system, and a persistent impression that families of color were both targeted and devalued by the system."[104] These youth built on their knowledge and comfort with each other and their co-authors—as well as their training and experience as youth advocates—to create a strong foundation for the complex and emotional discussions they had and the solutions they recommended. Ultimately one of them, Duane Price, posed the basic political question that summarized their demands: "If it was your family, would you all do the exact same thing, with the same rules and regulations, and stipulations to your family that you did to ours? If you had the opportunity to take what we received, would you accept it without any hesitation?"[105]

Symposium contributions from two leading movement collectives, the Movement for Family Power and RISE, similarly demand far more than fixing the system: they identify a different political and economic structure that centers their lives in the world they envision.[106] Youth, parents, and allies are producing concrete proposals for reshaping how families can be supported without being controlled. They demand taking the steps necessary to eliminate child and family poverty so that all families can flourish in robust communities that engage and support what all families need. These solutions must be merged with targeted but voluntary supports for families facing particular challenges. In moving toward a reconstruction of society, they imagine mutual aid, community organizing, parent and youth leadership, and a steady destruction of the systems that have done them such harm.

Since the juvenile court's earliest years, different voices have warned that the court cannot itself address the root causes of children and families finding themselves there. This book has identified study after study, report after report, commission after commission—all recommending that the surest way to keep people out of the family regulation system and family court is to address the poverty, racism, sexism, and classism (and homophobia and ablism) that send these families to court. The most recent reports are consistent with those earlier ones. Twenty studies of the child welfare and juvenile legal systems conducted over the last fifteen years by the Center for the Study of Social Policy found consistent barriers to reforming the systems in every jurisdiction. Those barriers include that racism shapes the systems, especially stereotypes of Black families; that child welfare systems do not and cannot provide the assistance families need; that communities assume families get help from child welfare agencies when they do not; that family relationships are undermined rather than supported; that "reasonable efforts" is an undefined legal construct that is not consistently used; that reliable, quality representation is not available to parents; that parents experience interventions as coercive and unclear; that the system is built on compliance to tasks rather than engagement with help; and that the systems are not held accountable when they fail.[107] The Center for the Study of Social Policy has now decided to abandon its reformist strategy and instead become part of a collaborative network, the upEND Movement, to dismantle the family regulation system and replace it with "human-centered, anti-carceral responses to mental health, substance use, and domestic violence through supportive services that strengthen families and maintain children with their parents."[108] There is already a strong model to build on.

Communities Are Primary Prevention

Communities are key to primary prevention. The U.S. Advisory Board on Child Abuse and Neglect in the 1990s called for a neighborhood-based strategy to change the way people acted and lived in their communities. Since then, pilot initiatives have been developed that build on the belief that support should be so readily at hand that people don't have to ask. The Strong Communities/Strong Families initiative that grew out of the U.S. Advisory Board's recommendations had a "basic principle that people should be able to get help where they are, when they need it, and with ease and without stigma."[109] This required community outreach to engage many people, organizations, and businesses in the community to share in that belief and take action to support families so all children in the community would be safe. Once the community shouldered that responsibility, families were encouraged to join voluntarily in mutual assistance to build a strong social support network, understand parents as leaders of mutual support, and help each other, when necessary, with professional support and direct services. Points of entry into the community network included pediatricians, kindergartens, and community organizations and businesses that could become centers of family activities. These activities included play groups, parent–child fun groups, parents' night out, and workshops or chats with volunteer professionals. One of the key findings of the initiative was the willingness of communities and volunteers to build and sustain involvement to support families. A second finding was that individuals committed to this approach can engage neighbors in adopting a supportive model to create normative changes in the community based on expectations of care for one another, including greater safety for children. Even in high-need communities, the support families most needed was often already there to be accessed through creative transformation of existing facilities and assistance. Thus, the firehouse became a community center, and the businessman donated a building that became a toy library staffed by Scouts.[110] Remarkably, the initiative showed that "significant changes in social support, collective efficacy, in-home child safety, observed parenting practices, parental stress, and rates of substantiated child maltreatment and child injuries [were] effective in preventing child maltreatment in both high and low resource communities."[111]

The designers of Strong Communities/Strong Families have long argued for a large-scale replication of the initiative given the preliminary successes. Subsequent studies of other prevention programs targeting neighborhood processes also identified activities that improved neighborhoods and schools as components for stable transformation of families and reducing child maltreatment. Early identification of "food insecurity, inadequate housing, inaccessible health care[,] and problematic child care at the community level" can address child maltreatment. In the decades since the U.S. Advisory Board completed its work, lessons have been learned to create modern prevention practices. These include assuring the diversity of social supports for at-risk families; the challenge of enhancing social support—both formal and informal—to improve parenting and monitor child well-being; and the recognition that recipients' reactions to assistance from others can be complex.[112] The complexity in creating prevention that incorporates these findings is apparent in developing secondary prevention.

Targeted Assistance Is Secondary Prevention

As the current reporting and investigating system is ended and many fewer families are brought to court, there has to be robust secondary assistance offered by the schoolteachers, police officers, social workers, doctors, and neighbors who used to just pick up the phone to call in a report and be done. Secondary prevention is not compulsory or integrated into child protection services. CPS agencies' sole purpose is investigating and addressing the serious allegations of "abuse and neglect" as redefined in CAPTA.

Professor Michael Wald has suggested that we build on nationally recognized and funded programs like Head Start and Home Visiting to reach families parenting very young children who may need more intensive support. The strong constituencies and fiscal base for these established programs can assist a variety of local programs to develop and provide an opportunity for parent and community engagement and leadership in the programs.[113] Older children are also at risk of CPS involvement, and Wald (among others) reconsiders how schools can be transformed from the highest percentage of hotline reporters to centers to support children and families. This is challenging, as schools have become so entwined with law enforcement and involved in suspending and expelling children through zero-tolerance policies. Nevertheless, the scholars and advocates Brianna Harvey, Josh Gupta-Kagan, and Christopher Church believe that schools can be transformed into centers to support and not report families. They identify concrete ways that schools can collaborate with families and community resources. Schools are already aware of the financial needs of children through lunch programs and requirements for homeless children. Schools could assist families to ensure that they receive other public benefits they are entitled to including nutritional, health, and housing benefits. For more complex problems, schools could partner with legal services organizations, much like medical providers do in medical-legal partnerships; there are examples already of legal services offices and pro bono organizations placing lawyers in schools to assist families and children with family-related legal, housing, immigration, and benefits issues. Schools can serve as a source of access to health care through referrals or school-based clinics to address the mental and behavioral health issues that can lead to

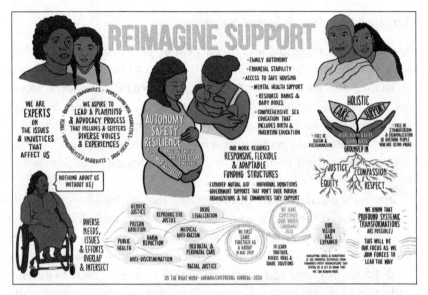

Figure 10.1. Reimagine Support by Adriana Contreras. Courtesy of the Movement for Family Power.

family disruption. In a CPS system that has radically reduced reporting, social workers can be redeployed to be sources of support and access to assistance outside schools. Replacing school police with social workers will elevate the educational and developmental purposes of schools and reduce the punitiveness found in so many underserved school systems. Finally, schools can strengthen community organizing and the development of peer mentors for parents by supporting grassroots efforts to address the inequality in underserved schools and communities, ultimately improving school policies and parent participation.[114]

Secondary prevention applies equally to status offenses and delinquency. With court jurisdiction eliminated or reduced, voluntary community-based resources must be readily available for youth and their parents. Many of these are the same resources that have been urged since the court began, and some are more recent: after-school programs in myriad areas of interest to young people; neighborhood recreational opportunities; school- and community-based educational programming; community-service projects and restorative justice programs; youth-led community organizing and community enhancing ventures;

and employment and paid internships. Financial and organizational support must be provided to youth-led as well as professionally led programs. Probation officers, social workers, and school peace officers, among others, can be retrained and redeployed to staff programs outside of CPS and the court. At the same time, youth requiring more targeted assistance should have ready access to mental and physical health services, substance use or behavioral treatment, and specialized programming for challenges related to family functioning. Situating multiple resources in youth centers where young people are willing to hang out—like The Door in New York City, which stresses communal values among the participants—increases the likelihood that youth will take advantage of the other opportunities and resources the centers offer.

Toward Equality and Full Participation in Democracy

Primary and secondary prevention leads toward fundamental transformation. As families are strengthened in their communities, receive the supports they need, and are unentangled from family regulation and court systems, they will be empowered to demand greater equality. During the COVID pandemic, income supports lifted more families out of poverty. Fewer children were reported to CPS, and yet physical abuse did not increase, building on earlier research that highly correlates poverty with child maltreatment. Recent research suggests that the relationship is causal.[115] Increased state spending on public benefit programs has been found to reduce reporting, substantiation, foster care placements, and even fatalities.[116] Increased minimum wage at the state level was associated with fewer screened-in cases, especially of neglect.[117] States that expanded Medicaid coverage under the federal Affordable Care Act saw a decline in child neglect; states that did not take advantage of the option did not.[118] Clearly the addition of income and benefits supports would vastly improve the lives of families and are an important step in reducing the poverty-related explanations that underlie so many of the cases in family court. Yet the other factors that bring families to court and our attitudes toward them must also change.

Professor Nancy Dowd has called for a "New Deal for Children," which proposes a "proactive, affirmative approach to establish the structures, policies and funding necessary to ensure the maximum development of every child," as it acknowledges that "under the current deal, [children] face a reality of unfairness, inequality, differential valuing, and the potential risk and harm from the state."[119] Unfairness, inequality, differential valuing, and harm have been a part of the family court since its inception. It is one of the structures that has to be dismantled if we are truly going to value all of our children. Many of the elements in Dowd's New Deal have been considered throughout this book: For children to be equal, to be treated equally and to have an equal chance, we have to accept the reality that children have always been and still are unequal; families, neighborhoods, and communities must be prioritized if children will have the opportunity to develop equally; parents and children must be liberated to fully engage in that transformation; none of the structures and policies that prevent families from having control over their lives are sacred; and to create this New Deal, a radical imagination is essential.

The Abolition of Family Court

As I was finishing this book, another report about the New York City Family Court was released, filled with valid complaints about the administrative disasters afflicting family court that were heightened by the COVID-19 pandemic. The report intended "to shed light on the crisis in the Family Court," acknowledging "most Family Court stakeholders are keenly aware of the deep inequities in that historically under-resourced Court" and seeking "to contribute to the critically important question of how to improve the reliability and effectiveness of a court that serves mostly poor, disenfranchised New Yorkers" by recommending and supporting "changes that we believe are achievable and necessary and already subject to broad consensus among Family Court stakeholders."[120] This report followed two others in quick succession. The first concluded that family court, along with other under-resourced trial courts, painted a picture "[of] a second-class system of justice for people of color in New York State."[121] The second identified how the most compelling problem was the continuing resistance to simplifying New York's state court system, which would finalize the process of unifying the family court with the state trial court of general jurisdiction.[122]

There is no question that court merger would improve the administrative efficiency of family court, relieving litigants from having to appear in multiple venues and improving the ability of judges to manage their caseloads. There is also no question that the subsequent recommendations in the COVID-19 report to modernize the court's technological capacity would also improve the efficiency and experience of litigants and court personnel. But therein lies the rub: like so many *crisis* reports before them, the goal is to make the court work better, to move cases more efficiently and effectively, to reduce delays, to issue orders more quickly, and to make the experience better for litigants. Nothing in these reports question whether these litigants belong in court. The "second-class system of justice for people of color" and the second-class system of justice for marginalized families around the country finding themselves in family court are not going to be changed by making the court work better. Change occurs only by recognizing that most of what these litigants need belongs outside court. Fixing the court will not serve their deserved ends. Instead, abolish the court. Abolish the court. Abolish it.

ACKNOWLEDGMENTS

In a book of such long fruition, acknowledgements inevitably will leave someone out. I have tried to keep a record of the many people who helped along the way, but I'm certain there will be a glaring error. If that includes you, please forgive me (and I hope there's a second printing).

When I began writing this book, I imagined it on a very short shelf with other books critiquing the juvenile and family courts every twenty years or so, particularly since the middle of the twentieth century. Surprisingly I found that, almost from the very beginning of the juvenile court, there were warnings about the use of a therapeutic, problem-solving, and socialized court with its potential and proven harms. During the final years of my exploration, abolition became a viable alternative, spurred by other abolition movements. But without understanding the earliest warnings about this court, I would not have been able to fully embrace an abolitionist stance. In addition, the scholarship of three chroniclers of the juvenile court—Barry Feld, David Tanenhaus, and Geoff Ward—were critical in my understanding of the history and practices of the court. This book was further motivated by the work of Walter Gellhorn and Alfred Kahn, both of whom I knew and admired at the end of their long careers at Columbia and the beginning of mine. Their insights in the 1950s were essential in shaping my thinking.

My abolitionist perspective was deeply informed and inspired by my clients, their families, and their activist communities. I am especially grateful to the youth writers and their editors at *Represent* and the parent advocates and activists at the Child Welfare Organizing Project and later at RISE who helped me teach my students for many years. They have demanded and deserve a different approach to injustice, inequality, precarity, and dignity—in essence, a different political and economic democracy. I hope they will see this book as a small step in creating that democracy.

My earliest efforts to analyze the family court were spurred by the openness and honesty of colleagues at the Stephen J. Ellmann Clinical

Theory Workshops, especially the late Steve Ellmann. The most sustained support and analysis came from the participants of the New York Area Family Law Scholars Workshops, created and nurtured by Solangel Maldonado and Edward Stein. Year after year I would present parts of this book, and year after year those critiques would make it better. I'm also grateful to colleagues who asked me to present my ideas at the Washington School of Law at American University, the Mid-Atlantic Clinical Theory Workshop, the Sayra and Neil Meyerhoff Center for Families, Children, and the Courts at the University of Baltimore School of Law, CUNY Law School, the Association of American Law Schools, Law and Society, University of Tennessee Law School, and the Frederic G. Levin Law School at the University of Florida.

A slew of research assistants made this book possible and more fun to write. If memory serves, I have included them all here. Thank you all for your sustained and dedicated work: Adia Coley, Sarah Deibler, Ellie Dupler, Melanie Jolson, Prakriti Luthra, Tanvi Mirani, Magdalena Oropeza, Jacqui Pitt, Robert Rhodes, Daniel Sack, Nicholas Schwarz, Abby Shamray, Tessa Silverman, Ashley Sullivan, Caitlin Tardio, and Christine Wang.

Two Columbia Law School deans—David Schizer and Gillian Lester—were personally committed to this project while also giving me time and financial assistance, especially through the Faculty Research Fund. I am deeply grateful for their support. The reference librarians and IT wizards at Columbia Law School worked their magic time and again. My clinic colleagues at the law school—both old and new—inspired me to work harder. My students gave me the best reason to go to work. The clinic staff—Brenda Eberhart, Mirlande Mercier, and Misty Swan, and my two partners in crime, Michelle Ellis and Elizabeth Gloder—were always there to make everything go right. And my colleague, forever neighbor, and dear friend Philip Genty fits into all the categories of thanks that appear below.

So many colleagues and friends have provided support, encouragement, and insight over the years whether or not they agreed with my views. I would especially like to thank, Barbara Babb, Wendy Bach, Amy Berlin, Steve Cohen, the late Robert Fergusen, Marty Guggenheim, Paul Holland, David Kelly, Elliott Milstein, Wally Mlyniec, Judy Moran, Jane Murphy, Nancy Polikoff, Diane Redleaf, Dean Rivkin, Dorothy Roberts, Ann Shalleck, Jana Singer, Nancy Sinkoff, Kendall Thomas, the late Charles Tilly, Judy Waksberg, Michael Wald, and Richard Wexler. Each of you have helped me in big and small ways.

Some colleagues have read more than their fair share of these chapters and provided excellent direction, detailed advice, and unflagging enthusiasm. I would especially like to thank Melissa Breger, Matt Fraiden, Cynthia Godsoe, Clare Huntington, and Mae Quinn for sticking with me as the years went by. In addition, I was fortunate that New York University Press sent my manuscript to Jana Singer to review; she twice provided detailed recommendations that were beyond wonderful.

As this book was nearing completion, two people buckled down and did the hard work of deep editing while sustaining my intentions and approach. Nancy Dowd encouraged me to submit my manuscript for the Families, Law, and Society series she edits at New York University Press, then conducted several reads to help me get this right. My friend and colleague Carol Sanger, in the midst of so much else, read with dedication and flare to enliven and improve my vision and my writing. Thanks, Turnip.

At New York University Press I would especially like to thank Clara Platter for her enthusiasm from my first submission and her dedication to my ideas right through the final version. I would also like to thank the copy editor, Jon Howard, Veronica Knutson, Martin Coleman, and the rest of the team at New York University Press for their hard work and professionalism in bringing this book to publication.

Special friends deserve special mention. Thanks to Liz McNamara and Barbara Noble, Joanie Bernstein and Barry Auskern, and more recently Riv-Ellen Prell and Steven Foldes for being my cheerleaders.

This book has a two-part dedication. It honors my mother, father, and brother, who believed in me and would be so proud to see their daughter and sister publish this book. But foremost the book is for Warren and Briggin, my husband and daughter, who dedicate every day to making their small parts of the world fairer, more just, more equitable, and more fun. With their love, they have made for me a life worth savoring every moment.

NOTES

INTRODUCTION

1 Van Waters 1925.
2 Knupfer 2001.
3 Cabot 1925, 246.
4 Ryerson 1978, 40–43.
5 Feld 1999, 26; Bullard 2013.
6 Polsky 1991; Knupfer 2001.
7 Murphy and Singer 2015.
8 McCloud 2015, 1156; Kaba 2021, 133.
9 Schur 1973.
10 Eliot 1914a.
11 Tilly 2006a, 64.
12 Gardner 2006.
13 Feeley 1983.
14 Dobbs 1949, 26.
15 Abbott 1936, 235.
16 Eastman 1934, 76.
17 Schwartz, Weiner, and Enosh 1998, 548–52.

1. THE GREAT IDEA OF THE JUVENILE COURT

1 Ketcham 1962, 26.
2 Mack 1925, 312.
3 Hoffman 1925, 266.
4 Hoffman 1925, 260.
5 Rosenheim 1962, 1; Tanenhaus 2002, 42.
6 Tappan 1962, 144, 149–50; Keve 1962, 172–77.
7 Breckinridge 1912, 11.
8 Polsky 1991, 66–71.
9 Baker 1920, 115.
10 Breckinridge 1912, 9; 12.
11 Harrington 1982, 36–39, 43; Pound 1912, 331–33; Pound 1913, 322; Pound 1945.
12 Platt 2009, 144.
13 Anderson 1925, 108, 116.
14 *Commonwealth v. Fisher* 1905; Ryerson 1978, 38–39, 67–68.

15 *Commonwealth v. Fisher* 1905, 213.
16 Tanenhaus 2002, 50–53.
17 *Lassiter v. Dep't of Social Services of Durham County, North Carolina* 1981; *Turner v. Rogers* 2011.
18 Eliot 1914b, 154–58.
19 Lindsey 1914, 140.
20 Day 1928, 105.
21 Day 1928, 111.
22 Waite 1923, 229.
23 Waite 1923, 234.
24 Waite 1923, 235; *Nicholson v. Scoppetta* 2004.
25 Lindsey 1914, 145.
26 Paulsen 1966, 696.
27 Paulsen 1966, 698.
28 Bullard 2013, 102–04, 111–13.
29 Bullard 2013, 88–89; Ward 2009, 225, 228–30.
30 Ward 2012, 78–103.
31 Gustafson 2013, 340.
32 Polier 1941, 77.
33 Flexner and Baldwin 1914, x–xi.
34 Rymph 2017, 28–30.
35 Rosenheim 1962, 10–12.
36 Tanenhaus 2002, 47.
37 Lathrop 1925, 290–91.
38 Lathrop 1925, 295.
39 Bowen 1925, 298, 304.
40 Bowen 1925, 305.
41 Bowen 1925, 309.
42 Knupher 2001, 53.
43 Hoffman 1925, 257.
44 Ryerson 1978, 87.
45 "Our History," https://nationalcasagal.org.
46 Ryerson 1978, 101.
47 Flexner 1910, 272.
48 Tanenhaus 2002, 14.
49 Tanenhaus 2002, 140–41.
50 Kahn 1953, 173.
51 "Our History," https://nationalcasagal.org.

2. THE GREAT IDEA AND THE THERAPEUTIC IMPULSE

1 Edwards 2004, 169.
2 Edwards 2004, 170.
3 Resnik 1982, 374.

4 N.Y. Family Court Act §141.

5 Edwards 2004, 170.

6 Platt 1969, 142.

7 Platt 1969, 142–43.

8 Baker 1920, 114.

9 Baker 1920, 109.

10 Baker 1920, 114.

11 Baker 1920, 116.

12 Polsky 1991.

13 Polsky 1991, 66–71.

14 "Navy as a Reform School," New York Times 1900, 3.

15 Lenroot 1949, 9.

16 Baker 1920, 116.

17 Ryerson 1978, 24–27.

18 Grossberg 2002, 32–34.

19 Polsky 76–80; Eliot 1914a.

20 Platt 2009, 138.

21 Ryerson 1978, 37.

22 Platt 2009, 141–45.

23 Ryerson 1978, 38.

24 Ryerson 1978, 45.

25 Ryerson 1978, 46–47.

26 Perkins 1919, 380.

27 Belden 1920, 8; Lenroot 1949, 213.

28 Cohen 2011, 99–100 (citing Pound 1913, 311).

29 Tanenhaus 2004, 118–24.

30 Healy 1922, 26.

31 Healy 1922, 9.

32 Perkins 1919, 378–79.

33 Perkins 1919, 381.

34 Perkins 1919, 381.

35 Lindsey 1914, 140.

36 Ryerson 1978, 39.

37 Perkins 1919, 381.

38 Eliot 1914a, 70.

39 Tanenhaus 2004, 48; Ryerson 1978, 38–41.

40 Lindsey 2004, 30.

41 Eliot 1937, 252.

42 Lenroot 1923, 216.

43 Tanenhaus 2004, 17.

44 Tanenhaus 2004, 34–36, 39–41.

45 U.S. Department of Justice, 2015b, 2.

46 Belden 1920, 56.

47 Breckinridge 1943, 12–13.

48 Belden 1920, 9.

49 Belden 1920, 13, 51; Rosenthal 1986, 306.

50 Eliot 1914b, 149.

51 Kahn 1953, 138.

52 Rosenthal 1986, 307–08; Chute 1923, 223–24.

53 Belden 1920, 51.

54 Rosenthal 1986, 307–08.

55 Waite 1921, 340.

56 Lenroot 1949, 10; Juvenile Court Standards 1923.

57 Platt 2009, 147–52. Rosenheim 1962, 15–16; Tanenhaus 2002; Tanenhaus 2004, 35, 47.

58 Ryerson 1978, 138.

59 Addams 1925.

60 Platt 2009, 143.

61 Mack 1925, 315.

62 Abbott 1925, 267.

63 Abbott 1925, 267–68.

64 Abbott 1925, 269.

65 Eliot 1925, 102.

66 Eliot 1914a, xi.

67 Eliot 1914b, 153–54.

68 Eliot 1914b, 156.

69 Eliot 1925, 103.

70 Eliot 1914b, 155.

71 Eliot 1925, 102–07.

72 Mack 1925, 312.

73 Platt 2009, 148.

74 Platt 2009, 139, 146.

75 Tanenhaus 2004, 32–34; Platt 2009, 146–52.

76 Belden 1920.

77 Lenroot and Lundberg 1925, 27, 159–60, 226,

78 Feld 1999, 71.

79 Kirchwey 1925, 331, 334–35.

80 Belden 1920; Ryerson 1978, 82.

81 Lenroot 1949, 217.

82 Ward 2012; Butler 2013, 1335.

83 Mack 1925, 313.

84 Belden 1920, 41.

85 Belden 1920, 42.

86 Secretary of Labor 1934, 93.

87 Children's Bureau 1932: foreword; Rosenthal 1986, 309–11.

88 Children's Bureau 1932, 30.

89 Rosenthal 1986, 310–12.

90 Abbott 1925, 235–37.

91 Nutt 1939, 159.

92 Nutt 1939, 161–62.

93 Nutt 1939, 169.

94 Rosenthal 1986, 312–14.

95 Smyth 1939, 179–80.

96 Smyth 1939, 183.

97 Westwick 1939, 186.

98 Westwick 1939, 194.

99 Westwick 1939, 195.

100 Pound 1945.

101 Pound 1945, 16–17, 20–22.

102 "History of the National Council of Juvenile Court Judges" 1955, 63.

103 "History of the National Council of Juvenile Court Judges" 1955, 1–3.

104 Laub 2002, 182–83, 201.

105 "History of the National Council of Juvenile Court Judges" 1955, 3–6.

106 Eastman 1934, 78–79.

107 Eastman 1934, 80.

108 "History of the National Council of Juvenile Court Judges" 1955, 5.

109 Eastman 1934, 81–83.

110 "History of the National Council of Juvenile Court Judges" 1955, 6, 27–30.

3. THE GREAT IDEA FOR BLACK CHILDREN

1 Abbott 1925, 268.

2 Feld 1999, 34–35; Bullard 2013, 88; Knupfer 2001.

3 Ward 2012, 10; Ward 2009, 225; Roberts 2005, 957.

4 Ward 2012, 66–70.

5 Ward 2012, 72–76; Billingsley and Giovannoni 1972, 26–31.

6 Trost 2005, 38–39; Ward 2012, 72–76.

7 Sterling 2013, 622.

8 Billingsley and Giovannoni 1972, 72–73.

9 Rymph 2017, 29.

10 Ward 2012, 132–33.

11 Ward 2012, 148–61.

12 Trost 2005, 38–39, 47–48.

13 Ward 2012, 149.

14 Ward 2012, 127, 160; Roberts 2005, 957, 960.

15 Ward 2012, 82–83, 93–99, 115–16.

16 Ward 2012, 101.

17 Butler 2013, 1364–68, 1372.

18 Chicago Commission on Race Relations 1923, 622–23.

19 Chicago Commission on Race Relations 1923, 335; Butler 2013, 1369–70.

20 Bowen et al. 1913, 1.
21 Bowen 1914, 195.
22 Bowen et al. 1913, 9.
23 Joint Committee on Negro Child Study in New York City et al. 1927; Sobie 2012 [1987], 129.
24 Lovejoy 1932, 12–13.
25 Joint Committee on Negro Child Study in New York City et al. 1927, 6.
26 Joint Committee on Negro Child Study in New York City et al. 1927, 6, 18, 23.
27 Joint Committee on Negro Child Study in New York City et al. 1927, 20.
28 Joint Committee on Negro Child Study in New York City et al. 1927, 11.
29 Joint Committee on Negro Child Study in New York City et al. 1927, 13, 21, 23.
30 Joint Committee on Negro Child Study in New York City et al. 1927, 23.
31 Bernstein 2001, 52–55, 326; Hildreth 1934, 6.
32 Bernstein 2001, 54–56.
33 Hildreth 1934, 6.
34 Joint Committee on Negro Child Study in New York City et al. 1927, 24; Hildreth 1934, 7.
35 Joint Committee on Negro Child Study in New York City et al. 1927, 7–8.
36 Billingsley and Giovannoni 1972, 80.
37 Thurston 1930; White House Conference 1930; White House Conference 1933.
38 White House Conference 1933, 278.
39 White House Conference 1933, 279, 286; Billingsley and Giovannoni 1972, 81–84.
40 White House Conference 1933, 289–90, 299–303.
41 White House Conference 1933, 281–82.
42 Ward 2012, 185; Hildreth 1934, 6–12.
43 Ward 2012, 190.
44 Lovejoy 1932, 35.
45 Hildreth 1934, 1.
46 Boyle 1934, 3.
47 Boyle 1934, 3.
48 Hildreth 1934, 8.
49 Brooklyn Eagle 1934, 1.
50 Hildreth 1934.
51 Lovejoy 1932, 34–48.
52 Diggs 1940, 313–16.
53 Diggs 1940, 317.
54 Diggs 1940, 319–20.
55 Ward 2012, 148–52; Ellis 1937, 362.
56 Roberts 2005, 362.
57 Butler 2013, 1363.
58 Butler 2013, 1376.
59 Ellis 1937, 363.
60 Ellis 1937, 362.

61 Ellis 1937, 363.
62 Ellis 1937, 363.
63 Nielsen 2020; Washburn 1981, 73.
64 Suddler 2019, 20.
65 McLeod 2016, 47.
66 McLeod 2016, 64–66.
67 McLeod 2016, 62–65.
68 McLeod 2016, 55.
69 Welfare and Health Council of the City of New York 1957, 45.
70 Newsweek 1957, 25; McIntyre 1960, 59; Barnosky 2006, 314.
71 Harrison 1959, 72.
72 Henning, Nanini, and Ward 2018, 31.
73 Dowd 2018, 19–27.
74 Suddler 2019, 79–83.
75 Suddler 2019, 110–11.
76 Kahn 1951, 8.
77 Feld 2017, 46–47.
78 Welfare and Health Council of the City of New York 1957, 6.
79 Welfare and Health Council of the City of New York 1957, ii, 54, 70–71.
80 Welfare and Health Council of the City of New York 1957, 76–77.
81 Katz 2020, 1566–70.
82 Clark 1959, 240.
83 Clark 1959, 241–47.
84 Clark 1959, 249–51.
85 Clark 1959, 251.

4. RATIONALIZING AND CONSOLIDATING COURT POWER
1 Tilly 1997, 45.
2 Lenroot 1923, 222.
3 Wolcott 2005, 169–72.
4 Lenroot 1949, 9.
5 Reinemann 1949, 36–38.
6 Healy 1949, 19.
7 Dobbs 1949, 24.
8 Deutsch 1950, 234.
9 Dobbs 1949, 26.
10 Chute 1949, 7.
11 Lenroot 1949, 12.
12 Schramm 1949, 20.
13 Perlman 1949, 67.
14 Schramm 1949, 23.
15 Cohen 2011, 101–03.
16 Katz 2019, 1281.

17 Quinn 2008, 741.
18 Quinn 2008, 744, 754–55.
19 N.Y. Fam. Ct. Act §846a.
20 MacDowell 2015, 489–90.
21 MacDowell 2015, 490.
22 Perkins 1919, 378.
23 Perkins 1919, 381.
24 Alexander 1944, 39.
25 DiFonzo 1994, 544–46, 555.
26 DiFonzo 1994, 544.
27 Alexander 1952, 243; Gellhorn, Hyman, and Asch 1954, 24; Cohen 2011.
28 Ryerson 1978, 37.
29 Fradkin 1962, 118, 121.
30 Elson 1962; National Probation and Parole Association 1959, 20–21.
31 Standard Family Court Act 1959, Foreword 3.
32 Tappan 1962, 157.
33 Tappan 1962, 144, 156–57.
34 Alexander 1952, 269.
35 Alexander 1952, 262.
36 Alexander 1952, 261.
37 Alexander 1952, 262–64.
38 Kephart 1955, 66.
39 Kephart 1955, 67–69, 72; Glueck and Glueck 1939.
40 Gellhorn, Hyman, and Asch 1954, 24.
41 Gellhorn, Hyman, and Asch 1954, 382.
42 Gellhorn, Hyman, and Asch 1954, 384.
43 Gellhorn, Hyman, and Asch 1954, 388.
44 Gellhorn, Hyman, and Asch 1954, 81–88.
45 Johnson 1953, vii.
46 Kahn 1953, 269.
47 Kahn 1953, 98.
48 Kahn 1953, 115.
49 Kahn 1953, 115.
50 Kahn 1953, 98–115.
51 Kahn 1953, 117.
52 Kahn 1953, 103, 116–23.
53 Kahn 1953, 277.
54 Kahn 1953, 281.
55 Kahn 1953, 106.
56 Kahn 1953, 269.
57 Kahn 1953, 265.
58 Sobie 2012 [1987], 158–62.
59 N.Y. Fam. Ct. Act §141.

60 N.Y. Fam. Ct. Act §141.
61 Ketcham 1962, 26.
62 Ketcham 1962, 26.
63 Ketcham 1962, 32–37.
64 Kahn 1962, 218–19.
65 Paulsen 1962, 47–48.
66 Paulsen 1962, 53.
67 Paulsen 1962, 52.
68 *In re Gault*, 387 U.S. 1 (1967)
69 Paulsen 1962, 66–68.
70 Studt 1962, 211.
71 Studt 1962, 215.
72 Kahn 1953, 281.
73 Allen 1964, 49.
74 Allen 1964, 60–61.
75 Alexander 1962, 92.

5. THE GREAT IDEA MEETS DUE PROCESS

1 *Joseph McKeiver v. Commonwealth of Pennsylvania* 1968.
2 *Joseph McKeiver v. Commonwealth of Pennsylvania* 1968.
3 *In the Matter of Joseph McKeiver* 1969; *McKeiver v. Pennsylvania* 1971.
4 Feld 1999, 90–97.
5 *Kent v. United States* 1966, 541.
6 Tanenhaus 2000, 14–16; Feld 1999, 73.
7 *Kent v. United States* 1966, 543.
8 *Kent v. United States* 1966, 555.
9 *In re Gault* 1967.
10 Tanenhaus 2011, 33;44–45.
11 Guggenheim 2005, 259.
12 *In re Gault* 1967, 17.
13 *In re Gault* 1967, 18.
14 *In re Gault* 1967, 14.
15 *In re Gault* 1967, 13–27.
16 MacFaden 1969, 96.
17 *In re Gault* 1967, 35–40.
18 Alexander 1962, 88.
19 *In re Gault* 1967, 51.
20 *In re Gault* 1967, 28.
21 *In re Gault* 1967, 60.
22 *In re Gault* 1967, 79.
23 *In re Winship* 1970.
24 *In re Winship* 1970, 375.
25 *In re Winship* 1970, 376.

26 *In re Winship* 1970, 376.

27 *In re Terry* 1970.

28 *In re Terry* 1970, 347.

29 *In re Terry* 1970, 355.

30 *In re Terry* 1970, 349.

31 *In re Terry* 1970, 347.

32 *In re Terry* 1970, 350.

33 *In re Terry* 1970, 349.

34 President's Commission on Law Enforcement and Administration of Justice 1967.

35 *In re Terry* 1970, 349–50.

36 *In re Terry* 1970, 351–55.

37 *DeBacker v. Brainard* 1969, 33–38.

38 *In the Matter of Joseph McKeiver* 1969, 760; *In the Matter of Edward Terry* 1969, 762; *In re Barbara Burrus* 1969, 523.

39 *McKeiver v. Pennsylvania* 1971, 539–40.

40 *McKeiver v. Pennsylvania* 1971, 543.

41 *McKeiver v. Pennsylvania* 1971, 544.

42 *McKeiver v. Pennsylvania* 1971, 546.

43 *McKeiver v. Pennsylvania* 1971, 546.

44 President's Commission on Law Enforcement and Administration of Justice 1967, 80–85.

45 President's Commission on Law Enforcement and Administration of Justice 1967.

46 Task Force Report: Juvenile Delinquency and Youth Crime 1967, 40.

47 *McKeiver v. Pennsylvania* 1971, 547.

48 *McKeiver v. Pennsylvania* 1971, 551.

49 *McKeiver v. Pennsylvania* 1971, 551.

50 Allen 1964, 49, 60.

51 Feld 1999, 158.

52 *McKeiver v. Pennsylvania* 1971, 536.

53 *McKeiver v. Pennsylvania* 1971, 537.

54 *McKeiver v. Pennsylvania* 1971, 537–38.

55 *In re Barbara Burrus* 1969, 527.

56 Sterling 2013, 653.

57 *In re Barbara Burrus* 1969, 528.

58 Society for the History of Children and Youth 2004.

59 *McKeiver v. Pennsylvania* 1971, 556.

60 *In re Barbara Burrus* 1969, 532.

61 Kapp 2007.

62 Freeman 1996; "Susie Sharp Papers #4898" (Sharp's papers contain no record of the case either); Hayes 2009 (nor is it discussed in her biography).

63 Summey 2017, 214.

64 Sterling 2013.

65 U.S. Commission on Civil Rights 1965.

66 *McKeiver v. Pennsylvania* 1971 (Brief for Petitioners).

67 *McKeiver v. Pennsylvania* 1971 (Reply Brief for Petitioners).

68 See chapter 3, "The Court and Black Children," in this volume.

69 Sterling 2013.

70 *In re Barbara Burrus* 1969, 525–26.

71 *Kent v. United States* 1966, 556.

72 Feld 1999, 247.

73 *McKeiver v. Pennsylvania* 1971 (Reply Brief for Petitioners).

74 Feld 1999; Feld 2007.

75 Ward 2012, 205–08.

76 U.S. Commission on Civil Rights 1965, 80–83.

77 U.S. Commission on Civil Rights 1965, 80.

78 U.S. Commission on Civil Rights 1965, 80–83.

79 U.S. Commission on Civil Rights 1965, 80.

80 *In re Gault* 1967, 19; Paulson 1966, 700.

81 Feld 1999, 129.

82 Dawson 2000, 66.

83 Butts and Mears 2001.

84 Dawson 2000.

85 Redding and Howell 2000, 146.

86 Dawson 2000, 47.

87 Henning 2009, 1116–21.

88 Office of Juvenile Justice and Delinquency Prevention 2013.

89 Zimring 2000, 208–14.

90 Behrman et al. 1996, 4–28.

91 Schwartz, Weiner, and Enosh 1998, 550.

92 Schwartz, Weiner, and Enosh 1998, 551.

93 Allen 1964, 60.

94 Guggenheim and Hertz 2016, 661.

95 Feld 2007, 217, 222.

96 Guggenheim and Hertz 2016, 661.

97 Feld 2007, 219.

98 Guggenheim and Hertz 2016, 662; American Bar Association 1995 [rpt. 2005].

99 Feld 2007, 220.

100 Guggenheim and Hertz 2016, 662.

101 Feld 1999, 221.

102 Office of Justice Programs, Department of Justice 2004, 3.

103 Office of Justice Programs, Department of Justice 2004, 9–11.

104 Office of Justice Programs, Department of Justice 2004, 17.

105 Office of Justice Programs, Department of Justice 2004, 19.

106 Office of Justice Programs, Department of Justice 2004, 21.

107 Zimring 1998.

6. STATUS OFFENSES AND THE RISE OF THE FAMILY COURT

1 *Rule v. Geddes* 1904, 31.
2 *Rule v. Geddes* 1904, 50–51.
3 Platt 1969; Tanenhaus 2004; Sobie 2012 [1987]; Allen 1964, 46.
4 Teitelbaum 2002, 158.
5 D.C. Code § 16–2301(8)(3).
6 D.C. Code § 16–2305.01(1).
7 *Rule v. Geddes* 1904, 38.
8 *Ex parte Crouse I* 1838, 27.
9 *Rule v. Geddes* 1904, 51.
10 *Rule v. Geddes* 1904, 50.
11 *Rule v. Geddes* 1904, 50–51.
12 *In re Sippy* 1953, 455.
13 D.C. Code, § 11–901 et seq. (1951).
14 Ketcham 1964, 16–18.
15 Elson 1962, 100.
16 *In re Sippy* 1953, 459.
17 *Matter of Kenneth J.* 1980, 821; *Matter of Leif Z.* 1980, 209.
18 Hockenberry and Puzzanchera 2020.
19 Juvenile Justice Geography, "Policy, Practice and Statistics," www.jjgps.org.
20 Coalition for Juvenile Justice 2020.
21 President's Commission on Law Enforcement and Administration of Justice 1967; Task Force Report: Juvenile Delinquency and Youth Crime 1967.
22 Scott and Steinberg 2008.
23 President's Commission on Law Enforcement and Administration of Justice 1967, 55.
24 President's Commission on Law Enforcement and Administration of Justice 1967, 57.
25 Gellhorn, Hyman, and Asch 1954; New York State Bar Association 2012; New York County Lawyer's Association 2010.
26 Allen 1964, 45.
27 Allen 1964, 34.
28 Allen 1964, 35.
29 Allen 1964, 37.
30 President's Commission on Law Enforcement and Administration of Justice 1967, 84.
31 Tonry 1976, 289.
32 *Kent v. United States* 1966, 556.
33 *In re Gault* 1967, 1.
34 President's Commission on Law Enforcement and Administration of Justice 1967, 80.

35 President's Commission on Law Enforcement and Administration of Justice 1967, 80.

36 Lemert 1967b, 93.

37 President's Commission on Law Enforcement and Administration of Justice 1967, 82.

38 President's Commission on Law Enforcement and Administration of Justice 1967, 82.

39 Tonry 1976, 281.

40 President's Commission on Law Enforcement and Administration of Justice 1967, 15.

41 Tonry 1976, 291–93.

42 U.S. National Advisory Commission on Criminal Justice Standards and Goals 1973, 169–70.

43 U.S. National Advisory Commission on Criminal Justice Standards and Goals 1973, 168.

44 U.S. National Advisory Commission on Criminal Justice Standards and Goals 1973, 169.

45 U.S. National Advisory Commission on Criminal Justice Standards and Goals 1973, 169.

46 Schur 1973.

47 Platt 1969.

48 Schur 1973, 153.

49 Schur 1973, 133, 166–70.

50 Flicker 1982.

51 Flicker 1982, 17–20.

52 Shepherd 1996, 39–40.

53 Kahneman 2011.

54 Flicker 1982, 11.

55 Flicker 1982, 275.

56 Platt 2009, 134–35.

57 Tilly 1997, 45.

58 Allen 1964, 46.

59 Institute of Judicial Administration 1977a.

60 *In re Snyder* 1975, 182.

61 Institute of Judicial Administration 1977a, 37 (emphasis added).

62 Institute of Judicial Administration 1977a, 2 (emphasis added).

63 Flicker 1982, 51.

64 Flicker 1982, 12.

65 Flicker 1982, 11.

66 Report of the California Assembly Interim Committee on Criminal Procedure 1971, 7.

67 Flicker 1982; Institute of Judicial Administration 1977a, 13.

68 Allen 1964, 52.

69 Institute of Judicial Administration 1977a, 5.

70 Institute of Judicial Administration 1977a, 61–66.

71 Rosenheim 1976, 44, 52.

72 Castellano 1986, 479, 482.

73 Schneider 1984, 347, 351.

74 Schneider 1984, 352.

75 Schneider 1984, 353.

76 Schneider 1984, 354.

77 Castellano 1986, 496; Institute of Judicial Administration 1977a, 67.

78 Schneider and Schram 1986, 211, 229.

79 Schneider 1984, 361; Castellano 1986, 497.

80 Schneider 1984, 368.

81 Castellano 1986, 486.

82 Castellano 1986, 487.

83 Schneider 1984, 365; Castellano 1986, 486–87.

84 Empey 1973, 13.

85 Hornberger 2010, 16.

86 Feld 1999, 176.

87 Office of Juvenile Justice and Delinquency Prevention 1995, 1992.

88 Feld 1999, 174.

89 Feld 1999, 175.

90 Nejelski 1976, 110, 114.

91 Sobie 2012 [1987], 7.

92 Sobie 2012 [1987], 161.

93 Flicker 1982, 53.

94 Juvenile Court Judges Journal 1967–68, 106–08.

95 Juvenile Court Judges Journal 1967–68, 106–08.

96 Waite 1921, 340 (emphasis in original).

97 Juvenile Court Judges Journal 1967–68, 106–08.

98 Alexander 1962, 92.

99 Juvenile Court Judges Journal 1967–68, 106–08.

100 Gilman 2012.

101 USHR 1980, 136 (emphasis added).

102 Feld 2009, 245.

103 Feld 1999, 174–75.

104 Feld 2017, 158.

105 Teitelbaum 2002, 168.

106 Feld 2009, 245.

107 Chesney-Lind and Shelden 2004, 53–54.

108 Cohen and Spinak 2018, 269.

109 Chesney-Lind and Shelden 2004, 35, 62.

110 Chesney-Lind and Shelden 2004, 53; Feld 1999, 251.

111 Feld 1999, 253.

112 Feld 1999, 257.
113 President's Commission on Law Enforcement and Administration of Justice 1967, 57.
114 Puzzanchera et al. 2003, 15–17, 53.
115 Chesney-Lind and Shelden 2004, 298–99.
116 Grossmann 1998, 21.
117 Grossmann 1998, 18.
118 Grossmann 1998, 21.
119 Allen 1964, 56.
120 Eggers 1998, 220–25.
121 Eggers 1998, 220–25.
122 Eggers 1998, 231.
123 Eggers 1998, 231.
124 Eggers 1998, 234; Wash. Rev. Code Ann. § 13.32A.040.
125 Wash. Rev. Code Ann. § 13.32A.030.
126 Wash. Rev. Code Ann. § 13.32A.015.
127 Wash. Rev. Code Ann. § 13.32A.140; 13.32A.150.
128 Pitman 1998–1999, 394.
129 *In re M.B.* 2000, 437–38.
130 Pitman 1998–1999, 412.
131 Arthur and Waugh 2008, 561.
132 Santos, 2016.
133 *In re the Dependency of A.K.* 2007, 655.

7. CREATING A FAMILY COURT INDUSTRY

1 Roberts 2002, 174–76.
2 Rosenthal 1986, 313.
3 Rosenthal 1986, 313–14.
4 Roberts 2002, 174–76; Rosenthal 1986, 312–13; Polsky 1991, 159.
5 Lawrence-Webb 1997, 11–21; Roberts 2002, 176–77; L. Briggs 2021, 621–27.
6 Lawrence-Webb 1997, 11–21; Roberts 2002, 176–77.
7 L. Briggs 2021, 611, 618–27.
8 Polsky 1991, 158–64.
9 Polsky 1991, 158–64; Costin, Karger, and Stoesz 1996, 108–12; Sanders 2002, 55.
10 Costin, Karger, and Stoesz 1996, 110; Lindsey 2004, 274–76.
11 Sanders 2002, 55–56, 61–62.
12 Rymph 2017, 159.
13 Rymph 2017, 160.
14 Chambers and Wald 1985, 70.
15 Rymph 2017, 95.
16 Lindsey 2004, 121–22; Costin, Karger, and Stoesz 1996, 113–16.
17 Waldfogel 1998, 72; Lindsey 2004, 122–23.
18 Melton 2005, 9–11.

19 Waldfogel 1998, 7.
20 Children's Bureau 2021b, 7.
21 Fong 2020, 615.
22 Children's Bureau 2021b, 7–8, 91.
23 Child Abuse Prevention and Treatment Act ("CAPTA"), P.L. 93–247, 88 Stat. 4 (1974), *amended by* P.L. 104–35, 110 Stat. 3063 (1996).
24 Wald 2012, 91.
25 Guggenheim 2005, 184–85.
26 Gil 1976, 54.
27 Gil 1976, 54.
28 Dowd 2018, 136.
29 Raz 2020, 13–14; Guggenheim 2005, 184–85; Pelton 1978, 613.
30 Pelton 1978, 613.
31 Platt 1969, 142.
32 Gellhorn, Hyman, and Asch 1954, 382–89; Sobie 2012 [1987], 160.
33 Tolchin 1964, 24.
34 Alexander 1962, 82.
35 Paulsen 1962, 44–81, 63–73.
36 Flicker 1982: xii.
37 Flicker 1982, 52.
38 Flicker 1982, 53.
39 Flicker 1982, 53.
40 Flicker 1982, 58–59.
41 Wald 1976, 641.
42 Eliot 1914b, 154–56; Eliot 1925, 102; Rosenthal 1986, 309–11.
43 Institute of Judicial Administration 1977b, 184–86.
44 Dembitz 1978, 1940.
45 Dembitz 1978, 1944.
46 Lindsey 2004, 35–41.
47 Lindsey 2004, 47–52.
48 Institute of Judicial Administration 1977b, 6.
49 *Hearing on Child Protection Issues Before the Subcommittee on Human Resources of the House Committee on Ways and Means, 108th Congress.* 2003, 34–66.
50 Liebmann 2006, 141–43.
51 Paulson 1966, 694; Ketcham 1977, 201; Nuuernberger and Van Duizend 1977, 3.
52 Goldstein, Freud, and Solnit 1973.
53 Goldstein, Freud, and Solnit 1973, 53–64.
54 Goldstein et al. 1986, 20–21.
55 Mnookin 1975, 226.
56 Goldstein et al. 1986, 104–05.
57 Goldstein et al. 1986, 93–94.
58 Goldstein et al. 1986, 111–13.
59 Goldstein, Freud, and Solnit 1979, 71.

60 *Smith v. Organization of Foster Families* 1977, 840.

61 Chambers and Wald 1985, 110.

62 *Smith v. Organization of Foster Families* 1977, 844.

63 *Smith v. Organization of Foster Families* 1977, 846–47 (emphasis added).

64 *Smith v. Organization of Foster Families* 1977, 823.

65 *Smith v. Organization of Foster Families* 1977, 854.

66 Goldstein, Freud, and Solnit 1979.

67 Sanders 2002, 62.

68 Pub. L. No. 96–272, 94 Stat. 500 (codified as amended in scattered sections of 42 U.S.C.) [hereinafter P.L. 96–272]

69 P.L. 96–272; Herring 2000, 332–33.

70 Lindsey 2004, 82.

71 Lindsey 2004, 83.

72 Kamerman and Kahn, 2002, 83; Guggenheim 2005, 188.

73 Costin, Karger, and Stoesz 1996, 123.

74 Sanders 2002, 69.

75 Edwards 2018.

76 Armstrong et al. 1997.

77 Lindsey 2004, 84–85; Guggenheim 2021, 722.

78 Crossley 2003, 285; Office of Inspector General, Department of Health and Human Services. 1994, 22.

79 Crossley 2003, 285.

80 Crossley 2003, 287.

81 Herring 2000; Kamerman and Kahn 2002.

82 Kamerman and Kahn 2002, 17.

83 Costin, Karger, and Stoesz 1996, 128.

84 Kamerman and Kahn 1990, 15; Ellet and Leighninger 2007, 3.

85 Lindsey 2004, 215, 231.

86 Lindsey 2004, 232–33; 253; 257.

87 Pelton 1999, 131; Minoff 2018, 16.

88 Kamerman and Kahn 1990, 13–15.

89 Swan and Sylvester 2009, 309.

90 Young and Gardner 2009.

91 Polsky 1991, 195–99.

92 Schwartz, Weiner, and Enosh 1999, 129.

93 Gagliardo 1971, 57; Polier 1975.

94 Braverman and Ramsey 1997, 458.

95 See www.childrensrights.org.

96 Ellet and Leighninger 2007, 13–17.

97 Carnochan et al. 2007, 121–22 (2007).

98 *Lassiter v. Dep't of Social Services of Durham County, North Carolina* 1981.

99 *Santosky v. Kramer* 1982.

100 Sankaran 2011, 13; *N.Y. Cnty. Lawyers' Ass'n v. State* 2002, 388–89.

101 Murphy 2010, 891.

102 Peters 2006, 997–1002.

103 Tanenhaus 2002, 47–48.

104 Knupfer 2001, 53.

105 "Our History," www.casamsc.org.

106 Mulzer and Urs 2016, 38.

107 Mulzer and Urs 2016, 38 (citing Child Abuse Prevention and Treatment Act Amendments of 1996 (CAPTA), Pub. L. No. 104–235, 110 Stat. 3063 (1996) (codified at 42 U.S.C. § 5106a(b)(2)(B)(xiii)).

108 Ellet and Leighninger 2007, 27.

109 Mulzer and Urs 2016, 24–26.

110 Murphy 2010, 904.

111 Mulzer and Urs 2016, 37.

8. THE FEDERAL FAMILY COURT

1 Worley and Melton 2013, 103, 105.

2 Bergman 2013, 63, 66–67.

3 Johnston 2017.

4 Melton and Thompson 2002, 3.

5 U.S. Advisory Board on Child Abuse and Neglect 1990, 1–10.

6 Melton and Thompson 2002, 13–15.

7 Lindsey 2004, 83–84.

8 Pub. L. No. 105–89, 111 Stat. 2115 1997.

9 Golden and Macomber 2009, 10.

10 Golden and Macomber 2009, 18–19; Gittler 2002, 116–41.

11 Lindsey 2004, 262–63; 275.

12 Lindsey 2004, 312.

13 Golden and Macomber 2009, 18–19.

14 Golden and Macomber 2009, 28; Huntington 2014, 242.

15 Mangold and Cerulli 2009, 365.

16 Mangold and Cerulli 2009, 370.

17 42 U.S.C. § 671(a)(15) 2018.

18 Lindsey 2004, 170–72, 310–12.

19 Crossley 2003, 284–88; Children's Bureau, n.d., ; Jones 2006; U.S. Government Accountability Office 2004, 11; D. Kelly 2021.

20 *Troxel v. Granville* 2000, 66.

21 Fraidin 2013, 916.

22 Fraidin 2013, 923.

23 Fraidin 2013, 944, 947, 963.

24 Fraidin 2013, 930.

25 Bean 2005, 334.

26 Bean 2005, 334; Crossley 2003; *In re Kaliyah S. et al.* 2015, 533.

27 Bean 2005, 334–38.

28 *In re N.J.* 2001.
29 *In re N.J.* 2001, 2.
30 *In re N.J.* 2001, 3.
31 *In re N.J.* 2001, 4.
32 Bean 2005, 334.
33 American Law Institute 2021; Edwards 2022, 97–98.
34 Bean 2005, 352–55; Kemper 2006, 173.
35 Bean 2005, 351–53.
36 Bean 2005, 337–38.
37 Bean 2005, 362.
38 Children's Bureau 2021b, 7; Children's Bureau 2020c, 68–72.
39 Bean 2005, 358.
40 Bean 2005, 365–66.
41 American Law Institute 2021; Edwards 2022, 97–98.
42 Braverman and Ramsey 1997, 458.
43 Children's Rights, Inc., www.childrensrights.org.
44 *B.K. v. McKay*, Class Actions, Children's Rights, Inc., www.childrensrights.org.
45 *Santosky v. Kramer* 1982, 763.
46 Pub. L. No. 105–89, 111 Stat. 2115 1997.
47 Guggenheim 2021, 722.
48 Children's Bureau 2018.
49 Schalick 2014, 473.
50 Schalick 2014, 475–77.
51 Herring 2000, 332–33; Allen and Davis-Pratt 2009, 70.
52 Strengthening Abuse and Neglect Courts Act of 2000, 42 U.S.C. § 670; Gatowski and Portune 2009.
53 Strengthening Abuse and Neglect Courts Act of 2000, 42 U.S.C. § 670; SEC. 2. Findings.
54 Children's Bureau, n.d.
55 Congressional Research Service 2006, 1, 11.
56 Congressional Research Service 2006, 11.
57 Children's Bureau 2005.
58 National Council of Juvenile and Family Court Judges 2004; Conference of Chief Justices 2004.
59 Children's Bureau 2012.
60 Breger 2010, 55.
61 Testa 2004, 501.
62 Golden and Macomber 2009, 20–21.
63 Huntington 2014, 242–43.
64 North American Council on Adoptable Children 2020.
65 Godsoe 2013a, 1116–17; Godsoe 2013b, 32.
66 Godsoe 2013a, 1123–26.
67 Godsoe 2013a, 1127.

68 Allen and Davis-Pratt 2009, 71–72, 74; Golden and Macomber 2009, 13.

69 Godsoe 2013a, 1127–28, 1136.

70 Godsoe 2013a, 1120; North American Council on Adoptable Children 2020.

71 Godsoe 2013b, 17.

72 Smith 2014; Post and Zimmerman 2012, 437.

73 Schalick 2014, 472; Adams 2014, 225; Casey Family Programs 2008.

74 Albert et al. 2021, 861.

75 Adams 2010, 338–44.

76 National Council of Juvenile and Family Court Judges 2012.

77 *Fostering Connections to Success and Increased Adoptions Act of 2008* 42 U.S.C.; N.Y. Fam. Ct. Act §1091.

78 Mandelbaum 2015, 265–67.

79 Mandelbaum 2015, 284–85.

80 Post and Zimmerman 2012; Mandelbaum 2015; *Nicholson v. Williams* 2002, 153.

81 Post and Zimmerman 2012.

82 National Council of Juvenile and Family Court Judges, n.d.-b.

83 Smith 2014.

9. THE FAILURE OF REFORM

 1 Edwards 2004, 169.

 2 N.Y. Fam. Ct. Act §141.

 3 Mulvey 1982, 51.

 4 Babb and Moran 2018.

 5 Dembitz 1978, 1940.

 6 USHR 1980, 136.

 7 Conference of Chief Justices 2017a. Conference of Chief Justices 2017b.

 8 Harrington 1982, 62.

 9 Abel 1982, 270, 280.

10 Feld 1999, 174.

11 Lee 2016, 49.

12 Abel 1982, 271 (emphasis added).

13 Babb and Moran 2018, 114.

14 Murphy and Singer 2015, 37–38.

15 Murphy 2020, 632–36.

16 Murphy 2020, 630.

17 Abel 1982, 307.

18 Babb and Moran 2018, 7.

19 Murphy 2020, 630.

20 Fund for Modern Courts Family Court Task Force 2009; New York State Bar Association 2012.

21 Scheiber 1993, 2052–53, 2055–56, 2069–70.

22 Feeley 1983, 194–95, 205.

23 Feeley 1983, 23–26.
24 Tilly 2006a, 34.
25 Gardner 2006, 17.
26 Stashenko 2008, 1.
27 Stashenko 2008, 1.
28 Feeley 1983, 202.
29 Tilly 2006b.
30 Feeley 1983, 206.
31 Babb and Moran 2018, 16–24.
32 U.S. Department of Justice, n.d.
33 U.S. Department of Justice, n.d.
34 *In re Gault* 1967, 26–27.
35 U.S. Department of Justice 2012, 10.
36 U.S. Department of Justice 2012, 1–5, 46–50.
37 U.S. Department of Justice 2015a, 11, 16; U.S. Department of Justice 2015b, 1–3.
38 U.S. Department of Justice 2015a, 18–19.
39 U.S. Department of Justice 2012, 15–16.
40 *In re Gault* 1967, 28, 30.
41 U.S. Department of Justice 2012, 52, 56–59.
42 U.S. Department of Justice 2012, 22–46.
43 *U.S. v. City of Meridian et al.* 2012, 1–3.
44 *U.S. v. City of Meridian et al.* 2012, 8–9.
45 Summers 2016a; Summers 2016b.
46 Florida Department of Juvenile Justice, n.d., *Myths vs. Facts.*
47 *E.A.R. v. State* 2009, 632.
48 *E.A.R. v. State* 2009, 633.
49 *E.A.R. v. State* 2009, 628.
50 Juvenile Law Center, n.d., https://jlc.org.
51 Interbranch Commission on Juvenile Justice 2010, 6.
52 Interbranch Commission on Juvenile Justice 2010, 8.
53 Juvenile Law Center, n.d., https://jlc.org.
54 American Bar Association 2012;. Juvenile Law Center 2014.
55 Hockenberry and Puzzanchera 2014, 77, 80; Hockenberry and Puzzanchera 2019, 64.
56 Hockenberry and Puzzanchera 2019, 64.
57 Hockenberry and Puzzanchera 2019, 72–74.
58 Jafarian and Ananthakrishnan 2017.
59 Rivkin and Spinak 2015.
60 Hockenberry and Puzzanchera 2018, 63.
61 Coalition for Juvenile Justice 2018.
62 American Bar Association 2007.
63 American Bar Association 2007, 8.

64 American Bar Association 2007, 11–12.
65 National Council of Juvenile and Family Court Judges 2010.
66 Office of Juvenile Justice and Delinquency Prevention 2019.
67 Coalition for Juvenile Justice 2015, 8–9.
68 Act 4 Juvenile Justice 2019.
69 Flicker 1982, 12.
70 Coalition for Juvenile Justice 2012.
71 President's Commission on Law Enforcement and Administration of Justice 1967, 80.
72 Coalition for Juvenile Justice 2012, 5.
73 Coalition for Juvenile Justice 2012, 11.
74 Coalition for Juvenile Justice 2012, 8.
75 Byer and Kuhn 2003, 59.
76 Gellhorn, Hyman, and Asch 1954, 76.
77 *McKeiver v. Pennsylvania* 1971, 528.
78 Milner 2019.
79 Milner 2019.
80 Spinak 2009.
81 Office of Juvenile Justice and Delinquency Prevention 1999; Spinak 2009, 14.
82 National Council of Juvenile and Family Court Judges 2017, 1.
83 National Council of Juvenile and Family Court Judges, n.d.-a.
84 Bell 1999, 42.
85 New York State Permanent Judicial Commission on Justice for Children 2006.
86 Bell 1999, 43.
87 Bell 2003, vi, 35–36, 45, 47, 70.
88 National Evaluation of the Court Improvement Program 2007, 42–45.
89 National Evaluation of the Court Improvement Program 2010: Iv.
90 Child and Family Services Reviews Aggregate Report Executive Summary Round 3: Fiscal Years 2015–2018 iii.
91 Child and Family Services Reviews Round 3 Report for Legal and Judicial Communities 5.
92 Child and Family Services Reviews Round 3 Report for Legal and Judicial Communities 6, 11, 14, 17, 20.
93 Children's Bureau 2021d..
94 Gupta-Kagan 2020, 81.
95 Gupta-Kagan 2020, 59–64.
96 Gupta-Kagan 2020, 19–23.

10. ABOLITION

1 "'Incorrigibility' Label Eliminated from New York's Child Welfare Law," 2021, https://imprintnews.org.
2 Gottlieb 2020.
3 Cherone 2020.

4 Aguilera 2020 [updated 2021].

5 R. Briggs 2021.

6 Children's Bureau 2021b; Children's Bureau 2021c.

7 Langer 2020, 53–54.

8 upEND Movement 2021.

9 *Duchesne v. Sugarman* 1977, 828.

10 Guinier and Torres 2014, 2751–52.

11 Guinier and Torres 2014, 2749.

12 Institute of Judicial Administration 1977b, 67; Dembitz 1978, 1940.

13 Roediger 2021, 216.

14 Allen 1964, 60.

15 Roediger 2021, 226.

16 Zimring, 2002, 142.

17 Zimring 2002:156.

18 Scott and Steinberg 2008.

19 *Roper v. Simmons* 2005, 551; Moriearty 2015, 945–46.

20 *Roper v. Simmons* 2005, 571; Moriearty 2015, 946.

21 *Graham v. Florida* 2010, 73; Moriearty 2015, 951.

22 *Graham v. Florida* 2010, 69–70; Moriearty 2015, 952.

23 *Miller v. Alabama* 2012, 460, 477–78, 489 (2012).

24 *Jones v. Mississippi* 2021, 130.

25 *J.D.B. v. North Carolina* 2011, 261.

26 *J.D.B. v. North Carolina* 2011, 261, 268.

27 *J.D.B. v. North Carolina* 2011, 275–76.

28 *J.D.B. v. North Carolina* 2011, 273.

29 Institute of Judicial Administration 1977b, 67.

30 Polier 1967, 52–53.

31 Schur 1973, 155.

32 Schur 1973, 154, 166, 169.

33 Lemert 1967, 96–97.

34 Bridges 2011; Dowd 2018; Roberts 2002; Roberts 2022.

35 Davis and Aldieri 2021, 330.

36 Davis and Aldieri 2021, 332–33.

37 RISE 2022, 2.

38 Hockenberry and Puzzanchera 2020, 64–65, 72–74.

39 Irvine, Wilber, and Canfield 2017.

40 Jafarian and Ananthakrishnan 2017.

41 Irvine and Yusuf 2016, 2–4; U.S. Department of Education, Office for Civil Rights 2014, 1.

42 Coalition for Juvenile Justice, n.d..

43 Coalition for Juvenile Justice 2015, 7.

44 Anderson, Kreider, and Schnell 2021, 12–13.

45 Feld 2017, 273–75.

46 Feld 2017, 278.

47 Feld 2017, 278.

48 National Juvenile Justice Network 2020, 3, 6.

49 National Juvenile Justice Network 2020, 4; Clements 2021.

50 National Juvenile Justice Network 2020, 4–5.

51 National Juvenile Justice Network 2020, 11–12, 13–14.

52 Sapien 2017.

53 Juvenile Court Statistics 2018, 9.

54 Child Rights International Network, n.d., "Minimum Ages of Criminal Responsibility Around the World."

55 National Governors Association 2021.

56 Kinscherff et al. 2022, 2.

57 Feld 2000, 110–11.

58 National Governors Association 2021, 5.

59 Kinscherff et al. 2022, 27–35.

60 Ginsburg 2018, 155–62.

61 Quinn 2014, 2185.

62 Quinn 2014, 2211.

63 Quinn 2014, 2214–15.

64 Rixey 2009, 885.

65 *In re L.M.* 2008, 466.

66 *In re L.M.* 2008, 467–70.

67 *In re L.M.* 2008, 469–72.

68 Rixey 2009, 885, 908.

69 U. S. Advisory Board on Child Abuse and Neglect 1990, 80.

70 Fong 2020, 615.

71 Cecka 2014, 51.

72 Social Workers Against Mandates 2021.

73 Harvey, Gupta-Kagan, and Church 2021, 575–610.

74 Fong 2018, 1785.

75 Newport 2022.

76 Wald 2022, 716–17.

77 Wald 2022, 718, 722.

78 Wald 2022, 721–23.

79 *Lassiter v. Dep't of Social Services of Durham County, North Carolina* 1981, 57.

80 Spinak 2016, 171.

81 Gerber et al. 2019, 42.

82 National Council of Juvenile and Family Court Judges 2020.

83 ACFY-CB-PI-16-05 (Oct. 27, 2016)

84 Carter, Church, and Sankaran 2022: 510–13.

85 Fraidin and Trivedi 2022, 36.

86 42 U.S.C. § 5106a(b)(2)(B)(xiii).

87 L. Kelly 2021, 255–56.

88 QIC Child Rep., n.d.
89 QIC Child Rep., n.d.
90 Guggenheim 2020, 1.
91 Baynes-Dunning 2022, 16.
92 Guggenheim 2022, 54, 59.
93 Repeal ASFA.
94 Family Integrity & Justice Quarterly 2022.
95 Sankaran 2022, 26, 28–30.
96 Chapin Hall 2011, 113–14.
97 Briar-Lawson, Day, and Mountz 2022, 39–40.
98 Meyer 2022, 84, 91.
99 Testa 2022, 74, 81.
100 Albert and Mulzer 2022, 557.
101 Briar-Lawson, Day, and Mountz 2022, 34, 39–40.
102 Albert et al. 2021, 868.
103 Spinak 2018.
104 Hopkins et al. 2022, 460.
105 Hopkins et al. 2022, 476.
106 Albert et al. 2021; RISE 2022.
107 Weber and Bettencourt 2022, 688, 695–703.
108 Weber and Bettencourt 2022, 709.
109 Melton and McLeigh 2020, 131.
110 Melton and McLeigh 2020, 138–43.
111 Roygardner, Palusci, and Hughes 2020, 87–88.
112 Roygardner, Palusci, and Hughes 2020, 83–84.
113 Wald 2022, 723–25.
114 Harvey, Gupta-Kagan, and Church 2021, 599.
115 Sege and Stephens 2021; Slack, Berger, and Noyes 2017, 1–4 (2017).
116 Puls et al. 2021.
117 Sege and Stephens 2021; Slack, Berger, and Noyes 2017.
118 Fraidin and Trivedi 2022, 39.
119 Dowd 2018, 136–37.
120 New York City Family Court COVID Work Group 2022, 1–2.
121 New York City Family Court COVID Work Group 2022, 4.
122 Family Court Judicial Appointment & Assignment Process Work Group 2020.

BIBLIOGRAPHY

STATUTES, CODES, AND RESTATEMENTS OF LAW

Adoption Assistance and Child Welfare Act of 1980. Pub. L. No. 96–272, 94 Stat. 500 (codified as amended in scattered sections of 42 U.S.C.).

Adoption and Safe Families Act of 1997. Pub. L. No. 105–89, 111 Stat. 2115 (codified as amended in scattered sections of 42 U.S.C.).

American Law Institute. 2021. *Draft Restatement of Children and the Law Pt. I, Ch. 2. State Intervention for Abuse and Neglect, Protecting Family Integrity 1 § 2.30. Obligation of the State to Make Reasonable Efforts to Keep a Child in the Care of a Parent or Guardian § 2.30.*

———. 2021. *Reasonable Efforts to Keep a Child in the Care of a Parent or Guardian § 2.30.*

Child Abuse Prevention and Treatment Act. P.L. 93–247, 88 Stat. 4 (1974), amended by P.L. 104–235, 110 Stat. 3063 (1996).

D.C. Code § 16–2301(8)(3). Judiciary and Judicial Procedure: Proceedings Regarding Delinquency, Neglect, or Need of Supervision, Definitions.

D.C. Code § 16–2305.01(1). Judiciary and Judicial Procedure: Proceedings Regarding Delinquency, Neglect, or Need of Supervision, Findings.

Grants to States for Child Abuse or Neglect Prevention and Treatment Programs. 42 U.S.C. § 5106a(b)(2)(B)(xiii).

Juvenile Court Act. D.C. Code, § 11–901 et seq. (1951).

Juvenile Court Law of Allegheny County. 11 P.S. § 269–418.

N.Y. Fam. Ct. Act §141.

N.Y. Fam. Ct. Act §846a.

N.Y. Fam. Ct. Act §1091.

Strengthening Abuse and Neglect Courts Act of 2000. 42 U.S.C. § 670.

Wash. Rev. Code Ann. § 13.32A (West). Various sections. Family Division Proceedings.

CASES AND PLEADINGS

B.K. v. McKay, Class Actions. 2015. Children's Rights. www.childrensrights.org.

Commonwealth v. Fisher, 27 Pa. Super. 175 (1905).

DeBacker v. Brainard, 396 U.S. 28 (1969).

Duchesne v. Sugarman, 566 F.2d 817 (2d Cir. 1977).

E.A.R. v. State of Florida, 4 So.3d 614 (2009)

Ex parte Crouse, 4 Whart. 9, 27 (Pa. 1838).

Graham v. Florida, 560 U.S. 48 (2010).

In re Barbara Burrus, 4 N.C.App. 523 (1969).

In re Gault, 387 U.S. 1 (1967).

In re J.V.R., 81 M.M. 2008. *Legal Docket*, Juvenile Law Center. http://jlc.org.

In re Kaliyah S. et al., 455 S.W.3d 533 (2015).

In re L.M. 286 Kan. 460, 467–70 (2008).

In re M.B. 101 Wash.App. 425 (2000)

In re N.J., 2001 WL 488067 (Iowa Ct. Appeals 2001).

In re Sippy, 97 A.2 455 (D.C. Mun. Ct. 1953).

In re Snyder, 85 Wash.2d 182 (1975).

In re Terry, 438 Pa. 339 (1970).

In re the Dependency of A.K., 162 Wash.2d 632, 655 (Wash. 2007).

In re Winship, 397 U.S. 358 (1970) (Harlan, J., concurring).

In the Matter of Edward Terry, 438 Pa.S.Ct. 339 (1970).

In the Matter of Joseph McKeiver, 215 Pa.Super. 760 (1969).

J.D.B. v. North Carolina, 564 U.S. 261 (2011).

Jones v. Mississippi, 141 S. Ct. 130 (2021).

Kent v. United States, 383 U.S. 541 (1966).

Lassiter v. Dep't of Social Services of Durham County, North Carolina, 452 U.S. 18 (1981).

Matter of Kenneth J., 423 N.Y.S.2d 821 (1980).

Matter of Leif Z., 431 N.Y.S.2d 209 (1980).

McKeiver v. Pennsylvania, 403 U.S. 528 (1971).

McKeiver v. Pennsylvania, Brief for Petitioners, 403 U.S. 528 (1971) (No. 128), 1980 WL 121988.

McKeiver v. Pennsylvania, Reply Brief for Petitioners, 403 U.S. 528 (1971) (No. 128), 1970 WL 121994.

Miller v. Alabama, 567 U.S. 460 (2012).

N.Y. Cnty. Lawyers' Ass'n v. State, 745 N.Y.S.2d 376, 388–89 (N.Y. Sup. Ct. 2002).

Nicholson v. Scoppetta, 3 N.Y.3d 357 (2004).

Nicholson v. Williams, 203 F.Supp.2d 153 (E.D.N.Y. 2002).

Roper v. Simmons, 543 U.S. 551 (2005).

Rule v. Geddes, 23 U.S. App. D.C. 31 (1904).

Santosky v. Kramer, 455 U.S. 745 (1982).

Smith v. Organization of Foster Families, 431 U.S. 816, 840 (1977).

Troxel v. Granville, 530 U.S. 57, 66 (2000).

Turner v. Rogers, 564 U.S. 431 (2011).

U.S. v. City of Meridian et al., Civil Action No. 3: 13-CV-978-HTW-LRA, Complaint (October 24, 2012).

PUBLICATIONS

Abbott, Grace. 1925. "History of the Juvenile Court Movement Throughout the World." In *The Child, the Clinic, and the Court: A Group of Papers*, 267–73. New York: New Republic, Inc.

————. 1936. "The Juvenile Court and a Community Program for Treating and Preventing Delinquency." *Social Service Review* 10, 2: 227–42.

Abel, Richard L. 1982. "The Contradictions of Informal Justice." In *The Politics of Informal Justice*, edited by Richard L. Abel, 267–320. New York: Academic Press.

ACFY-CB-PI-16-05. 2016. "Instructions for State Courts Applying for Court Improvement Program (CIP) Funds for Fiscal Years (FYs) 2017–2021."

Act 4 Juvenile Justice. 2019. *Juvenile Justice and Delinquency Prevention Act (JJDPA) Fact Sheet Series*. www.act4jj.org.

Adams, LaShanda Taylor. 2010. "Resurrecting Parents of Legal Orphans: Un-Terminating Parental Rights." *Virginia Journal of Social Policy & the Law* 17: 318–72.

————. 2014. "Legal Orphans Need Attorneys to Achieve Permanency." *American Bar Association Child Law Practice* 3:225.

Addams, Jane. 1925. Introduction, in *The Child, the Clinic, and the Court: A Group of Papers*, 1–2. New York: New Republic, Inc.

Aguilera, Elizabeth. 2020 (updated 2021). "Juvenile Justice Overhaul: How the Governor's Plan Shifts Care of Serious Offenders to Countries." Cal Matters. https://calmatters.org.

Albert, Ashley, et al. 2021. "Ending the Family Death Penalty and Building a World We Deserve." *Columbia Journal of Race and Law* 11: 860–94.

Albert, Ashley, and Amy Mulzer. 2022. "Adoption Cannot Be Reformed." *Columbia Journal of Race and Law* 12(1): 557–600.

Alexander, Paul W. 1944. "Speaking as One Judge to Another." In *Cooperation in Crime Control, 1944 Yearbook, National Probation Association*, edited by Marjorie Bell, 23–40. New York: National Probation Association.

————. 1952. "What Is a Family Court, Anyway?" *Connecticut Bar Journal* 26: 243–78.

————. 1962. "Constitutional Rights in Juvenile Court." In *Justice for the Child: The Juvenile Court in Transition*, edited by Margaret K. Rosenheim, 82–94. Chicago: University of Chicago Press.

Allen, Francis A. 1964. *The Borderland of Criminal Justice: Essays in Law and Criminology*.

Allen, Mary Lee, and Beth Davis-Pratt. 2009. "The Impact of ASFA on Family Connections for Children." In *Intentions and Results: A Look Back at the Adoption and Safe Families Act* 70–82. www.urban.org.

American Bar Association. 1995 (reprinted in 2002). *A Call for Justice: An Assessment of Access to Counsel and Quality of Representation in Delinquency Proceedings*.

————. 2007. *House of Delegates Resolution 104C*.

Anderson, Nils. 1925. "Trial by Newspaper." In *The Child, the Clinic, and the Court: A Group of Papers*, 108–19. New York: New Republic, Inc.

Anderson, Nolan, Randy Kreider, and Kristen Schnell. 2021. *Injustice in the Lowest Courts: How Municipal Courts Rob America's Youth*. https://debtorsprison.jlc.org.

Armstrong, Molly, et al. 1997. "Vera Institute of Justice, New York State Family Court Improvement Study 23." In Jane M. Spinak, 2002 "Adding Value to Families: The Potential of Model Family Courts." *Wisconsin Law Review*: 331–75.

Arthur, Patricia J., and Regina Waugh. 2008. "Status Offenses and the Juvenile Justice and Delinquency Prevention Act." *Seattle Journal for Social Justice* 7: 555–76.

Babb, Barbara A., and Judith D. Moran. 2018. *Caring for Families in Court: An Essential Approach to Family Justice.* New York: Routledge.

Baker, Harvey H. 1920. "Judge Baker on the Procedure of the Boston Juvenile Court." In *Harvey Humphrey Baker, Upbuilder of the Juvenile Court* 107–20. Concord: Rumford Press.

Barnosky, Jason. 2006. "The Violent Years: Responses to Juvenile Crime in the 1950s." *Polity* 38: 314–44.

Baynes-Dunning, Karen. 2022. "Stop Blaming the 'Uncooperative Mother.'" *Family Integrity & Justice Quarterly* (Winter 2022): 14–25.

Bean, Kathleen S. 2005. "Reasonable Efforts: What State Courts Think." *University of Toledo Law Review* 36: 321–66.

Behrman, Richard E., et al. 1996. "The Juvenile Court: Analysis and Recommendations." *The Future of Children* 6: 4–28.

Belden, Evelina. 1920. *Courts in the United States Hearing Children's Cases: Results of a Questionnaire Study Covering the Year 1918.* Washington: Government Printing Office.

Bell, James. 1999. *Review and Analysis of State Program Reports Related to the Court Improvement Program* 42.

———. 2003. *Feasibility of Evaluating the State Court Improvement Program* vi, 35–36, 45, 47, 70. www.acf.hhs.gov.

Bergman, Abraham B. 2013. "A Pediatrician's Perspective on Child Protection." In *C. Henry Kempe: A 50 Year Legacy to the Field of Child Abuse and Neglect*, edited by Richard D. Krugman and Jill E. Korbin, 63–69. Lanham, MD: Rowman & Littlefield.

Bernstein, Nina. 2001. *The Lost Children of Wilder: The Epic Struggle to Change Foster Care.* New York: Pantheon Books.

Billingsley, Andrew, and Jeanne M. Giovannoni. 1972. *Children of the Storm: Black Children and American Child Welfare.* New York: Harcourt Brace Jovanovich, Inc.

Bowen, Louise de Koven. 1914. *Safeguards for City Youth at Work and at Play.* New York: MacMillan Company.

Bowen, Louise de Koven, et al. 1913. *The Colored People of Chicago: An Investigation Made for the Juvenile Protective Agency.* Chicago: Rogers and Hall.

Bowen, Mrs. Joseph T. (Louise de Koven Bowen). 1925. "The Early Days of the Juvenile Court." In *The Child, the Clinic, and the Court: A Group of Papers*, 298–309. New York: New Republic, Inc.

Boyle, Edward F. 1934. "Letter from Edward F. Boyle to Fiorello H. LaGuardia." In *The Negro Problem as Reflected in the Functioning of the Domestic Relations Court of the City of New York*, by Katharine Hildreth. New York: N.p.

Braverman, Dave, and Sarah Ramsey. 1997. "When Welfare Ends: Removing Children from the Home for Poverty Alone." *Temple Law Review* 70: 447–70.

Breckinridge, S. P. 1943. "Legal Problems of the Juvenile Court." *Social Service Review* 17: 12–14.

Breckinridge, Sophonisba P., and Edith Abbott. 1912. *The Delinquent Child and the Home*.1–12. New York: Russell Sage Foundation.

Breger, Melissa L. 2010. "Making Waves or Keeping Calm? Analyzing the Institutional Culture of Family Courts Through the Lens of Social Psychology Group Think Theory." *Law & Psychology Review* 34: 55–90.

Briar-Lawson, Katharine, Priscilla A. Day, and Sarah Mountz. 2022. "A Tipping Point for Change: Adoption and Safe Families Act Reform/Repeal." *Family Integrity & Justice Quarterly* (Winter 2022): 39–40.

Bridges, Khiara M. 2011. *The Poverty of Privacy Rights*. Stanford: Stanford Law Books.

Briggs, Laura. 2020. *Taking Children*. Oakland: University of California Press.

———. 2021. "Twentieth Century Black and Native Activism Against the Child Taking System: Lessons for the Present." *Columbia Journal of Race and Law* 11: 611–38.

Briggs, Ryan. 2021. "After Abuses at Residential Facilities, Philly to Create New Youth Ombudsperson Office." *WHYY PBS*. https://whyy.org.

Brooklyn Eagle. "Terror Reign Revealed by School Jury." 1934. 1.

Bullard, Katharine S. 2013. *Civilizing the Child: Discourses of Race, Nation, and Child Welfare in America*. Lanham, MD: Lexington Books.

Butler, Cheryl Nelson. 2013. "Blackness as Delinquency." *Washington University Law Review*. 90: 1335–1397.

Butts, Jeffrey A., and Daniel P. Mears. 2001. "Reviving Juvenile Justice in a Get-Tough Era." *Youth and Society* 169–198.

Byer, Judge Joan L., and Jeffrey Kuhn. 2003. "A Model Response to Truancy Prevention: The Louisville Truancy Court Diversion Project." *Juvenile and Family Court Journal* 59–66.

Cabot, Frederick P. 1925. "The Detention of Children as a Part of Treatment." In *The Child, the Clinic, and the Court: A Group of Papers*, 246–54. New York: New Republic, Inc.

Carnochan, Sarah, at al. 2007. "Child Welfare and the Courts: An Exploratory Study of the Relationship Between Two Complex Systems." *Journal of Public Child Welfare* 1: 117–36.

Carter, Melissa, Christopher Church, and Vivek Sankaran. 2022. "A Quiet Revolution: How Judicial Discipline Essentially Eliminated Foster Care and Nearly Went Unnoticed." *Columbia Journal of Race and Law* 12: 497–516.

Casey Family Programs. 2008. *How Have States Implemented Parental Rights Restoration and Reinstatement?* www.casey.org.

Castellano, Thomas C. 1986. "The Justice Model in the Juvenile Justice System: Washington State's Experience." *Law & Policy* 8: 479–506.

Cecka, Dale Margolin. 2014. "Abolish Anonymous Reporting to Child Abuse Hotlines." *Catholic University Law Review* 64: 51–98.

Chambers, David L., and Michael S. Wald. 1985. "*Smith v. Organization of Foster Families for Equality & Reform*." In *In the Interest of Children: Advocacy, Law Reform, and Public Policy*, by Robert H. Mnookin. New York: W. H. Freeman and Company, 110.

Chapin Hall. 2011. *Midwest Evaluation of the Adult Functioning of Former Foster Youth: Outcomes at 26*. www.chapinhall.org.

Cherone, Heather. 2020. "Pritzker Unveils Plan to 'Transform' Juvenile Justice in Illinois By Closing Large Facilities." *WTTW News*. https://news.wttw.com.

Chesney-Lind, Meda, and Randall Shelden. 2004. *Girls, Delinquency, and Juvenile Justice*. Belmont: Thomson Wadsworth.

Chicago Commission on Race Relations. 1923. *The Negro in Chicago: A Study of Race Relations and a Race Riot*. Chicago: University of Chicago Press.

Child Rights International Network. n.d. *Minimum Ages of Criminal Responsibility Around the World*. https://archive.crin.org.

Children's Bureau. 1932. *Facts about Juvenile Delinquency: Its Prevention and Treatment, Children's Bureau Publication no. 215*. Washington D.C.: Government Printing Office.

———. 2005. *Court Involvement in the Child and Family Services Review (CFSR), ACYF-CB-IM-05-05*.

———. 2012. *Court Improvement Program*. www.acf.hhs.gov.

———. 2018. *The AFCARS Report*. https://www.acf.hhs.gov.

———. 2020a. *Aggregate Report Executive Summary Round 3: Fiscal Years 2015–2018* iii.

———. 2020b. *Child and Family Services Reviews Aggregate Report: Round 3: Fiscal Years 2015–2018*.

———. 2020c. *Child Maltreatment 2018*. www.acf.hhs.gov.

———. 2021a. *CFSR Round 3 Report for Legal and Judicial Communities* 5, 6, 11, 14, 17, 20.

———. 2021b. *Child Maltreatment 2019*. www.acf.hhs.gov.

———. 2021c. *Child Maltreatment 2019: Summary of Key Findings*. www.childwelfare. gov/pubpdfs/canstats.pdf.

———. 2021d. *Trends in Foster Care and Adoption: FY 2011–2020*. www.acf.hhs.gov.

———. n.d. *Children's Bureau Fact Sheet for Courts*. "History of the CRSRS." www.acf. hhs.gov.

Children's Rights, Inc. "Class Actions." www.childrensrights.org.

Chute, Charles. 1923. "Juvenile Probation." *Annals of the American Academy of Political and Social Science* 105: 223–228.

———. 1949. "The Juvenile Court in Retrospect." *Federal Probation Journal* 13: 3–8.

Clark, Kenneth B. 1959. "Color, Class, Personality, and Juvenile Delinquency." *Journal of Negro Education* 28: 240–251.

Clements, Alyson. 2021. "Connecticut and New York Raise Minimum Age of Prosecution." National Juvenile Justice Network. www.njjn.org.

Coalition for Juvenile Justice. 2012. *Positive Power: Exercising Judicial Leadership to Prevent Court Involvement and Incarceration of Non-Delinquent Youth*. www.juvjustice.org.

———. 2015. *Status Offenses: A National Survey*. www.njjn.org.

———. 2018. *Improving Responses for Youth Charged with Status Offenses* (PowerPoint presentation on file with the author).

———. 2020. *Use of the Valid Court Order: State-by-State Comparisons*. www.juvjustice.org.

———. n.d. *SOS Project, Standards of Care for Non-Delinquent Youth, Section 1.11*. www. juvjustice.org.

Cohen, Amy J. 2011. "The Family, the Market, and ADR 2011." *Journal of Dispute Resolution* 91–126 (citing Roscoe Pound, *The Administration of Justice in the Modern City*, 26 *Harvard Law Review* 302 (1913)).

Conference of Chief Justices. 2004. *Conference of State Court Administrators, Resolution 18 In Support for Court Involvement in Audits Conducted by the Children's Bureau.* https://ccj.ncsc.org.

———. 2017a. *Resolution 1 In Support of Reauthorization of Court Improvement Programs.*

———. 2017b. *In Support of the Conference of Chief Justices' Resolution 1: In Support of Reauthorization of Court Improvement Programs.*

Congressional Research Service. 2006. *Child Welfare: State Performance on Child and Family Services Reviews.* https://crsreports.congress.gov. RL32968.

Costin, Lela B., Howard J. Karger, and David Stoesz. 1996. *The Politics of Child Abuse in America.* New York: Oxford University Press.

Crossley, Will L. 2003. "Defining Reasonable Efforts: Demystifying the State's Burden Under Federal Child Protection Legislation." *Boston University Public Interest Law Journal* 12: 259–315.

Davis, Benjamin P., and Eric Aldieri. 2021. "Precarity and Resistance, A Critique of Martha Fineman's Vulnerability Theory." *Hypatia* 36: 321–327, 330. Quoting Judith Butler, *Notes Toward a Performative Theory of Assembly*, 2015 at 33.

Dawson, Robert O. 2000. "Judicial Waiver in Theory and Practice." In *The Changing Borders of Juvenile Justice: Transfer of Adolescents to the Criminal Court*, edited by Jeffrey Fagan and Franklin E. Zimring, 45–81. Chicago: University of Chicago Press.

Day, Honorable L. B. 1928. "The Development of the Family Court." *Annals of the American Academy of Political and Social Science* 136: 105–111.

Dembitz, Nanette. 1978. "Two Views of a Project." *Harvard Law Review* 91: 1940–1951.

Deutsch, Albert. 1950. *Our Rejected Children.* Boston: Little, Brown & Co.

DiFonzo, J. Herbie. 1994. "Coercive Conciliation: Judge Paul W. Alexander and the Movement for Therapeutic Divorce." *University of Toledo Law Review* 25: 525–575.

Diggs, Mary Huff. 1940. "The Problems and Needs of Negro Youth as Revealed by Delinquency and Crime Statistics." *Journal of Negro Education* 9: 311–320.

Dobbs, Harrison Allen. 1949. "In Defense of Juvenile Court." *Federal Probation Journal* 13: 24–29.

Dowd, Nancy E. 2018. *Reimagining Equality: A New Deal for Children of Color.* New York: New York University Press.

Eastman, Harry. 1934. "The Juvenile Court Today." *YB* (1934): 76.

Edwards, Leonard P. 2004. "Remarks of Judge Leonard P. Edwards at the Presentation of the William H. Rehnquist Award for Judicial Excellence." In *Center for Families Children and Courts* 5: 169–180.

———. 2018. "Ignoring Reasonable Efforts: How Courts Fail to Promote Prevention." *The Imprint.* https://imprintnews.org.

———. 2022. "Reasonable Efforts and the Adoption and Safe Families Act: A Judicial Perspective." *Family Integrity & Justice Quarterly* 1 (Winter 2022): 94–103.

Eggers, Tiffany Zwicker. 1998. "The 'Becca Bill' Would Not Have Saved Becca: Washington State's Treatment of Young Female Offenders." *Minnesota Journal of Law and Inequality* 16: 219–258.

Eliot, Thomas D. 1914a. *The Juvenile Court and the Community*. New York: MacMillan Co.

———. 1914b. "The Trend of the Juvenile Court." *The Annals of the American Academy of Political and Social Science, Reform in Administration of Justice* 52: 149–58.

———. 1925. "The Project-Problem Method as Applied in Indeterminate Sentence, Probation, and Other Reeducational Treatment." In *The Child, the Clinic, and the Court: A Group of Papers*, 102–07. New York: New Republic, Inc.

———. 1937. "Casework Functions and Judicial Functions: Their Coordination." *YB* 137: 252–266.

Ellet, Alberta J., and Leslie Leighninger. 2007. "What Happened? An Historical Analysis of the De-Professionalization of Child Welfare with Implications for Policy and Practices." *Journal of Public Child Welfare* 1: 3–34.

Ellis, Elaine. 1937. "Our Delinquent Children." *The Crisis* 44: 362–363.

Elson, Alex. 1962. "Juvenile Courts and Due Process." In *Justice for the Child: The Juvenile Court in Transition*, edited by Margaret K. Rosenheim, 95–117. Chicago: University of Chicago Press.

Empey, LaMar T. 1973. "Juvenile Justice Reform." In *Prisoners in America*, edited by Lloyd E. Ohlin. Englewood, NJ: Prentice-Hall.

Family Court Judicial Appointment and Assignment Process Work Group. 2020. *The Family Court Judicial Appointment and Assignment Process*. www.nycbar.org.

Family Integrity & Justice Quarterly (Winter 2022 issue).

Feeley, Malcolm. 1983. *Court Reform on Trial: Why Simple Solutions Fail*. New York: Basic Books.

Feld, Barry C. 1999. *Bad Kids: Race and the Transformation of the Juvenile Court*. New York: Oxford University Press.

———. 2000. "Legislative Exclusion of Offenses from Juvenile Court Jurisdiction: A History and Critique." In *The Changing Borders of Juvenile Justice: Transfer of Adolescents to the Criminal Court*, edited by Jeffrey Fagan and Franklin E. Zimring, 83–144.

———. 2007. "A Century of Juvenile Justice: A Work in Progress of a Revolution that Failed?" *Northern Kentucky Law Review* 34: 189–256.

———. 2009. "Violent Girls or Relabeled Status Offenders? An Alternative Interpretation of the Data." *Crime & Delinquency* 55: 241–265.

———. 2017. *The Evolution of the Juvenile Court: Race, Politics, and the Criminalizing of Juvenile Justice*. New York: New York University Press.

Flexner, Bernard. 1910. "The Juvenile Court as a Social Institution." In *4 Correction and Prevention: Preventive Treatment of Neglected Children*, edited by Charles Richmond Henderson. New York: Russel Sage Foundation Publications.

Flexner, Bernard, and Roger N. Baldwin. 1914. *Juvenile Courts and Probation*. New York: The Century Co.

Flicker, Barbara Danziger. 1982. *Standards for Juvenile Justice: A Summary and Analysis, Second Edition.* Institute of Judicial Administration [and American Bar Association].

Florida Department of Juvenile Justice. 2017. *The Juvenile Justice System Improvement Project (JJSIP): An Overview of Delinquency, JJSIP, The Comprehensive Strategy, and Florida's Disposition Matrix.*

———. n.d. *Myths vs. Facts.* www.djj.state.fl.us.

Fong, Kelley. 2018. "Concealment and Constraint: Child Protective Services Fears and Poor Mothers' Institutional Engagement." *Social Forces* 97: 1785–1810.

———. 2020. "Getting Eyes in the Home: Child Protective Services Investigations and State Surveillance of Family Life." *American Sociological Review* 85(4): 610–638.

Fradkin, Howard E. 1962. "Disposition Dilemmas of American Juvenile Courts." In *Justice for the Child: The Juvenile Court in Transition*, edited by Margaret K. Rosenheim, 118–243. Chicago: University of Chicago Press.

Fraidin, Matthew I. 2013. "Decision-Making in Dependency Court: Heuristics, Cognitive Biases, and Accountability." *Cleveland State Law Review* 60: 913–974.

Fraidin, Matthew I., and Shanta Trivedi. 2022. "A Role for Communities in Reasonable Efforts to Prevent Removal." *Columbia Journal of Race and Law Forum* 12: 28–44.

Freeman, Franklin. 1996. *Presentation of the Portrait of Susie Sharp at the Supreme Court of North Carolina.*

Fund for Modern Courts Family Court Task Force. 2009. *A Call to Action: The Crisis in Family Court, Report to the Chief Judge of the State of New York, Recommendations for Leadership and Reform.* https://moderncourts.org.

Gagliardo, Angelo J. 1971. "Are Youth Bureaus the Answer." *Juvenile Court Judges Journal* 22: 57–59.

Gardner, Howard. 2006. *Changing Minds: The Art and Science of Changing Our Own and Other People's Minds.* Boston: Harvard Business School Press.

Gatowski, Sophia I., and Lisa Portune. 2009. "Court Performance Measures in Child Abuse and Neglect Cases: Implementation Guide." Washington, D.C.: U.S. Department of Justice, Office of Justice Programs, Office of Juvenile Justice and Delinquency Prevention.

Gellhorn, Walter, Jacob D. Hyman, and Sidney H. Asch. 1954. *Children and Families in the Court of New York City.* New York: Dodd, Mead & Co.

Gerber, Lucas A., et al. 2019. "Effects of an Interdisciplinary Approach to Parental Representation in Child Welfare." *Children and Youth Services Review* 102: 42–55.

Gil, David G. 1976. "Primary Prevention of Child Abuse: A Philosophical and Political Issue." *Journal of Pediatric Psychology* 54–57.

Gilman, David. 2012. Personal conversation with author, November 11, New York, NY.

Ginsburg, Nancy. 2018. "Raising the Bar: Improving the Model of Defense Representation for Adolescents Prosecuted in Adult Courts." In *Rights, Race and Reform: 50 Years of Child Advocacy in the Juvenile Justice System*, edited by Kristin Henning, Laura Cohen, and Ellen Marrus, 154–68. New York: Routledge.

Gittler, Josephine. 2002. "Efforts to Reform Child and Family Services: The Political Context and Lessons to be Learned." In *Toward a Child Centered, Neighborhood-*

Based Child Protection System: A Report of the Consortium on Children, Families, and the Law, edited by Gary B. Melton, Ross A. Thompson, and Mark A. Small. 116–41. Westport: Praeger.

Glueck, Sheldon, and Eleanor Touroff Glueck. 1939. *One Thousand Juvenile Delinquents: Their Treatment by Court and Clinic*. Cambridge, MA: Harvard University Press.

Godsoe, Cynthia. 2013a. "Permanency Puzzle." *Michigan State Law Review* 2013: 1113–1136.

———. 2013b. "Parsing Parenthood." *Lewis and Clark Law Review* 17: 113–170.

Golden, Olivia, and Jennifer Macomber. 2009. "Framework Paper." In *Intentions and Results: A Look Back at the Adoption and Safe Families Act*, 8–34. Washington, D.C.: Urban Institute.

Goldstein, Joseph, Anna Freud, and Albert Solnit. 1973. *Beyond the Best Interests of the Child*. New York: Free Press.

———. 1979. *Before the Best Interests of the Child*. New York: Free Press.

Goldstein, Joseph, et al. 1986. *In the Best Interests of the Child* (compendium volume). New York: Free Press.

Gottlieb, Chris. 2020. "Major Reform of New York's Child Abuse and Maltreatment Register." *New York Law Journal*, May 26. https://plus.lexis.com.

Grossberg, Michael. 2002. "Changing Conceptions of Child Welfare in the United States, 1820–1935." In *A Century of Juvenile Justice*, edited by Margaret K. Rosenheim, Franklin E. Zimring, David S. Tanenhaus, and Bernardine Dohrn. 3–41. Chicago: University of Chicago Press.

Guggenheim, Martin. 2005. *What's Wrong with Children's Rights*. Cambridge, MA: Harvard University Press.

———. 2019. "The History and Influence of the National Association of Council for Children—An Alternate Perspective." *Children's Legal Rights Journal* 39: 12–41.

———. 2021. "How Racial Politics Led Directly to the Enactment of the Adoption and Safe Families Act of 1997." *Columbia Journal of Race and Law* 11: 711–732.

———. 2022. "The Failure to Repeal the Adoption and Safe Families Act Will Long be a Stain on this Period of American History." *Family Integrity & Justice Quarterly* (Winter 2022): 54–61.

Guggenheim, Martin, and Randy Hertz. 2016. "Selling Kids Short: How 'Right for Kids' Turned Into 'Kids for Cash.'" *Temple Law Review* 88: 653–674.

Guinier, Lani, and Gerald Torres. 2014. "Changing the Wind: Notes Toward a Demosprudence of Law and Social Movements." *Yale Law Journal* 123: 2740–2804.

Gupta-Kagan, Josh. 2020. "American's Hidden Foster Care System." *Stanford Law Review* 72: 814–913.

Gustafson, Kaaryn. 2013. "Degradation Ceremonies and the Criminalization of Low-Income Women." *U.C. Irvine Law Review* 3: 297–358.

Harrington, Christine B. 1982. "Delegalization Reform Movements: A Historical Analysis." In *The Politics of Informal Justice*, edited by Richard L. Abel, 35–71. New York: Academic Press.

Harrison, Emma. 1959. "Wilkins Charges Delinquency Bias." *New York Times* 72.

Harvey, Brianna, Josh Gupta-Kagan, and Christopher Church. 2021. "Reimagining Schools' Role Outside the Family Regulation System." *Columbia Journal of Race and Law* 11: 575–610.

Hayes, Anna R. 2009. *Without Precedent: The Life of Susie Marshall Sharp*. Chapel Hill: University of North Carolina Press.

Healy, William. 1922. "The Practical Value of Scientific Study of Juvenile Delinquents." *U.S. Department of Labor, Children's Bureau Publication No. 96*.

———. 1949. "Thoughts About Juvenile Court." *Federal Probation* 13: 16–19.

Hearing Before the Subcommittee on Youth Violence of the Committee on the Judiciary, 105th Congress. September 1, 1998. Statement of Hon. David E. Grossmann on behalf of the National Council of Juvenile and Family Court Judges 16–23. Washington, D.C.: U.S. Government Printing Office, 1999.

Henning, Kristin. 2009. "What's Wrong with Victim's Rights in Juvenile Court? Retributive Versus Rehabilitative Systems of Justice." *California Law Review* 97: 1107–1170.

Henning, Kristen, Jenadee Nanini, and Geoff Ward. 2018. "Toward Equal Recognition, Authority, and Protection: Legal and Extra-Legal Advocacy for Black Youth in the Juvenile Justice System." *Rights, Race, and Reform*. 2018 edited by Kristin Henning, Laura Cohen and Ellen Marrus, 30–50.

Herring, David. 2000. "The Adoption and Safe Families Act—Hope and Its Subversion." *Family Law Quarterly* 34: 329–358.

Hildreth, Katharine. 1934. *The Negro Problem as Reflected in the Functioning of the Domestic Relations Court of the City of New York*. New York: N.p.

"History of the National Council of Juvenile Court Judges." 1955. *Juvenile Court Judges Journal* 6: 1–84.

Hockenberry, Sarah, and Charles Puzzanchera. 2014. *National Center for Juvenile Justice, Juvenile Court Statistics*.

———. 2018. *National Center for Juvenile Justice, Juvenile Court, 2016*.

———. 2019. *National Center for Juvenile Justice, Juvenile Court Statistics, 2017*.

———. 2020. *Office of Juvenile Justice and Delinquency Prevention, Juvenile Court Statistics, 2018*.

Hoffman, Charles. 1925. "Organization of Family Courts, with Special Reference to the Juvenile Court." In *The Child, the Clinic, and the Court: A Group of Papers*, 255–66. New York: New Republic, Inc.

Holland, Paul. 2012. Telephone conversation with author, November 26.

Hopkins, Marcia, et al. 2022. "Youth and Families Matter: Reconstructing the System One Youth at a Time from the Expertise of Youth Advocates." *Columbia Journal of Race and Law* 12: 459–576.

Hornberger, Nancy Gannon. 2010. "Improving Outcomes for Status Offenders in the JJDPA Reauthorization." *Juvenile and Family Justice Today* (Summer 2010): 16.

Huntington, Clare. 2014. "The Child-Welfare System and the Limits of Determinacy." *Journal of Law and Contemporary Problems* 77: 221–248.

"'Incorrigibility' Label Eliminated from New York's Child Welfare Law." 2021. *The Imprint*. https://imprintnews.org.

Institute of Judicial Administration and American Bar Association. 1977a. *Standards Relating to Noncriminal Misbehavior*.

———. 1977b. *Standards Relating to Abuse and Neglect, Tentative Draft*.

Interbranch Commission on Juvenile Justice. 2010. *Report to the General Assembly, Governor Edward G. Rendell and the Supreme Court of Pennsylvania 6*.

Irvine, Angela, and Aishatu Yusuf. 2016. *New Information About the School-to-Prison Pipeline: Up to Nine in Ten Juvenile Justice-Involved Youth Have Been Disciplined in School*. www.njjn.org.

Irvine, Angela, Shannan Wilber, and Aisha Canfield. 2017. *Lesbian, Gay, Bisexual, Questioning, and/or Gender Nonconforming and Transgender Girls and Boys in the California Juvenile Justice System: A Practice Guide*. https://perma.cc/3L9T-TMSB.

Jafarian, Masha, and Vidhya Ananthakrishnan. 2017. *Just Kids: When Misbehaving Is a Crime*. Vera Institute. www.vera.org.

Johnson, Kenneth. 1953. Foreword in *A Court for Children: A Study of the New York City Children's Court*, by Alfred J. Kahn. New York: Columbia University Press.

Johnston, Wm. Robert. 2017. *Historical Statistics on Adoption in the United States, Plus Statistics on Child Population and Welfare*. Johnston's Archive. www.johnstonsarchive.net.

Joint Committee on Negro Child Study in New York City et al. 1927. *A Study of Delinquent and Neglected Negro Children Before the New York City Children's Court*. New York: Joint Committee on Negro Child Study in New York City.

Jones, William G. 2006. "Working with the Courts in Child Protection." Washington, D.C.: U.S. Department of Health and Human Services, Children's Bureau Office on Child Abuse and Neglect.

Juvenile Court Standards, Department of Labor, Government Printing Office, Washington, D.C. 1923.

Juvenile Justice Geography. "Policy, Practice and Statistics." www.jjgps.org.

Juvenile Law Center. 2014. *Lessons From "Kids for Cash," Part 2: All Children Must Have Access to Legal Representation in Court*. https://jlc.org.

———.n.d. *Luzerne "Kids for Cash" Scandal*. https://jlc.org.

Kaba, Mariame. 2021. *We Do This 'Til We Free Us*. Chicago: Haymarket Books.

Kahn, Alfred J. 1951. *Police and Children: A Study of the Juvenile Aid Bureau of the New York City Police Department*. New York: Citizens' Committee for Children.

———. 1953. *A Court for Children: A Study of the New York City Children's Court*. New York: Columbia University Press.

———. 1962. "Court and Community." In *Justice for the Child: The Juvenile Court in Transition*, edited by Margaret K. Rosenheim, 217–34. Chicago: University of Chicago Press.

Kahneman, Daniel. 2011. *Thinking, Fast and Slow*. New York: Farrar, Straus and Giroux.

Kamerman, Sheila B., and Alfred J. Kahn. 1990. "Social Services for Children, Youth and Families in the United States." *Child and Youth Services Review* 12: 7–180.

———. 2002. *Beyond Child Poverty: The Social Exclusion of Children*. New York: The Institute for Child and Family Policy at Columbia University, 2002.

Kapp, M. Keith. 2007. *Presentation of the Portrait of J. Frank Huskins at the Supreme Court of North Carolina.* www.nccourts.org.

Katz, Elizabeth D. 2019. "Criminal Law in a Civil Guise: The Evolution of Family Courts and Support Laws." *University of Chicago Law Review* 86: 1241–1309.

———. 2020. "Racial and Religious Democracy." *Stanford Law Review* 72: 1467–1575.

Kelly, David. 2021. Email correspondence with the author, December 10.

Kelly, Lisa. 2021. "Abolition or Reform: Confronting the Symbiotic Relationship between Child Welfare and the Carceral State." *Stanford Journal of Civil Rights and Civil Liberties* 17: 255–320.

Kemper, Kurtis A. 2006. "Construction and Application by State Courts of the Federal Adoption and Safe Families Act and Its Implementing State Statutes." *American Law Reports 6th* 10: 173.

Kephart, William M. 1955. "The Family Court: Some Socio-Legal Implications." *Washington University Law Quarterly* 1955: 61–73.

Ketcham, Orman W. 1962. "The Unfulfilled Promise of the American Juvenile Court." In *Justice for the Child: The Juvenile Court in Transition*, edited by Margaret K. Rosenheim, 22–43. Chicago: University of Chicago Press.

———. 1964. "A Survey of Case Law Pertaining to the Juvenile Court of the District of Columbia." *Juvenile Court Judges Journal* 14: 16–23.

———. 1977. "National Standards for Juvenile Justice." *Virginia Law Review* 63: 201.

Keve, Paul W. 1962. "Administration of Juvenile Services." In *Justice for the Child: The Juvenile Court in Transition*, edited by Margaret K. Rosenheim, 172–99. Chicago: University of Chicago Press.

Kinscherff, Robert, et al. 2022. Center for Law, Brain & Behavior at Massachusetts General Hospital. *White Paper on the Science of Late Adolescence: A Guide for Judges, Attorneys, and Policy Makers.* https://clbb.mgh.harvard.edu.

Kirchwey, George W. 1925. "Institutions for Juvenile Delinquents." In *The Child, the Clinic, and the Court: A Group of Papers*, 331–37. New York: New Republic, Inc.

Knupfer, Anne Meis. 2001. *Reform and Resistance: Gender, Delinquency, and America's First Juvenile Court.* New York: Routledge.

Langer, Máximo. 2020. "Penal Abolitionism and Criminal Law Minimalism: Here and There, Now and Then." *Harvard Law Review* 134: 42–77.

Lathrop, Julia C. 1925. "The Background of the Juvenile Court in Illinois." In *The Child, the Clinic, and the Court: A Group of Papers*, 290–97. New York: New Republic, Inc.

Laub, John H. 2002. "A Century of Delinquency Research and Delinquency Theory." In *A Century of Juvenile Justice*, edited by Margaret K. Rosenheim, Franklin E. Zimring, David S. Tanenhaus, and Bernardine Dohrn, 179–205. Chicago: University of Chicago Press.

Lawrence-Webb, Claudia. 1997. "African American Children in the Modern Child Welfare System: A Legacy of the Flemming Rule." *Child Welfare* 76: 11–30.

Lee, Tina. 2016. *Catching a Case.* New Brunswick, NJ: Rutgers University Press.

Lemert, Edwin M. 1967. "The Juvenile Court—Quest and Realities." In *President's Commission on Law Enforcement and Administration of Justice, Juvenile Delinquency and Youth Crime, Task Force Report: Juvenile Delinquency and Youth*, App. D, 91. Washington D.C.: U.S. Government Printing Office.

Lenroot, Katharine F. 1923. "The Evolution of the Juvenile Court." *Annals of the American Academy of Political and Social Science* 105: 213–222.

———. 1949. "The Juvenile Court Today." *Federal Probation* 13: 9–15.

Lenroot, Katharine F., and Emma O. Lundberg. 1925. "Juvenile Courts at Work." Washington, D.C.: Department of Labor, U.S. Government Printing Office.

Liebmann, Theo. 2006. "What's Missing from Foster Care Reform? The Need for Comprehensive, Realistic and Compassionate Removal Standards." *Hamline Journal of Public Law and Policy* 28: 141–176.

Lindsey, Duncan. 2004. *The Welfare of Children*. New York: Oxford University Press.

Lindsey, Edward. 1914. "The Juvenile Court Movement." *Annals of the American Academy of Political and Social Science* 52: 140–148.

Lovejoy, Owen R. 1932. *The Negro Children of New York*. New York: Children's Aid Society.

MacDowell, Elizabeth L. 2015. "Reimagining Access to Justice in the Poor People's Courts." *Georgetown Journal on Poverty Law and Policy* 22: 473–543.

MacFaden, Judge William E. 1969. "Why a Family Court?" *Juvenile Court Judges* 20: 96–101.

Mack, Julian. 1925. "The Chancery Procedure in the Juvenile Court." In *The Child, the Clinic, and the Court: A Group of Papers*, 310–19. New York: New Republic, Inc.

Mandelbaum, Randi. 2015. "Re-Examining and Re-Defining Permanency from a Youth's Perspective." *Capital University Law Review* 43: 259–305.

Mangold, Susan V., and Catherine Cerulli. 2009. "Follow the Money: Federal, State, and Local Funding Strategies for Child Welfare Services and the Impact of Local Levies on Adoptions in Ohio." *Capital University Law Review* 38: 349–384.

McCloud, Allegra M. 2015. "Prison Abolition and Grounded Justice." *UCLA Law Review* 62: 1156–1239.

McIntyre, William. "Arsenal of Delinquency." *New York Times Magazine*, May 1, 1960, 59.

McLeod, Jacqueline A. 2016. *Daughter of the Empire State: The Life of Judge Jane Bolin*. Urbana: University of Illinois Press.

Melton, Gary. 2005. "Mandated Reporting: A Policy Without Reason." *Child Abuse and Neglect* 29: 9–18.

Melton, Gary B., and Jill D. McLeigh. 2020. "The Nature, Logic, and Significance of Strong Communities for Children." *International Journal of Child Maltreatment* 3: 131–161.

Melton, Gary B., and Ross A. Thompson. 2002. "The Conceptual Foundation: Why Child Protection Should be Neighborhood-Based and Child-Centered." In *Toward a Child-Centered, Neighborhood-Based Child Protection System*, edited by Gary B. Melton, Ross A. Thompson, and Mark A. Small, 3–27. Westport, CT: Praeger.

Meyer, Amelia Franck. 2022. "Harm Caused by the Adoption and Safe Families Act." *Family Integrity & Justice Quarterly* (Winter 2022): 84–93.

Milner, Jerry. 2019. *Hope for Families*. National Judicial Leadership Summit IV on Child Welfare. https://vimeo.com.

Minoff, Elisa. 2018. *Entangled Roots*. Center for the Study of Social Policy. https://cssp.org.

Mnookin, Robert H. 1975. "Child-Custody Adjudication: Judicial Functions in the Face of Indeterminacy." *Law and Contemporary Problems* 39: 226–293.

Moriearty, Perry L. 2015. "*Miller v. Alabama* and the Retroactivity of Proportionality Rules." *University of Pennsylvania Journal of Constitutional Law* 17: 929–990.

Mulvey, Edward P. 1982. "Family Courts: The Issue of Reasonable Goals." *Law and Human Behavior* 6: 49–64.

Mulzer, Amy, and Tara Urs. 2016. "However Kindly Intentioned: Structural Racism and Volunteer CASA Programs." *City University of New York Law Review* 20: 23–76.

Murphy, Jane C. 2010. "Revitalizing the Adversary System in Family Law." *University of Cincinnati Law Review* 78: 891–927.

———. 2020. "Rethinking the Role of Courts in Resolving Family Conflicts." *Cardozo Journal of Conflict Resolution* 21: 625–639.

Murphy, Jane C., and Jana B. Singer. 2015. *Divorced from Reality: Rethinking Family Dispute Resolution*. New York: New York University Press.

"National Council Matters Resolution." 1967. *Juvenile Court Judges Journal* 18: 106.

National Council of Juvenile and Family Court Judges. 2004. *Resolution in Support of Health and Human Services Program Improvement Plans*. www.ncjfcj.org.

———. 2010. *Resolution in Support of Reauthorization and Strengthening of the Juvenile Justice and Delinquency Prevention and Elimination of the Valid Court Order Exception*. www.ncjfcj.org.

———. 2012. *Resolution Calling for Judicial Action to Reduce the Number of Legal Orphans at Risk of Aging Out of Foster Care in the United States*. www.ncjfcj.org.

———. 2017. *Sustaining the Change: Lessons Learned from Judicial Leaders*. www.ncjfcj.org.

———. 2020. *Judge's Action Alert, Leveraging Federal IV-E Funding to Support Child and Parent Representation*. www.ncjfcj.org.

———. n.d.-a. *The Model Court Effect: Proven Strategies in Systems' Change*. www.ncjfcj.org.

———.n.d.-b. *Trauma-Informed Courts*. www.ncjfcj.org.

National Evaluation of the Court Improvement Program. 2007. *Synthesis of 2005 Court Improvement Program Reform and Activities* 2, 42–45. https://docplayer.net/10955439-The-national-evaluation-of-the-court-improvement-program-cip-synthesis-of-2005-court-improvement-program-reform-and-activities-final-report.html.

———. *Final Study Site Report*. 2010. iv. On file with the author.

National Governors Association. 2021. *Age Boundaries in Juvenile Justice Systems*.

National Judicial Leadership Summit IV on Child Welfare. 2019. https://vimeo.com.

National Juvenile Justice Network. 2020. *Policy Platform: Raise the Minimum Age For Trying Children In Juvenile Court* 3, 6.

National Probation and Parole Association. 1959. *Standard Family Court Act 20–21*.

"Navy as a Reform School." 1900. *New York Times*, December 19, 3.

Nejelski, Paul. 1976. In *Pursuing Justice for the Child: The Juvenile Court in Transition*, edited by Margaret K. Rosenheim and Robert Maynard Hutchins, 94–118. Chicago: University of Chicago Press.

New York City Family Court COVID Work Group. A Joint Project of the New York City Bar Association and The Fund for Modern Courts. 2022. *The Impact of COVID-19 on the New York City Family Court: Recommendations on Improving Access to Justice for All Litigants*. www.nycourts.gov/legacypdfs/court-research/NY-Family-Court-Report-1-22-2022.pdf.

New York State Bar Association. 2012. *Family Court Task Force Final Report*. https://nysba.org.

New York State Permanent Judicial Commission on Justice for Children. 2006. *Accomplishments: 15 Year Report*. www.courts.state.ny.us.

Newport, Anna Belle. 2022. "Civil Miranda Warnings: The Fight for Parents to Know Their Rights During a Child Protective Services Investigation." *Columbia Human Rights Law Review* (forthcoming).

Newsweek. 1957. "Why The Young Kill: Prowling the Juvenile Jungles of the Big Cities." August 19. 25.

Nielsen, Euell A. 2020. "The Double V Campaign." BlackPast. www.blackpast.org.

North American Council on Adoptable Children. 2020. https://nacac.org.

Nutt, Alice Scott. 1939. "The Future of the Juvenile Court as a Case Work Agency." *YB* 1939: 157–169.

Nuernberger, Wilfred W., and Richard Van Duizend. 1977. "Development of Standards of Juvenile Justice: An Overview." *Juvenile Justice* 28: 3–6.

New York County Lawyer's Association.. 2010. *Task Force on the Family Court*. New York: NYCLA.

Office of Inspector General, Department of Health and Human Services. 1994. *Oversight of State Child Welfare Programs* iii. https://oig.hhs.gov/oei/reports/oei-01-92-00770.pdf.

Office of Justice Programs, Department of Justice. 2004. *Juveniles in Corrections* 3. www.ncjrs.gov.

Office of Juvenile Justice and Delinquency Prevention. 1995. *Juveniles Taken Into Custody: Fiscal Year 1992*.

———. 2013. *Purpose Clauses for Juvenile Courts, 2012*. https://ojjdp.ojp.gov.

———. 2019. *State Use of Valid Court Exception, Fiscal Year 2016*. https://ojjdp.ojp.gov.

"Our History." *CASA of Morris and Sussex Counties, Inc.* www.casamsc.org.

Paulsen, Monrad G. 1962. "The Delinquency, Neglect, and Dependency Jurisdiction of the Juvenile Court." In *Justice for the Child: The Juvenile Court in Transition*, edited by Margaret K. Rosenheim, 44–81. Chicago: University of Chicago Press.

———. 1966. "Juvenile Courts, Family Courts, and the Poor Man." *California Law Review* 54:694–716.

Pelton, Leroy H. 1978. "Child Abuse and Neglect: The Myth of Classlessness." *American Journal of Orthopsychiatry* 48: 608–617.

———. 1999. "The Role of Material Factors in Child Abuse and Neglect." In *Protecting Children from Abuse and Neglect*, edited by Gary B. Melton and Frank D. Barry. New York: Guilford Press.

Perkins, Willis B. 1919. "Family Courts." *Michigan Law Review* 17: 378–381.

Perlman, I Richard. 1949. "The Meaning of Juvenile Delinquency Statistics." *Federal Probation* 13: 63–67.

Peters, Jean Koh. 2006. "How Children are Heard in Child Protective Proceedings, in the United States and Around the World in 2005: Survey Findings, Initial Observations, and Areas for Further Study." *Nevada Law Journal* 6: 966.

Pitman, Mistee R. 1998–1999. "The Becca Bill: A Step Toward Helping Washington Families." *Gonzaga Law Review* 34: 385–416.

Platt, Anthony M. 1969; 2009. *The Child Savers*. New Brunswick, NJ: Rutgers University Press.

Polier, Justine Wise. 1941. *Everyone's Children, Nobody's Child: A Judge Looks at Underprivileged Child in the United States*. New York: Charles Scribner's Sons.

———. 1967. "The *Gault* Case: Its Practical Impact on the Philosophy and Objectives of the Juvenile Court." *Family Law Quarterly* 1:47–54.

———. 1975. "The Future of the Juvenile Court." *Juvenile Justice* 26: 3–10.

Polsky, Andrew J. 1991. *The Rise of the Therapeutic State*. Princeton, NJ: Princeton University Press.

Post, Dawn, and Brian Zimmerman. 2012. "The Revolving Doors of Family Court: Confronting Broken Adoptions." *Capital University Law Review* 40: 437–515.

Pound, Roscoe. 1906. "The Causes of Popular Dissatisfaction with the Administration of Justice." *A.B.A. Reports* 29: 395.

———. 1912. "Social Problems and the Courts." *American Journal of Sociology* 18: 331–341.

———. 1913. "The Administration of Justice in the Modern City." 26 *Harvard Law Review* 302–328.

———. 1945. "The Juvenile Court and the Law." In *Cooperation in Crime Control, 1944 Yearbook, National Probation Association*, 490–504, edited by Marjorie Bell. New York: National Probation Association.

President's Commission on Law Enforcement and Administration of Justice. 1967. *The Challenge of Crime in a Free Society*. Washington, D.C.: U.S. Government Printing Office.

Puls, Henry T., et al. 2021. "State Spending on Public Benefits Programs and Child Maltreatment." *Pediatrics* 148: 5–10.

Puzzanchera, Charles, et al. 2003. *Juvenile Court Statistics 1998*. Washington, D.C.: Office of Juvenile Justice and Delinquency Prevention.

QIC Child Rep. n.d. *A National Report Card on Legal Representation for Abused & Neglected Children*. www.improvechildrep.org.

Quinn, Mae C. 2008. "Anna Moscowitz Kross and the Home Term Part: A Second Look at the Nation's First Criminal Domestic Violence Court." *Akron Law Review* 41: 733–762.

———. 2014. "Giving Kids Their Due: Theorizing a Modern Fourteenth Amendment Framework for Juvenile Defense Representation." *Iowa Law Review* 99: 2185–2217.

Raz, Mical. 2020. *Abusive Policies: How the American Child Welfare System Lost Its Way*. Chapel Hill: University of North Carolina Press.

Redding, Richard E., and James C. Howell. 2000. "Blended Sentencing in American Juvenile Courts." In *The Changing Borders of Juvenile Justice: Transfer of Adolescents to the Criminal Court*, edited by Jeffrey Fagan and Franklin E. Zimring, 145–79. Chicago: University of Chicago Press.

Reinemann, John Otto. 1949. "The Expansion of the Juvenile Court Idea." *Federal Probation* 13: 34–40.

Repeal ASFA. n.d. www.repealasfa.org.

Report of the California Assembly Interim Committee on Criminal Procedure. 1971. *Juvenile Court Processes* 7.

Resnik, Judith. 1982. "Managerial Judges." *Harvard Law Review* 96: 374–448.

RISE. 2022. "Centering Parent Leadership in the Movement to Abolish Family Policing." *Columbia Journal of Race and Law*. 12: 437–58.

Rivkin, Dean, and Jane M. Spinak. 2015. *The Hidden Pipeline to Prison: Reforming Juvenile Status Offenses*. On file with the authors.

Rixey, Cart. 2009. "The Ultimate Disillusionment: The Need for Jury Trials in Juvenile Adjudications." *Catholic University Law Review* 58: 885–912.

Roberts, Dorothy E. 2002. *Shattered Bonds: The Color of Child Welfare*. New York: Basic Books Inc.

———. 2005. "Black Club Women and Child Welfare: Lessons for Modern Reform." *Florida State University Law Review* 32: 957–972.

———. 2022. *Torn Apart*. New York: Basic Books Inc.

Roediger, Brendan D. 2021. "Abolish Municipal Courts: A Response to Professor Natapoff." *Harvard Law Review Forum* 134: 213–227.

Rosenheim, Margaret K. 1962. "Perennial Problems in the Juvenile Court." In *Justice for the Child: The Juvenile Court in Transition*, edited by Margaret Rosenheim, 1–21. Chicago: University of Chicago Press.

———. 1976. "Notes on Helping Juvenile Nuisances." In *Pursuing Justice for the Child*, edited by Margaret K. Rosenheim and Robert Maynard Hutchins, 43–66. Chicago: University of Chicago Press.

Rosenthal, Marguerite G. 1986. "The Children's Bureau and the Juvenile Court: Delinquency Policy." *Social Service Review* 60: 303–318.

Roygardner, Debangshu, Vincent J. Palusci, and Kelli N. Hughes. 2020. "Advancing Prevention Zones: Implementing Community-Based Strategies to Prevent Child Maltreatment and Promote Healthy Families." *International Journal of Child Maltreatment* 3: 81–91.

Ryerson, Ellen. 1978. *The Best-Laid Plans: America's Juvenile Court Experiment*. New York: Hill and Wang.

Rymph, Catherine E. 2017. *Raising Government Children: A History of Foster Care and the American Welfare State*. Chapel Hill: University of North Carolina Press.

Sanders, Deborah L. 2002. "Toward Creating a Policy of Permanence for America's Disposable Children: The Evolution of Federal Foster Care Funding Statutes from 1961 to Present." *Journal of Legislation* 29: 51–88.

Sankaran, Vivek. 2011. "No Harm, No Foul? Why Harmless Error Analysis Should Not Be Used to Review Wrongful Denials of Counsel to Parents in Child Welfare Cases." *South Carolina Law Review* 63: 13–41.

———. 2022. "Ending the Unnecessary Pain Inflicted by Federal Child Welfare Policy." *Family Integrity & Justice Quarterly* 1: 26–33.

Santos, Melissa. 2016. "Washington No. 1 for Jailing Noncriminal Kids, Spurred by Law Named for Tacoma Runaway." *News Tribune*, January 30. www.thenewstribune.com.

Sapien, Joaquin. 2017. "Dysfunction Disorder." *ProPublica*. www.propublica.org.

Schalick, Meredith L. 2014. "Bio Family 2.0: Can the American Child Welfare System Finally Find Permanency for 'Legal Orphans' with a Statute to Reinstate Parental Rights?" *University of Michigan Journal of Legal Reform* 47: 467–494.

Scheiber, Harry N. 1993. "Innovation, Resistance, and Change: A History of Judicial Reform and The California Courts, 1960–1990." *Southern California Law Review* 66: 2049–2120.

Schneider, Anne Larason. 1984. "Divesting Status Offenses from Juvenile Court Jurisdiction." *Crime & Delinquency* 30: 347–370.

Schneider, Anne Larason, and Donna D. Schram. 1986. "The Washington State Juvenile Justice System Reform: A Review of Findings." *Criminal Justice Policy Review* 1: 211–235.

Schramm, Gustav L. 1949. "The Juvenile Court Idea." *Federal Probation* 13: 19–23.

Schur, Edwin M. 1973. *Radical Non-Intervention: Rethinking the Delinquency Problem.* New Jersey: Prentice-Hall Inc.

Schwartz, Ira M., Neil A. Weiner, and Guy Enosh. 1998. "Nine Lives and Then Some: Why the Juvenile Court Does Not Roll Over and Die." *Wake Forest Law Review* 33: 533–552.

———. 1999. "Myopic Justice? The Juvenile Court and Child Welfare Systems." *Annals of the American Academy of Political and Social Science* 564: 126–141.

Scott, Elizabeth, and Laurence Steinberg. 2008. *Rethinking Juvenile Justice.* Cambridge, MA: Harvard University Press.

Secretary of Labor. 1934. *Twenty-Second Annual Report.* Washington, D.C.: U.S. Government Printing Office.

Sege, Robert, and Allison Stephens. 2021. "Child Physical Abuse Did Not Increase During the Pandemic." *JAMA Pediatrics*, 338–340.

Shepherd, Robert E., Jr. 1996. "ABA Juvenile Justice Standards: Anchor in the Storm." *Criminal Justice* 10: 39–40.

Slack, Kristen S., Lawrence M. Berger, and Jennifer L. Noyes. 2017. "Introduction to the Special Issue on the Economic Causes and Consequences of Child Maltreatment." *Child and Youth Services Review* 72: 1–4.

Smith, Susan Livingston. 2014. *The Donaldson Adoption Institute, Keeping the Promise: The Case for Adoption Support and Preservation.* www.celcis.org.

Smyth, George W. 1939. *Probation Yearbook*, 175–83.

Sobie, Merril. 2012 [1987]. *The Creation of Juvenile Justice: A History of New York's Children's Laws.* Albany: New York Bar Foundation.

Social Workers Against Mandates. 2021. *Mandated Supporting*. https://jmacforfamilies. org.

Society for the History of Children and Youth. 2004. "Youngest Combatants of the Second Civil War: Black Children on the Front Lines of Public School Desegregation, Part 6: 'Desegregation': More Than a Black Student Entering a White School." *Society for the History of Children and Youth Newsletter Summer 2004*.

Spinak, Jane M. 2009. "Reforming Family Court: Getting It Right Between Rhetoric and Reality." *Washington University Journal of Law and Policy* 31:11–38.

———. 2016. "Family Defense and the Disappearing Problem-Solving Court." *CUNY Law Review* 20: 171–202.

———. 2018. "They Persist: Parent and Youth Voice in the Age of Trump." *Family Court Review* 56(2): 308–330.

Stashenko, Joel. 2008. "Law Guardian Cases are Capped at 150." *New York Law Journal* 239: 1.

Sterling, Robin Walker. 2013. "Fundamental Unfairness: *In re Gault* and the Road Not Taken." *Maryland Law Review* 72: 607–681.

Studt, Elliot. 1962. "The Client's Image." In *Justice for the Child: The Juvenile Court in Transition*, edited by Margaret K. Rosenheim, 200–16. Chicago: University of Chicago Press.

Suddler, Carl. 2019. *Presumed Criminal: Black Youth and the Justice System in Postwar New York*. New York: New York University Press.

Summers, Tim Jr. 2016a. "Henley-Young Must Release Kids After 21 Days; Some Disappearing?" *Jackson Free Press*, June 8. www.jacksonfreepress.com.

———. 2016b. "Youth Judge Now Adhering to Fed Regs." *Jackson Free Press*, August 17. www.jacksonfreepress.com.

Summey, Virginia. 2017. "Fighting Within the Bar: Judge Elreta Alexander and Civil Rights Advocacy in Greensboro, North Carolina." Ph.D. diss., University of North Carolina at Greensboro.

Susie Sharp Papers #4898. Southern Historical Collection, The Wilson Library, University of North Carolina Chapel Hill. www2.lib.unc.edu.

Swan, Christopher, and Michelle Sheran Sylvester. 2006. "The Foster Care Crisis: What Caused Caseloads to Grow?" *Demography* 43: 309–335.

Tanenhaus, David. 2000. "The Evolution of Transfer out of the Juvenile Court." In *The Changing Borders of Juvenile Justice: Transfer of Adolescents to the Criminal Court*, edited by Jeffrey Fagan & Franklin E. Zimring, 13–43. Chicago: University of Chicago Press.

———. 2002. "The Evolution of Juvenile Courts in the Early Twentieth Century: Beyond the Myth of Immaculate Construction." In *A Century of Juvenile Justice* edited by Margaret K. Rosenheim, Franklin E. Zimring, David S. Tanenhaus, and Bernardine Dohrn, 42–73. Chicago: University of Chicago Press.

———. 2004. *Juvenile Justice in the Making*. New York: Oxford University Press.

———. 2011. *The Constitutional Rights of Children*. Lawrence: University Press of Kansas.

Tappan, Paul W. 1962. "Juridical & Administrative Approaches to Children with Problems." In *Justice for the Child: The Juvenile Court in Transition*, edited by Margaret Rosenheim, 144–71. New York: The Free Press.

Task Force Report: Juvenile Delinquency and Youth Crime 1967. President's Commission on Law Enforcement and the Administration of Justice Task Force on Juvenile Delinquency. 1967. Washington, D.C.: U.S. Government Printing Office.

Teitelbaum, Lee. 2002. "Status Offenses and Status Offenders." In *A Century of Juvenile Justice* edited by Margaret K. Rosenheim, Franklin E. Zimring, David S. Tanenhaus, and Bernardine Dohrn, 158–76. Chicago: University of Chicago Press.

Testa, Mark F. 2004. "The Quality of Permanence—Lasting or Binding? Subsidized Guardianship and Kinship Foster Care as Alternatives to Adoption." *Virginia Journal of Social Policy and Law* 12: 499–534.

———. 2022. "Disrupting the Foster Care to Termination of Parental Rights Pipeline: Making a Case for Kinship Guardianship as the Next Best Alternative for Children Who Can't Be Reunified with their Parents." *Family Integrity & Justice Quarterly* (Winter 2022): 74–82.

Thurston, Henry W. 1930. *The Dependent Child; A Story of Changing Aims and Methods in the Care of Dependent Children*. New York: Columbia University Press.

Tilly, Charles. 1997. *Roads From Past To Future*. Lanham, MD: Rowman & Littlefield.

———. 2006a. *Why?* Princeton, NJ: Princeton University Press.

———. 2006b. "Reasons for (and in) Organizational Performance, Address to the New York City Family Court Conference." October 26, 2006 (in author's possession).

Tolchin, Martin. 1964. "Experts Wonder if Family Court Is Doing Its Job." *New York Times*, 24.

Tonry, Michael H. 1976. "Juvenile Justice and the National Crime Commissions." In *Pursuing Justice for the Child*, edited by Margaret K. Rosenheim and Robert Maynard Hutchins, 281–98. Chicago: University of Chicago Press.

Trost, Jennifer. 2005. *Gateway to Justice: The Juvenile Court and Progressive Child Welfare in a Southern City*. Athens: University of Georgia Press.

U.S. Advisory Board on Child Abuse and Neglect. 1990. *Child abuse and neglect: Critical first steps in response to a national emergency*. Washington, D.C.: U.S. Government Printing Office.

U.S. Commission on Civil Rights. 1968. *A Report on Equal Protection in the South (1965); Report of the National Advisory Commission on Civil Disorders*, 303.

U.S. Department of Education, Office for Civil Rights. 2014. *Civil Rights Data Collection Data Snapshot: School Discipline, Issue Brief No. 1*. www2.ed.gov.

U.S. Department of Justice. 2008. *Court Performance Measures in Child Abuse and Neglect Cases: Implementation Guide*. www.acf.hhs.gov.

———. n.d. *Rights of Juveniles*. www.justice.gov.

U.S. Department of Justice. 2012. *Investigation of the Shelby County Juvenile Court*, 10.

———. 2015a. *Statement of Interest of the United States, N.P. et al. v. the State of Georgia*.

———. 2015b. *Investigation of the St. Louis County Family Court, St. Louis, Missouri*.

————. n.d. "Juvenile Justice" section of the "Special Litigation Section Cases and Matters" page on the DOJ website. https://www.justice.gov/crt/special-litigation-section-cases-and-matters/download#juv

U.S. Department of Juvenile Justice Research and Planning. 2014. *Briefing Report Direct Commitments.*

U.S. Government Accountability Office. 2004. *GAO-04-333, Child and Family Services Reviews: Better Use of Data and Improved Guidance Could Enhance HHS Oversight of State Performance*, 11.

U. S. House of Representatives, Committee on Education and Labor. 1980. Juvenile Justice Amendments of 1980. Washington, D.C.: U.S. Government Printing Office.

U.S. National Advisory Commission on Criminal Justice Standards and Goals. 1973. *A National Strategy to Reduce Crime.* Washington, D.C.: U.S. Government Printing Office.

upEND Movement. 2021. *How We endUP: A Future Without Family Policing.* https://upendmovement.org.

Van Waters, Miriam. 1925. "The Juvenile Court from the Child's Viewpoint. A Glimpse of the Future." In *The Child, the Clinic, and the Court: A Group of Papers*, 217–37. New York: New Republic, Inc.

Waite, Edward F. 1921. "How Far Can Court Procedures Be Socialized without Impairing Individual Rights?" *Journal of the American Institute of Criminal Law and Criminology* 12: 339–348.

————. 1923. "The Outlook for the Juvenile Court." *Annals of the American Academy of Politics and Social Sciences* 105: 229–242.

Wald, Michael S. 1976. "State Intervention on Behalf of 'Neglected' Children: Standards for Removal of Children from Their Homes, Monitoring the Status of Children in Foster Care, and Termination of Parental Rights." *Stanford Law Review* 28: 623–700.

————. 2012. "Taking the Wrong Message: The Legacy of the Identification of the Battered Child Syndrome." In *C. Henry Kempe: A 50 Year Legacy to the Field of Child Abuse and Neglect*, edited by Richard D. Krugman and Jill E. Korbin, 89–101. Lanham, MD: Rowman & Littlefield.

————. 2022. "Replacing CPS: Issues in Building an Alternative System." *Columbia Journal of Race and Law* 12: 713–33.

Waldfogel, Jane. 1998. *The Future of Child Protection: How to Break the Cycle of Abuse and Neglect.* Cambridge, MA: Harvard University Press.

Ward, Geoff K. 2009. "The Other Child Savers: Racial Politics of the Parental State." In *Anthony Platt, the Child Savers: The Invention of Delinquency*, 225–41. New Brunswick, NJ: Rutgers University Press.

————. 2012. *The Black Child-Savers: Racial Democracy & Juvenile Justice.* Chicago: University of Chicago Press.

————. 2016. "Microclimates of Racial Meaning: Historical Racial Violence and Environmental Impacts." *Wisconsin Law Review* 2016: 575.

Washburn, Patrick S. 1981. "The Pittsburgh Courier's Double V Campaign in 1942." *Am. Journalism* 3: 73.

Weber, Kristen, and Bill Bettencourt. 2022. "Different Year, Different Jurisdiction, but the Same Findings: Reform Isn't Enough." *Columbia Journal of Race and Law* 12: 688–711.

Welfare and Health Council of the City of New York. 1957. *Fact Book on Children in New York City: Characteristics of the Child Population and Welfare, Health, and Education Services for Children.*

Westwick, Atwell. 1939. *Probation Yearbook*, 184–202.

White House Conference on Child Health and Protection. 1930. *Preliminary Committee Reports, The Century Co., New York.*

———. 1933. Section IV. *The Handicapped: Prevention, Maintenance, Protection; Dependent and Neglected Children, D. Appleton-Century Co., New York.*

Wolcott, David B. 2005. *Cops and Kids: Policing Juvenile Delinquency in Urban America.* Columbus: Ohio State University Press.

Worley, Natalie K., and Gary Melton. 2013. "Mandated Reporting Laws and Child Maltreatment: The Evolution of a Flawed Policy Response." In *C. Henry Kempe: A 50 Year Legacy to the Field of Child Abuse and Neglect*, edited by Richard D. Krugman and Jill E. Korbin, 103–18. Lanham, MD: Rowman & Littlefield.

Young, Nancy, and Sid Gardner. 2009. "Twelve Years Later: The Issue of Substance Abuse." In *Intentions and Results: A Look Back at the Adoption and Safe Families Act*, 93–101. Washington, D.C.: Urban Institute.

Zimring, Franklin E. 1998. "The 1990s Assault on Juvenile Justice: Notes from an Ideological Battleground." *Fed. Sent'g Rep.* 11: 260–261.

———. 2000. "The Punitive Necessity of Waiver." In *The Changing Borders of Juvenile Justice: Transfer of Adolescents to the Criminal Court*, edited by Jeffrey Fagan and Franklin E. Zimring, 208–14. Chicago: University of Chicago Press.

———. 2002. "The Common Thread: Diversion in the Jurisprudence of a Century of Juvenile Justice." In *A Century of Juvenile Justice*, edited by Margaret K. Rosenheim et al., 142–57. Chicago: University of Chicago Press.

INDEX

Page numbers in *italics* indicate Figures

AACWA. *See* Adoption Assistance and Child Welfare Act

ABA. *See* American Bar Association

Abbott, Edith, 19

Abbott, Grace, 37, 44, *45*, 49–51, 57

Abel, Richard, 229–30

abolition, 8, 12–13, 121, 225, 264–65; of family court, 4–6, 256–59, 292–93, 295; Feld on, 268–69; of jurisdiction, 5–6, 46, 55, 137–38, 141–44, 146, 190, 227, 246, 255, 258–59, 266–67, 276, 283–84, 287, 290

abuse. *See* child abuse

Abuse and Neglect volume, 143, 172–75, 179. *See also* Juvenile Justice Standards Project; American Bar Association (ABA)

activists, 3, 116–17; as African-Americans, 71, 73; as community, 255, 258, 265, 285–86, 295; as young civil rights, 10, 116–18

ADC. *See* Aid to Dependent Children

adjudication, 46, 84, 95, 253, 267, 279; ages for, 269–72; process after, 107, 110; requirement for, 8, 13. *See also* due process; lawyers or attorneys

adolescence: broad delinquency definition of, 76; "juvenile nuisances" of, 149; misbehavior in, 128; normal behavior of, 63, 133–34; "stupid behavior" of, 245; treating children differently and, 260–63, 270–72. *See also* misbehavior; noncriminal misbehavior

adoption, 1; ASFA for, 12, 200–201, 206, 210, 212–13, 217–20, 282–83; broken, 218–20, 282; and "celebration days," 212–13; eliminating, 283; financial incentives for, 200; judges on, 206; legal guardianship after, 217–18; numbers of, 252; numbers for Black children, 76, 210; parental rights termination and, 206, 216–19; permanency and, 283; stable kin or, 218; Title IV-E funding for, 200–202, 283

Adoption and Safe Families Act (ASFA), 11–12, 214; on AACWA and reasonable efforts, 199, 203–4, 207, 211; for adoption, 12, 200–201, 206, 212–13, 217, 247, 282–83; Clinton era with, 11–12, 198–99, 285; family court and, 201–3, 206–7, 210; family destruction under, 4–5, 219; on family reunification, 204, 210, 212; faux permanency under, 216–21; federal mandates by, 205–8, 210–11, 216–18, 220–21, 248; on hearings, 279; informal coercion in, 228–29; NCJFCJ and, 213; permanency under, 200–201, 203–8, 216–21; reasonable efforts required by, 206–11, 279–80; repeal of, 247–48, 281–82, 284–85; reunification and, 201, 203–7, 210, 212, 282; safety and, 199, 203–5, 220–21; on well-being, 199, 206, 210–11, 213, 216, 248

Adoption Assistance and Child Welfare Act (AACWA), 182–84, 187–91; ASFA on reasonable efforts and, 199, 203–4, 207, 211; federal mandates from, 190–91, 199; foster care under, 182, 187, 190–91, 210; on reasonable efforts, 182–84, 199, 203–4; for reunification, 188, 199

Advisory Board on Child Abuse and Neglect (U.S. Advisory Board), 11–12, 198–200, 275, 287–88

AFDC. *See* Aid to Families with Dependent Children

age of legal responsibility, 269–72

aging out, of foster care, 218–220, 281

Aid to Dependent Children (ADC), 165–66

Aid to Families with Dependent Children (AFDC), 165–66, 172, 199–200

Alabama, 72, 261

Alexander, Paul W., *84*; for confessions, 104–5; court reinvigoration by, 85, 95, 155, 171; on due process, 98–99; for family courts, 86, 89; on informality, 88, 228

Allen, Francis, 122, 144, 147, 159; court concern by, 98, 135–36, 258; on "reacting against old errors," 111–12

American Bar Association (ABA):s f and juvenile justice standards 142–43, 146, 156; *Noncriminal Misbehavior* and, 144, 149–50, 242; on status offenses, 242–43; *Abuse and Neglect* 143, 172–75, 179

Anti-Drug Abuse Act (1986), 189–90

Arizona, 96, 103–4, 208–9

ARY. *See* "at-risk youth" petitions

ASFA. *See* Adoption and Safe Families Act

Ashby, Karen, 245

assimilation norms, 1, 5, 8, 27, 101. *See also* middle-class values

"at-risk youth" (ARY) petitions, 160–61

Bad Kids and the Transformation of Juvenile Court (Feld), 268

Baker, Harvey H., 19, 34–36, 51–52, 54

Baldwin, Roger, 28

Barnes, Albert, 36–37

Bean, Kathleen, 206–7

Becca Bill, 160–62

Before the Best Interests of the Child (1979), 177–80

Belden, Evelina, 42, 47–49

Berger, Warren, 105–6

Bergman, Abraham, 197–98

"best interest of the child" (BIOC), 32, 221, 257; CASAs and,194; definition of, 178–79, 182, 203; elimination of, 284; family autonomy and, 174; family court and, 172, 177, 193, 203, 280, 284–85; foster care and, 176–81; *GALs* for, 32, 193, 280–81; Goldstein, Freud and Solnit on, 177–81; judge obligation to community and, 82; legal interests instead of, 280; parent lifestyle and, 96; poverty and, 172; permanency as, 182

Beyond the Best Interests of the Child (1973), 177–78

"binding or lasting," 216–18, 220, 283

BIOC. *See* "best interest of the child"

Black, Hugo, 105, 108

Black children: adoption rates for, 210; Black child-savers for, 57–60, 70, 115; blamed for delinquency as, 75; "born criminal" on, 61, 69, 71, 77–79; CASAs and, 280; as civil rights activists, 114–17; Clark on, 77–79; community on delinquency and, 77–79, 115; discrimination on, 62–65, 72, 77–78, 115; disproportionality of treatment as, 32, 61–62, 68–69, 240, 269; disparate impact of systems on, 61, 115, 123–24, 235–37, 266–67; "disruptive" children and families as, 113; executed, 61, 72; goal of citizenship for, 57; Great Idea on, 9, 57–79; harshness on, 9, 151, 237, 245; juvenile court on, 10, 48, 71–72, 116–17, 269–70; numbers experiencing CPS investigations, 168, 275; placement on, 68–69, 74; poverty of, 71, 77–79, 151, 199–200; prisons for, 58–59, 61–62, 65, 69, 71–72, 115, 123–24; punitive treatment of, 58–61, 64, 74; racism and poverty on, 71, 77–79, 151; removal from families of, 166; reports on the needs and treatment of, 61–65, 67–70, 76; reunification with family for, 200, 216–17; segregation on delinquency and, 77–78; vocational or reform school on, 58–60; surveillance of, 75–76; White House Conference on (1909), 28, 58–59; White House Conference on (1930), 65–67; Ward, G., on excluding, 57, 59, 295. See also children of color; discrimination; integration; racism; segregation of Black children

Blackmun, Harry, 108–12, 124, 135, 246, 277

Blacks, 28, 74, 76, 168; activists as, 71, 73; community by, 9, 59–60, 115; courts with families of, 32, 201; discrimination influencing, 62–66, 70; "disruptive" children and families as, 113; family policing on, 4, 285; houses of refuge and, 58–59, 64; immigrants or, 48, 61, 84–85, 134; mothers' aid and, 66; police on, 61–63, 72, 75, 114; precarity of families of, 265; on racism preventing reform, 287; on segregation, 67, 72–73; slavery influencing, 3, 5, 58, 65–67, 69, 71; solidarity and, 66; state intervention into family, 84–85, 178; surveillance increase of, 72; white child-savers not seeing, 57–58; women child-savers as, 57, 115; women's clubs of, 59, 70–71, 115. See also discrimination, integration; racism; segregation of Black children

blended sentences, 120–21, 123, 218, 268, 270

Bolin, Jane, 73–74, 76

Boston, 2, 19, 34, 38, 54–55
Bowen, Louise de Koven, 30, 62
Boyle, Edward, 67–69
Breckinridge, Sophonisba, 19
Breger, Melissa, 214
Brennan, William, 113
Briggs, Laura, 166
Bronner, Augusta, 54–55
Brown v. Board of Education, 77, 114, 117, 165
Bullard, Katherine, 27
Burnley, Jane, 187
Bush, George H. W., 11
Butler, Cheryl, 71
Byer, Joan, 246

Cabot, Frederick, 2, 54–55
Cabot, Richard C., 54
California, 33, 52, 104, 147, 255, 269; court system report and, 230; on dispositions, 95–96
CAPTA. See Child Abuse Prevention and Treatment Act
Carroll, Richard, 58–59
CASAs. See court-appointed special advocates
casework, 18, 35–36, 88, 176, 191; by Blacks, 70; case histories reliance in, 89, 98; casework model, 40; Children's Bureau for, 50, 166; of CPS, 197–98, 214; Dembitz on, 175–76; juvenile court and, 49–51; therapeutic impulse in, 35, 40, 45, 166
Cecka, Dale Margolin, 275
Center for the Study of Social Policy, 287
A Century of Juvenile Justice (Zimring), 260
CFSRs. See Child and Family Services Reviews
The Challenge of Crime in a Free Society (Johnson Commission report), 133–34, 266
Chambers, Julius, 114–15

Chesney-Lind, Meda, 157–58

Chicago, 31, 44, 47, 62, 65; Black children in, 61, 63; Flowers of, 29, 193; juvenile court in, 29, 35–36, 38, 40, 135

child abuse, 32, 167, 291; CAPTA on, 168–70, 176–77, 276, 289; definition of, 169, 276–77; dependency definition and, 87, 96; emergency on, 11, 26–27; family court shrinking steps on, 284–85; JJ Standards on, 175; Kempe discovering, 167–68, 170; by parent, 87; as sexual abuse, 160, 168, 173, 179, 204–5, 276; in wealthy families, 26–27. *See also* reporting

Child Abuse Prevention and Treatment Act (CAPTA, 1974), 168, 198; on child abuse, 168–70, 176–77, 276, 289; child protection legislation and, 168–170, 280; concern on, 176, 178, 182–183, 280; definitions in, 168, 176, 276; *GALs* requirement by, 193–94; lawyers and, 280–81; on maltreatment proceedings, 276–77; on neglect, 168, 170, 172–73, 176–77, 182, 193, 289; state action through, 170, 172, 182–83, 220

Child and Family Services Reviews (CF-SRs), 211–13, 251–52

child maltreatment proceedings, 32, 168; CAPTA on, 276–77; judges on, 176; poverty for, 172, 291; reporting for, 37, 197, 255–56; social failure or, 169–71, 183, 207; standards for, 173, 278–79; substantiation for, 275, 288; *See also* child abuse; child neglect; reporting

child neglect, 11; CAPTA on, 168, 170, 172–73, 176–77, 182, 193, 289; definition of, 18–19, 96, 144, 153, 172, 175, 266, 276–77, 284; 1961 California rules on, 95–96; dependency definition and, 28–29, 87, 96; decriminalization to, 153; family court shrinking steps on, 284–85; JJ Standards on, 175, 179; parents and, 23, 34, 87–88, 132–33, 166, 169,

184–85, 253; poverty and, 189, 221, 291; *See also* dependency; reporting

child protection, 11–12, 58, 192, 289; on abuse, 167; CAPTA and, 168, 280; definition of, 2168, 176, 276; 1980s increase in, 121–22. *See also specific topics*

child protective services (CPS), 196, 205, 277, 289, 291; attorneys of, 195, 214; caseworkers of, 197–98, 214; for reporting, 275–76, 290

The Child, the Clinic, and the Court: A Group of Papers, 44–49; background of, 42–44

children. *See specific topics*

children, citizen-building of, 27, 57–59

children, "disruptive," 1, 8, 113, 127, 181, 266–67, 269

children in need of services (CHINS), of Washington, 161

children in need of supervision (CHINS), of Massachusetts, 154

children of color: assimilation and not, 27; delinquency blame on, 74; families and, 11, 32, 115, 134, 181, 265; New York family court report on, 292–93; 1930s on, 65; poverty and, 189, 201, 203, 263–65; punitive treatment of, 124, 158; recidivism and, 238; school suspensions on, 267; status offenses on, 158; transfer laws and, 123. *See also* Black children

children, different treatment of, by the Supreme Court, 260–63, 268–69, 271–72

Children's Aid Society, 69

Children's Bureau (U.S.), 41–42, 57, 71, 164–65, 211–14, 246–47; Abbott, G., of, 37; Belden and, 42, 47–49; Burnley of, 187; for casework, 50, 166; and CFSR, 212–13, 251–252; juvenile court survey from, 38; Lathrop of, 19, 29–30, 30, 62; Lenroot of, 50–51, 51, 80–81, 97, 164; Model Juvenile and Family Court Standards of, 104; reporting and, 38, 166–167; on Title IV-B and IV-E funding mandates, 211–14, 283; on treatment, 38, 49, 51–52, 174; on volunteers, 42

Children's Rights, Inc. (CRI), 208–9

Children's Village (agency), 64

child-savers, 2, 37, 47; as attorneys, 281; as Black, 57–60, 70–71, 115; for child removal, 35–36; white female reformers as, 2, 29–30, 57–58, 62, 165, 194, 280

The Child Savers (Platt), 47, 141

child support: payment of, 1, 5, 22–24, 83–84, 171, 230, 234; U.S. Advisory Board for, 11–12, 198–200, 287–88. *See also* mothers' aid

child welfare, 2, 9, 11, 50–52, 188–90, 201; agencies instead of courts, 50–52, 95; ASFA and family court administering, 199, 201–3, 210; broken system of, 188–91, 247–52; CAPTA paradigm of, 18; Children's Bureau on, 50–52, 95; 246; court supervision of, 210–13, 220; families without court and agencies of, 191, 278–80; as foster care, 164–67; New York on collaboration and, 212; 1950s and 1960s on, 164; permanency paradigm of, 81, 182; poverty on, 189; reimagined, 274–283; systems sued, 191, 208–9; Social Security Act for, 165; worker expertise in, 191–92. *See also specific topics*

CHINS. *See* children in need of services; children in need of supervision

Church, Christopher, 289

Chute, Charles, 80–82

Ciavarella, Mark, 239–40

CIP. *See* Court Improvement Project

civil rights, 39, 101; activists on, 10, 116–17; judges violating, 117–18, 235; North Carolina on, *112*, 113–14; U.S. on rights of children, 235–39

Clark, Kenneth, 77–78

Clinton, Bill, 11–12, 198–201, 285

coercion, 9, 101, 104–5; benevolent, 111–12, 150; court as instrument of, 92; in informal processes, 228–29; jurisdiction as, 152–53; with mothers' aid, 36; on parents, 252–53

Cohen, Herbert, 108, 110–11

Colorado, 242

Colored Orphan Asylum, 64

The Colored People in Chicago (Bowen), 30, 62

Commission on Civil Rights (1965), 117–18

Commonwealth v. Fisher, 21

community, 4, 82, 147, 165, 267; activists as, 255, 258, 265, 295; alternative system to court intervention, 215, 226, 258, 277, 286; help for Black child delinquency, 77–79, 115; as change warriors, 285–87; Children's Bureau for, 49, 51; complex needs of, 71, 75; as crisis intervention, 148–49; courts taking resources from, 13, 138; Eliot for services in, 5–6, 24, 40, 45–46, 50; assistance in, 6, 8, 10–12, 18, 27–28, 46, 81, 142, 226, 267, 272; Johnson Commission for assistance in, 110, 138–39; judges and, 33; neighborhood-based protection as, 198, 287; JJ Standards for assistance in, 148–49, 174, 176, 242; Nixon Commission for bureaus and, 140; as prevention, 51, 215, 242, 287–88; as primary prevention, 287–88; problem-solving in, 5–6, 139, 141–44, 148–51; safety for, 53, 82, 97–98, 120–21, 244–46; support through, 5–6, 9, 11, 165, 176, 183, 189, 258; surveillance by, 11, 18; for targeted assistance in, 289–91; for treatment, 46, 55; U.S. Advisory Board on, 198, 200; volunteers as, 288, 290–91

Conferences of Chief Justices and State Court Administrators, 213, 227, 248

Connecticut, 208, 269

constitutional rights, 20–21, 27–28, 99,103, 114, 118, 123, 156, 202–3, 236. *See also* due process

Cooke, Emily, 250

Cotton, Tom, 243

court-appointed special advocates (CASAs), 31–32, 193–95, 214, 277, 280, 284

Court Improvement Project (CIP), 249–51

court reform efforts, 23–24, 27, 150–57, 255; as administrative, 12, 43–44, 57, 230–31; crises and, 230–34; "do good" hampering, 234, 256; failure of, 254–56; for judge consolidation, 32, 53, 80–81, 85; for court merger, 293; socialized courts and, 19–20; by white females, 2, 27, 29–30, 58, 62

court reinvention, 6–9, 85, 95, 122, 155, 171, 225–26

court specialization, 149, 191–92, 226; by judges, 87, 90; reform efforts on court, 23–24

court unification, 23–24; ASFA and, 248; CIP funding on, 249–51; cooperative bureaucracy in, 233–34; Gellhorn for, 90–92, 94, 246; issues gathered in, 23, 226; in New York, 170; School Part exception to, 91, 98, 246

courts. *See specific topics*

CPS. *See* child protective services

CRI. *See* Children's Rights, Inc.

criminal court, 1, 17, 20, 36–37, 45, 109, 155, 227, 230, 260; as applied to Black adults and children, 61; blended sentences into, 120–21, 123, 218, 268, 270; charged as adult in, 119; judge restrictions on, 102; 1970s and 1990s juveniles into, 119–20; purpose of, 21; returning children to, 110; roots applied in family court, 82–84; transfer policies to, 87, 102, 119–21, 123, 137, 237, 268, 270; and youth court practices, 270–72

criminal laws, 82–84, 87, 101–2, 119; adolescence and, 260–61, 270–72; Black children transfer and, 237; drug offenses and, 241, 272; family court shrinking steps on, 284–85; Great Idea and children under, 95, 260; sexual activity on, 243

Davenport, Donna, 269–70

Day, L. B., 24–25

"deconstitutionalization of poverty," 27–28

decriminalization, 4, 151–54

deinstitutionalization of status offenders (DSO), 151–52, 158–59, 161, 189

Delaney, Hubert, 76

delinquency, 2, 7, 2,10,; definition of, 76, 87,129, 163–64; family court after due process in, 190–91; fundamental fairness and, 10, 105, 154; get-tough era (1990s) and, 96, 119–20, 121, 142, 157, 268; Healy, W., on, 38–39, 54–55; incorrigible in, 118, 128, 154; juvenile court not preventing, 49, 53–56, 259–60; after *McKeiver* 119–124; 1950s on, 74–76; 1961 California rules on, 95–96; as normal adolescent behavior, 63, 133–34, 147, 149; Paulson on, 26–27, 96, 118; problematizing of behavior as, 149; poverty and racism and Black child, 28–29,71, 77–79, 151; sexual activity as, 83, 88; status offenses as, 131, 138; VCOs for status offenders and, 156–57; privileged whites as, 78.

The Delinquent Child and the Home, 19

Dembitz, Nanette, 175–76

demosprudence, 258

dependency, 32, 50–51, 153; causes of, 35, 38; court on, 1, 22, 24–26, 172, 259–60; definition of, 19, 28–29, 87, 96; judicial leadership and, 247–54; See also child neglect

The Dependent Child (Thurston), 65

detention home, 29–30, 47–48, 117, 245
Diggs, Mary Huff, 69–70
discrimination. 5; on Black child delin-
    quency, 62, 65, 72, 77–78, 115, 117, 147;
    on Black parents, 65–66, 70; juvenile
    court and, 5, 9–10, 61–62, 73, 78–79,
    115, 117, 263; in private child care agen-
    cies, 74, 76. See also specific topics
dispositions, 32, 34, 95, 119, 139; alterna-
    tives to, 109, 131, 271–72, 284; ASFA
    and, 201; on Black children, 237; with-
    out due process, 155; Florida judges
    and, 238–39; for foster care, 185–86,
    240; judges and, 92–93, 96, 104, 120,
    263; New York and, 184; as punish-
    ment, 133; status offenses and, 147
disproportionality, 4, 9, 11, 32, 61, 68–69,
    76–78,114, 117, 123, 158, 168, 181, 201,
    210, 237, 265–66, 277
diversion, 121, 133, 151–52, 133, 242, 246,
    268, 272; informal processes in, 228;
    for law breakers, 137–38; as "leaving
    alone," 140; police and, 153; and worse
    outcomes, 153, 157, 190, 228
Dobbs, Harrison, 81
doll studies, 77
domestic violence court, 83
The Door (youth center), 291
Douglas, William O., 108
Dowd, Nancy, 169, 291–92, 297
DSO. See deinstitutionalization of status
    offenders
due process, 415, 8, 10, 17; concerns about
    not providing (1950s and 60s), 95–97;
    as elusive, 226; entitlement to lawyers,
    96, 104, 120, 145, 185, 239–40, 277–78;
    and fundamental fairness, 105–18, 120,
    122, 272–73; and Great Idea, 10, 100–
    124; hearings, and, 117, 152, 163, 192,
    235–37, 249–50; informality or, 228–
    29; judges resisting, 33, 98–99, 123,
    234–40; Lassiter on parental, 277–78;
    need to ensure in family court and,

277–81; proof beyond a reasonable
    doubt, 105–6; rights of children,101–6,
    108–19; right to counsel and, 122–23,
    137, 163. See also specific topics and
    cases

E.A.R. v. State of Florida, 238–39
Eastman, Harry L., 54–55
Edna McConnell Clark Foundation, 248
education. See schools
Edwards, Leonard, 33–34, 98, 225
Eisenhower, Dwight, 165–66
Eliot, Thomas D., 6, 24, 40, 45–46, 50
Ellis, Elaine, 71–72, 77
Empey, Lamar, 151–52
equality, 4–5, 13, 170, 266, 291–92; racism
    and lack of, 61–62, 65, 68–69, 71–73,
    115, 235, 237, 269–70; therapeutic
    mantle disguising, 36, 257
extension-of-placement hearings, 186–87

Fact Book on Children in New York City
    (1957), 76
families, 2, 13, 65, 187, 285–86; ASFA
    terminating, 12, 210, 247; children
    of color and, 11, 32, 115, 134, 181, 265;
    equality for, 291–92; investigations
    of, 179, 188–89, 207, 256, 275; judges
    authority over, 37–39, 86–87, 229;
    jurisdiction on, 24–26, 85, 94–95, 226;
    juvenile court expansion over, 22–23,
    88, 147; lawyers or attorneys for, 277–
    78, 280–81; as marginalized, 4, 11–13,
    32, 69, 85, 168, 170, 200, 255–57; Native
    Americans on customary adoption
    and, 283; precarity of, 264–65; radi-
    cal nonintervention in, 139, 148–51,
    259–60, 264; reasonable efforts and,
    199–205, 207; removal from, 35–36,
    181–82, 185–86, 228, 274; surveillance
    on, 256–59, 274; U.S. Advisory Board
    for, 11–12, 198–200, 287–88; well-being
    of, 201, 263–64

family court: as cooperative bureaucracy, 233–34; concern about, 49, 54; Allen with court, 98, 135–36, 258; on BIOC, 177–78; case histories about effectiveness of, 89, 98; caseloads, 230–33; on CASAs and volunteers, 194–95; consolidation in, 82–87; 90, 94–95, 97, 233–234; for court abolition, 121–122; on court constitutional basis, 103; on court self-reinvention, 6–9, 85, 95, 122, 155, 171, 225–26; and "do good," 2, 3, 5–6, 234, 256–57, 259, 263; on Great Idea and court power, 42–46, 53, 81–82, 95–97; groupthink mentality and, 214; as industry, 164, 168; Johnson Commission on, 135–37; on judges, 39, 202, 225–26; on juvenile court, 1, 43–44, 286–87; Kephart on, 89–90, 98; Platt on, 47, 107, 141; on shrinking, 8, 13, 227, 256–59, 265, 274, 284–85; on states and resources, 202, 208, 225; *See also* court unification; interventionist tenets

Family Court of Lucas County, Toledo, Ohio, *86*

family integrity, 179, 208, 287; constitutional right of, 202–3; destruction on, 4–5, 219; as priority, 215, 226, 234, 253–54, 278, 282; support and, 13, 148, 165–67, 170, 182, 186–89, 191, 198–202, 207, 215, 247, 259–60, 270, 277, 289

family regulation, 4, 11, 164, 216, 218, 234, 247, 254–55, 265–66, 281, 284–85, 287, 291. *See also* child welfare; *specific topics*

Farve, Trent, 248

federal funding, 11, 213–14; CAPTA for, 168; federal mandates for, 204, 211–12, 251; foster care systems from, 166–67; judges attracting, 190; preventive efforts or, 188, 211, 242; reasonable efforts for, 184–85, 200–202, 279; reduction of, 183, 187–88; Title IV-E review process

as, 187, 200–202, 211, 219, 278, 281; unintended incentives from, 253

federal mandates: from AACWA, 190–91, 199; by ASFA, 205–6, 208, 217, 248; and CFSRs 211–13, 251–52; on due process, 23–24, 152–53, 163, 234–40; on family courts, 11, 164,1 67–70, 249–52; on judges, 201, 220–21; Southern states on integration, 165

Feeley, Malcolm, 230–31, 233, 250

Feld, Barry, 101, 111–12, 116, 122, 153, 268–69

Ferguson, James E., II, 113

Flemming, Arthur, 165–66

Flexner, Bernard, 28, 31

Flicker, Barbara, 144, 146, 154, 172–73

Florida, 118, 238–39, 261

Flowers, Lucy, 29, 193

formalism, 97, 139, 152, 231; fallacy of, 231

Fortas, Abe, 101–9, 114, 116, 118, 137, 236–37

foster care: AACWA and, 182, 187, 190–91, 210; "aging out" of, 218–20, 281; Anti-Drug Abuse Act increasing, 189–90; BIOC and, 177–81; child welfare as, 164–67; drift in, 167, 176; funding and, 182–83, 188, 192, 198, 200, 202, 219, review hearings and, 184–85, 187; impact of incarceration, 189–90; numbers in, 167, 182–83, 187, 198, 200, 210, 252; permanency hearings and, 210; psychological parent theory in, 177–81, 184; publication on youth and, 215; religious-affiliated agencies and, 64, 76, 148; removal from, 180–81; *Smith v. OFFER* and, 180–181; states hiding, 252–54; Title IV-E review process for, 187, 200–202, 211–13, 219, 251, transfer policies in, 253; youths on, 285–86

Fostering Connections to Success and Increased Adoptions Act (2008), 219–20

Fraidin, Matthew, 203

Freud, Anna, 177–79, 181–82, 184

fundamental fairness, 155; delinquency and, 10, 105, 154; *In re Gault* and, 109–10, 120, 122–23; jury trials and, 108, 110; race and, 112–15, 118; right to counsel and, 122, 137, 163; U.S. Supreme Court on, 142, 171, 272–73

funding: for placement, 167; prevention or, 188, 211, 242; for probation officers, 47; for reunification, 183, 253. *See also* federal funding

The Future of Juvenile Court as a Case Work Agency (Nutt), 50–52, 54

GALs. See *guardians ad litem*

Gault, Gerald, 96, 102–3, 262. See also *In re Gault*

Geddes, Helen, 127–29, 136, 141, 143, 147–48, 246; hearing right and, 130, 145; *Rule v. Geddes* and, 131

Gellhorn, Walter, 90–92, 94, 246

Georgia, 236–37

get-tough era (1990s), 96, 119–20, 121, 142, 157, 268

Gil, David, 169–70

Gilman, David, 156

girls: behavior of, 157–58; Black, 63, 67–68, 267; Hudson Training School for, 68–69; as incorrigible, 128, 143, 145, 149, 157–58, 161, 245, 255; LGBTQ+, 267; placement on, 68–69, 129–33; reform school for, 128–31, 136, 145; sexual activity and, 158, 160; status offenders and, 157–58, 266; treatment and, 83; Wayward Minors Court for, 83. *See also specific topics*

Glueck, Eleanor, 54–55, 89

Glueck, Sheldon, 54–55, 89

Godsoe, Cynthia, 217–18

Goldstein, Joseph, 177–79, 181–82, 184

Graham v. Florida (2010), 261

Gray, Ernestine, 279–80

Great Idea, 1–3, 6, 8–10; for Black children, 9, 57–79; *The Child, the Clinic,* *and the Court* on, 42–44, 49; concern on court power for, 42–46, 53, 81–82, 95–97; court power for, 9, 89, 92; on criminal laws and children, 95, 260; due process in, 10, 100–124; failure of, 254; *In re Burrus* challenging, 10, 108, 112, 114–19; of juvenile court, 8, 17–32, 97–99; persistence of, 97–99, 225, 254, 256; probation officers and, 40–41; status offense jurisdiction and, 127; therapeutic impulse and, 8, 33–56

Greenberg, Jack, 114–15

Grossmann, David, 158–59

groupthink mentality, 214

Guanier, Lani, 258

guardians ad litem (GALs), 206, 281, 285; lawyers as, 193–94, 277; as volunteers, 31–32, 193–95, 214, 280, 284.

Gupta-Kagan, Josh, 252–53, 289

Gutowicz, Theodore S., 100, 106, 262–63

Hall, Livingston, 156

Harlan, John, 105

Harrington, Christina, 228

Harvey, Brianna, 289

Head Start, 289

Healy, Thomas, 80–81

Healy, William, 38–39, 54–55

hearings, 130, 145, 250, 256; as adversarial, 11, 20; ASFA on, 211, 279; on child protection, 192; confidentiality of, 4, 29, 274; due process and, 117, 152, 163, 192, 235–37, 249–50; as extension-of-placement, 186–87; as formal, 139, 152; in foster care systems, 184–85, 187; judges in, 87; on permanency, 210–11; phases of, 92; request for open, 113–14. *See also* adjudication

Hedman, Becca, 160–62

Hellman, Lillian, 7

hidden foster care, 252–54

Hildreth, Katherine, 67–70

Hoffman, Charles, 17–18
Home Term court, 83–84
Home Visiting, 289
Hooks, Julia, 59, 60
houses of refuge, 18, 21, 129; Blacks and, 58–59, 64
Hoyt, Franklin Chase, 62–63
Hudson Training School for Girls, 68–69
Huskins, J. Frank, 113–14

"if it was your family," 285–87
IJA. See Institute of Judicial Administration
Illinois, 26. See also Chicago
immigrants, 1, 3, 8, 27–28, 48, 57, 61, 76
incarceration: 3; alternatives to, 235; of Black children, 58–59, 61–62, 65, 69, 71–72, 115, 123–24; crimes and, 130, 155, 157; effect on foster care, 189–90; of juveniles, 107, 123, 235, 256, 274; school to prison, 237; status offenses and, 155, 244, 267; treatment or, 228; VCO and, 243; "youth part" or, 271–72. See also prisons
incorrigible: in delinquency, 46, 118, 154; girls as, 128, 143, 145, 149, 157–58, 161, 255; as not for courts, 46, 150, 255; sentences and, 261; youth as, 134. See also status offenses
"Incorrigibles," 126
individualized justice, 105; failures on, 124; investigations and treatment in, 43; judges for, 34–35, 53, 103, 228; punishment or, 119
informal processes, 230; Alexander on, 88, 228; belief in, 226; as cajoling or threatening, 23; due process or, 228–29; poverty control by, 20; socialized courts with, 22, 32, 228
In re Burrus, 10, 108, 112, 114–19
In re Gault, 96, 102, 104, 117–18; due process lack in, 102–7, 114, 137, 153–55, 227, 235–36, 272; fundamental fairness and,

109–10, 112, 120, 122–23; Polier on, 263; Roberts, S., on, 106–7
In re N.J., 204–5
In re Terry, 108, 112
In re Winship (1970), 105–6
Institute of Judicial Administration (IJA), 142, 172
integration, 73; Southern states on, 165. See also segregation
interventionist tenets, 136; of family court, 5–6, 162, 256; Flicker on, 144, 146, 154, 172–73; on girls, 157–58; Healy, W., on, 38–39, 54–55; JJ Standards on, 146–47; judges for, 156; of juvenile court, 140; as not proven effective, 226; parens patriae with, 101, 144, 150; reduction of, 258–59; Schur on, 5, 141–42, 254, 264. See also surveillance
investigations, 11, 43, 62, 268; CAPTA and, 182, 220; by courts, 40, 42, 102–3, 185–86, 214–15; of families, 179, 188–89, 207, 256, 275; JJ Standards and, 175; maltreatment proceedings as, 168, 179, 255–56; by probation officers, 37, 40; reduction of, 258–59, 276; by U.S. Department of Justice., 235–37, 242, 258
Iowa, 204, 206, 216

J.D.B. v. North Carolina (2011), 261–62
JJDPA. See Juvenile Justice and Delinquency Prevention Act
JJ Standards. See Juvenile Justice Standards Project
JLC. See Juvenile Law Center of Philadelphia
Johnson, Lyndon, 133, 199–200
Johnson Commission. See President's Commission on Law Enforcement and Administration of Justice
"Joint Study on the Negro Child in New York" (1920s), 62–65
Jones v. Mississippi (2021), 261
JPA. See Juvenile Protective Association

Judge Baker Foundation Clinic, 5

judges: discretion excess for, 235, 237–38; European inquisitorial tradition for, 39; on formal rules, 19; intuitive decisions by, 203; justifications by, 24–26, 51–56, 89, 154, 159, 176, 190, 227, 258, 263–64; "keystone of the arch," as, 85, 88, 94, 98, 155; as managerial, 34, 225; suitability of, 48–49, 91–93, 96; supervision by, 36; as unqualified, 50; U.S. Supreme Court on, 103–4

judicial leadership: 1, 33, 51, 86, 93, 121, 213–216, 225, 227–28; by applying the law, 278–80; family courts as, 214; protection and dependency, 247–54; solution or enlightened, 244–48

judicial power: judges abusing, 227–28, 234, 237–40; of juvenile court judges, 23–24, 38–39, 88–89, 93, 104, 119–20, 123, 152, 159, 225, 260; of *parens patriae*, 129, 144; of parents, 131; of probation officers, 41; separation of, 216; of states, 82, 127, 178–79; U.S. on judge, 102, 171, 235. *See also* coercion

judicial problem-solving, 5, 19, 83, 164, 203, 216, 226–29, 233; as not for courts, 256–57

judicial waiver, 119, 122

jurisdiction, 22, 43, 86–87, 102, 119, 211; abolition of, 5–6, 46, 55, 137–38, 141–44, 146, 190, 227, 246, 255, 258–59, 266–67, 276, 283–84, 287, 290; ASFA transforming, 201; Black children in court, 9, 48, 63; blended sentences and, 120; categories lack, 2, 37, 49; as coercive control, 152–53; on families, 24–26, 85, 94–95, 226; family court expanding, 10, 18, 22, 44, 52–53, 79, 82, 122, 177, 191, 234; Johnson Commission on, 137–38; judges on, 150, 156, 159, 170–76, 227, 258, 263; maximum age of , 270–72, 284–85; minimum age of, 269–70, 284–85; on misbehavior, 147;

on poor families, 11, 26–28; restriction of, 93, 110, 140–41, 149, 191, 244–45, 263; states on court offenses and, 240–41; on status offenses, 127, 130–31, 133, 135, 141, 149, 151, 154, 158, 160–62, 240, 255, 283. *See also* "wayward youth" laws

jury trials, 100–12, Cohen on, 108, 110–11; *In re Burrus* and, 113–15, 118; Johnson Commission and, 107, 109–10; after *McKeiver v. Pennsylvania*, 273–74; right to, 9, 21–22, 100–101, 105–6, 273–274. See also *McKeiver v. Pennsylvania*

juvenile court: beginnings of, 1, 17, 22–24; common law tradition or, 37–38; as family court, 1–2, 82; issue types in, 18–19, 22–23; medical metaphor of, 34, 68, 99; 50-year anniversary of, 80–81; securing resources for, 43; rural areas, 44–45, 48, 57; "purposes" clauses, 120–121; as urban courts, 25, 57, 107, 154. *See also specific topics*

Juvenile Court Act (District of Columbia), 131

juvenile delinquency. See *delinquency*

Juvenile Justice and Delinquency Prevention Act (JJDPA, 1974), 152, 156, 161; reauthorization of, 243; VCO and, 243

Juvenile Justice Standards Project (JJ Standards), 141–150, 154, 172–76, 179; after project, 242–44; Gilman on, 156; Polier on, 174–75, 263; rebuffing of, 191. See also *Abuse and Neglect* volume; *Noncriminal Misbehavior* volume

Juvenile Law Center of Philadelphia (JLC), 239–40

Juvenile Protective Association (JPA), 62

Kagan, Elena, 261

Kahn, Alfred, 31, 91–94, 97, 295

Kahneman, Daniel, 143–44

Kansas Supreme Court, 273–74

Katz, Elizabeth, 83–84

Kelly, David, 250

Kempe, C. Henry, 167–68, 170
Kennedy, Anthony, 260–61
Kennedy, John F., 199–200
Kent, Morris, 101–2, 119
Kentucky, 31, 246
Kent v. United States (1966), 101, 104, 116, 137, 227
Kephart, William M., 89–90, 98
kinship caregivers, 148, 217–18, 252–53, 283
Kirchwey, George, 48
Kross, Anna Moscowitz, 83

labeling, 2–4, 13, 78, 138, 141, 151, 157, 163, 169, 243, 255; theory of, 138
La Guardia, Fiorello, 68, 73, 174
Lassiter v. Department of Social Services (1981), 277–78
Lathrop, Julia, 19, 29–30, *30*, 62
Law Enforcement (1965), 117–18
lawyers or attorneys, 31; child caseloads, 231–32; for children, 100–101, 106, 108, 113–16, 131–32, 258, 289–90; concern on, 287; of CPS, 195, 214; due process and entitlement to, 96, 104, 120, 145, 185, 239–40, 277–78; for families, 277–78, 280–81; as GALs or CASAs, 193–94, 277; judges on, 88, 100, 192, 228; as rare, 17, 84, 92, 103, 171, 231–33, 236
legal guardianship, 217–18. *See also* permanency
legal orphans. *See* orphans
Lemert, Edwin, 264
Lenroot, Katherine, 50–51, *51*, 80–81, 97, 164
Lewis, Amelia, 103
LGBTQ+ youth, 266
Lindsey, Ben, *16*
Lindsey, Duncan, 176, 183, 189
Lindsey, Edward, 24, 26
Lindsay, John, 175
Louisiana, 165

MacDowell, Elizabeth, 84–85
MacFaden, William E., 104

Mack, Julian, 46–48, 51, 98
Mandelbaum, Randi, 220
marginalized families and communities, 4, 11–13, 32, 69, 85,168, 170, 200, 255–57, 259, 271, 274, 293
Massachusetts, 154, 269; Boston, 2, 19, 34, 38, 54–55
maximum age of jurisdiction, 270–72, 284–85
McKeiver, Joseph, 100–101, 106, 108, 111–12, 115, 262–63
McKeiver v. Pennsylvania, 5, 10, 22, 108–17, 120–23; Blackmun and, 108–12, 124, 135, 246, 277; *In re Burrus* and, 113–19; on juvenile court, 108–12, 119, 227, 246; due process and, 112; Feld on, 111, 116; jury trials after, 273–74
Mexican, 28, 59, 65
Michigan, 39, 85, 208
middle-class values, 1–3, 8, 164–66; Clark on Blacks with upper-class and, 78; delinquency and, 26–28; juvenile courts, judges for, 85; progressive efforts and, 3, 27, 57; for social work, 85; as white, 85, 194, 280. *See also* assimilation norms
Miller, George, 187
Miller v. Alabama (2012), 261
Milligan, John R., 156, 227
Milliken, O. J., 61–62
Milner, Jerry, 247
minimum age of jurisdiction, 269–70, 284–85
Minnesota, 25, 43, 247
Miranda v. Arizona, 104
misbehavior: in adolescence, 128; court perpetuation on, 127, 144; delinquency or, 46–47, 141–42; interventionist tenets and, 147; Johnson Commission on, 136–37; juvenile court perpetuation and, 127; as juvenile nuisances, 149; net-widening practices, 150–57; racism and, 134–35

Mississippi, 237, 248, 261
Missouri, 236
Mnookin, Robert, 178–79, 181
model courts, 12, 247–54
Model Juvenile and Family Court Standards (Model Standards Act), 87,104
Mondale, Walter, 170
mothers' aid, 18, 28, 36, 50, 66, 164–65
Movement for Family Power, 286, *290*
Mulvey, Edward, 225
Mulzer, Amy, 194
Murphy, Jane, 5, 229

NAACP, 71, 74–75, 114
National Advisory Commission on Criminal Justice Standards and Goals (Nixon Commission, 1973), 139–41
National Council of Juvenile and Family Court Judges (NCJFCJ), 156, 158–59, 213, 219, 227, 248; model courts and, 12, 247–54
National Council of Juvenile Court Judges (NCJCJ), 53–54, 104, 154–56
National Probation Association (NPA): Alexander and, 86; Chute of, 80–82; judges break with, 51–56; NCJCJ and, 53–54; Pound and, 53, 85; Smyth of, 52; standardization by, 41–42
National Summit on Judicial Leadership in Child Welfare (2019), 247
Native Americans, 65; status offenses percentage of, 240, 266; assimilation and citizenship not for, 27; and 1909 White House Conference, 59; in court disproportionately, 32, 269; and customary adoption, 283; family policing on, 4, 285; investigations of, 168
Navy (U.S.), older boys to, 35
NCJCJ. *See* National Council of Juvenile Court Judges
NCJFCJ. *See* National Council of Juvenile and Family Court Judges

Nebraska, 24–25, 108
neglect. *See* child neglect
Negro. *See* Blacks
The Negro Children of New York (1932), 69
The Negro in Chicago (1919), 61
"The Negro in the United States" (Reid), 65–67
The Negro Problem (Hildreth), 67–70
Negro Reform Association, 59
neighborhood-based child protection, 198, 287–91
Nejelski, Paul, 153
"New Deal for Children," 291–92
New Jersey, 208
Newsom, Gavin, 255
New York, 170, 249, 255; Black children and juvenile court of, 67–68; on children of color, 292–93; court reform in, 230–32; discrimination in, 76; diversion of, 272; The Door in, 291; family courts of, 90–94, *163*, 194–95, 292; "Joint Study on the Negro Child" and, 62–65; on minimum age of legal responsibility in, 269; for parents, 181; on reasonable efforts, 184; reunification and, 212–13
New York Family Court Act (1962), 94, 104, 170–71; PINS of, 140–41
Nicole, 204–6, 210, 216–18
Nixon, Richard, 108–9, 139–41, 146, 170
Nixon Commission. *See* National Advisory Commission on Criminal Justice Standards and Goals
noncriminal misbehavior, 121, 140; delinquency and, 131–33, 143; family court on, 190, 266–67; JJDPA and states on, 151–54; JJ Standards Project on, 146–47, 152, 174, 227; Johnson Commission on, 134, 137–38, 266; Nixon Commission on, 140; radical nonintervention on, 148–151; without court appearances, 272

Noncriminal Misbehavior (1970s) volume, 141–44, 146–47, 149–50, 174, 242; Polier on, 150, 263; on status-offenses proceedings, 242; Washington State using, 149–50. *See also* Juvenile Justice Standards Project

North Carolina, 261–62; on civil rights movement, *112*, 113–14; *In re Burrus*, 108; racism and, 71–72

North Dakota, 122

NPA. *See* National Probation Association

Nutt, Alice Scott, 50–52, 54

Obama, Barack, 235

OFFER. See *Smith v. Organization of Foster Families for Equality and Reform*

Ohio, 17, *86*, 171

Oklahoma, 208

One Thousand Juvenile Delinquents (Glueck and Glueck), 54–55, 89

Oregon, 24

orphans, 18; as Black children, 64; courts for, 22, 106; as legal, 216–20

"Our Delinquent Children" (1937), 71

parens patriae, 21, 37, 116, 227; Cohen on, 108, 110–11; courts with, 129–30, 155, 175; Dembitz for, 175–76; due process or, 108, 129–32; critique of, 101, 144, 150; Kansas Supreme Court on, 273–74

parents, 2, 28, 92, 127, 139, 197, 276; as change warriors, 257–58, 265, 275, 285–87; Camille Sippy and, 131–32; Becca Hedman and, 160–62; Cindy Snyder and, 144–48; diminished absolute power of, 131; courts judging, 92–93, 95–96, 132–33, 145; due process and, 96, 103, 277–78, 280–81; Helen Geddes and, 127–29; judges substituting judgment for, 17, 35, 52, 133, 155, 159, 164; Nicole and Sherry as, 204–6, 210, 216–18; not following

rules of, 87–88; listened to and, 96–97; psychological parent theory for foster, 177–81, 184; negating rights of, 166, 172–74, 178–79, 192, 234; restored parental rights and, 218–20; "safety plans" and, 252–53; trauma of, 96–97, 282; U.S. Supreme Court on counsel and, 192

Paulson, Monrad, 26–27, 96, 118

Pelton, Leroy, 170

Pennsylvania, 10, 24, 26, 108, 112, 129; power abuse in, 239–40; Supreme Court of, 21–22, 101–2, 106

Perkins, Willis B., 39–40, 51–52, 85

permanency: adoption and, 182–90, 200, 210, 283; under ASFA, 199–201, 203–6, 210, 216–18; as binding or lasting, 216–18, 220, 283; CFSR report on, 251–52; family court reorientation steps on, 284–86; faux, 216–218; legal guardianship as, 217–18; Nicole without, 204–6, 210, 216–18; and parental rights reinstated, 218–20; personalized justice, 1, 3, 24, 27, 29, 38, 40; challenge to, 94; formality or, 97; judges for, 81, 155; Pound and, 20; therapeutic impulse for, 94. *See also* individualized justice

personalized justice: and permanency 1, 3, 24, 27, 29, 38, 40; and the therapeutic impulse, 38. *See also* individualized justice

"persons in need of supervision" (PINS), 140–41, 154

PIP. *See* Program Improvement Plan

placement, 129, 167; BIOC and, 177–79; outcomes on Black children, 68–69, 74; court review of, 210–12; extension of, 183–89; in foster care, 174–75; on girls, 68–69, 129–33; JJ Standards on, 148–49; kinship, 217–18, 283; numbers in, 123, 152, 240; permanency alternatives to, 217; as punitive, 50;

for recidivism, 238; after removal, 174–75

Platt, Anthony, 47, 107, 141

police, 3–4; abuse by, 241, 262, 266; on Black children, 61–63, 72, 75, 114; diversion and, 153; reporting to, 27; in schools, 262, 266, 273, 289–90; surveillance by, 75–76

Polier, Justine Wise, 27–28, 76, 150, 174–75, 263

Polikoff, Nancy, 284–85

Polsky, Andrew, 3, 35, 135–36, 190

Positive Power (2012), 244–47

Pound, Roscoe, 20, 38, 53–54, 82, 84–85

poverty, 3–5, 32, 96, 116, 266; abuse and neglect relation to, 168–70, 172–74, 189; of Black children, 71, 77–79, 134, 151, 199–200; children blamed for, 169; children of color and, 189, 201, 203, 263–65; "deconstitutionalization of," 27–28; drawn in court for, 11, 26–28, 32, 96, 221, 257, 266; Fleming Rule and, 165–66; income supports and, 199–200

The Practical Value of Scientific Study of Juvenile Delinquents (Healy, W.), 38–39, 54–55

precarity, 4, 264–66, 295

presidential commissions, 133–41

President's Commission on Law Enforcement and Administration of Justice 1967 (Johnson Commission), 139–40, 154–55, 158, 245, 268; on concern, 135–37; on due process, 110–11; on jurisdiction, 137–38; on jury trials, 107, 109–10; on juvenile courts, 135–37; on noncriminal misbehavior, 134, 138, 266. See also *The Challenge of Crime in a Free Society*

prevention, 124, 282, 287–91; as community-based, 51, 215, 242, 287–88; funding for, 188, 211, 242. See also *specific topics*

Price, Duane, 286

prisons, 123–24, 157; abolition of, 4–5; Black children in, 58–59, 61–62, 65, 69, 71–72, 115, 123–24, 237; children into, 18, 47–49, 119; detention home and reform school as, 47–48; school to prison, 237; status offenders and, 243–44. See also incarceration

Pritzker, J. B., 255

probation, 1, 8, 35; for adults, 81; officers as Blacks, 65, 70; funding for, 47; investigations by, 37; judges with, 8, 17, 20, 40–42; middle-class values for, 85; physician's junior as, 40–42; racial assignments of, 74; as retrained, 290; as social work profession, 54; as treatment, 8–9, 40, 42; as volunteers, 30. See also National Probation Association

problem-solving, 83; in communities, 5–6, 139, 141–44, 148–51; by court, 5, 19, 164, 203, 216, 226–29, 233; families without court, 278–80; as not for courts, 256–57. See also judicial problem solving

Program Improvement Plan (PIP), 251

prosecutors, 119–20, 151

psychiatric practices, 43, 46, 91, 131, 157

psychological parent theory, 177–81, 184

Puerto Ricans, 65, 75–76, 171

punitive treatment and punishment, 48, 52, 118; of Black children, 9, 58–62, 64–65, 69, 71–72, 74, 115, 123–24, 237, 245; early examples of, 47–48; of children of color, 124, 158; Children's Bureau on, 47–50; Ciavarella and private, 239–40; in Clinton era, 285; dispositions as, 133; investigations as, 11; Johnson Commission on, 110; on young children, 269–70; 1990s and, 119–24; shift in approach, 8–9, 36, 47–49, 116, 119, 124, 131, 260; U.S. Supreme Court ignoring, 116–17. See also *specific topics*

Quinn, Mae, 83, 272–73, 297

racism: ADC and, 165–66; assimilation standards with, 27; and Black child delinquency, 71, 77–79, 151; Black child harsh treatment as, 9, 237, 235–38; 245; "born criminal" in, 61, 69, 71, 77–79; CAPTA denial of, 170; in CPS systems, 287; family court with, 4–5, 286, 292; fundamental fairness and, 112–19; *In re Burrus* and, 10, 108, 112, 114–19; Johnson Commission on, 134–35, 139, 147; juvenile court and, 4–5, 56, 174; *The Negro in Chicago* on, 61; probation department; and, 74; punishment and, 268; treatment as, 61–62, 65, 68–69, 71–73, 115, 235, 237, 269–70; trauma and stress of, 75, 77–79, 169: U.S. Supreme Court on due process and, 10, 79, 92, 114; of whites, 71, 75, 77–79, 115. *See also specific topics*

radical nonintervention, 5, 141–44, 226, 259–60, 264; as community problem solving, 5–6, 139, 141–44; diversion is not, 152, 190; as framework for abolition, 259–60, 164; trying, 148–51; "deal evenly" rules, 142; giving up on, 160–62; as "leaving alone," 5, 139–42

Reagan, Ronald, 183

reasonable efforts, AACWA on, 182–87, 199, 203–4, 210; ASFA requiring, 199–201, 210–11, 279–80; courts and, 201–9, 211, 217, 219; families and, 199–205, 207; federal funding on, 184–85, 201–2, 279; as ICWA active efforts, 282; proper application, 279–80; as lackluster, 182, 282, 287; to prevent legal orphans, 219; narrowed definition of, 199, 204, 217; permanency on, 200; state resources and, 208–10; undefined, 184, 287

recidivism, 7, 238, 242–43

reform efforts. *See* court reform efforts

reform school: Black children with, 58–60; boys to, 19, 96; for girls, 128–31, 136,

145; judges ordering, 25–26; as prison, 47–48

rehabilitation: 107–8, 110; community based, 138; failed model of, 156; as incarceration for Black children, 115–16, 124; judicial leadership for, 121; problem-solving court for, 5, 19, 164, 203, 216, 226–28, 233; punishment and, 121; to retribution, 119; as run amuck, 149–50; segregated institutions in, 59

Reid, Ira De Augustine, 65–67

removal: from family, 35–36, 181–82, 185–86, 178, 228, 274; from foster care, 180–81; placement after, 174–75; reasonable efforts preventing, 201, 279; return after, 279, 282

reporting: abolish, 275–76; CAPTA and, 172, 182–83, 198; Children's Bureau for, 167; CPS system for, 197–98; ending of, 253, 255–56, 275–76, 284, 288–91; family court shrinking steps on, 284–85; quick growth of, 168; as mandated, 172, 179, 192, 197–98, 208, 255–56

Resnik, Judith, 34

restorative justice movement, 120

reunification, 183, 207, 253; AACWA and, 182–83, 188, 199; ASFA and, 201, 204, 207, 210, 212, 220, 282; *Before the Best Interests* on, 178, 182; BIOC and, 182; Black children without, 216–17; community for, 215; decreasing, 12, 200, 216–17; failure in, 184–87, 210, 216–17, 252; lack of funding for, 183, 199, 217; no "reunification days," 212–13;

Richmond, Mary, 40

right to counsel, 122–23, 137, 163, 272–73, 277–78. *See also* due process; lawyers or attorneys

RISE, 265, 286, 295

Roberts, Dorothy, 284–85

Roberts, Samuel J., 106–7, 111
Roediger, Brendan, 258–59
Roosevelt, Theodore, 28, 58–59, 65
Roper v. Simmons (2005), 260–61
Rosenheim, Margaret Keeney, 28, 149
Rule v. Geddes, 131

safety: AFDC for child as, 199–200; ASFA and, 199–201, 203–7, 213, 221, 248; carceral state for, 5; for child, 148, 161, 175, 179, 185, 197, 206–7, 251–53, 282, 288; CFSRs and, 251: due process and, 277–78; for public and community, 80, 82, 97, 102, 119–20, 137, 159, 244–46, 248; "safety plans," 253
SANCA. *See* Strengthening Neglect and Abuse Courts Act
Scheiber, Harry, 230
schools, 96; and courts on truancy, 266–67, 269; support from, 289–90
Schur, Edwin, 5, 141–42, 254, 264
secondary prevention, 289–91, *290*
Second Circuit Court of Appeals (U.S.), 257
segregation of Black children, 58–59, 62–64,67, 69, 71–74, 76–78
sexual activity: abuse or, 168, 173, 179, 204–5, 235, 276; criminal offenders in, 243; as delinquency, 83, 88; girl control and, 158, 160; punishments on, 121, 143
Sharp, Susie, 114
Shattered Bonds (Roberts, D.), 284–85
Shelden, Randall, 157–58
Singer, Jana, 5, 229
Sippy, Camille, 131–33, 141–43, 245–46
Skinner, William, II, 237–38
Smith v. Organization of Foster Families for Equality and Reform (*OFFER*), 180, 182
Smyth, George W., 51–53
Snyder, Cindy, 144–49, 161, 245–46
social control: of adolescents, 133–34; of "disruptive" children, 127; maltreatment proceedings and, 169–71, 183,
207; reporting as, 40, 167–68; treatment for, 93, 97; "wayward youth" laws for, 128–29
socialized courts, 8, 25, 84, 229–30; consolidation of, 53, 82–83, 85; criminal elements into, 82–84; family court as, 263–64; with informal processes, 22, 32, 228; judges for, 156; juvenile court as, 18, 32, 50; Polier for, 27–28, 76, 150, 174–75, 263; poverty and, 28–29, 84; reduction of, 259, 263–64; as reform movement, 19–20; warnings on, 295
Social Security Act (1935), 165
social work, as court alternative, 165–67; for families, 65; for holistic representation, 278; insufficient federal funding for, 188; insufficient training and experience of, 191; Richmond and, 40; middle-class values for, 85; as profession, 30, 51–55, 166, 188, 191, 195, 280; as retrained, 290
Society for the Prevention of Cruelty to Children, 18, 64
Solnit, Albert, 177–79, 181–82, 184
Sotomayor, Sonia, 262
Soucup, David, 193–94
Standard Juvenile Court Act (1923), 43
state intervention in families, 2, 4–5, 11; ASFA and family integrity with, 202; court as central to, 225–27; on families, 36–37, 179; disparate impact on poor, marginalized and families of color, 84–85, 134; failed approach to safety, 274; judges central for, 37–39; hidden foster care as, 252–53; informal processes part of, 228–230; JJ Standards and sharp limits on power of, 143, 146–47, 172–175; judge excessive power as, 235–240, 269–70; Model Standards Act and, 87; therapeutic justification for, 135. *See also specific topics*

status offenses, 2, 10–11, 121, 127–62, 240–247, 266–268; ABA on, 242–43; Black and Native American children and, 266; on children of color, 158; purpose of court for, 127, 259–60; crisis intervention instead of, 148–50; decriminalization and, 153; definition of, 2, 10, 129; as delinquency, 131, 138; dispositions and, 147; elimination of, 266–68; diversion and 153; DSO and, 151–52, 158–59, 161, 189; in early 2000s, 240; Geddes, Helen, 127–29, 136, 141, 143, 147–48, 246; Hedman, Becca, 160–62; JJ Standards Project on, 142–147, 149, 263; Johnson Commission on, 134, 138–39, 266; judges support of, 10–11, 121, 154, 171–72; neglect and, 132; NCJCJ on, 154–57; Nixon Commission on, 139–41; punishments for, 121, 134, 136, 147, 151, 153, 157, 162; radical nonintervention and, 141, 148–50; Sippy, Camille, 131–33, 141–43, 245–46; Snyder, Cindy, 144–49, 161, 245–46; truancy and, 133, 241–42, 266–67; valid court order (VCO) and, 156–57, 243–44, 267. *See also* non-criminal misbehavior; *Non-Criminal Misbehavior*

Stewart, Potter, 105

Strengthening Neglect and Abuse Courts Act (2000, SANCA), 211

Strong Communities/Strong Families, 287–88

Studt, Elliot, 96–97

Suddler, Carl, 75

support: adoption financial incentives as, 200; through community, 5–6, 9, 11, 176, 183, 189, 258; court jurisdiction on child, 27, 82; from CPS, 290; families without, 13, 148, 165–67, 170, 182, 186–89, 191, 198–202, 207, 215, 247, 259–60, 270, 277, 289; after aging out, 219–20; for kinship caregivers, 252–53; payment of child, 1, 5, 22–24, 83–84, 171, 230, 234; from schools, 289–90; secondary prevention and targeted, 289–91, 290; from states, 291. *See also* child support

Supreme Court (U.S.): 10, 22, 24; Blackmun support of juvenile court, 109, 111, 246; on *Brown v. Board of Education*, 77, 114, 117, 165; on "children are different" cases, 260–63; on clear and convincing evidence in termination of parental rights, 209; due process rights of children, 101–6, 108–19; Fortas concern about juvenile court, 101–4; and fundamental fairness, 105–18, 120, 122, 272–73; on parents and counsel, 277–78; on proof beyond a reasonable doubt, 105–6. *See also* due process, *specific cases*

surveillance: community-based help or, 11, 18; on families, 256–57, 274; increase of Black, 72; informal processes for, 229; by judges, 3, 18, 36, 257; by police, 72, 75–76; privacy rights or, 265; reduction of, 258–59

Swan, Christopher A., 189

Sylvester, Michelle Sheran, 189

Tanenhaus, David, 31, 47, 295

Tappan, Paul W., 87–88

Tennessee, 235–36, 240, 259

termination of parental rights (TPR), 200, 204–5, 207, 209, 277–78, 282–83

Teske, Steve, 245

Testa, Mark, 216–17, 220, 283

therapeutic impulse: 3, 33–56; in casework, 40, 45; for what child needs, 43, 155; to control youth, 135; for divorce system, 85–86; inequities disguised by, 36, 257; at 50-year anniversary, 80–81; Great Idea and, 8, 33–56; judges fight to keep, 51–56; prescription for juvenile court, 33, 35, 39, 94; and personalized justice, 38; progressive reformers and, 36

Thinking Fast and Slow (Kahneman), 143–44

Thomas, Kendall, 257–58

Thurston, Henry W., 65

Tilly, Charles, 6, 80–81, 144

Title IV-E review process, 187, 200–202, 219, 278, 281; Children's Bureau on, 211–12, 283

Tonry, Michael, 139

Torres, Gerald, 258

tough on crime, 96, 119–20, 121–24; alternative to, 268; "deal evenly" instead of, 142; limits of due process on, 235–240; and younger children 157

TPR. *See* termination of parental rights

transfer policies: to adult courts, 87, 102, 119–21, 123, 137, 268, 270; Black children and criminal court, 237; on children of color, 123; and legal responsibility, 271; in foster care, 253; Chicago psychopathic institute, therapeutic treatment at, 44; Children's Bureau on, 38, 49–51, 174; community for, 46, 55, 287–291; court unable to provide or accomplish, 46, 49–51, 55, 81, 83, 95, 102–3, 107, 130, 137–38, 140, 165, 174, 221, 246, 263; girls and, 83, 157; goal of court as, 10, 21, 38, 40, 43–44, 91, 93, 97, 111, 123, 159, 163, 170; as individualized, 43, 103, 105; probation as, 8–9, 40, 42, 274; punishment or, 8–9, 36, 46–49, 83, 116, 119, 131, 133, 151, 165, 228, 235, 260; rehabilitative ideal and, 135, 138; therapeutic intervention for, 35, 81–82; types of, 128, 135, 157, 160, 170, 173, 188, 195, 226, 228, 291; voluntary provision of, 139, 153, 242

truancy: 62–63, 68, 76; as an original basis for court intervention,18–19; School Part for, 91, 98, 246; status offenses and, 133, 241–42, 266–67; in Washington State, 150, 160–61

unification of courts. *See* court unification.

United States Department of Justice (DOJ); on violations of child civil rights, 235–39; investigations by, 235–38. *See also* due process

upEND Movement, 287

Urs, Tara, 194

U.S. Advisory Board. *See* Advisory Board on Child Abuse and Neglect

Utah, 269

valid court order (VCO), 156–57, 243–44, 267

Van Waters, Miriam, 1–2

VCO. *See* valid court order

volunteers, 8–9, 29–32; Children's Bureau on, 42; as community based, 288, 290–91; *GALs* and CASAs as, 193–95, 214, 280–81, 284

Waite, Edward F., 25–26, 28, 43, 155

Wald, Michael, 173, 178, 276–77, 289

Walker Sterling, Robin, 114–15

Ward, Geoff, 57, 59, 295

Ward, Hallett S., 113, 116

Warren, Earl, 22, 101, 113–14

Washington, Booker T., 58–59

Washington, D.C., 130–31, 208, 231

Washington state, 144–45, 148–51, 160–62, 208

Wayward Minors Court for Girls, 83

"wayward youth" laws, 35, 116, 130; Black girls as, 63; laws for child control, 128–30; delinquency and dependency in, 87; presidential commissions on, 133–41

The Welfare of Children (1994), 189

well-being: ASFA on, 210–11, 213, 248; assurance for, 288; of children, 130, 206, 210, 216, 283; failure on, 252; of families, 201, 263–64; judges on, 136, 175; as middle-class, 166; perverted approach to, 4

West Virginia, 96

Westwick, Alton, 51–53

White House Conference on Children (1930), 65, 67, 69

whites: avoiding court as, 71; CASAs as, 280; children as, 58–60, 63–66, 68–70, 74, 76; child-savers as, 2, 29–30, 57–58, 62, 115, 165, 194, 280; corporal punishment for, 72; court created for, 57–58, delinquents as, 69; female reformers as, citizens as, 27; 58, 62; as immigrants, 3, 28, 48, 61, 76; judges as, 270; middle-class as, 85, 101, 194, 280; mothers as, 28; mothers' aid for, 164; parents as, 64, 67; privilege of, 26, 78; racism of, 71, 75, 77–78, 115, 123, 267, 285. *See also* racism; segregation of Black childdren

Wilkins, Roy (child), 72

Wilkins, Roy (NAACP), 74–75

William H. Rehnquist Award for Judicial Excellence, 33

Wisconsin, 208

World War II, 53; and aftermath, 72–76, 80

Wyoming, 41

"youth part," 268–69, 271–72; and maximum age of jurisdiction, 271, 284

Zimring, Franklin, 260

ABOUT THE AUTHOR

JANE M. SPINAK is the Edward Ross Aranow Clinical Professor Emerita of Law Emerita at Columbia Law School, where she directed clinical programs in family regulation for forty years. Spinak also served as the attorney-in-charge of the Juvenile Rights Division of the Legal Aid Society of New York and was the founding chair of the board of the Center for Family Representation. She co-chaired the Task Force on Family Court created by the New York County Lawyers Association. She has received numerous awards for her work on behalf of children and families, including being named a Human Rights Hero by the ABA Human Rights Journal in 2005.